3

Contents

4

Natural Environment Research Council

INSTITUTE OF TERRESTRIAL ECOLOGY

Trees and wildlife in the Scottish uplands

ITE symposium no. 17
Banchory Research Station
4 and 5 December 1985

Edited by
DAVID JENKINS

Banchory Research Station
Hill of Brathens, Glassel
BANCHORY
Kincardineshire

Printed in Great Britain by
Lavenham Press Ltd, Lavenham, Suffolk
© NERC Copyright 1986

Published in 1986 by
Institute of Terrestrial Ecology
Administrative Headquarters
Monks Wood Experimental Station
Abbots Ripton
HUNTINGDON
PE17 2LS

BRITISH LIBRARY CATALOGUING-IN-PUBLICATION DATA
Trees and wildlife in the Scottish uplands – (ITE symposium,
    ISSN 0263-8614; no. 17)
    1. Forest management – Scotland
    I. Jenkins, D. (David). 1926–. II. Institute of Terrestrial Ecology.
    III. Series
    ISBN 0 904282 97 X

ACKNOWLEDGEMENTS
The expenses of the foreign visitors to the symposium were met by Fountain
Forestry Ltd who also gave a generous grant towards other costs of organizing
the meeting, including the provision of the colour plates. This help is gratefully
acknowledged. All the papers were typed by Mrs L M Burnett, ITE, Banchory.
Considerable help during the symposium was received from Dr N G Bayfield,
Mr J W H Conroy and Mr A D Littlejohn. Mrs L M Burnett and Mrs S Oliver
helped with the organization of the symposium. Mrs Jean King checked all the
references and Mrs P A Ward liaised with the printers and helped with the final
editing and proof reading. The photographs were selected by Mr N Picozzi. The
symposium was planned by a Steering Committee composed of Professor D
Jenkins and Dr J Miles (ITE), Mr M A Ashmole (Fountain Forestry Ltd) and
Professor H G Miller (University of Aberdeen).

COVER ILLUSTRATION
Deeside west of Ballater, Aberdeenshire, showing natural regeneration of pine
and birch, extensive conifer plantations and a remnant of native pine forest
(Photograph N Picozzi)

The *Institute of Terrestrial Ecology (ITE)* was established in 1973, from the
former Nature Conservancy's research stations and staff, joined later by the
Institute of Tree Biology and the Culture Centre of Algae and Protozoa. ITE
contributes to, and draws upon, the collective knowledge of the 14 sister
institutes which make up the *Natural Environment Research Council*, spanning
all the environmental sciences.

The Institute studies the factors determining the structure, composition and
processes of land and freshwater systems, and of individual plant and animal
species. It is developing a sounder scientific basis for predicting and modelling
environmental trends arising from natural or man-made change. The results of
this research are available to those responsible for the protection, management
and wise use of our natural resources.

One quarter of ITE's work is research commissioned by customers, such as
the Department of Environment, the Commission of the European
Communities, the Nature Conservancy Council and the Overseas Development
Administration. The remainder is fundamental research supported by NERC.

ITE's expertise is widely used by international organizations in overseas
projects and programmes of research.

Professor D Jenkins
Institute of Terrestrial Ecology
Banchory Research Station
Hill of Brathens, Glassel
BANCHORY
Kincardineshire
AB3 4BY
033 02 (Banchory) 3434

Preface

Forestry and its effects on our countryside are very much in the news. The concern of Scottish ecologists was expressed through the organization of at least 3 conferences during November and early December 1985. Our meeting is just one of them. It is nonetheless timely, and it brings together a wider range of people than the other 2 meetings. The first, organized by the Scottish Ornithologists' Club, discussed the interactions of commercial forestry with birds. The second, under the auspices of the Countryside Commission for Scotland, was concerned mainly with broadleaved trees. We are concerned with wider aspects, including both birds and broadleaved trees, although primarily with conifer plantations in the Scottish uplands. However, it is impossible to consider the impact of any aspect of afforestation in isolation; forestry in the Scottish uplands is not a separate industry from forestry in the lowlands, and the industry is international.

The concern of foresters to integrate their management policy with the requirements of the rest of the rural community is obvious. The new policy of the Forestry Commission with regard to broadleaved trees has arisen at least partly as a result of public concern. The economic demand for more home-produced timber may be satisfied only by planting up open hillsides and spoiling views which many people have come to regard as part of their heritage. It may be necessary, though this is still unproven, to afforest part of the habitat of upland birds which are rare in Britain. Decisions on some of these points may be political, but the widespread public concern remains.

This concern is about integrating the need for timber with maintaining the richness of the Scottish upland countryside, of which the forests are very much a part. Nature conservationists and animal and plant ecologists already have a great deal of practical knowledge on the management of semi-natural habitats, but their knowledge of the fauna of commercial forests is, in some cases, not as great as they would wish. The purpose of this meeting is to bring together foresters, conservationists and other ecologists to discuss the status and future growth of Scottish forests, to identify ways in which forests can be managed to optimize their conservation of wildlife and amenity and recreation values, and to learn from experience elsewhere. If gaps in our knowledge are exposed, discussion of them will help this Institute of the Natural Environment Research Council in planning a programme of research on the requirements for managing woodland for wildlife and amenity in British uplands, and lay the foundations for future co-operation with foresters and other ecologists.

David Jenkins
Brathens
December 1985

The nature of British upland forests in the 1980s

A A ROWAN
Forestry Commission, Edinburgh

1 Introduction

If anyone had reviewed the status of British upland forests in 1885, he would have found little to write about; the fundamental feature of these forests today is that they exist. The restoration of forest cover to a substantial part of the uplands must be one of the most dramatic land use changes experienced in these islands. Such a change represents a significant technical achievement, which stands comparison with the great successes in improved agricultural production. The forests are, understandably, very different in character from the woodlands lost in earlier times, in much the same way that modern agriculture differs from, say, mediaeval farming. Understanding the present status of these forests requires an appreciation of how they were, and are being, created.

The forests exist very largely as a consequence of a consistent Government policy of forest expansion which had its origins in Committees of Enquiry in 1885–87, 1902 and 1912, the Royal Commission on Coast Erosion and Afforestation in 1909, and the Forestry Sub-Committee of the Reconstruction Committee 1916–17, better known as the Acland Committee (Ministry of Reconstruction 1918). The 1909 Royal Commission proposed 2 alternative schemes for state afforestation. One involved the planting of 4.2 Mha in 60 years, and the other 2.8 Mha in 80 years. The Acland Committee estimated that the area of rough grazing capable of growing first-class timber was at least 1.2 Mha, and probably more than 2 Mha. The Committee considered that the afforestation of 0.81 Mha would diminish home production of meat by less than one per cent. In order to render the United Kingdom independent of imported timber for 3 years in an emergency, it was necessary to afforest 0.72 Mha, allowing for an improved yield from existing woods. It was recommended that two-thirds of this area should be planted in the first 40 years (Ministry of Reconstruction 1918). In 1918, the United Kingdom included the whole of Ireland.

The story of how the Government acted on the Acland Committee's Report, setting up the Forestry Commission (FC) in 1919, is fairly well known. Despite the financial stringencies of 1922 and 1931, the work of land acquisition and planting went ahead. By the outbreak of war in 1939, the Commission had acquired approximately 88% of the 'Acland' programme and had planted 75% (147 kha). A major review of forest policy (Forestry Commission 1943) assessed the areas of rough grazing and woodland from 1938 statistics, as shown in Table 1. This review, recognizing the wholesale exploitation of woodland from 1939 on-wards, proposed that a forest area of 5 million acres (2.03 Mha) was required, for national safety and as reasonable insurance against future stringency in world supplies. It was estimated that this area could be secured by afforestation of 3 million acres (1.22 Mha) and 2 million acres (0.81 Mha) from those existing woodlands 'better suited for forestry than for any other national purpose'. This statement implied that 0.44 Mha of existing woodland would not form part of the productive forest estate. The pre-war rate of planting was considered manifestly inadequate, and emphasis was placed on rapid expansion with new planting rates of up to 30 kha yr^{-1} in the second and third decades (ie 1955–75) against an average rate of new planting over the 50-year period of 24 kha yr^{-1}.

It is interesting to note that the 50-year target of 2.03 Mha of productive forest and woodland was reached in 1985, after 40 years of work. While part of this land use change has been carried out by the owners of the land, all the Forestry Commission's expansion has been carried out without recourse to powers of compulsory purchase. This development represents a great number of acquisition transactions, all of which have gone through, as have the many private forestry acquisitions, after negotiation between willing seller (or lessor) and buyer. This smooth transition, moreover, has caused minimal reduction in agricultural output, even in those areas where expansion has been greatest.

Given the land pattern of Britain, it was inevitable that the great bulk of forest expansion would be in the uplands, where the rough grazings lay.

2 The upland forests

2.1 Definitions

The term 'upland' is not precise. Taking an altitudinal measure, such as 230 m above Ordnance Datum, gives some indication of where the uplands lie, but increased latitude gives recognizable upland con-

Table 1. Land and woodland area (Mha) of Great Britain, 1943 (source: Forestry Commission 1943)

	England & Wales	Scotland	GB
Total land area	15.10	7.75	22.85
Area of rough grazings	2.28	4.25	6.54
Area of common grazing included above	0.57	negligible	0.57
Forest and woodlands	0.83	0.42	1.25
Forest as percentage of total area	5.5	5.4	5.5

ditions almost at sea level. These conditions give rise to the predominant upland husbandry of rough grazing on soils which severely limit the agricultural options open to the occupier. Although there are lowland rough grazings, eg on the Dorset heaths, the 1938 figures for these areas (Table 1) are probably as good a measure of 'upland', in relative terms at the very least, as one is likely to obtain.

Locating forest areas in relation to upland also presents difficulty. Forest statistics are not collected in terms which answer the questions of where, and of what extent and composition, are Britain's upland forests. Some indication is obtained by using data from the woodland census of 1979–82 for the FC Conservancies which then existed (Forestry Commission 1984). The Scottish and Welsh Conservancies, together with North-East England, can be taken as 'upland', while East, South-East and South-West England are not. North-West England covers a wide range from true upland in Cumbria and the Pennines to typical lowlands in the English midlands, and has to be regarded as being intermediate.

Census results showing the extent and composition of forest and woodland, both FC and privately owned, in these Conservancies are given in Table 2.

2.2 Distribution
Always bearing in mind that these figures relate to total woodland area, upland and lowland, within these Conservancies, Table 2 confirms what one might expect regarding the distribution of forest. The high proportion of woodland in Scotland is in line with the proportion of rough grazings, as in Wales.

The proportion of land surface under trees is now appreciable, particularly in West and South Scotland, in British terms if not in European. The proportions are nowhere extraordinary, however; Dumfries and Gallo-way, with 21% of its land surface under woodland, is still very much an agricultural region, as are west Glamorgan and Moray, each with 20%, putting them in the same league as Belgium.

2.3 Age structure
The most striking feature of today's upland forests is their youth. The major period of expansion in England and North Wales was immediately post-war, while in Scotland and South Wales the period since 1960 shows the greatest change. By far the largest proportion of conifer forest in West and South Scotland is under 40 years old, with more than two-thirds under 20 years old. This can be seen as a clear response to Government policy of forest expansion, and the technical ability to put it into effect.

2.4 Species
The importance of spruce in upland forests stands out clearly, particularly in the wetter areas of West Scotland and North Wales. The high proportion of pine in East Scotland and North-East England might be expected; in North Scotland, the pine proportion highlights the extent to which expansion took place in the drier eastern areas of the Conservancy and the substantial use of lodgepole pine (*Pinus contorta*). The use of species other than pines or spruces is much more a feature of English and Welsh forests than Scottish, with larches (*Larix* spp.) or Douglas fir (*Pseudotsuga menziesii*) predominating in this category.

3 How the upland forests were established
3.1 Extent
Efforts to extend the area of woodland by the improving landlords of the 18th century were largely directed to the lowlands, most often as part of agricultural improvement. The extensive hill plantations on the Atholl estates were a pioneering example, not followed on any great scale elsewhere. Various

Table 2. Areas (kha) of forest and woodlands in 'upland' Conservancies, 1980 (source: Forestry Commission 1984)

Conservancy 1	Total woodland area 2	Column 2 as % of total land and inland water area 3	Area of conifer high forest 4	Column 4 as % of column 2 5	Conifer age distribution: % of area in column 4				Main conifer species: % of column 4		
					0–20	21–40	41–60	Over 60	Pine	Spruce	Other
N (Scotland)	245	9.2	199	81	59	26	9	6	60	31	9
E (Scotland)	218	12.2	176	81	41	38	12	9	49	35	16
W (Scotland)	190	15.3	156	83	69	23	7	1	8	81	11
S (Scotland)	267	16.3	235	89	68	26	4	2	14	73	13
NE (England)	177	7.6	115	65	38	45	14	3	30	50	20
N (Wales)	121	11.0	87	73	41	45	13	1	9	67	24
S (Wales)	120	12.3	81	67	50	39	10	1	12	57	31
NW (England)	169	5.6	77	45	42	37	17	4	35	35	30
Scotland	920	12.6	766	83	60	28	8	4	33	55	12
England	948	7.3	382	41	42	37	17	4	38	31	31
Wales	241	11.6	168	70	45	43	11	1	10	62	28
Great Britain	2108	9.4	1317	62	53	32	11	4	32	49	20

factors account for this trend, such as the relative profitability of upland stock rearing, the greater attraction of agricultural rather than forest investment for available capital, and, in the 19th century, ready access to cheap timber from overseas. Upland areas which had retained a certain amount of forest cover from earlier times, such as the valleys of the eastern Highlands and the broadleaved woods of Cumbria, usually remained under some form of management. New planting was carried out successfully on the better upland sites, particularly when these areas retained some of the characteristics of earlier woodland conditions. Afforestation of the wetter and more exposed sites presented severe technical difficulties, however.

3.2 Species availability

Solutions to these difficulties lay in 2 directions. The first was to find species suitable for the sites. That the range of native British tree species was inadequate had been recognized before the 17th century. Early introductions from Europe of European larch (*Larix decidua*), Norway spruce (*Picea abies*) and European silver fir (*Abies alba*) provided a valuable addition to Scots pine (*Pinus sylvestris*), oak (*Quercus* spp.), beech (*Fagus sylvatica*) and sycamore (*Acer pseudoplatanus*), particularly on lower ground, but all had limitations. Exposure and site limitations were apparent with all these species, and planting at high elevations was rarely attempted. The introduction of western North American conifers in the 19th century was an essential element in the development of upland afforestation, with Sitka spruce (*Picea sitchensis*) (introduced in 1831) quite outstanding. The techniques of site classification began to be applied in the British uplands between 1914 and 1920 under the direction of R L Robinson, and were progressively refined. They are described well in Anderson's book *The selection of tree species* (Anderson 1950). Work on species selection went hand-in-hand with the second, and principal, developmental thrust, that of altering the site itself.

3.3 The heaths

The drier upland heaths, part of the Callunetum of western Europe, had been the subject of periodic planting in the 19th and early 20th centuries, almost exclusively with Scots pine. These plantations were generally of low production, and on poorest ground a satisfactory crop was not obtained. These heaths are generally in the east of Britain, with predominantly siliceous soils on which shallow podzols have developed, typified by 2 more or less impermeable layers, a thin surface peat and an ironpan, leading to waterlogging and anaerobic soil. The degraded condition is the result mainly of human action in destroying the forest cover by felling and burning, and of uncontrolled grazing which brought about the dominance of heather (*Calluna vulgaris*). On the least fertile areas, even heather exists only in an impoverished form (Zehetmayr 1960). In addition to Scots pine, a number of other species have been tried experimentally, but the key to successful afforestation lay in mechanical cultivation.

The importance of cultivating the heathlands had long been recognized, notably in the afforestation of the Jutland heaths from about 1800. Beginning with hand digging of holes or strips, or simple ploughing, as early as 1870 deep ploughing to 50 cm with a horse-drawn plough was being done by the Danish state forest service and the Heath Society. This method broke the pan and leached layers and mixed them with the surface peat, giving a favourable planting medium. The FC embarked on a renewed attempt to afforest the British upland heaths from 1920 onwards, and soon confirmed that disturbance of the surface peat to promote its aeration and breakdown was the vital factor, together with breaking the pan when it is near the surface as in typical iron or peaty podzols. Site preparation on these lines by hand in the 1920s gave way to ploughing from 1930 onwards, first on the boulder-free heaths of north Yorkshire, and later on more difficult sites as suitable ploughs and the machines to draw them became better developed. The progression has been towards deep-subsoiling tines with shallow mouldboards, in place of earlier deep single-mouldboard ploughs.

3.4 The peatlands

The upland peatlands presented similar problems. They lie in the higher rainfall areas, and those available for afforestation are of the acid 'moss' or bog types, developed over rocks which are for the most part acid, hard and ancient. The Carboniferous series is the youngest to bear this type of peat over any great area.

For forestry purposes, any depth of organic remains over 15 cm can be regarded as peat. The peatlands generally merge, mosaic fashion, into the heaths as one goes eastward, depending on rainfall and topography. Some of the peatlands are of the basin or 'raised bog' variety, and, while in many areas these may be found suitable for forestry, their extent and importance are much less than that of the climatic peats which form a large proportion of the land available for afforestation.

Numerous attempts had been made from the 18th century onwards to afforest peatland. When peats were better, ie carrying a vegetation of grass or rushes, there were successes; but on the more 'difficult' peats, notably those with heather/cottongrass/club-rush (*Calluna/Eriophorum/Scirpus*) vegetation, these attempts usually failed to establish a crop. Early attempts were handicapped by a lack of suitable species, and a failure to appreciate the necessity for using different techniques from those which gave good results on mineral soils. There appears to have been little attempt at extensive afforestation of difficult land, and few improvements in technique up to the end of the 19th century. One interesting exception was the use of Sitka spruce on peat at Durris, Kincardineshire, in the 1880s. Sitka spruce was used extensively at Moorburnhead, Dumfriesshire, where from 1913 onwards the Duke of Buccleuch planted a considerable area of moorland which was covered by peat about 30 cm deep. Planting in the Crown Plantations at Inverliever, Argyll, where much of the land was peat-covered, went on from 1909. Sitka spruce was used only on a very small scale at first, but, as the unsuitability of Norway spruce on many sites was apparent by the 1920s, Sitka became the preferred species for planting on peat. Scots pine was relatively little used on peatland by this time, having shown its unsuitability. European larch was equally unsuitable, though Japanese larch (*Larix kaempferi*) was used to a greater extent. A little use was made of *Abies* species, and early experimental work by the FC encompassed a wide range of possible species.

The Belgians carried out pioneer work, evolved from older Prussian methods, on the technique of turf planting and intensive drainage on the moor-grass (*Molinia*) moors of Hertogenwald from 1836 onwards, but it was not until 1907 that Stirling-Maxwell (1907) published an account of his turf planting experiments at Corrour, Inverness-shire. He had been planting at Corrour since 1892, and his great work laid the foundation for most of the subsequent development in the afforestation of peat (Zehetmayr 1954). The forest at Moorburnhead had been established by direct planting, and the FC used this method in its early years. By 1923, the poor growth of direct-planted spruce on peat was obvious; further experimental work confirmed the advantages of turf planting, which became adopted as the standard establishment method. As early as 1925, it was envisaged that hand digging of drains and turfs would be superseded at some future date by suitable ploughs and caterpillar tractors. Draining ploughs and adequate tractors became available just before the war, being first used on any scale in south Scotland in 1939–40. Early ploughs were of the Solotrac type, replaced for the most part by the draining ploughs developed first by Cuthbertson of Biggar and by Clark of Parkgate. These developments are fully described by Neustein (1976–77), and it is noteworthy that the FC Research Branch was able to specify what would be required of these machines from the results of remarkably successful 'mock ploughing' experiments from 1928 onwards, whereby furrows were turned over by hand to simulate single furrow or complete ploughing.

3.5 Fertilizers and herbicides

Another major development was the use of fertilizers, particularly at the time of establishment. This method had been applied at Corrour, using phosphatic fertilizer with the Belgian turf system, and top-dressing of checked stands with high-grade basic slag was carried out there from 1907 onwards (Stirling-Maxwell 1925). The FC laid down manuring trials at Inchnacardoch in 1925. These trials later confirmed the efficacy of a phosphate dressing, essential on the poorest peat types (Zehetmayr 1954). Basic slag, later replaced by ground mineral phosphate, was used with some caution, and it was not until the 1960s that low-cost aerial application became possible. Davies, working in west Scotland, was instrumental in developing this technique on a wide scale, not only for application at the time of planting but at periodic intervals, roughly 7 years, in the early life of the crop. Fertilizer regimes covered the application of potassium on deep peats, in addition to the standard phosphate. Application rates were in the region of 375 kg ha^{-1}, and are still being used (Davies 1969; Dannatt *et al.* 1971). Phosphate applications are particularly valuable in maintaining the growth rate of spruce in the face of the heather competition which commonly arises on grassy moorland when grazing ceases. Complementary to the fertilizers were the herbicides, first used on any scale in the 1960s, which made effective and cheap heather control possible to an extent unattainable by hand weeding.

3.6 Recent developments

By the late 1960s, therefore, the following lines of development were well established.

— *Cultivation and drainage* of both heaths and peats, well researched and understood, with equipment available to tackle the majority of sites.
— *Fertilizers*, also well researched, with low-cost means of application.
— *Herbicides*, to provide a degree of vegetation control not previously possible.
— *Species* well understood, particularly the ability of Sitka spruce to produce satisfactory crops on a wide range of sites.

The combined effect of these factors was to make upland afforestation possible on a much greater scale. Sites which had previously been considered too infertile or intractable could be manipulated and planted successfully; given some sort of rooting medium, the limits to afforestation became those of exposure and possible wind damage. The expansion of the forest area from 1960 onwards was the result, and the 1979–82 census highlights the importance of Sitka spruce, as shown in Table 3.

4 The importance of research

While upland forest can now be established with a high degree of certainty, some technical problems remain or have become apparent. Chief of these problems is undoubtedly stability. The deeper single-mouldboard plough furrows of the post-war period made for easier establishment on the peaty gleys, but gave a more restricted root-plate and greater susceptibility to windthrow than the spaced turfs of the old hand draining days. Windthrow and windbreak have, of course, been a cause for concern for as long as trees have been cultivated, particularly on poorly drained soils. Research by FC since the war provided informa-

Table 3. Proportion of Sitka spruce in planting since 1961 (source: Forestry Commission 1984)

	Sitka spruce as % of total area planted	
	1961–70	1971–80
North Scotland	35	57
East Scotland	30	52
West Scotland	73	88
South Scotland	62	84
North-East England	29	61
North Wales	62	71
South Wales	51	63
North-West England	21	40
Scotland	50	68
England	14	30
Wales	57	68
Great Britain	38	68

tion on the incidence of wind damage in relation to gales and on the aerodynamics of individual trees and crops (Fraser & Gardiner 1967). By 1977, Booth had put forward an empirical method of assessing wind-throw hazard in terms of altitude, exposure, soil conditions and regional windiness, which gave some general prediction of the height a crop was likely to reach before wind damage became appreciable (Booth 1977).

This method has proved to be a most useful management tool. Just as it became clear that tall trees are more prone to windthrow than small trees, it became apparent that nothing holds trees up better than other trees, and, contrary to earlier belief, thinning can increase the risk of windthrow. Realization of this fact led to the designation of substantial areas of crops as 'non-thin', particularly on the higher-lying peaty gleys on the west side of the country. Forest managers have now learned how to build the uncertainty of wind-throw into management plans, and how to deal with it efficiently; but the truncation of crop rotation by windthrow can have serious financial consequences, particularly if the trees have not attained sawmilling size in sufficient quantity. Any measure which increases stability is therefore valuable, and the development of techniques which give improved roothold is obviously desirable. Besides the questions of stability and thinning (or lack of it) are spacing and its relation to timber quality; experiments laid down in 1935–36 are now yielding valuable information as the trees reach maturity. There is also further potential for crop improvement through tree breeding, which, though not peculiar to upland forestry, is of great importance to it. As the older stands reach felling age, restocking assumes even greater importance, and regeneration techniques are capable of refinement.

The great success of Sitka spruce has raised the question of whether we now rely on it, and to a lesser extent lodgepole pine, overmuch. Wood (1974) pointed out that, with the exception of Norway spruce, all the chief afforestation species are intolerant trees belonging to the early ecological succession in their native habitats. The tolerant late succession species have (understandably) proved difficult to establish in bare land planting, but there is interest in the north-west American tolerants, especially grand fir (*Abies grandis*), western hemlock (*Tsuga heterophylla*) and western red cedar (*Thuja plicata*). The extent to which these and other species ought to be used to diversify the present upland forests is a matter for investigation. Profitability of produce is an important criterion, but by no means the only one.

The central role of the Forestry Commission research in laying the foundations on which upland forestry in the 1980s is based will be apparent. Research has been very largely task-orientated, and in 1921 the FC grouped the problems confronting it under the following 4 heads:

   i. establishment of plantations
   ii. improvement of production: thinning, pruning, etc
   iii. protection
   iv. the peat soils

The objective of pre-war research on afforestation was to find the cheapest effective method of establishing a healthy crop. As a result, experimentation concentrated on the difficult marginal sites as a means of bringing large areas of cheap ground into forestry (Wood 1974). The results of this research have been incremental and demonstrate the importance of a sound scientific base of experimental work, capable of validation, and providing a reliable foundation from which practical conclusions can be drawn.

5 The upland forest landscape
Even on the plateau lands, upland forests are a very visible entity in the landscape. There is no denying that some of the pre-war, and some of the post-war, planting was unsympathetic, to say the least. There were reasons for the choice of both area and species, notably the economic necessity to plant every last acre, and as quickly as possible, and it is not always possible to avoid uniformity where the underlying land form is relatively featureless. Some of the more attractive upland forests lie on varied, broken ground, when the original species selection was equally varied, or when failures or check brought uneven texture. The present position is rather different, with uniform stretches of forest being broken, whether by felling or windthrow, and a much better understanding by foresters of the necessity for, and the techniques of, good forest design. The appointment of Dame Sylvia Crowe as landscape consultant to the Forestry Commission in 1963 was a milestone in this respect, and the principles of forest landscape set out by her (Crowe 1966) continue to provide sound guidance for the many foresters wishing to manage forests which are both productive and pleasing to the eye. Good design and layout can do a great deal to integrate new

afforestation into the landscape, but the upland forest of the 1980s is, first and foremost, *young*. The full potential for variety and interest in these forests will be realized when the regeneration phase begins, and the age class distribution widens. Positive management will be required to achieve this potential.

6 Upland forest wildlife

Considering its extent, the present upland forest is probably the least well-known habitat for wildlife. It is unquestionably man-made, just as the treeless ground it replaced was largely the consequence of human action, but it is no less deserving of study and recognition for what it is, rather than for what it is not.

What is increasingly evident is that upland forests are richer and more varied than those unacquainted with them might suppose. In many respects, the conservation of forest wildlife parallels the landscape position; the foresters of the 1980s show increasing awareness of the non-timber aspects of the forest entity, and the means whereby those features of conservation interest can be safeguarded at the time of afforestation are better understood. One example is the treatment of watercourses, researched by Mills for the Forestry Commission. Following publication of his recommendations (Mills 1980), sound watercourse management is now standard practice.

The importance of broadleaves in upland forests, both for landscape purposes and as habitat, is recognized in the Government's policy for broadleaves (Forestry Commission 1985). The 'guideline' aim of a proportion of broadleaves in these forests will form part of forest management plans from now on. A wide range of conservation aspects require further research, for example in habitat management. This work is likely to be an important part of the activity of the Research Division of the FC for some time to come.

The potential for measures to increase habitat diversity within today's upland forests is considerable, and this is recognized in the Code of Guidance prepared by Timber Growers United Kingdom (1985). There exists a substantial body of practical knowledge and experience among the Wildlife Rangers of the Forestry Commission and private forestry, of which the FC *Wildlife ranger's handbook* contains many examples (Springthorpe & Myhill 1985). The development of this aspect of forest management is one of the most striking features of upland forestry in this decade.

7 Access and recreation

People like visiting forests for a wide variety of reasons, particularly if they are pleasant, attractive places. The upland features of landscape and wildlife interest are of obvious importance. Visitors have always been welcome in FC forests and in a great many private woodlands, forest operations permitting. Numbers of visitors coming to forests steadily increase, and the popularity of visitor centres, forest walks, and wayfaring trails continues. The sport of orienteering is very largely forest- or woodland-based, with particular emphasis on the upland areas. These forests have 2 valuable attributes: they can accommodate much greater numbers of visitors, without appearing crowded, than can the same area of treeless country; and the shelter afforded to walkers is much appreciated when conditions on the open hill are inclement. There may be some conflict of interest between public access and the need to protect the most important conservation sites (the sanctuary areas), but this protection can be achieved by zoning appropriate areas of the forest.

8 Conclusions

The forests of the uplands have gone through a number of stages. The first, colonizing, post-glacial forest gave way to the forests which were exploited by man up to and beyond mediaeval times, and of which only semi-natural remnants are left. We still have examples of the efforts by landowners to replace woodland, from the 18th century onwards. Their successors are the 20th century plantations established by means of well-developed techniques, often on land which has not carried trees for centuries. We are now, in the 1980s, at a dynamic, transition stage, as these plantations develop into what we would all recognize as forests. The major ecological shift from bare land to full forest diversity of structure, appearance, habitat and wildlife takes time to develop, and what we see today is no more than a snapshot of a continuing process.

The forests change, as do people's requirements of them. The productive use of land makes good sense nationally, and the creation of a renewable resource on this scale is no more than good husbandry, fully consonant with the principle of the World Conservation Strategy, ie of resource conservation for sustainable development. The changes brought about by the creation of forest are welcomed by those to whom it brings employment and prosperity, but may not be welcome to those who prefer to see familiar surroundings remain unaltered. Forest expansion may also be seen as a threat to other interests, whether farming or nature conservation, or to the existing social pattern within the countryside. It is, however, within the range of possibilities to establish and manage forests in such a way that a number of different requirements can be accommodated, particularly if the various interests and concerns can be identified and examined objectively. Achieving a balance between the needs of timber production and other interests is a duty of the Forestry Commission under the Wildlife and Countryside (Amendment) Act 1984. This duty is taken very seriously, and welcomed; given this reasonable balance, the forests will serve the needs of Britain in many ways into the next century and beyond.

9 References

Anderson, M.L. 1950. *The selection of tree species.* Edinburgh: Oliver & Boyd.

Booth, T.C. 1977. *Windthrow hazard classification.* (Research information note no. 22.) Farnham: Forestry Commission.

Crowe, S. 1966. *Forestry in the landscape.* (Forestry Commission booklet no 18.) London: HMSO.

Dannatt, N., Davies, E.J.M. & McCavish, W.J. 1971. Kilmory: 1971: An investigation into fertiliser response. *Scott. For.,* **25,** 100–109.

Davies, E.J.M. 1969. Further experiences with aerial fertilization in the West (Scotland) Conservancy. *Scott. For.,* **23,** 87–101.

Forestry Commission. 1943. *Post–war forest policy.* (Cmd 6447.) London: HMSO.

Forestry Commission. 1984. *Census of woodlands and trees.* Edinburgh: Forestry Commission.

Forestry Commission. 1985. *The policy for broadleaved woodlands.* (Forestry Commission policy and procedure paper no. 5.) London: HMSO.

Fraser, A.I. & Gardiner, J.B.H. 1967. *Rooting and stability in Sitka spruce.* (Forestry Commission bulletin no. 40.) London: HMSO.

Mills, D.H. 1980. *The management of forest streams.* (Forestry Commission leaflet no. 78.) London: HMSO.

Ministry of Reconstruction. 1918. *Final report of the Reconstruction Committee – Forestry Sub–Committee.* (Cd 8881.) London: HMSO.

Neustein, S.A. 1976–77. A history of plough development in British forestry. Parts I–IV. *Scott. For.,* **30,** 2–15; 89–111; 253–274; & **31,** 2–12.

Springthorpe, G.D. & Myhill, N. 1985. *Wildlife ranger's handbook.* Edinburgh: Forestry Commission.

Stirling-Maxwell, Sir J. 1907. The planting of high moorland. *Trans. R. Scott. arboric. Soc.,* **20,** 1–7.

Stirling-Maxwell, Sir J. 1925. On the use of manures in peat planting. *Trans. R. Scott. arboric. Soc.,* **39,** 103–109.

Timber Growers United Kingdom. 1985. *The forestry and woodland code.* London: TGUK.

Wood, R.F. 1974. *Fifty years of forestry research.* (Forestry Commission bulletin no. 50.) London: HMSO.

Zehetmayr, J.W.L. 1954. *Experiments in tree planting on peat.* (Forestry Commission bulletin no. 22.) London: HMSO.

Zehetmayr, J.W.L. 1960. *Afforestation of upland heaths.* (Forestry Commission bulletin no. 32.) London: HMSO.

The status of native woods in the Scottish uplands

G F PETERKEN
Nature Conservancy Council, Peterborough

1 Introduction

Scotland's native woodlands were long ago reduced by felling, burning, grazing and retrogressive soil changes to a small fragment of their original natural extent (eg Rymer 1980). Some measure of their reduced state comes from the Forestry Commission census of 1980, which recorded 119 kha* of woodland dominated by native broadleaf trees and shrubs, 1.6% of the area of Scotland. Quantitatively, these remnants are swamped by modern conifer plantations, but their importance as features in the landscape and as semi-natural habitats remains high.

Descriptions of these native woods are available in a number of publications. McVean (1964) provides a general account of the flora and structure of the main woodland types. Gordon (1911) also describes a number of types in his search for the characteristics of the original woodland. The woodland sections of Ratcliffe (1977) provide both a general review and detailed descriptions of important sites. Classification and descriptions of all or part of the range of types are available in Birks (1973), Birse *et al.* (1976), Bunce (1982), Goodier and Ball (1974), McVean and Ratcliffe (1962), and Peterken (1981). Steven and Carlisle (1959) comprehensively review the history and natural history of the native pinewoods. Detailed studies of the ecological development of individual woods are available for a few sites such as Beinn Eighe (Durno & McVean 1959), Abernethy (O'Sullivan 1973), Rannoch (Lindsay 1974), and Loch Lomond (Tittensor 1970). The massive historical compilation by Anderson (1967) gives numerous historical references to the composition and state of native woods.

2 Rassal Ashwood

Before considering the status of upland native woods in general, it is worth focusing attention on one, not particularly typical, example, Rassal Ashwood. This wood lies just to the north of Kishorn village in Ross district (NG 845431), and it is notable as the most northerly example of 'true' ashwood (Ratcliffe 1977). It occupies a gentle, west-facing slope of Durness limestone, which is divided into an irregular mosaic of ridges and hollows. The ridges are formed by outcrops of limestone, thinly covered by organic alkaline loam, whereas the hollows are filled with heavy, neutral clay loam, which is mostly freely drained but locally

*Calculated from figures given in Forestry Commission (1983) by taking the area of coppice; coppice-with-standards; high forest and scrub composed of oak, ash, birch, elm, alder, hazel and willow; 75% of the area of 'other' and 'mixed' broadleaf high forest and scrub; and adding 10 kha for native pinewoods

flushed. The site is heavily grazed by sheep and mostly covered by a mixed sward of grasses and small herbs, and by dense drifts of bracken (*Pteridium aquilinum*). The trees are mostly thinly scattered, mature, open-grown ash (*Fraxinus excelsior*), forming an irregular parkland, with a few old hazel (*Corylus avellana*), rowan (*Sorbus aucuparia*) and hawthorn (*Crataegus monogyna*).

Even though this is a National Nature Reserve, a prior wayleave existed which resulted in the felling of a limited number of trees on at least 2 occasions, and enabled the age of the trees to be determined (Table 1). Most trees had very slow growth phases and some had hollow cores, so the absolute ages given are unlikely to be completely accurate. Futhermore, the age at felling of tree 8 is likely to be substantially less than that given, as it is improbable that it maintained a very slow growth rate for 200 years. Ignoring this tree, it appears that the present stand originated between 1750 and 1820, with a particularly high initiation rate in the late 18th century. Certainly, there has been little or no recruitment for more than a century, and the youngest stem counted was a stool shoot of hazel dating from the mid-19th century. No ring counts of rowan are available, but, as these trees are clearly old, half decayed and often lie prostrate with rejuvenated crowns, they are surely contemporaries of the ash.

Speculating on the conditions under which the stand was initiated, natural regeneration seems more likely than planting because there is no obvious even-aged cohort, and the ashes are present on the limestone outcrops but absent from the intervening deeper soils. Early growth of most trees was slow or very slow, which suggests a prolonged fight against grazing and browsing. Indeed, some of the old ash are double-stemmed, which reinforces this possibility. Growth rates cannot, however, have been solely determined by the degree of browsing, for slow initial growth was maintained for many decades, by which time the trees were well out of reach. In fact, the General Roy map of 1750 shows the site as woodland, which indicates that they grew up within a pre-existing stand. Their wide-spreading form suggests, however, that the stand must have been open-canopied. Their growth history is highly individualistic, and some (notably tree 9) show a clear rejuvenation late in life. The tentative conclusion is that the present stand originated slowly by natural regeneration during a period of reduced grazing either side of 1800.

In an attempt to rejuvenate the wood, the Nature

Table 1. Estimates of age and year of origin of trees felled in Rassal Ashwood

	Species	Rings counted	Missing rings	Therefore, age at death (years)	Year of origin	Notes on growth pattern
1968 counts (felled *c*1966)						
1	Ash	181	—	181	1785	0–105 slow; 106–160 moderate; 161–181 slow
2	Ash	178	5*	183	1788	6–140 slow; 141–183 moderate
3	Hazel	114	—	114	1852	Slow
4	Ash	152	—	152	1814	0–40 moderate; 41–152 very slow
5	Ash	178	—	178	1788	Moderate
6	Ash	206	—	206	1760	0–40 very slow; 41–206 moderate
1985 counts (felled *c*1984)						
7	Ash	107	33*	140	1844	34–81 slow; 82–140 moderate
8	Ash	96	*c*200*	*c*300	1684	200–221 very slow; 222–296 moderate, becoming very slow
9	Ash	184	—	184	1800	0–98 very slow; 99–143 moderate; 144–164 fast; 165–184 slow

*Estimated by extrapolation from the innermost surviving growth rings

Conservancy enclosed 2 ha of open ash/hazel woodland in 1957. In the subsequent 28 years, mixed woodland developed slowly at first and then vigorously, so that it now presents a marked contrast to the unenclosed elderly parkland. Within the enclosure, the old ash remain with no perceptible change in their vigour, but they are now embedded in vigorous regrowth of the hitherto moribund old hazels, and natural regeneration, some of which has now grown to 10 m, almost as high as the old ash. Interestingly, ash is not well represented in the new regeneration, though it is present in patches and growing well. The main regenerants are rowan, hazel and goat willow (*Salix caprea*): there is a suspicion that some of the willows were planted. Regeneration has been particularly copious on the limestone outcrops, but in the hollows the growth of bracken, grasses and tall herbs has been vigorous enough to exclude most regeneration, and these areas remain as clearings. The ground vegetation has also reverted from pasture to a woodland character: the pasture grasses have gone; tall herbs such as meadowsweet (*Filipendula ulmaria*) and hogweed (*Heracleum sphondylium*) flourish; and shade-bearing herbs prevail, such as upland enchanter's-nightshade (*Circaea intermedia*), bluebell (*Endymion non-scriptus*), wild strawberry (*Fragaria vesca*), herb Robert (*Geranium robertianum*), water avens (*Geum rivale*), wall lettuce (*Mycelis muralis*) and primrose (*Primula vulgaris*).

The pattern of recent regeneration has repeated that of the late 18th century, in so far as colonization has been slowest on the deeper soils. The composition, however, is different. To some extent, the difference could be due to age (if willow had regenerated in the late 18th century, it would now be dead), but the higher proportion of hazel and rowan in present regeneration, combined with the lower density of ash, implies that conditions for regeneration were different. Recent regeneration, in fact, tends to support the notion that the old ashwood did not regenerate in an older, closed woodland.

The woodland described is not completely isolated. A small burn, the Allt Mor, flows in a deeply incised, wooded valley about 0.5 km to the east and south, and this woodland almost links with Rassal Ashwood along the margins of the Kishorn floodplain. This valley is likely to have been a permanent refuge for woodland species and a possible source from which Rassal Ashwood could have been reconstituted, though in fact many of the woodland herbs grow in the grazed pasture. Part at least is ash/hazel woodland on alkaline clay loam, with a ground flora similar to that which has developed within the exclosure.

3 Habitat continuity and isolation

Rassal Ashwood may or may not be ancient, but other woods have been demonstrated to be primary. For example, the mixture of pine and birch at Beinn Eighe was shown by Durno and McVean (1959) to be continuous back to at least the boreal period, even though the amount of woodland and the relative importance of pine (*Pinus sylvestris*), birch (*Betula* spp.) and alder (*Alnus glutinosa*) have fluctuated sharply. They found, also, that the amount of oak in the district has possibly not changed greatly either, a point which is confirmed by historical records of all these woodland types in the 16th and 17th centuries (Anderson 1967). Comparison of late 19th century and modern Ordnance Survey maps indicates that the birch fringes of Letterewe oakwood are recent, but the core of this wood must be ancient. The pattern of woodland in this district has been stable in general terms, but fluctuations in distribution and composition appear to be a characteristic of the system.

The concept of a woodland core around which the detailed nature of woodland fluctuates is perhaps the key to understanding upland natural woods. This core can be seen in a strictly geographical sense of the woodland boundary and indeed location, which has expanded, contracted and even moved bodily over long periods (Fenton 1985). It can also be seen in terms of composition, in that a wood has a core of principal species, but the relative importance of each can vary within wide limits.

Some types, notably those composed principally of birch (Kirby 1984) and/or pine, can fluctuate so much that the cores may be difficult to define. Miles (1978) has studied birchwood development on heathland and found that such woods have a limited duration. If they are not destroyed by some extraneous disturbance, they eventually degenerate back to heathland. This characteristic implies a cyclical relationship between birchwood and heathland in which continuity of woodland on one spot is abnormal. Continuity, however, exists on a larger scale. Alternatively, birch may be replaced by shade-bearing trees such as rowan, but only if the successors are present within colonizing distance. Some birchwoods appear to be inhibited in their succession by isolation. Craigellachie, for example, has a soil range and altitude which ought to be suitable for hazel, ash, wych elm (*Ulmus glabra*) and oak, but these are not colonizing.

Native pinewoods illustrate the core concept admirably. They were identified as the woods with pine continuity since at least the 17th century, but the amount and distribution of pine within them have varied. At Abernethy, there are simultaneously areas of pine parkland containing only old trees where the woodland is retreating, and isolated patches of young saplings where it is advancing. This amoeboid habit is not just a product of recent land use changes, but prevailed in prehistoric times (O'Sullivan 1973), albeit at a greater density and amount of woodland. The Black Wood of Rannoch has certainly been harshly treated in historical times, through felling, grazing, burning and planting with alien trees, but the main cores of pine woodland have been little altered over the centuries (Lindsay 1974). The total extent and boundaries have fluctuated, and so particularly have the composition and stocking.

The broadleaf woodlands of oak, hazel, ash, wych elm and/or alder have rather more stable cores than the birch- and pinewoods, and probably fewer fluctuations in their boundaries. With the possible exception of acid oakwoods and floodplain alderwoods, these are naturally more stable types, well able to regenerate within themselves. Heavily reduced by grazing, many are now restricted to steep slopes, broken ground and narrow valleys, where they are naturally protected from further reduction. Requiring richer soils, they are more closely associated than other types with the farmed landscape, and have thus been corseted within fixed boundaries, like the woods of the English lowlands. Those which survived until recent times have mostly been coppiced, which itself has tended to stabilize their composition and boundaries. Indeed, those which were not managed had largely vanished by the early 20th century (Gordon 1911), except in truly inaccessible sites, such as the coastal cliffs of Trotternish, or the gorge at Dundonnel.

To what extent the woodland plants and animals keep pace with woodland fluctuations is largely a matter of conjecture. The flora of heathy birchwoods appears to be adapted to change by a variety of methods: survival in unwooded heathland; rapid colonization; dormant, buried seed (Miles 1986). Native pinewoods are said to have their distinctive herbs, but these can survive felling and planting of pine (eg at Golspie) and can colonize distant pine forests (eg at Culbin). The flora of mixed broadleaf woods probably includes more species which are genuinely immobile, but even here many species and communities have an obvious capacity to survive clearance and replanting (Gordon 1911), and grow successfully in unwooded habitats, such as rock outcrops, cliffs and bracken brakes. Crowson (1962) found that certain beetles were incapable of colonization, but Wormell (1977) found a steady build-up of species in remote broadleaf plantations on Rhum. The general impresion is that habitat continuity is less important as an ecological factor than it is in lowland England, though it certainly must be significant. Scots pine plantations in Scotland occupy 13 times the area occupied by native pinewoods, but it seems highly improbable that they contain the 93% of the population of coralroot orchid (*Corallorhiza trifida*), creeping lady's-tresses (*Goodyera repens*) and one-flowered wintergreen (*Moneses uniflora*) which might be expected if habitat continuity were insignificant.

4 Age, structure, management and composition
The ash trees of Rassal give the impression of being gnarled survivors from prehistoric antiquity, but in fact they are less than 200 years old. This is not unusual: the great majority of trees in the semi-natural woods are of 19th and 20th century origins. Surprisingly, among the older stands may be numbered some of the northern birchwoods. Unexceptional trees felled about 1980 on the south shore of Loch Rannoch and at Dunbeath Water (Caithness) were aged respectively 209 and 180 years. Truly ancient trees are quite rare. The Black Wood of Rannoch contains many 'granny' pines over 300 years old, the oldest known of which was 396 years when felled in the late 1970s. Some parkland trees may be equally old; Gordon (1911) quotes the case of Lochwood (Dumfries), where one of the old parkland oaks was 230 years old when felled in 1773, and its apparent contemporaries survived until modern times.

Clearly, if these woods are relics, they have continued to rejuvenate themselves. The structure of many is essentially even-aged, and most of those which are mixed-aged contain obvious even-age cohorts (McVean 1964). Regeneration has clearly taken place in pulses, initiated by changes in management (as at Rassal), temporary disturbances and planting, between which there has been little or no regeneration.

The impression gained from Anderson (1967) is that planting has long been a common practice in Scotland's broadleaf woods, but it seems likely that this practice has affected the policies rather than the woods now regarded as semi-natural. Admittedly, many woods now contain beech (*Fagus sylvatica*) and sycamore (*Acer pseudoplatanus*), which owe their presence either directly to planting within the wood or indirectly to seeding from trees planted elsewhere. Furthermore, substantial alteration in the balance between native species has occurred in some woods by both planting and cleaning. For example, the pure oak coppices at Twentyshilling Wood (NN 761225) and Craig Wood (NO 033427) appear to be the product of planting. Conversely, alder was cut out of the Black Wood of Rannoch (Lindsay 1974), and it is now very rare there. On moist, base-rich soils, oak is often present only as large trees, which suggests that this species' presence is due more to coppice management than to natural factors. Nevertheless, most semi-natural woods have no obvious signs of planting, and historical studies generally indicate that planting was insignificant in the coppiced woods (Lindsay 1975) and, until recently, in the native pinewoods (Steven & Carlisle 1959).

The degree to which semi-natural woodland composition has been altered by man is perhaps, exemplified by Methven Wood (NO 054266). In the 18th and 19th centuries, this appears to have been treated as coppice-with-standards on a 26-year rotation, and the modern wood still clearly retains this structure. Most is pedunculate oak (*Q. robur*) standards over hazel coppice with abundant birch, but parts have sessile oak (*Q. petraea*) standards, and other parts have some alder in the underwood. Mid-19th century recollections of management by the gardener and land steward of the Smythe family (see insert) show not only his perception of the distant origin of the wood, but the subtle shuffling of native species and the introduction of exotics by planting and natural regeneration.

The coppicing exemplified by Methven Wood came late to the Highlands and retreated early, but its influence on modern woodland structure was strong. As Lindsay (1975) says, 'The self-sown deciduous woodland of Scotland was coppiced to such an extent that the terms "coppice" and "natural wood" came to be regarded as interchangeable'. Many woods still have a coppice-with-standards structure which is every bit as clear as it is in south-east England. The oakwoods on the eastern shores of Loch Lomond had a long history of coppicing and, until forestry recently brought about changes, their structure and composition reflected the age at which they were last cut and singled, and the intensity with which uncommercial species had been cleaned out (Tittensor 1970). Many woods have not been treated as coppice since the mid-19th century, but still have a cohort of dominant old oaks in a matrix of younger growth (eg Milton of Drimmie valley, NO 169505). The abandoned coppice-with-standards commonly has 2 age classes, the older standards of 100–200 years, and coppice regrowth of as recent as 30–40 years, but usually older.

The wood of Methven
'This beautiful remainder of Caledonian Scenery had its first growth in very distant Ages without the Aid or help of Man either to plant or protect it, and in latter ages had extended very considerably to the Westward, and has often afforded shelter to the Brave as well as concealment to the Unworthy – and hath been considered by its late and worthy proprietors as a Bank established on the firmest footing.

From an old survey it seems to contain nearly 200 acres of Ground – and the fine Scotch firs interspersed in the south wood appear to have arisen from seeds scattered by the winds from a belt of the same trees that had formerly been planted on the south side thereof. And the Larch, Spruce and Silver fir trees which so greatly ornament the front and summit of the South wood were planted therein by Lord Methven, and a few Norway Spruce have lately been planted by Mr Smythe in the North wood, who has also caused all the places deficient of oak stools to be filled up by young oak plants as the yearly cutting advances, which will add greatly to the value of the wood in time coming. Due care has also been taken to encourage the growth of seedling oaks by cutting away from them the other sorts of timber that is likely to injure them, and the cutting down of Birch in Winter seems greatly to prevent its growing again.

Note: From a survey of grounds around Methven Castle made by Mr Thos Winter in 1744 the wood of Methven is stated to contain 172 acres, 3 floods and 26 falls – to which extent several additions have since been made in which several plants of the Quercus sessiliflora have found a place and also imported within the old boundaries – the whole of the original stock being that of the Q. pedinculata.'

(source: Bishop, T. 1851. *Memorabilia de Methven*, pp 18–20)

Grazing is now perceived as the most significant factor in the ecology of upland semi-natural woods. In the past, indiscriminate grazing in unenclosed woodland undoubtedly contributed to the loss of great tracts of native woodland, and this process continues today, so that some sites which have borne woodland in historical times now have few trees, or none (Gordon 1911). However, most of the surviving semi-natural woods (which are not relatively recent in origin) have been managed, and, as part of this management, grazing was necessarily controlled or excluded. Indeed, many woods exist because they were managed, and it is the breakdown of management and the spread of sheep husbandry in the 19th century which threaten their survival (Lindsay 1977). Reduction of grazing, which today is often associated with afforestation of adjacent ground, provides an opportunity for new recruitment. This process may even be facilitated by grazing, which provides the bare spots necessary for seedling establishment (Miles & Kinnaird 1979), even though it forbids subsequent growth. As at Rassal, subsequent growth may be a mixture of seedling regeneration and rejuvenation of old trees and shrubs. Exclosures at Morrone Birkwood have enabled birch to regenerate in both fashions, regeneration of aspen, juniper (*Juniperus communis*) and rowan, and colonization by bird cherry (*Prunus padus*) (D Batty pers. comm.). Lack of recent regeneration is a common feature of upland woods, but is not always due solely to grazing: many woods have a closed canopy which may be the main limiting factor.

The existing native woods have clearly been shaped and structured by largely artificial factors. They are not natural, but they have responded naturally, and this may have allowed them to return towards their original natural state. Lacking woods which have been free of unnatural disturbance and management (or, rather, if natural woods exist, they are in specialized locations such as steep cliffs and ravines, which tell us little about the generality of woods), we can only speculate on the nature of natural woods. However, natural woodland survives elsewhere in the northern hemisphere, and this indicates that the natural disturbance regime of pine and northern birchwoods is likely to differ from that of mixed broadleaf stands (Jones 1945; White 1979). The former are part of the boreal forests, which exist largely as even-aged stands whose age mosaic is determined by violent disturbances (fire, diseases, ice storm) on an irregular periodicity of decades or a century or so. The latter form part of the temperate broadleaf forests, which, though not immune to violent disturbance, often remain undisturbed for long enough to initiate gap phase regeneration. If this assessment is correct, the modern structure of native pine- and birchwoods may be close to natural, whereas the structure of the mixed broadleaf woods remains essentially artificial.

The lesson from modern studies of disturbance as a natural factor in forest ecology is that substantial fluctuations are possible at a local scale in the composition of natural stands and the distribution of species between age classes. Management and other artificialities have undoubtedly caused such changes in Highland woods, and the response of woods to withdrawal of human influence shows that further changes will occur. Nevertheless, the fluctuations take place amongst a largely fixed group of species, and it was undoubtedly reasonable for McVean and Ratcliffe (1962) to reconstruct the original-natural distribution of Scotland's native woods from their knowledge of modern remnants.

5 Conclusion

It is easy to regard the native woods of Scotland as so fragmented, modified and degraded that they are (i) no more than an out-of-date crop, which can be replaced by an up-to-date crop, and (ii) incapable of recovery without artificial stimulus and resuscitation. However, the capacity of these woods to recover has been demonstrated at Rassal and many other sites. They are undoubtedly modified, but natural processes have continued and many may not be far removed from a natural state. They have been hugely reduced, but most of their original variety appears to have survived. They should be given more chance to recover by themselves, and we should not pre-judge the direction which this recovery will take.

6 Summary

The native woodlands of the Scottish uplands are described in a wide range of publications, some of which are listed: this paper concentrates on the dynamic nature of these woods. One stand, Rassal Ashwood NNR, originated in the late 18th century during a period of reduced grazing pressure, probably in open woodland adjacent to a small wooded ravine. Although the wood had long been heavily grazed, abundant regeneration took place in an exclosure built in 1957, and by 1985 the woodland ecosystem within the exclosure was re-established. This and other examples demonstrate that upland woods should not be seen as static entities, but as communities which fluctuate in size, shape and composition to various degrees. The fluctuations occur both naturally and under the influence of changing management and exploitation. However, a core area or condition can usually be recognized which remains, despite these changes. Many of the existing woods may be more nearly natural and more capable of rejuvenation than is often supposed, and they should be allowed more chance to recover by themselves, without planting or excessive grazing.

7 Acknowlegements

Dr Rosalind Smith brought the historical notes on Methven Wood to my attention. David Batty, Dr Keith Kirby, Ray Collier and Graham Walker supplied useful information.

8 References

Anderson, M.L. 1967. *A history of Scottish forestry.* London: Nelson.

Birks, H.J.B. 1973. *Past and present vegetation of the Isle of Skye.* Cambridge: Cambridge University Press.

Birse, E.L., Robertson, J.S. & Durno, S.E. 1976. *Plant communities and soils of the lowland and southern upland regions of Scotland.* (Monograph, Soil Survey of Scotland.) Aberdeen: Macaulay Institute for Soil Research.

Bunce, R.G.H. 1982. *A field key for classifying British woodland vegetation. Part 1.* Cambridge: Institute of Terrestrial Ecology.

Crowson, R.A. 1962 Observations on Coleoptera in Scottish oak woods. *Glasg. Nat.,* **18,** 177–195.

Durno, S.E. & McVean, D.N. 1959. Forest history of the Beinn Eighe nature reserve. *New Phytol.,* **58,** 228–236.

Fenton, J. 1985. *The SWT Highland birchwood survey.* Edinburgh: Scottish Ecological Consultants on behalf of Scottish Wildlife Trust.

Forestry Commission. 1983. *Census of woodlands and trees 1979–82. Scotland.* Edinburgh: Forestry Commission.

Goodier, R. & Ball, M.E. 1974. The management of upland broadleaved woodlands for nature and landscape conservation. *Forestry,* **47,** (Supplement), 59–71.

Gordon, G.P. 1911. Primitive woodland and plantation types in Scotland. *Trans. R. Scott. arboric. Soc.,* **24,** 153–177.

Jones, E.W. 1945. The structure and reproduction of the virgin forest of the north temperate zone. *New Phytol.,* **44,** 130–148.

Kirby, K. 1984. Scottish birchwoods and their conservation – a review. *Trans. bot. Soc. Edinb.,* **4,** 205–218.

Lindsay, J.M. 1974. *The use of woodland in Argyllshire and Perthshire between 1650 and 1850.* PhD thesis, University of Edinburgh.

Lindsay, J.M. 1975. The history of oak coppice in Scotland. *Scott. For.,* **29,** 87–95.

Lindsay, J.M. 1977. Forestry and agriculture in the Scottish highlands, 1700–1850: a problem in estate management. *Agric. Hist. Rev.,* **25,** 23–36.

McVean, D.N. 1964. Woodland and scrub. In: *The vegetation of Scotland,* edited by J.H. Burnett, 144–167. Edinburgh: Oliver & Boyd.

McVean, D.N. & Ratcliffe, D.A. 1962. *Plant communities of the Scottish highlands.* London: HMSO.

Miles, J. 1978. The influence of trees on soil properties. *Annu. Rep. Inst. terr. Ecol. 1977,* 7–11.

Miles, J. 1986. What are the effects of trees on soils? In: *Trees and wildlife in the Scottish uplands,* edited by D. Jenkins, 55–62. (ITE symposium no. 17.) Abbots Ripton: Institute of Terrestrial Ecology.

Miles, J. & Kinnaird, J.W. 1979. The establishment and regeneration of birch, juniper and Scots pine in the Scottish highlands. *Scott. For.,* **33,** 102–119.

O'Sullivan, P.E. 1973. Pollen analysis of mor humus layers from a native Scots pine ecosystem, interpreted with surface samples. *Oikos,* **24,** 259–272.

Peterken, G.F. 1981. *Woodland conservation and management.* London: Chapman & Hall.

Ratcliffe, D.A., ed. 1977. *A nature conservation review.* Cambridge: Cambridge University Press.

Rymer, L. 1980. Recent woodland history of north Knapdale, Argyllshire, Scotland. *Scott. For.,* **34,** 244–256.

Steven, H.M. & Carlisle, A. 1959. *The native pinewoods of Scotland.* Edinburgh: Oliver & Boyd.

Tittensor, R.M. 1970. History of Loch Lomond oakwoods. *Scott. For.,* **24,** 100–118.

White, P.S. 1979. Pattern, process and natural disturbance in vegetation. *Bot. Rev.,* **45,** 229–299.

Wormell, P. 1977. Woodland insect population changes on the Isle of Rhum in relation to forest history and woodland restoration. *Scott. For.,* **31,** 13–36.

Whither forestry? The scene in AD 2025

F T LAST[1], J N R JEFFERS[2], R G H BUNCE[2], C J CLARIDGE[3], M B BALDWIN[3] and R J CAMERON[3]
1 Institute of Terrestrial Ecology, Edinburgh
2 Institute of Terrestrial Ecology, Grange-over-Sands
3 Highland Regional Council, Inverness

1 Introduction

When thinking about the future of forestry, it is necessary to recognize that the form of the landscape in the year 2025, or at least the significant forestry element, has already been largely determined. Even though trees tend to grow faster in the UK than in most countries of the European Communities, those planted between now and 2025 will have less impact on the landscape than those already planted. Further, it should be appreciated that the use of land is strongly influenced by political decisions which are inevitably determined by events, both national and international. Thus, although the UK economy is freer than many, it is not a free economy; land use reflects, in large measure, the availability of grants, concessions, tax exemptions and intervention payments. Without the annual support given to the agricultural industry by the British government, which amounted to £970M in 1981–82 (Ministry of Agriculture, Fisheries and Food 1983), much of the British agriculture would be unprofitable compared to energy farming and forestry (Mitchell et al. 1983). Britain, as a member of the Commission of the European Communities (CEC), is obliged to take cognizance of the needs and views of the other members of the Commission and, predictably, these are likely to have an increasing impact, particularly in relation to land use.

1.1 The wilderness concept

When debating the future of the Scottish Highlands, it is essential to consider the mosaic of uplands and lowlands, the use of the one impinging on that of the other. Further, it is necessary to recognize that the use of both the uplands and lowlands influences, and is influenced by, the distribution of the resident population and the movements of visitors which, in turn, reflect regional infrastructures. Thus, it is worthless to consider the well-being of forests and wildlife without being mindful of the requirements of the human population.

Two years ago, at a conference concerned with 'Wilderness – the way ahead', many speakers strongly argued the merits of the 'wilderness concept'. In doing so, they referred to the Wilderness Act, passed in the USA in 1964, which aims 'to assure that increasing population, accompanied by expanding settlement and growing mechanisation, does not occupy and modify all areas within the U.S.' (Block 1984). As defined by Zunino (1984), the philosophy of the wilderness concept accepts 'the balanced use of natural resources based on the idea of creating an environmental heritage for posterity; it entails imposing limits on human developments in order to preserve an everlasting space for nature and its wild creatures'. While being firmly embedded in the virtues of resource conservation, the concept encompasses a sociological or spiritual desire, namely the need to have wild and free space so as to commune with nature. To some, this desire may seem to be an unnecessary affectation, but to an increasing number of others it is an absolute necessity.

Although it could legitimately be argued that the Highlands, like the rest of Britain, have already been comprehensively altered by the activities of man, anyone ignoring 'wilderness' as a legitimate land use when considering the future of the Highlands will do so at his peril. How will the owners of designated wilderness areas be compensated for the loss of 'improvement'? If we are willing to pay for unwanted agricultural excesses, there is doubtless a way to facilitate the maintenance of wilderness, always pre-supposing that the proponents of wilderness have sufficient political backing to present widely acceptable arguments.

1.2 Agriculture

Until the Mansholt plan was unveiled about 17 years ago, it was tacitly assumed that most agricultural land within the European Communities would continue to be used for agriculture in perpetuity (MacKerron & Rush 1976). Now, however, our judgements are being challenged. The forecasts suggested that the UK would be self-sufficient in 1984 in wheat (producing 104% of its requirements), barley (143%), oilseed rape (112%), beef and veal (101%), skimmed milk powder (224%), and full-cream milk powder (667%). In many instances, the forecast for the European Communities suggested even larger surpluses. Of the major agricultural crops, UK growers under-supply only potatoes and sugar, but, within the Communities, the outputs of these crops were expected to reach 99% and 123% respectively of anticipated requirements (Melchett 1985).

When contemplating the significance of these data, other considerations should be taken into account. As noted at the 1985 Oxford Farming Conference by Mr Fawcett, the Managing Director of Dalgety Agriculture, food production in the developed world is increasing rapidly, often as a result of 'improved efficiency', while consumption (in the developed world) is lagging behind. Within the UK, total cereal production has doubled in the last 15 years; yields of barley increased from 8.5 Mtonnes to about 11 Mtonnes despite a decrease of 10% in the area planted, while milk output has increased by more than 30% (mainly as a result of enhanced yields per cow). On the other hand, consumption, except of vegetables and fruits, has been either static or declining, eg decreases of 40% in the domestic consumption of sugar (which has not been offset by a matching increase in the use of sugar in manufactured foods), 30% in the consumption of butter between 1960 and 1981, and 21% in the consumption of UK beef, veal and lamb. Taken together, these trends of increasing 'efficiency' and over-production and of decreasing consumption inevitably lead to the conclusion that changes are needed in the ways in which we steward our land resources.

A range of estimates has been made of the areas of the European Communities that need to be removed from existing agricultural usages, if surpluses are to be minimized. Giraud (1985) suggested 9 Mha by 1990, Strehler (1985) proposed 8 Mha, while Buckwell, of Wye College, London, in addition to estimating 5.25 Mha for the Communities, detailed losses within the UK of 0.5 Mha of wheat, 0.4 Mha of barley and 0.03 Mha of sugar beet.

Should the Commission of European Communities continue to spend 40% of its agricultural budget disposing of food surpluses (Dalsager 1983)? If not, would the probable decrease in cattle and sheep enable the present artificially depressed tree-line in the Cairngorms to rise, eg from 600 m to 700 m (Pears 1967)? However, before turning our attention from an agricultural land use, is it conceivable that 'new' plant and animal crops may be found, possibly for industrial uses, eg the supply of starch, biofuels, fibres, natural dyes and a range of feedstocks for chemical industries? If they were found, would any of them be suitable for the lowlands and uplands of the Scottish Highlands?

1.3 Forestry

Following discussion of the Mansholt plan, the Commission of the European Communities published its *Forestry policy in the European Community* (CEC 1979). It was suggested that 5 Mha of land, submarginal for agriculture, should be transferred to forestry, recognizing that the change could be reversible. But why to forestry? When discussing the UK timber industry, Bradley (1985) indicated that imports in 1983 of round- and sawnwood, wood manufactures and reconstituted wood, wood pulp and waste paper, and paper and board amounted to £937M, £569M, £420M and £1,906M, giving a total of £3,832M. This amount in 1983 was equivalent in value to about 90% of the timber and timber-based products used in Britain: the European Communities (including the figures for Britain) import 60% of their timber needs (Centre for Agricultural Strategy 1980). In short, the Communities have a very large timber deficit which,

even accepting the need for goods to sustain trade, is probably putting an excessive long-term pressure on the timber resources of those countries that export.

In considering a strategy for the UK forest industry, the contributors to the report prepared by the Centre for Agricultural Strategy (CAS), Reading, bluntly stated that timber production should be increased (CAS 1980). They suggested that the increase should be achieved by (i) the selection of genetically superior planting stock and more productive silvicultural and harvesting procedures, (ii) the conversion of unproductive woodland, and (iii) the addition of sizeable areas to the UK forest estate. They recognized that an annual increase of 60 000 ha yr^{-1} was likely to lead to 26% self-sufficiency in timber by AD 2025, when 16% of Britain would be afforested, compared with 8% at present.

The report suggested that hardwoods should not be entirely ignored in the uplands, where production cannot be expected to be high but where conservation and landscape interests are important. It also assumed that the bulk of the broadleaved planting would take place in the lowlands, where it would form only a small part of the total. The aim should be to increase the ratio of areas planted with broadleaved trees to those planted with conifers from 1:30 at the present to 1:20 by 2025.

The balance of the 'new' areas, ie the vast majority, would be afforested with conifers, it being tacitly assumed that Sitka spruce (*Picea sitchensis*) would be the favoured species. When the report was published in 1980, it was also assumed that only the poorer land would be afforested, ie those areas graded 'V' in England and Wales (Agricultural Development and Advisory Service 1974) and 'D' in Scotland (Scottish Development Department 1981), and considered to be 'marginal for agriculture', which are not constrained by rocky outcrops, by uneconomically slow growth rates attributable to high altitudes, or by the danger of adversely affecting water yields, and so on. As a result, it was suggested that the tree cover in the former East, West and North Conservancies of the Forestry Commission might increase from 13%, 16% and 8% to 26%, 40% and 20% by the year 2030. All 30 of these Conservancies include areas of what is collectively known as the Highlands (Figure 1).

In the CAS report, it is clear that the authors did not wish to be straightjacketed by 'either/or' statements; instead, they attempted to develop a range of options or scenarios but, in doing so, they did not provide a framework on which to insert and judge the merits of changed uses of land.

2 Framework for assessing land use options

To consider and assess the comparative merits of a range of options, it is desirable to have a system in which the different uses, such as forestry, agriculture,

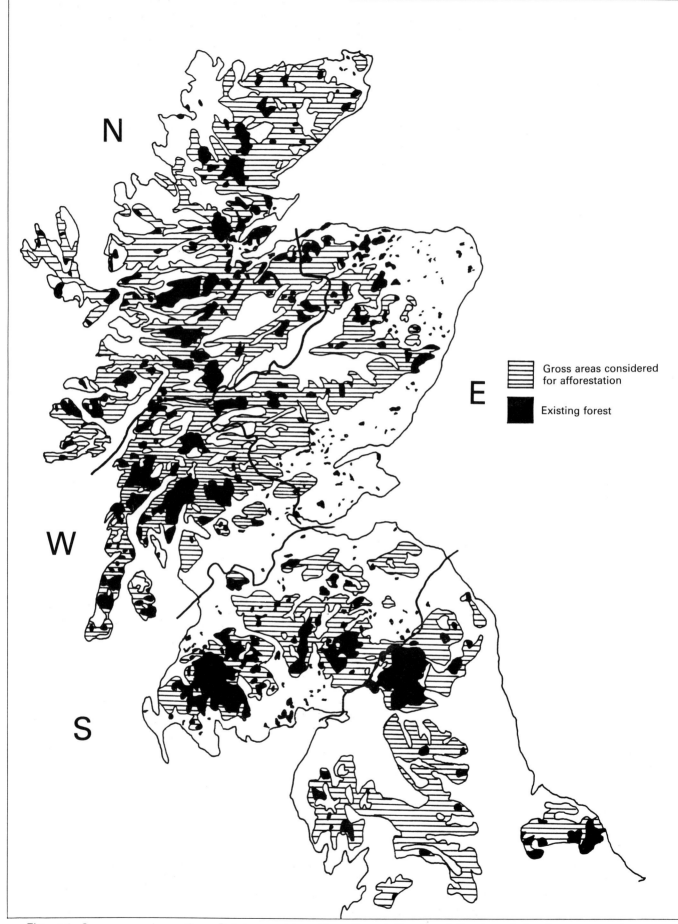

Figure 1. Gross areas in northern Britain considered for afforestation in relation to existing forests, scenic areas and water constraints (source: CAS 1980). Boundaries refer to former Forestry Commission Conservancies in Scotland

the conservation of water and/or wildlife, can be inter-related. For, whatever we may think, these options are still over-ridingly influenced, except for political considerations, by environmental factors. Anderson and Fairbairn (1955) recognized that different types of silvicultural practices were developed in response to the influences of sunshine, wind, rain . . . but, with the data handling techniques available to them, they found it 'extremely difficult, if not impossible, to combine more than 2 factors'. Times have changed. With a variety of more recently evolved statistical procedures, including cluster analysis (Howard & Howard 1980), it is now possible to derive land classifications using complexes of extant map-readable information related to geological, topographical and climatological features.

Using data derived from the central one kilometre square of each of the 1228 squares (15 km x 15 km) into which Great Britain can be divided, Bunce and his colleagues have, with the application of Indicator Species Analysis (Hill *et al.* 1975), evolved 32 land classes (Plate 9). The data employed included:

— mean numbers of days with snow falling
— mean daily minimum temperature in January
— mean daily duration of bright sunshine
— maximum elevation
— distance to west coast – a measure of longitude and oceanicity
— distance to south coast – a measure of latitude and associated changes, eg daylength
— details of solid, and drift, geology

Some of the land classes are mainly located in England and Wales, eg classes 1–8, whereas Scotland is dominated by land classes 17–32 (Bunce *et al.* 1981; Bunce & Last 1981). As the descriptions of land classes 21, 24, 28 and 29 indicate, it is possible to provide a detailed assessment of the environments which plants and animals would experience in the different land classes (Table 1). By consulting the appropriate records and/or exercising judgement, it is then possible to attach 'performance functions' to each of a wide range of plants for the differing conditions of each land class. Additionally, it is possible to attach costs of inputs, including interest on capital expenditure, and value of outputs for each crop in each land class, so enabling judgements to be made of likely net costs.

In recent years, this system of land classification has been developed and exploited by the Planning Department of the Highland Regional Council (HRC), Scotland, whose data-bases are attuned to 1 km squares (HRC 1985a). Broadly speaking, the Region can be divided into 2 parts: a coastal array of lowland land classes 25–32 which are characteristic of the northern half of Britain, and an inland zone of land classes 17–24, sorted primarily by altitude. Some of the latter land classes are shared with upland areas wherever

Table 1. Characteristics of the more abundant land classes in the Highland Region, Scotland (source: Bunce *et al.* 1981)

LAND CLASS 21 (23% of the area of the Region)
Central and northern Scotland
Steep hillsides predominate, but there are some moderate slopes
Bleak upland landscapes, sometimes enclosed and afforested
Open-range grazing or forest, moorland and peatland vegetation
85% at altitudes of 199–488 m, 2% over 488 m, slope 8°

Mean minimum January temperature	0.0°C
Mean number of days on which snow falls	54.3
Mean daily duration of bright sunshine	4.1 h

LAND CLASS 24 (12.5% of the area of the Region)
Central and western Scotland
Precipitous and extremely steep slopes with land at high altitude
Rugged mountain scenery, often rocky, with fast-flowing streams
Limited open-range grazing, mainly peatland with some moorland vegetation
56% at altitudes of 199–488 m, 31% over 488 m, slope 18°

Mean minimum January temperature	0.1°C
Mean number of days on which snow falls	51.4
Mean daily duration of bright sunshine	4.1 h

LAND CLASS 28 (12.9% of the area of the Region)
South and north-east Scotland
Mostly flat land but with some gentle gradients at medium to low altitudes
Heterogeneous landscape, from enclosed farmland to open moors
Pasture and rough grazing but with some good grassland, also peatland
89% at altitudes of less than 199 m, 11% at 199–488 m, slope 4°

Mean minimum January temperature	0.2°C
Mean number of days on which snow falls	45.3
Mean daily duration of bright sunshine	4.3 h

LAND CLASS 29 (9.6% of the area of the Region)
West Scotland
Indented coastlines, uneven topography, with some steep slopes
Complex scenery with many contrasting elements
Mainly open-range grazing, some crofting, peatland and moorland, also some bracken
95% at altitudes below 199 m, 5% at 199–488 m, slope 13°

Mean minimum January temperature	1.7°C
Mean number of days on which snow falls	31.5
Mean daily duration of bright sunshine	4.6 h

they occur in Britain. The Highland Region has comprehensive collections of data concerned with the environment, land uses, infrastructure, the human population and artefacts for its 27 915 squares.

Importantly, the system of land classification is arranged so that policy options can be considered and, to an extent, tested. For this strategic purpose, it is not necessary to have a complete enumeration of every square within a Region. Instead, experience has shown that adequate approximations are obtained using data from 8 randomly selected squares of each land class.

At present, the Highland Region is dominated by moorland. This habitat occupies 63% of the land area; grassland/pasture accounts for 17%, arable 3%, commercial woodland 13% and amenity woodland 4% (Figure 2) (HRC 1985c). Setting aside, for the time being, political aspects of the question 'Should a greater area be afforested?', is it possible to decide if there *could* be larger areas of productive forests in the Highland Region?

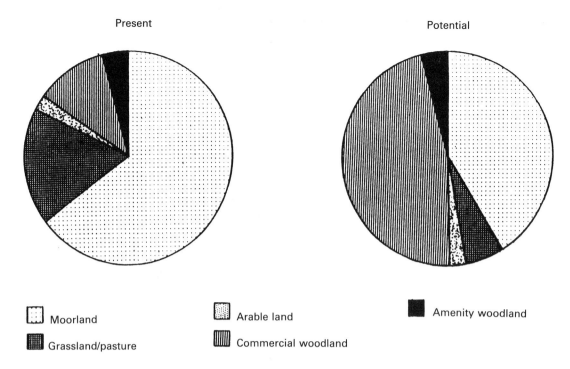

Present · Potential

Moorland · Arable land · Amenity woodland

Grassland/pasture · Commercial woodland

Figure 2. Present and potential land uses in the Highland Region, Scotland, judged on present-day yield expectations and costs, and assuming a discount rate of 3% (source: HRC 1985c)

This question can be answered in a number of ways, but first it is necessary to identify the land which is theoretically suitable for afforestation, by excluding those areas of the different squares judged to be physically unplantable because they are sea, intertidal, loch/lochan, sea cliff, urbanized, already afforested (Figure 3) or above the tree-line (an altitudinal arbiter which varies in different parts of the Region, ranging from 200–250 m in the north and west to 600 m in the south-east). It is then possible to proceed by deleting areas designated by the Nature Conservancy Council as (i) Sites of Special Scientific Interest (SSSIs) and (ii) National Nature Reserves (NNRs), and by assuming that the present uses of commercial peat deposits and land in Macaulay Land Capability Classes 1–5 (Bibby *et al.* 1982) and crofting tenure will not be altered. However, is this a prudent way to proceed when the values of different land uses are likely to change relative to each other?

It is widely accepted that forestry prices will increase against those of agriculture. The preferred approach is to minimize the number of assumptions and instead attempt to obtain an objective estimate by examining the net costs of different options. For each land class in the Highland Region, 14 possible forest enterprises, including the planting of Sitka spruce, lodgepole pine (*Pinus contorta*), Japanese larch (*Larix kaempferi*), Douglas fir (*Pseudotsuga menziesii*) and Corsican pine (*Pinus nigra* var. *maritima*), were compared with a range of existing land uses, including the cultivation of barley, oats, wheat, potatoes, turnips, swedes, rough grass, short-term grass and permanent grass. It was found that significant areas of present-day grassland/ pasture and moorland could be converted remuner-

atively, at present-day prices, to commercial afforestation, so as to increase the existing commercially afforested areas within the Region from 13% to about 40% assuming a discount rate of 3%, or to 24% with a discount rate of 5%.

With the land class system it is possible, as the maps show (Figure 3), to pinpoint with a degree of certainty those areas in which land uses might change. But, for the future, should we concern ourselves solely with the maximization of monetary return? Ever since the oil crisis, greater concern has been expressed for the proper stewardship of our non-renewable resources, with a movement towards optimization instead of maximization.

3 Forestry scenarios

Changes in the use of land must be considered against a range of possible scenarios, partly because we cannot be certain that any one scenario is likely to be correct, but also to enable us to test the sensitivity of the factors influencing our decisions against the different possibilities. Most of the factors needing to be considered have already been mentioned, and they include the increased importance of timber production relative to the production of food. There is already a world shortage of many kinds of timber, and the rate at which mature timber is being felled will almost certainly trigger a sharp rise in timber prices. Faced with both increased prices and real shortages of the kinds of timber which we have traditionally imported, it will be necessary to reconsider our established dependence on imported supplies. Similarly, changes in the availability of timber will themselves have an effect on the practical uses that we make of wood. Bulk use

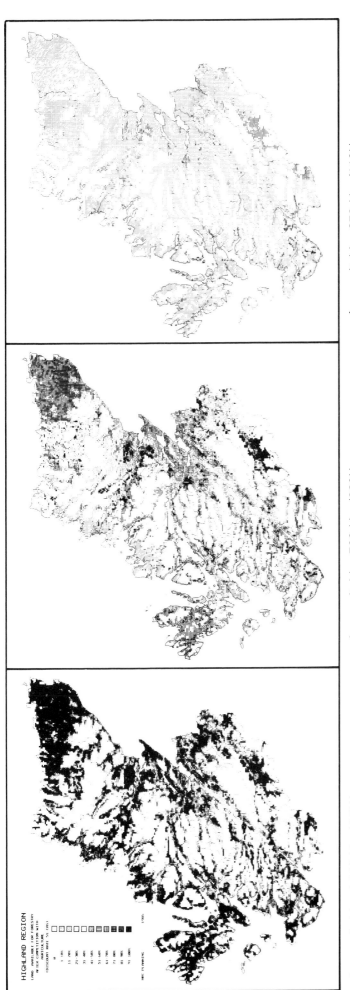

Area suitable: 1 110 kha (44%)

Excludes areas judged to be physically unplantable (sea, intertidal, loch, land cliff, seacliff, urban land or existing woodland and that above stipulated altitudinal limits)

Area suitable: 700 kha (28%)

Judged against agricultural options, assuming a discount rate of 3%

Area suitable: 279 kha (11%)

Judged against agricultural options, assuming a discount rate of 5%

Figure 3. Areas of the Highland Region which are not afforested but could be profitably, compared with existing land uses, at discount rates of 3% and 5% (source: HRC 1985c)

of inferior timber may well be replaced by more specialized and craft uses of higher quality timbers, leading to a new balance being struck between the demands for softwoods and hardwoods. The rapid development of electronic communications also seems likely to reduce greatly our demand for pulpwood, at least for the making of paper.

By far the most influential factor will be the future cost of energy. Almost all current operations in forestry and agriculture have been made possible by the availability of energy, as fossil fuels, at ridiculously low prices, bearing in mind the fact that these fuels are not renewable in a timescale which bears any relationship to the rate at which they have been used. There are only limited reserves of fossil fuels, and the creation of energy by alternative methods is never likely to provide energy at prices lower than those of today, especially for the transport of people and materials.

Figure 4 illustrates 4 scenarios used recently by the Forestry Research Co-ordinating Committee as a basis for planning forestry research. The first of the scenarios, that of least change, assumes the continuation of the existing forest poly in Britain, with no very marked increase in the area of forest, and an unchanged balance between the areas devoted to growing hardwoods and softwoods. This scenario assumes no marked increase in the proportional cost of energy, and that recreation, amenity and wildlife

conservation will be given equal value to the production of timber.

There are 2 forest production scenarios, differing only in the extent to which there is a marked increase in the proportional cost of energy. In both of these scenarios, increased importance is given to forest production, with the area of forest being increased to at least 10% of the total land surface. The production of wood is assumed to be given higher value than recreation, amenity and wildlife conservation. Possibly greater emphasis will be given to hardwoods, and to the closer integration of forestry with agriculture.

The final scenario is one of world shortages of timber, leading to an increase of the forest area to 15% or more of the total land surface of the UK. With the value of wood higher than that of most foods, hardwoods and softwoods are assumed to be of about equal importance. Energy costs are assumed to be high, especially for motive energy, and the emphasis will be on resource conservation rather than on wildlife conservation.

It is, of course, impossible to predict which, if any, of these scenarios is likely to be closest to the truth, but the most unlikely scenario is that of least change. Whatever choice of total forest area results from the combination of pressures that create our countryside, forest policy will itself have to adapt to the needs of

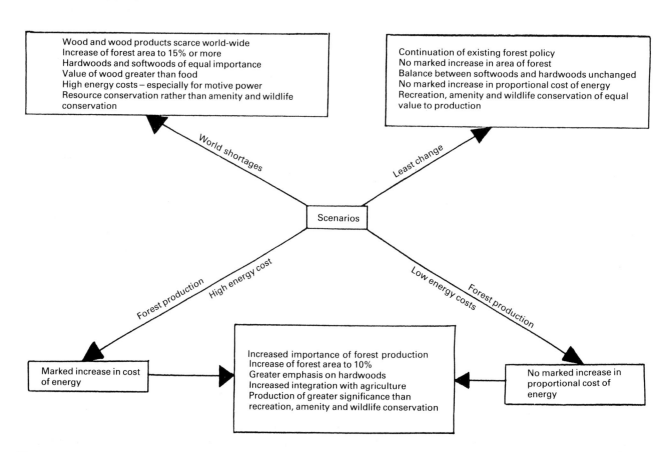

Figure 4. Four scenarios used recently by the Forestry Research Co-ordinating Committee as a basis for planning UK forestry research

British society. Four possible forest policy scenarios are given in Table 2. Again, the first of these scenarios assumes the continuation of the *status quo*, with the social and economic pressures for and against forestry continuing more or less as at present, and with the principal emphasis on softwood production and only a very marginal interest in hardwoods, mainly expressed as a continuing demand for broadleaved woodland devoted to amenity, wildlife conservation and sport.

Table 2. Four possible forest policy scenarios based on the assumption that the afforested area of the UK will be increased

Scenario 1. *Status quo*, assumes that social and economic pressures for and against forestry will continue more or less as at present, with the principal emphasis on softwoods and only very marginal interests in hardwoods, but a continuing demand for broadleaved woodland for amenity and sporting interests.

Scenario 2. *High-yield policy*, concentrating on a narrow range of conifer species grown so as to produce the highest possible yield. Hardwoods mainly of interest as energy and fuelwood crops, apart from a limited area kept for amenity or sport. Many broadleaved woodlands replanted as conifers.

Scenario 3. *High-quality policy*, switching attention from yield *per se* to timber of high quality, whether softwood or hardwood, but particular emphasis on hardwood because of reduced supplies of tropical hardwoods. Timber properties emphasized rather than yield.

Scenario 4. *Agro-forestry policy*, supplementing conventional forestry, mainly in the uplands, by a new style of lowland, mixed or broadleaved, forestry combined with agriculture, sport and energy farming.

An alternative high-yield policy would concentrate attention on a narrow range of conifer species, grown to produce the highest possible yield. Apart from limited areas of hardwoods for amenity and sport, broadleaved species would mainly be grown as energy and fuelwood crops. Many existing areas of broadleaved woodland would probably be replanted with conifers. A high-quality timber policy would switch attention from yield *per se* to the production of timber with the highest possible quality. Both hardwoods and softwoods would be produced, with a strong emphasis on hardwoods because of the scarcity of tropical hardwoods. Finally, but not necessarily exclusively, forest policy might embrace a strong agro-forestry element, where conventional upland forestry would be supplemented by a new style of lowland mixed or broadleaved forestry combined with agriculture, amenity, sport and energy farming.

Whatever the scenario for the future may be, there is certain to be change, and the change may be both extensive and rapid. As pointed out by Seligman (1985) at the 3rd Energy from Biomass Conference of the European Communities, the world is becoming more conscious of its environment every day. In the UK, we have relied far too long on being able to obtain our essential timber supplies from overseas, and principally from the developing countries. Wood is an essential commodity in the Third World, and there is certain to be a strong demand from developing countries for us to grow a bigger proportion of the wood we need, rather than to continue exploiting their reserves. We should recognize that we have a responsibility to increase our self-sufficiency in timber and wood products so as to relieve the pressure on forests in developing countries (Campbell 1984).

4 Some factors constraining the forestry options
In using the land classification system, it has been shown that future forestry developments are, to a very considerable extent, determined by habitat features, but there are other constraints which should be considered and which are equally identifiable in advance. These constraints include the need to avoid (i) NNRs and SSSIs which may have been designated to conserve assemblages of plants and animals or specific species, and (ii) areas where forest canopy interception losses may deleteriously affect the yields of water from catchments or mini-catchments (Calder 1985). It is also desirable to obviate conflicts with deer and grouse and to minimize risks of increasing the acidification of fresh waters.

4.1 Silvicultural factors
In considering the impact of optimizing the utilization of resources, we have questioned some aspects of the future development of commercial forestry, but the advisability of concentrating on the use of Sitka spruce can be challenged from considerations of wildlife and landscape; it also requires continual reassessment when considering the threat of potential pests and pathogens. Unlike most agricultural crops, forest trees are outbreeding and, as a result, there are continuing opportunities for maintaining populations which are heterogeneous except for the attributes upon which selection is based.

Nonetheless, forestry is tending to follow agriculture, but on a greatly extended timescale. Inevitably, forest crops are likely to become less variable, a trend that might be hastened by the desire for quick genetic gains using vegetatively propagated clones. This process might be facilitated by micro-propagation. While we sometimes tend to forget that commercial forestry is, in reality, an extended form of agricultural cropping, there is no doubt of the advisability of seeking alternative tree crops and, in doing so, it would be foolish to disregard the increasing environmental interest in broadleaved trees.

Can we really say that we have exactingly examined the potential of our native species, notably birch (*Betula* spp.)? Brown (1984) suggested that 'sophisticated silviculture allied to breeding superior cultivars of birch could quite readily produce home grown veneer quality trees'. He also believes that the multiple-use management of birch woodlands would benefit forester, farmer, sportsman and tourist. Is it conceivable that exotic broadleaved species with sufficient frost and cold tolerance can be selected for conditions in the Highlands (Murray *et al.* 1986)?

4.2 Water conservation

The quality of water in headwater streams of the River Forth in central Scotland is greatly affected by afforestation where these streams drain mini-catchments overlying slowly weathering bedrock (Harriman & Morrison 1982). Streams draining 'basins' whose catchments were more than 50% covered by Sitka spruce more than 15 years old were significantly and continuously more acidic than those draining unafforested moorland basins or where the trees were less than 15 years old. This variation in the effect of trees of different ages suggests that the increased acidity is not attributable to soil disturbance during and following site preparation and planting. Instead, the effect has been attributed, to different extents, to the greater dry deposition of gaseous and particulate atmospheric pollutants on trees than on moorland rough grazings, and to alterations in the amounts of evapotranspiration and base cation uptake. However, the impact of these influences will be predictably greater where ground and surface waters lack alkalinity (Henriksen *et al.* 1984), the 'cut-off' separating sensitivity from tolerance being greater (100 mg $CaCO_3$ l^{-1}) for ground waters (Edmunds & Kinniburgh 1986) than for surface waters (Stoner *et al.* 1984). Acidic waters occur where (i) soils are acid, or glacial drift is thin or absent, (ii) carbonate minerals are absent, and (iii) the residence time of water is short.

Edmunds and Kinniburgh (1986) have been able to

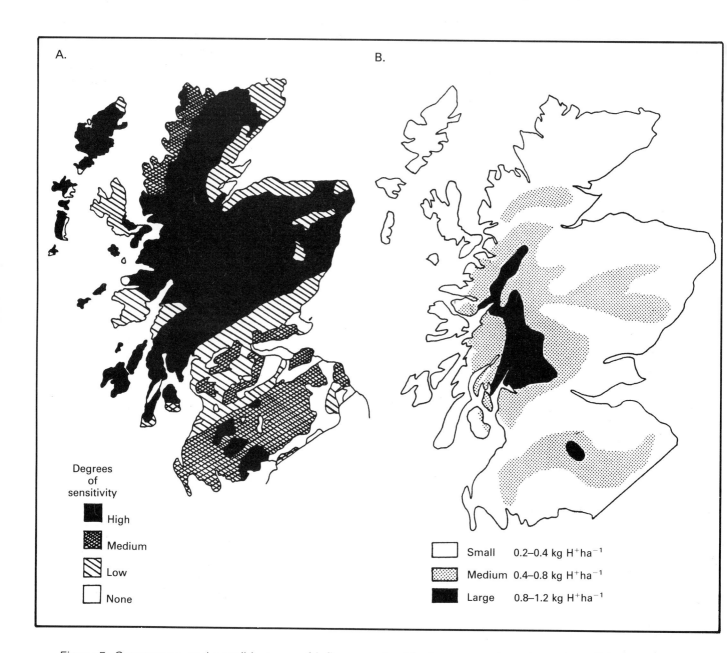

Figure 5. Occurrence, and possible areas of influence, of acid rain sensu stricto, *in northern Britain. A. Ground waters in Scotland with different sensitivities to acidic deposition (source: Edmunds & Kinniburgh 1986). B. Mean hydrogen ion inputs in wet precipitation, 1978–80 (source: Last* et al. *1984)*

produce a map of the likely distribution of sensitive and tolerant ground waters. If this is overlain by maps showing the predictable occurrence of wet and dry acidic deposition, it is possible to identify areas where afforestation may exacerbate the degree of acidity, with concomitant changes in freshwater biota, including the loss of salmonids. The areas affected include parts of south-west Scotland and, more importantly for this symposium, the west central Highlands (Figure 5). Should these locations be afforested? If they were to be afforested, can the risks of intensified acidification be minimized?

4.3 Wildlife

Because systems of forestry and woodland management in the Highlands are greatly concerned with the damage caused by deer, notably red deer (*Cervus elaphus*), it is worth considering if some areas of future afforestation, which will inevitably encroach on deer forest, may be at greater risk from their attack than others. The term 'deer forest' was first applied to areas of land that were used exclusively for deer stalking. Originally, they were devoid of agricultural interest but, in order to gain from agricultural subsidies, landowners introduced sheep, a trend which is now being reversed.

In 1957, there were 183 deer forests in Scotland, mostly in the Highlands, occupying 1.13 Mha (DAFS 1959): in 1982, the gross incomes from stags (trophy and carcase) and hinds (carcase) were £200–£240 and £45–£55 respectively, compared with £25–£40 for a brace of grouse (Jenkins & Matthew 1984). Although the winter distribution of red deer may, in future, be altered by the increasing areas of maturing plantation forests, repeat surveys made in 1972–73 and 1984–85 of the South Ross and West Inverness Districts of the Highland Region show that the winter distribution of red deer can be described in terms of land class. Thus, a much larger proportion of the 1 km squares of land classes 18, 19 and 24 were 'occupied' by red deer than of land classes 20, 25, 27 and 28. On the other hand, a greater proportion of the squares of land classes 26, 27 and 28 were estimated to be capable of profitable afforestation than those of land classes 18, 23 and 24 (Figure 6). By combining the 2 sets of data, it is apparent that relatively large proportions of land classes 25, 26, 27 and 28 are potentially afforestable with possibly minimal initial interference from red deer, but nonetheless it would be necessary to institute control measures to prevent their later multiplication.

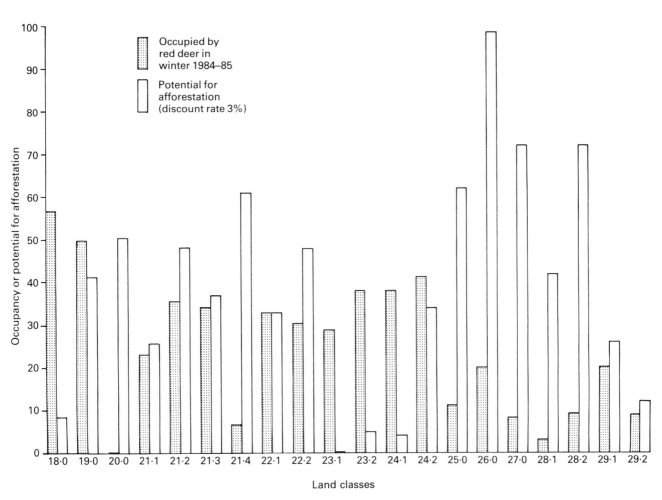

Figure 6. Proportions of different land classes in the Highland Region, Scotland, that (i) were occupied by red deer in winter 1984–85 and (ii) might be afforested profitably, assuming a discount rate of 3% (source: data held by the Red Deer Commission and Highland Regional Council, both at Inverness)

5 Commentary

There is no doubt that the future of forestry will be decided politically, whether regionally, nationally, within the European Communities, or by other 'external' forces. We envisage that there will be a diversion of funds from the maintenance of agricultural excesses to the enhanced production of wood, whether for structural timber, furniture, pulp or fuelwood. While pursuing these objectives, foresters should not underestimate the importance of 'amenity' trees. During 1984, surveyors in the Highland Regional Council categorized 19 different types of 'woodlands', ranging from roadside trees to major commercial plantings (Table 3). The list of 'woodlands' gives some idea of the niches occupied by trees, and, at the same time, indicates the relevance of amenity and landscape, in addition to single-minded production.

As would be expected, the dominant trees in the different types of woodland differ, eg hawthorn (*Crataegus monogyna*) and beech (*Fagus sylvatica*) in hedgerows, compared with birch and alder (*Alnus* spp.) alongside rivers and streams, and lodgepole pine and Sitka spruce in man-made forests. While some of the more 'worthy' assemblages of these trees are found in SSSIs and NNRs, and therefore subject to continuing management, the majority, which have a disproportionately large and beneficial visual impact, remain largely untended.

In thinking about the 'commonplace', most people would not wish to see the present-day list of trees altered by the intrusion of non-native incomers. Instead, the mix should remain much as it is today, perhaps with the more frequent planting of our native cherries, gean (*Prunus avium*) and bird cherry (*P. padus*), species which are greatly under-rated. Foresters would be ill advised not to accept responsibility for sustaining and augmenting the commonplace, sometimes irreverently regarded as unproductive. These species are productive but their productivity is measured in terms of visual impact; they enhance diversity and, very importantly, by allowing the growth of understorey vegetation, they provide a foliage height diversity which seems to favour a wide range of bird species (Newton & Moss 1981) (Figure 7).

Production forestry, in essence long-term agriculture, possibly involving a mixture of trees, and of trees with shorter-term vegetation, may spread to a greater variety of more fertile sites than heretofore and, in doing so, may replace traditional agriculture. Will it be recognized that forest plantations ('agricultural forests') and semi-natural stands are equally productive, the one in terms of timber and energy, and the other in relation to conservation and amenity. But, what proportion of each use is ideal, and in what kind of mosaic? The answer has still to be given, but at least it is possible to show in a predictable manner, using the system of land classification, what would, or would not, be sustainable in the physical environments of the different land classes of the Scottish Highlands. Additionally, the system of land classification provides a useful framework for judging economic implications, while facilitating the examination of many predictable constraints related to conservation (wildlife and water), 'acid rain' and amenity. For such analyses, it is becoming increasingly urgent to establish a comprehensive multi-land use advisory service, covering the management of conservation, forestry, agriculture, recreation, wildlife and water (see Campbell 1984).

Landscapes are dynamic. They have been continually evolving over the centuries. Are our 'institutions'

Table 3. Distribution, within urban and rural areas of the Highland Region, Scotland, of (i) different types of 'woodland' and (ii) the most numerous tree species (source: HRC 1985b)

Types of 'woodland'	Average area (ha km^{-2}) of each woodland within the different types	Area occupied by each type of woodland as % of		Most numerous tree species
		total woodland within Highland Region	total area of Highland Region	
Coniferous plantations	11.6	72.4	10.6	Lodgepole pine, Sitka spruce, Scots pine
Semi-natural coniferous woodlands	6.3	0.8	<0.1	Scots pine, birch, goat willow
Semi-natural broadleaved woodlands	3.9	11.8	1.7	Birch, goat willow, oak
Semi-natural mixed woodlands	4.3	2.5	0.4	Birch, Scots pine, juniper
Broadleaved woodlands underplanted with conifers	3.5	1.7	0.2	Birch, Scots pine, European larch
Mixed plantings	2.0	0.6	<0.1	Beech, Scots pine, birch
Multi-stemmed stands	2.8	0.4	<0.1	Hazel, birch, wych elm
Policy woodlands	0.9	0.4	<0.1	Lime, Scots pine, birch
Semi-natural copses	—	0.2	<0.1	Birch, goat willow, Scots pine
Semi-natural clumps	—	0.1	<0.1	Birch, goat willow, Scots pine
Shelterbelts	0.6	0.3	<0.1	Scots pine, European larch, Douglas fir
Hedgerows	0.8	0.3	<0.1	Hawthorn, beech
Roadside trees	0.6	0.6	<0.1	Birch, beech, wych elm
Riverside trees	1.4	2.0	0.3	Birch, alder, rowan
Railway-side trees	1.9	0.2	<0.1	Birch, ash, beech
Others	—	2.6	0.4	Scots pine, birch, rowan

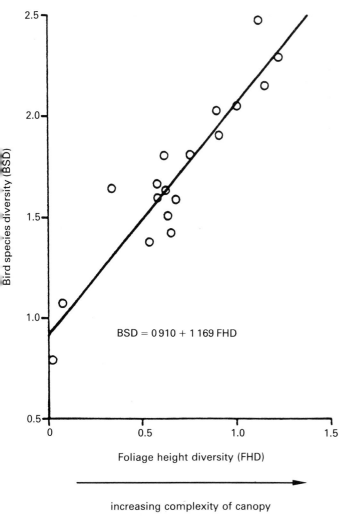

$$BSD = 0.910 + 1.169 \, FHD$$

increasing complexity of canopy

Figure 7. Relationship between bird species diversity and foliage height diversity when examining a variety of mature woods with broadleaved or coniferous species or mixtures (source: Newton & Moss 1981)

become a reality, remembering that land use is influenced greatly by political factors? On the one hand, the overwhelming dependence of the UK on outside sources of timber, and the over-production of many agricultural products (for which demand is steadily decreasing) suggest that land should be converted to production forestry. On the other hand, it is essential to recognize the importance of conservation (wildlife and water) and amenity, and the desire to maintain landscape linked with the 'wilderness concept'.

Assuming that these political considerations, linked to the availability of grants, concessions and tax exemptions, can be resolved to permit further afforestation, it is suggested that the type of afforestation needs to be attuned to changing conditions, in which the cost of energy may be over-riding and in which the balance of softwoods to hardwoods may change in favour of the latter.

The outcome of political issues cannot be predicted. However, it is possible to predict the location of some ecological factors likely to constrain future afforestation, eg those areas where (i) afforestation may unduly exacerbate the risk of freshwater acidification, or (ii) young plantings may be subject to possibly severe damage by red deer.

Irrespective of what happens between now and then, the forestry element which will have a major impact on the landscape in the year 2025 has already been planted. However, the role of 'non-productive' woodlands and amenity trees in relation to (i) landscape and (ii) the provision of niches for wildlife must be acknowledged more widely, as well as the need to take more positive steps to enhance these resources of trees, preferably of native species.

sufficiently imaginative to ensure that they collaborate to guide and prevent the abuse of the Highlands? Are they, and those responsible for political decisions, adequately briefed and sympathetic? Do they realize that the results of many of their decisions can be predicted? If not, there is a need for ecologists to assume a greater educative role.

6 Summary

By analysing 'plant performance functions' and 'assessments of net management costs' for a range of intensive and extensive agricultural crops and a variety of managed forests/woodlands, it is suggested that a greater monetary return would be obtained if large areas of the uplands were to be afforested. Within the Highlands Region, it is suggested that 700 kha could be converted remuneratively at a net discount rate of 3%; at a discount rate of 5%, the area would be 279 kha.

There is, therefore, a very considerable potential for afforestation, but will this potential, or should it,

7 References

Agricultural Development and Advisory Service, Land Service. 1974. *Agricultural land classification of England and Wales.* London: Ministry of Agriculture, Fisheries and Food.

Anderson, M.L. & Fairbairn, W.A. 1955. *Division of Scotland into climatic sub-regions as an aid to silviculture.* (Forestry Department bulletin no. 1.) Edinburgh: University of Edinburgh.

Bibby, S. J., Douglas, H. A., Thomasson, A.J. & Robertson, J.S. 1982. *Land capability classification for agriculture.* (Soil Survey of Scotland.) Aberdeen: Macaulay Institute for Soil Research.

Block, J. 1984. Evolution of the wilderness concept in the US. In: *Wilderness: the way ahead,* edited by V. Martin & M. Inglis, 74–77. Forres, Inverness: Findhorn; Lorian.

Bradley, R.T. 1985. The UK timber industry. *Commonw. Forest. Rev.,* **64**, 181–186.

Brown, I.R. 1984. *Management of birch woodland in Scotland.* Perth: Countryside Commission for Scotland.

Bunce, R.G.H. & Last, F.T. 1981. How to characterize the habitats of Scotland. *Annu. Rep. Edinb. Cent. rural Econ. 1980/81,* 1–14.

Bunce, R.G.H., Barr, C.J. & Whittaker, H.A. 1981. *Land classes in Great Britain: preliminary descriptions for users of the Merlewood method of land classification.* (Merlewood research and development paper no. 86.) Grange-over-Sands: Institute of Terrestrial Ecology.

Calder, I.R. 1985. Influence of woodlands on water quantity. In: *Woodlands, weather and water,* edited by D.J.L. Harding & J.K. Fawell, 31–46. London: Institute of Biology.

Campbell, J. 1984. Excellence in Britain's forestry. In: *Ecology in the 80s,* edited by J.N.R. Jeffers, 22–34. Cambridge: Institute of Terrestrial Ecology.

Centre for Agricultural Strategy. 1980. *Strategy for the UK forest industry.* (CAS report no. 6.) Reading: CAS, University of Reading.

Commission of the European Communities. 1979. *Forestry policy in the European Community.* (COM (78) 621 FINAL.) Luxembourg: CEC.

Department of Agriculture and Fisheries for Scotland. 1959. *Agricultural statistics 1957: Scotland.* Edinburgh: HMSO.

Dalsager, P. 1983. Agriculture and forestry biomass – an energy source for Europe? In: *Energy from biomass, Proc. 2nd E.C. Conf.,* edited by A. Strub, P. Chartier & G. Schleser, 3–6. London: Applied Science.

Edmunds, W.M. & Kinniburgh, D. 1986. The susceptibility of UK groundwaters to acidic deposition. *J. Geol. Soc. Lond.,* Thematic issue. In press.

Giraud, A. 1985. La biomasse dans la compétition énergétique. In: *Energy from biomass, Proc. 3rd E.C. Conf.,* edited by W. Palz, J. Coombs & D.O. Hall, 6–14. London: Elsevier Applied Science.

Harriman, R. & Morrison, B.R.S. 1982. Ecology of streams draining forested and non-forested catchments in an area of central Scotland subject to acid precipitation. *Hydrobiologia,* **88,** 251–263.

Henriksen, A., Skogheim, O.K. & Rosseland, B.O. 1984. Episodic changes in pH and aluminium-speciation kill fish in a Norwegian salmon river. *Vatten,* **40,** 255–260.

Highland Regional Council. 1985a. *HRC/ITE land classification system.* (Planning Department information paper no. 5.) Inverness: HRC.

Highland Regional Council. 1985b. *Amenity woodland survey.* (Planning Department information paper no. 7.) Inverness: HRC.

Highland Regional Council. 1985c. *Forestry model.* (Planning Department display note.) Inverness: HRC.

Hill, M.O., Bunce, R.G.H. & Shaw, M.W. 1975. Indicator species analysis, a divisive polythetic method of classification and its application to a survey of native pinewoods in Scotland. *J. Ecol.,* **63,** 597–613.

Howard, P.J.A. & Howard, D. 1980. Methods of classifying map data with particular reference to indicator species analysis and K-means clustering. *Annu. Rep. Inst. terr. Ecol. 1979,* 34–42.

Jenkins, D. & Matthew, E.M. 1984. The wildlife resource and its use. In: *The World Conservation Strategy and Grampian Region. Report of the Braemar Workshop, 1982,* edited by J.A. Forster, 83–97. Aberdeen: Grampian Regional Council and Nature Conservancy Council.

Last, F.T., Fowler, D. & Cape, J.N. 1984. Fossil fuels and the environment: their interrelationship. *Coal Energy Q.,* **41,** 14–23.

MacKerron, G. & Rush, H.J. 1976. Agriculture in the EEC: taking stock. *Food Policy,* **1,** 286–300.

Ministry of Agriculture, Fisheries and Food. 1983. *Annual review of agriculture 1983.* (Cmnd 8804.) London: HMSO.

Melchett, Lord. 1985. Farming for the public, not for ourselves. *Proc. Br. Crop Prot. Conf. – Weeds, 5th,* **1,** 3–19.

Mitchell, C.P., Brandon, O.H., Bunce, R.G.H., Barr, C.J., Tranter, R.B., Downing, P., Pearce, M.L. & Whittaker, H.A. 1983. Land availability for production of wood for energy in Great Britain. In: *Energy from biomass, Proc. 2nd E.C. Conf.,* edited by A. Strub, P. Chartier & G. Schleser, 159–163. London: Applied Science.

Murray, M.B., Cannell, M.G.R. & Sheppard, L.J. 1986. Frost-hardiness of *Nothofagus procera* and *Nothofagus obliqua* in Britain. *Forestry.* In press.

Newton, I. & Moss, D. 1981. Factors affecting the breeding of sparrowhawks and the occurrence of their songbird prey in woodlands. In: *Forest and woodland ecology,* edited by F.T. Last & A.S. Gardiner, 125–131. Cambridge: Institute of Terrestrial Ecology.

Pears, N.V. 1967. Present tree-lines of the Cairngorm Mountains, Scotland. *J. Ecol.,* **55,** 815–830.

Scottish Development Department. 1981. *Land use summary sheet 1: Agriculture.* (SDD national planning series.) Edinburgh: SDD.

Seligman, R.M. 1985. Biomass fuels in a European context. In: *Energy from biomass. Proc. 3rd E.C. Conf.,* edited by W. Palz, J. Coombs & C.O. Hall, 15–22. London: Elsevier Applied Science.

Stoner, J.H., Gee, A.S. & Wade, K.R. 1984. The effects of acidification on the ecology of streams in the Upper Tywi catchment in west Wales. *Environ. Pollut. A,* **35,** 125–157.

Strehler, A. 1985. Biomass availability and use in the industrial regions of the EC. In: *Energy from biomass, Proc. 3rd E.C. Conference,* edited by W. Palz, J. Coombs & D.O. Hall, 60–65. London: Elsevier Applied Science.

Zunino, F. 1984. A wilderness concept for Europe. In: *Wilderness: the way ahead,* edited by V. Martin & M. Inglis, 61–65. Forres, Inverness: Findhorn; Lorian.

Whither forestry? The scene in AD 2025

R S D OGILVY
Fountain Forestry Limited, Inverness

1 Introduction

The over-riding principle directing the structure and extent of forest development is economics, although there are certainly woodlands where other factors are the prime consideration. These factors include shelter and protection, amenity or cover for game. However, there seems little prospect of significant new areas being planted solely for sport or amenity. Although these factors will have a strong influence upon design, we can assume that most future forests will have been created for commercial purposes. This paper addresses itself to them.

In common with all industry, in order to maintain favourable conditions for expansion, forests must be considered to be environmentally acceptable. In this respect, every factor can be related back to economics. Some factors are of direct economic importance, eg the volume and quality of timber, and others are of indirect economic importance, eg design for wildlife and conservation. Although design for conservation may reduce the basic timber productivity, it may also reduce vulnerability to damage by browsing animals.

In assessing the future structure, I first consider the internal forest characteristics, analyse the influences affecting internal forest design, and project a model of the typical composition and internal physical structure of our future forests. Having established the internal physical characteristics, I then consider the broader picture, and attempt to determine the shape and extent of the future forests within the uplands and to build up a composite picture of forestry in the landscape.

2 Internal forest structure

The factors influencing internal forest design can be defined under the following objectives:

  i. primary economic, seeking to maximize financial yield;
  ii. secondary economic, seeking to minimize risk from natural influences, while pursuing objective (i);
  iii. non-economic, only seeking to maintain forestry as environmentally acceptable.

2.1 Primary economic factors

2.1.1 Volume increment

The prime objective of foresters is to maximize the financial return from the forest. It requires the production of the maximum volume of timber of the highest quality in the shortest possible time. Within the Scottish Highlands, Sitka spruce (*Picea sitchensis*) is the tree which out-performs all others in both productivity and quality. It has been planted extensively since it was introduced by Douglas in 1832, and the way it performs under Scottish conditions is well understood.

Vigorously growing Sitka spruce demand more nitrogen, potash and phosphorus than most upland soils can provide and the application of additional fertilizers has been common practice. Recent research has shown, however, how the use of 'nurse' species can compensate for mineral deficiencies, especially nitrogen on deep peats. The high energy consumption involved in the production of nitrogenous fertilizers makes them increasingly expensive. Given that the dilution of spruce by other species has a minimal effect upon the final yield, it seems likely that sites which are expected to exhibit N-deficiency if planted with pure Sitka spruce will be planted in an intimate mixture of Sitka spruce with a nurse species, usually Scots pine (*Pinus sylvestris*), lodgepole pine (*Pinus contorta*) or Japanese larch (*Larix kaempferi*).

The pre-eminence of Sitka spruce as a timber tree in the UK has focused attention on improvement through tree breeding. The controlled pollination between selected clones has now advanced to the stage where the improved plants are available for forest use. The timescale for such breeding programmes is such that it could be 20 years before similarly improved material for other species becomes available. Hence, the predominance of Sitka spruce in planting schemes seems likely to continue.

2.1.2 Timber quality

In order to obtain the best financial return while maximizing the volume production, it is necessary to ensure that the timber achieves an acceptable quality. The following 2 factors determine this quality:

  i. the size and form of a log
  ii. the physical characteristics of the timber

Although the EEC requirement for small roundwood will continue to increase, the energy efficiency of sawmilling compared with particle board construction suggests that logs suitable for sawn timber production will always carry a premium over smaller categories. The strength, durability and working qualities of timber cannot be influenced by the conversion process, and the management of woodlands will be heavily orientated towards maintaining acceptable timber quality while maximizing volume production.

The principal log characteristics which can be influenced by stand management are:

  i. knot size and quantity
  ii. proportion of juvenile wood
  iii. taper
  iv. individual log volume
  v. ring width

The first 2 both require an initial stand density of no less than 2500 trees ha^{-1} to limit the size and persistence of side branches and effectively to limit the crown within which the juvenile wood is laid down. This planting density also minimizes stem taper. However, stocking levels must be reduced at some point in the rotation, if diameter growth is not to be significantly reduced. This reaction can be achieved by thinning, and the increasing demand for small roundwood will ensure that all forests are thinned to some degree unless stability is considered to be an overriding factor.

Several forest systems have been developed in the hope of achieving an acceptable compromise. *'Oceanic'* forestry opens up the plantations at an early age, giving selected stems room to develop. This system produces the large-diameter log sooner, but at the expense of quality with high taper, a high proportion of juvenile wood, persistent branching and large knots. *'No thinning'* regimes plant at a normal spacing of around 2300–2500 ha^{-1}, wide enough to give adequate individual stem size yet close enough to obtain minimum knot size and finer growth through early branch suppression and close competition. *'Respacing'* systems seek to obtain the best of both worlds by planting closely spaced, followed by very early opening up at any age preceding normal thinnings. The natural reluctance of any forester to plant a tree and then spend money again to remove it seems sufficient to nullify the already tenuous economic arguments.

'Chemical thinning' is also being practised in crops which, although requiring thinning for silvicultural reasons, have a stem size too small for easy economic harvesting, or where the physical removal of thinnings might result in instability. I do not expect that this practice will continue for the following reasons.

  i. Forest pathogens have traditionally been controlled by good stand hygiene. With anxiety from many sources on the use of pesticides liable to lead to restrictions on their use, the provision of extensive breeding material appears unacceptable.
  ii. It is economically unnecessary. At present prices, the returns on a thinning can pay for the harvesting cost. This is a feature of our managment in similar plantations.

I see only a very limited role for chemical thinning in future British forestry, but it may be useful where stands are considered to be too susceptible to windblow to be thinned conventionally.

The most encouraging development in reconciling these conflicting demands is the afore-mentioned mixture using a nurse species where, by careful selection of the nurse, a *'self-thinning'* regime can be created. In this system, the nurse not only provides an enhanced nutritional base for the main crop, but, by the careful selection of species and provenance, the nurse ultimately becomes over-topped and suppressed by the main crop although competing sufficiently to shape and clean the timber. This system allows a gradual increase in the space available for the crop to develop, giving the requisite size of individual stem and maintaining regular growth and light side branching.

This utopian concept, although difficult to achieve, offers sufficient attraction to become the mainstay of upland afforestation. The benefits of such mixtures in growing Sitka spruce can be summarized as follows.

  i. The avoidance of heather check.
  ii. Enhanced nutritional status giving lower fertilizer inputs, especially nitrogen.
  iii. Improved site utilization with differing but complementary rooting patterns.
  iv. Opportunity for self-thinning.
  v. Reduction in the risk of total loss by forest pathogens.
  vi. Conservation benefits through better light reaching the forest floor, with wider ranges of host material.
  vii. More acceptable aesthetically than monocultures of Sitka spruce.

2.1.3 Establishment costs

The costs of afforestation and production have a direct bearing on the financial yield, and foresters are always bound to seek economies. Most improvements in efficiency have little effect on forest structure, eg the use of helicopters for fertilizing, using containerized trees for planting, chemical in place of hand weeding, etc. All these methods improve efficiency but they have no effect on the final forest design.

However, better production machinery has allowed timber to be extracted economically at a greater distance from forest roads, and modern forests have only 30% of the roads which were previously considered essential. In many Forestry Commission forests such as Glen Urquhart and Port Clair, 3 roads formerly traversed a hillside where only one would now be considered necessary.

2.1.4 Financial and fiscal incentives

The government influences development patterns through financial inducements or penalties, and all investment managers have to adapt to make the best use of the incentives available. The major influence is on the scale of forestry expansion rather than on the internal forest structure, but, through the application of the forestry grant and broadleaved woodland schemes, developments perceived to be in the public interest are encouraged. As a result, there will be increasing interest in the use of broadleaves, although even the enhanced grant will be insufficient to make traditional broadleaves commercially viable. In 1987, however, the first commercial quantities of silver birch (*Betula pendula*) will become available from the birch breeding programme at Aberdeen University. This programme promises to provide trees of fine quality and vigour, producing a yield class between 6 and 8 which is comparable with conifers on some sites. The combination of the higher broadleaved grant with improved productivity of this species will ensure a dramatic increase in the planting of birch in commercial plantations.

2.2 Secondary economic factors
2.2.1 Windblow
This will be the most important limiting factor influencing forest structure. It determines the terminal height of the stand, and whether it will be thinned, the style of ground preparation, the silvicultural system and choice of species. The principal effect upon the forest is in the imposition of a clearfelling silvicultural system. Irregular canopies increase the risk of windblow, and individual woods will stand or fall together, with the pattern of clearfelling and replanting remaining a permanent feature.

The more sensitive use of watercourses and natural features as breaks in the plantation will provide the boundaries for clearfelling coupes. These will thus become more irregular and naturally defined than has been common up to now.

2.2.2 Red deer and other browsing animals
The failure to allow room within enclosures has led to notable forest failures, eg at Slattadale and Fuinary where large areas of Sitka spruce had to be felled prematurely because of bark stripping and because numbers of red deer (*Cervus elaphus*) could not be reduced due to poor internal forest design. Although total exclusion using deer fences is normal for afforestation, colonization by red deer is inevitable once the tree canopy closes. Accordingly, all current and future forests will be designed in such a way as to accommodate deer and relieve pressure upon the planted crop.

The requirements for deer complement the more general wildlife considerations. They can be summarized as leaving open ground within the woodlands, especially around water and grazing meadows. Typically, this ground amounts to 10–15% of the total area. Such measures reduce the risk of unacceptable damage, but allow normal control by rifle. They may also generate additional income from sporting use.

We recognize that the permanent exclusion of deer from our forests is impossible, but we accept that deer fencing is necessary in the Scottish uplands to allow the re-establishment of woodland. Red deer in woodlands often produce calves annually as against biennially on the open hill. They become fecund at one year instead of 2 and have lower calf mortality. As the productivity of red deer in many woodlands is often higher than that on the open hill, about one-fifth of the adult deer population can be culled annually while maintaining the adult numbers at a steady level (Ratcliffe 1984). If the newly planted extensive forests use good internal design, it will be possible to reduce deer numbers permanently. It is our contention that by the year 2025 there will be no distinction between deer and forest land, with deer moving freely between forest and hill and both deer and stalkers adapting to a truly integrated environment.

2.2.3 Climatic effects
Foresters manage woodlands in such a way as to minimize the impact of climate. However, the climate has a direct impact upon the forest and will affect its final structure and appearance.

Wind has the most pernicious effect and within plantations we will always see trees blown singly or in groups and lines. Extraction of limited areas is often uneconomic, and dead and rotting trees will always be found within the forest. Wind also manifests itself as exposure, so that, as one progresses from the bottom of a wood to the top, growth falls away until the tree-line is reached, at which point only shrub-like specimens can be found. Frost shapes plantations when cold air collects in frost hollows, and spruce in particular may take many years to grow above the damaging level.

The use of Sitka spruce is, of course, a response to the local climatic conditions, as less tolerant species such as Douglas fir (*Pseudotsuga menziesii*) will only grow well on the more favoured sites.

2.2.4 Soils
Within the Highlands, the majority of soils are acidic. Although they can be subdivided into such categories as podzols, ironpans and gleys, often with varying depths of peat, the modern practice is to grow Sitka spruce on all, even where brown earths are encountered.

Many of our existing forests were planted with much more specific attention to ground variation, so that we see Sitka spruce in the flushes, lodgepole pine on the blanket peats, Scots pine and European larch (*Larix decidua*) on the mineral heaths, Norway spruce (*Picea abies*) on the drier grass lands, and Douglas fir, hemlock fir (*Tsuga canadensis*) or cypress (*Cupressus* spp.) on the brown forest earths. Many of these, particularly lodgepole pines on peat, will be replaced by Sitka spruce after clearfelling.

2.2.5 Weed competition

The vegetation below the tree-line on the Scottish moors is an artificial climax maintained by burning or grazing. When enclosed for planting, the normal development to natural climax begins, aided by the site improvement consequent on the afforestation activities. This development is less apparent in the first rotation, but when the first crop is cleared and the ground is later replanted, the woodland conditions allow the rapid colonization by indigenous woody species which have already become partly re-established within the original enclosure. Inevitably, open spaces develop within the crop on the rougher sites and native broadleaves may establish themselves throughout the crop, creating difficulty for the forester in getting the planted crop established. Nevertheless, the mixture will become a normal feature of all our coniferous forests and will persist, even if actively discouraged.

2.2.6 Pests and diseases

We have already mentioned how vital it is to design forests to allow effective deer control if serious damage is to be avoided. More insidious are the effects of fungal and insect pests, but, although they will certainly continue to take their toll of individual trees or of some groups, I do not expect them to have a significant impact upon the woodland structure.

2.2.7 Fire

Fire is included here as it is essentially a natural influence, although generally started by people. In the past, woodland design to minimize fire risk has been most evident in the use of larch belts through and around many plantations. Such belts can resist the passage of a crown fire but their use on plantation edges does not stop a ground fire and lines of larches can have a negative effect on the visual amenity. Forest design will continue to rely on perimeter fire traces and will make greater use of unplanted watercourses and internal hardwood strips as fire breaks. The creation of more imaginative fire ponds will provide additional benefits for amenity, wildlife and recreation.

2.3 Non-economic influences

These are the factors which influence the structure of the forest but which have no direct benefits to the crop. However, they minimize hostility to forest development.

2.3.1 Visual amenity

For most people, the impact of forestry in the countryside is visual. It will remain normal practice to harmonize plantations within the overall landscape and to enhance their detailed appearance by careful design. It also becomes an economic consideration where planning requirements have to be accommodated to obtain the benefits of the Forestry Grant Scheme.

The following are typical points considered.

   i. The avoidance of straight lines, either boundaries or internal rides, with upper planting limits in harmony with the topography. Harsh transitions between moorland and forest are mitigated wherever possible.
   ii. The maintenance of viewpoints from roads, parking places, picnic sites, paths and prominent features.
   iii. The breaking up of monotonous monocultures by using alternative species, especially larch and broadleaves, usually on prominences within the plantation or to break up the woodland edges.
   iv. The maintenance of points of interest such as hillocks, lochs and river margins, or archaeological sites of interest.

2.3.2 Conservation of wildlife

Foresters are blamed for damaging the flora and fauna of moorland sites. To meet such criticism, foresters adopt codes of practice to ensure that wildlife damage is minimized. The measures adopted complement other criteria such as deer management, fishery management and visual amenity, but the most important additional feature is tree species diversity, and in particular the use of native broadleaves.

The use of these native trees is much favoured by naturalists (who may forget that the Scots pine is also native). Their use protects and maintains the indigenous flora, and especially the fauna associated with them. With intensifying pressure from conservation groups, the incentives to use native broadleaves will be maintained. In addition, the general awareness engendered by various conservation groups ensures that most forestry investors are conscious of their responsibilities, which, when allied with the financial support, will result in greater use being made of native species in afforestation programmes.

2.3.3 Acidification of watercourses

Although there has been no detectable damage from 'acid rain' to the actual forest crop in Scotland, neither is there likely to be, coniferous trees are less able to neutralize acidic precipitation than open moorland. In addition to the present practice of planting back from watercourses, we see this factor as adding weight to the case for greater use of broadleaves, especially the improved birch, in sensitive water catchments.

Many of the streams and lochs emanating from afforested catchments in Galloway are virtually devoid of fish because the pH is too low for fish eggs to develop. Planting birch in wide swathes around the principal streams has been shown to have a marked neutralizing effect.

3 External forest characteristics

Having studied the influences shaping the internal forest structure, we can now examine those which may affect the future scale of afforestation and its integration with other land uses.

The principal factors influencing the scale of expansion are classified under the following 3 headings:

i. relative economics of different land uses
ii. political perceptions
iii. basic forest economics

3.1 Relative economics of different land uses

3.1.1 Agriculture

It is extremely difficult realistically to compare economics of forestry and agriculture because both receive arbitrary subsidy. Given the broader level of support generally given to both agriculture and forestry throughout the EEC, I consider it unlikely that the levels of government support for either will reduce in real terms.

As a result of the present levels of support, there is over-production of agricultural produce, whereas timber production only provides 40% of EEC requirements. With UK forestry expansion only achieving 50% of government targets, it seems certain that agricultural support will decrease relative to forestry support.

At the present level of subsidy, to obtain a 6% return on capital, a good-quality sheep farm can rarely place a value in excess of £150 ha^{-1} on the best ground. To achieve the same return, forestry could afford to pay over £500 ha^{-1}. This situation implies a steady progression of grazing land to forestry, although such a trend will be limited by the large amounts of land held under agricultural tenancy or crofting tenure, where the occupier has security and little incentive for change of use. This is especially true in situations of common grazing where many individuals have only minor shares in a common. However, legislation which allows crofters to buy their crofts and seek apportionments of common grazings has led to a trickle of land to forestry, and this trend is seen as continuing.

3.1.2 Deer stalking

This land use generally makes little return on capital, only paying its annual running costs, although the popularity of the sport usually ensures that the capital value is maintained in real terms. As discussed earlier, deer are more productive in woodlands than on moors and, as the best stalking is on the higher, more rugged ground, I believe that the opening of forests to deer will lead to continued forest expansion into former deer forests, with true integration following.

3.1.3 Grouse moors

It is proving difficult to maintain high levels of red grouse (*Lagopus lagopus*) by the control of predators. Inevitably, many grouse moors have seen the numbers of grouse dwindle from tick-borne diseases. It is also becoming less acceptable to slaughter raptors as these birds are highly regarded by naturalists. Food production from grouse moors is negligible and only the enthusiasm of sporting proprietors can maintain the tradition. The most productive grouse moors often occupy the best plantable land, but, as grouse moors can be maintained at altitudes beyond the tree planting limits, I see the pattern of development very much as for deer forests, with the continued expansion of woodlands on to former grouse moors.

3.1.4 Water catchments

While not a principal land use, large areas of plantable land act as catchments for salmon rivers, hydro-electric schemes and domestic water supplies. Forests reduce runoff by up to 25% and produce greater sedimentation than bare moorland. The former effect is serious for hydro-electric schemes and water supplies, and the latter for salmon fisheries along with the acidification effects previously described. Until now there has been little effect on afforestation expansion but, with the increasing awareness of the potential effects, increased anxiety downstream could hinder afforestation programmes. In one recent case, DAFS anxiety over river gravel deposition led to great difficulty in obtaining planting consents.

3.1.5 Nature reserves

Both the Nature Conservancy Council (NCC), through the application of Sites of Special Scientific Interest (SSSIs), and the Royal Society for the Protection of Birds (RSPB), through their reserves, hold large areas as sacrosanct and allow no development. As a result of the Wildlife and Countryside Act, economic realities in the application of SSSI will probably have less effect on forestry expansion than might be inferred from recent cases. In 2 instances, the NCC paid in total over £0.5M to prevent afforestation on less than 2000 ha. With the government's expressed desire to increase our home timber base, it is hard to imagine continuing expenditure at this level to maintain land in its unproductive state.

It should be noted that both the NCC and the RSPB are opposed to further upland afforestation, and, with the support of nervous politicians, they present the most significant threat to major expansion.

3.1.6 Peat resources

Many planning officials consider peat to be a resource worthy of exploitation, and, although very little other than personal peat cutting is done, they wish to leave such 'peat core' areas undisturbed in the hope of developments yet to come. The environmental effect of large-scale peat development could attract even greater criticism from conservationists than afforestation, eg Duich Moss. As timber, unlike peat, is a viable renewable resource, it is hard to see how a policy of retaining areas of peat cores can be sustained.

3.2 Political considerations

Foresters grow trees because economic assessments based on the UK's vulnerable position of dependence on imported supplies suggest a secure base for investment. The UK imports 90% of its wood and wood-based products, and, against a background of shrinking overseas supplies and escalating energy costs of transport, there is little doubt that the future produce will find a ready sale.

The climate for attracting investment is manipulated by government through fiscal policies. It is only through government recognition of our vulnerability that large-scale afforestation has been encouraged. Governments of differing political colours are all agreed on the need to reduce dependence on overseas supplies, although differing views are held on the pattern of ownership and incentives.

For the purposes of this paper, it matters not who does the planting or how the incentives are constructed. What is important is the recognition of continuing government encouragement through fiscal incentives to expand UK forests. Of the government's target for new afforestation, only 50% is currently being achieved. Scottish coniferous high forest presently extends to 870 kha, and at the present rate of planting will rise to only 1.5 Mha by the year 2026. I believe that our continued expansion will certainly not be less than this figure.

3.3 Forest economics

The channelling of investment to forestry is influenced in total terms by fiscal strategy, but, as the level of planting grant is constant for all sites over 10 ha, other site factors dictate the location and scale of the investment. Land is subject to the laws of supply and demand. At present, a strong market means that all plantable land finds a ready sale, albeit with variable prices dictated by considerations such as potential timber production, distance from ports or consumers, and the costs of afforestation and production.

Regardless of its geographical location, I believe that, on the basis of the current investment criteria, all plantable land will ultimately find an investor, with varying economic factors being accommodated in the land price. The forest industry in the UK is too small to sustain the scale of wood-using industries which would allow us to compete internationally. The ludicrous situation exists whereby we export our small roundwood from Inverness and other east coast ports and import the resultant pulp for our papermills.

As the scale of forestry increases, the economics will improve, so that the industry will be better able to locate locally and to provide stable employment within the forests from continuous felling and replanting programmes. I believe that the momentum for planting will increase as the forests reach the critical mass and really start to generate local demand on an economic scale.

4 Conclusion

Considering the influences affecting internal forest design, and although no 2 forests will ever be the same, I can visualize the appearance of a typical forest in the year 2026. It will be unfenced, lightly roaded, growing genetically selected clones of Sitka spruce in an intimate mixture with Scots or lodgepole pine and hybrid larch, and with these trees covering only 85% of the woodland area. The 15% of open rides, watercourse margins and clearing will carry heavy regeneration of rowan (Sorbus aucuparia), birch and other local broadleaves, which will provide popular deer browsing. Here and there, fairly large blocks will be under genetically improved birch.

Clearfelling will be the normal termination of the production cycle, with coupes extending to wind-firm edges. These areas may be fenced temporarily until replanted trees become established.

Herds of red deer will roam the forest, with their total body weights 50% higher than is normal today, and with proportionately increased antlers.

Within the overall upland scene, I foresee the continuing expansion of forests on all cultivatable land below the commercial tree limit, which, subject to topography , ranges from 300 m in the north and west to 500 m in the south and east. The harsh outlines of solitary plantations will be lost as additional planting embraces them or as restocking employs better forest design techniques. In the year 2026, I do not foresee blocks of forestry on a moorland landscape, but the stark moorlands of SSSIs and common grazings isolated in a forest scene.

The world-wide scarcity of timber will have dramatically increased the value of the resource, and wood-using industries, particularly sawmills and particle board mills, will provide a ready market, with greatly increased economic activity in the rural communities. The cycle of felling and replanting will provide continuity of employment within such communities, although as many rangers will be employed as forestry workers, controlling deer and managing the sport and leisure activities within the forest.

Sheep and cattle will continue to graze the bottom land, benefiting from the shelter afforded by the extensive forests around.

These forests I describe are not based on hope or guess work. They are the forests Fountain Forestry is planting today.

5 Summary

In trying to visualize the forests of the year 2025, we have attempted to identify the various influences affecting the internal forest structure and design and the scale and integration within the landscape.

We see a doubling of the existing forest area by 2025, with the new forests comprising genetically improved Sitka spruce growing on 85% of the woodland area in an intimate mixture with pines and larch.

The balance of the area will support a diversity of self-sown indigenous broadleaves, especially birch, rowan and gean (*Prunus avium*), and large areas, especially in salmon river catchments, will be planted with genetically superior clones of birch.

The accepted silvicultural system will use deer fences only temporarily for restocking after clearfell. Deer will move freely between forests and hill, living within the forest where they will grow to become 50% heavier, with proportionally increased antlers.

The rural communities will include a tradition of woodland employment consequent upon the sustained production provided by the expanded forest.

Farming, forestry and sporting will no longer be seen as conflicting land uses, just the natural use of land.

6 Reference

Ratcliffe, P.R. 1984. Population dynamics of red deer (*Cervus elaphus* L.) in Scottish commercial forests. *Proc. R. Soc. Edinb.*, **82B,** 291–302.

The history of native woodlands in the Scottish Highlands

R F CALLANDER
Haughend, Finzean, Aberdeenshire

1 Introduction

This paper discusses the contribution of historical information to the management of native woodlands in the Scottish Highlands. These native woodlands are of a predominantly different ecological character from those in the rest of Britain. Boreal woodlands dominated by birch (*Betula* spp.) and pine (*Pinus sylvestris*) represent the natural tree cover throughout most of the Highlands (McVean & Ratcliffe 1962). The Highlands are defined as the mainland area north of the Highland Boundary Fault and west of the eastern edge of the Grampians (Hechter 1975; McVean & Ratcliffe 1962). The land area of the Highlands is just over half of Scotland's 7.7 Mha, twice the size of Wales and equivalent to nearly one-third of the area of England.

The first part of the paper describes what history can reveal about the present status, condition and distribution of the native woodlands in the Highlands, and how this information relates to the management of these woods. There has been relatively little use so far of historical information for this purpose in the Highlands. However, the Highlands have the most distinctive native woodland history of any region in Britain (Peterken 1981). The second half of the paper reviews current knowledge of the history of Highland woods, and considers how further historical research might contribute to management of native woodlands in the Highlands.

2 Native woodlands and historical information

Woodlands in the Highlands can be classified as 'native' in 3 different ways, and it is necessary in the management of any 'native' woodland to identify which of these definitions is to be used. They are as follows.

    i. The trees in the wood are species that became established in the Highlands without human influence during the post-glacial period (Tivy 1973).

    ii. Each tree species is also 'likely to be a past-natural component of woodland on the site under consideration' (Peterken 1981).

    iii. The wood is only 'genuinely native' if the trees have also 'descended from one generation to the next by natural means' (Steven & Carlisle 1959).

For management, it is necessary to decide first whether stocking will rely on natural regeneration or on planting, and, second, if planting is to be done, what species and provenance will be suitable. The definition employed need not be the same for all parts of a site or necessarily for each tree species involved. The management decisions to be made will depend on the priority given to different objectives including, for example, nature conservation and timber production.

The native woodlands discussed in this paper are those defined by Steven and Carlisle (1959). These self-sown woods of local provenance are the most natural woodlands in the Highlands. However, they are all semi-natural because, as in the rest of Britain, no woods have escaped some degree of human influence (Peterken 1981). The following sub-sections describe how historical records can be used to identify native woodlands and to explain their species composition, age structure, individual extent and overall distribution.

2.1 Woodland origin

The use of historical records is more important for identifying native woodlands in the Highlands than in other regions of Britain. Site continuity is less significant in the ecology of these boreal woodlands than elsewhere in Britain, and this fact can make it more difficult in the Highlands to distinguish by fieldwork between primary and secondary woodlands (Peterken 1981). As a result, historical records can provide the only method of separating semi-natural and planted woods.

Scots pine and oak (*Quercus* spp.) are the 2 native species that have been most extensively planted in the Highlands. The survey of Steven and Carlisle (1959) demonstrated the use of historical records to identify native pinewoods. Their list does not include all native pinewoods (eg Creag Ghuibhais, Deeside, NO 315957*), but there has been no equivalent survey for native oakwoods. Historical work has been done at some oak sites in the Highlands (eg Lindsay 1974, 1975; Rymer 1980; Scott 1974; Tittensor 1970). Scott demonstrated at Dinnet Oakwood (Deeside, NO 463983) that, while the origin of some oakwoods can be identified by fieldwork, there may be great difficulty in distinguishing the status of others without historical records.

Other native species have also been planted in the past in the Highlands, but mainly at house and farm sites. Small numbers of other valued species may have been planted into native woods. For example, Finzean Estate papers show that larch (*Larix* spp.) was planted into gaps in self-sown pine/birchwoods in the mid-19th century (Callander 1985).

*Map reference is for the north-east corner of the wood

The management of native woodlands will be influenced by their condition, including species composition, age structure and extent. These attributes have usually been affected by timber extraction and/or browsing pressure, and historical records can help to reveal the degree to which they have been altered.

2.2 Species composition

Both the absence of a tree species from a native woodland and the relative abundance of species within the wood can result from the selective removal of particular species in the past. For example, Lindsay (1974) described the clearance of less valued species like birch from coppiced oakwoods in the 19th century. He also identified the importance of the selective felling of valued species, like oak and ash (*Fraxinus excelsior*), within other native woodlands in the Highlands.

The influence of browsing animals has also been of particular significance in the Highlands. Kirby (1986) suggests that most native woodlands in Britain owe their survival to past management, mainly enclosure and coppicing. These practices were less common in the Highlands than in other regions, as most native woodlands have been unmanaged except for exploitation*, and have been left unenclosed against livestock and deer. They have survived by natural regeneration, which has resulted in the selective survival of those species that sow themselves most readily and are least susceptible to browsing. The scarcity of birch and other native broadleaves in native pinewoods is, for example, attributed to past browsing pressure (Steven & Carlisle 1959).

Browsing pressure is an important constraint on natural regeneration in native woodlands in the Highlands and its influence through successive generations at particular woods has favoured pine rather than other native tree species. Most native woodlands in the Highlands are now species poor, though sites like the Tullich glen (NO 380992) in Deeside show an intermix of pine, birch and a dozen other native species within a small area. The character of the Highland landscape, with marked changes in soil quality, altitude and exposure over very short distances, indicates that such local species diversity and intermixes of woodland types would be more common, without the impoverishing effect of heavy browsing.

2.3 Age structure

The age of trees in a native woodland can sometimes be related to timber extraction or coppicing (Tittensor 1970; Steven & Carlisle 1959). In some cases, age can only be established from historical sources, while in others evidence in the field may provide clues. For example, 140-year-old pines in Glenferrick wood, Finzean (NO 573918), are concentrated along the

*'The intermittent or sustained removal of timber and other woodland products without regard to the replacement of losses' (Lindsay 1974)

edges of old drag tracks. Estate records show that this wood was felled in the early 1840s, except for the stunted trees on the upper slopes (Callander 1985).

Browsing has also been a particularly important influence on age structure. Changes in cattle, sheep, deer, rabbit or hare numbers have all determined when natural regeneration was able to occur. Watson (1983) related the present age of pine stands on upper Deeside to increases in deer numbers during the late 18th century.

Fire and windblow are both considered to be natural events in boreal and taiga woodlands. Fire has had a greater influence on the age structure of native woodlands in the Highlands than in other regions of Britain. It can create a favourable seed bed for natural regeneration, but it also has a destructive influence on native woodland structure, as can be seen where muirburn has burned patterns into and through existing areas of natural regeneration (eg Pannanich Hill, Deeside, NO 398958). Historical records can often provide details of major fires and windblows. Diack (no date), for example, describes 6 major fires in the Glen Tanar pinewood between 1688 and 1920. At least 4 of these fires occurred in June.

Even-aged stands formed by the natural regeneration of birch and pine characterize native woodlands in boreal regions. Differences in age between such stands, their extent, density and composition may suggest the factors that have affected the development of the woods. Woods of uniform age are an artificial feature, due perhaps to browsing, fire or felling. An intermix of different-aged trees and stands in a mosaic of varying complexity is more natural. The size of the wood is an important variable, with birch and pine tending to regenerate outside even-aged stands, either at the edge of the wood or where sufficient internal canopy openings have developed.

2.4 Extent

The age structure of native woodlands in the Highlands often indicates that the boundaries of woods are changing. Expansion occurs where natural regeneration spreads on to open ground away from older stands, and contraction occurs where widely spaced older trees are dying out, around more fully stocked, mixed-aged woodland. Both these trends can occur in and around the same wood.

Peterken (1986) has used historical records to show that expansions and contractions of woods can have occurred in the same area for centuries. As a result, he characterized native woodlands in the Highlands as having boundaries that fluctuate around a core area, noting that with birch and pine in particular the core areas themselves change their locations through successive generations. This echoes the old saying that 'these Highland fir woods gradually shift their stances' (Michie 1901 in Steven & Carlisle 1959).

Such changes in extent contrast with the records for native woodlands in lowland areas, where historical map sequences tend only to show a pattern of contraction (Rackham 1980; Peterken 1981). In those areas, native woods are usually ancient, with a history of continuous woodland since at least 1600. The more dynamic character of native woodlands in the Highlands, with the relative lack of ecological distinction between recent and ancient native woods, suggests that a different approach is required to define a woodland site. In contrast to the well-defined island woods of the lowlands, native woodlands in the Highlands might be considered a part of the same habitat complex as open areas of moor- and grassland that have no tree cover at present.

Historical records not only reveal the mobile character of Highland woods but can also explain their present extent. These typically unenclosed and unmanaged woods are, as their self-sown status suggests, a consequence rather than an intention of unrelated land use practices. The dominant influence of these practices and the full extent of the dynamic pattern of native woodlands in the Highlands are demonstrated by studies of the changing distribution of native woodlands.

2.5 Distribution

The distribution of native woodlands in the Highlands shows a similar history of expansion and contraction to that demonstrated for individual woods. The full extent and significance cannot be recognized without the use of historical sources. McKenzie (1985) and Wightman (in progress) have shown this for birchwoods, McKenzie studying 150 ha of birch spread over a single parish, and Wightman studying several thousand ha in Deeside. The present age structure of the birchwoods in each location suggests that there has been a major expansion in their total area during the last 40 years. Historical research confirmed that there had been an expansion on to new sites, but the increase in the total area of birchwoods was much less than expected, because in both locations around half the area that was under birch 40 years ago is no longer birchwood.

This major interchange of sites in a short period demonstrates the dynamic character of the pattern of native woodlands in the Highlands. Figures quoted by Peterken (1986) showing relatively little change in the total area of native woods in 1947–82 cannot be assessed so easily as equivalent data for lowland areas. The results from the studies by Wightman and McKenzie suggest that these native woodlands are more usefully viewed as a population of wild trees rather than a collection of habitats, which tends to be the legacy of managing the more stable lowland pattern. The wildlife population survives according to circumstances or the interplay between its ecology and other land use factors.

Wightman's work will allow the influence of different land uses to be identified for a wide area during a short period. In McKenzie's study area, estate forestry had been the most important factor affecting the extent of birch, and he traced this relationship back over 300 years. On the basis of a cyclical pattern between the area of birch and both the extent and maturity of the estate's plantation, he concluded that, unless there was a change in management, the present area of birch was about to decline sharply, despite its net 15% increase since 1947 and the vigorous age structure of the present woods.

The dynamic pattern of native birch- and pinewoods, and the importance of the factors determining their distribution, can only be understood by using historical records. If only a limited number of native woods can be protected in designated sites, and yet it is hoped to maintain or increase the overall area of native woodlands (Kirby 1986), the woods will need to be managed at a locality scale. Peterken's (1986) idea of cores and fluctuating boundaries for individual woods will need to be applied over wider areas. These areas could be defined by the distribution of woods and range from a parish to major river valley systems like Deeside, where native woodlands are interlinked in the main valley and over many of the subsidiary catchments. Wightman's study shows that, while there has been little change in the overall extent of birch in Deeside during the last 40 years, the interchange of sites has also involved major shifts in distribution. Net declines in upper and lower Deeside have only been balanced by the scale of the net gains in mid-Deeside.

These examples show that the changing pattern of native woodlands in the Highlands can only be understood through the history of factors affecting it, and the next section examines the existing state of this knowledge before discussing the scope for further research.

3 Native woodland history

3.1 The historical background

The dominant influences on native woodlands in the Highlands are extensive sheep, cattle and deer grazing, plantation forestry, and commercial sport. The influence of these land uses started after the large-scale exploitation of native woodlands in the Highlands during the 17th and 18th centuries. In contrast to the rest of Britain, the native woodlands in the Highlands appear to have been more or less intact at the beginning of the 17th century (Carlisle 1975). These woods have been collectively labelled 'The Caledonian forest' (Steven & Carlisle 1959) or 'The great wood of Caledon' (Darling & Boyd 1964), after the forest area shown on Ptolemy's map of the 2nd century AD. Forest animals present in the 17th century appear to have included European brown bear (*Ursus arctos*), beaver (*Castor fiber*) and wild boar (*Sus scrofa*) (Ritchie 1920; Thompson 1978), whereas in England the bear and beaver had already been extinct for over 600 years and wild boar was last recorded in 1260 (Rackham 1980).

43

The history of this forest is mentioned in most academic and general books which deal with the Highlands, but the knowledge presented might be described as 'The legend of the forest of Caledon'. The theme of the destruction of extensive self-sown woods is consistently repeated, yet the impressions of the former extent and distribution of these woods and the significance of different phases and causes in their destruction vary widely (Lindsay 1974). However, prior to the 17th century, there had been little exploitation of these woods. The small indigenous human population did not have large demands for fuelwood or timber and the impact of livestock was limited by their small numbers, particularly of sheep, and potentially by the regenerative capacity of the boreal woodlands. There had been little external influence, with only limited exploitation from outside the region on the Highland fringes, from the 15th century (Shaw 1984). The cultural isolation of the Highlands was delineated by the Gaelic language frontier that had formed along the Highland boundary by the 14th century (Nicholson 1974). Roman and, later, English armies only skirted the Highlands and the distinct character of the region's woodland history before the 17th century is indicated by the absence of Royal Forests or church lands (Gilbert 1979).

The large-scale exploitation that started in the opening decades of the 17th century resulted from fuelwood and timber shortages in England and lowland Scotland (James 1981; Gilbert 1979). Exploitation started in the east and west Highlands at the same time and reached its peak in the 18th century after the final suppression of the Jacobites. Records of sawmills and blast furnaces reflect the pattern of exploitation and its changing scale.

Sawmills are almost exclusively recorded from the east and central Highlands (Shaw 1984). The first was installed in 1630 and by 1700 there were a dozen operating, all sited at the woods. In the 18th century, there were over 60 mills operating on native timber. Larger mills were based at river mouths as a result of the extensive development of river floating. Some mills operated water wheels and 30–40 frame saws. There was little iron smelting in the east (eg the short-lived enterprise in Speyside), but, in the west, ironworks were the main form of development (Stell & Hay 1984). The first blast furnace operation was established around 1610 and a second before 1700. Four were then established between 1718 and 1728, and the 2 largest ironworks in the Highlands were set up in the 1750s. A major tanbark trade focused on Perthshire, and Argyll was also associated with the ironworks throughout the 18th century.

The exploitation had passed its peak by the end of the 18th century and declined during the first half of the 19th century. It was the first in a series of major land use changes that have swept over the Highlands during the last 300 years, each following a similar 'boom and bust' cycle. The cattle trade built up rapidly in the second half of the 18th century and then declined sharply before the mid-19th century. Sheep husbandry, which had grown on the newly deforested lands since 1760 (Darling 1955), swelled rapidly to displace both the cattle and some local communities. The profitability of sheep was already over by the 1870s, by which time 'deer forests' were rapidly expanding towards their peak in the early decades of this century. In their decline, deer forests are being replaced by coniferous afforestation, beginning after the First World War and more rapidly since 1945.

The impact of the period of direct exploitation and the subsequent influences of the different land uses are the principal ingredients in understanding the present extent, condition and changing pattern of native woodlands in the Highlands. However, there has been little attempt so far to study these relationships. Reports on woodlands, for example, usually contain pages on bioclimatic factors but only a few repeated anecdotes of historical information, despite the dominant influence of anthropogenic factors in shaping native woods in the Highlands. Similarly, the native woodland history of the Highlands has received scant and dismissive treatment in recent major works (Rackham 1976, 1980; Peterken 1981).

3.2 Further research

The survey work for the Ancient Woodland Inventory (AWI) of the Nature Conservancy Council will only provide a map of the longest established semi-natural woodlands in the Highlands (Kirby et al. 1984). The AWI is intended as a basis for the conservation and management of all native woods. However, its criteria and classification were based on experience in lowland England, and further research will be required to achieve its objectives in the Highlands.

The main criterion for the AWI has been site continuity, using map sources at approximately 100-year intervals back to the 17th century. The lack of adequate map sources in Scotland from the 17th and 18th centuries meant that the existing AWI's classification of semi-natural woodlands in England and Wales had to be hastily modified for Scotland. For example, 'ancient woodlands' will date from 1750, not 1600, and other woods will be listed under new headings. However, no changes have been made because site continuity has less value as a measure of semi-natural woods in the Highlands than elsewhere in Britain. The nomenclature is also ill-fitting. Semi-natural woodlands have been traditionally described as 'native woodlands' in the Highlands for at least 150 years (eg Grigor 1839), and the woods with the longest site continuity would be more appropriately labelled 'native Caledonian' woods, following the classification of Steven and Carlisle (1959). 'Ancient woodlands' are a product of England's woodland types and its distinctive woodland history.

Further use of historical map sequences will be required for the classification of native woods in the Highlands to identify changing patterns. This classification will need to include all existing native woodlands and also former woodlands that have not shown site continuity. It will need to employ map sources with shorter time intervals than those used in the AWI. A 100-year spacing would not show the cycles of woodland area revealed by McKenzie (1985), or the rapidity of change that was also shown by Wightman (in progress). Studies can, for example, use the Forestry Commission 1947 census maps, together with the sequence provided by editions of the Ordnance Survey, to cover the last 120 years.

These studies should be done on a local scale to extend the map sequence. The richest period for estate maps is from the first edition of the Ordnance Survey map series back to the late 18th century. Roy's survey (1750) and Blaeu's mid-17th century atlas also become more valuable at a local scale, as their reliability can be assessed in conjunction with other local sources. In interpreting the map results, the influence of different land uses can be analysed most effectively at a local level, even when centralized data are available. A clear account of native woodland history in the Highlands during the 17th and 18th centuries will only be built up from local studies.

The scarcity of historical work on either the pattern of native woodlands or individual woods in the Highlands does not reflect a lack of sources. However, the range of sources and their respective values can be different from other regions. Similarly, methods of research in Scotland, involving the Scottish Record Office and the National Register of Archives, can be unfamiliar to those with experience only of England. Anderson (1967) has been widely quoted by ecologists, but his work is mainly a compilation of historical information from published secondary sources. His achievement can be a useful starting point, but estate papers, for example, were beyond his scope and yet they will be central in the contribution of history to native woodland management.

The value of estate papers in Scotland is enhanced by 2 particular features of land ownership. First, land ownership is the level at which land management is co-ordinated and the pattern of land ownership provides the scale and degree of continuity in records. The Highlands of Scotland have the most concentrated pattern of private land ownership in Europe, which incorporates a correspondingly high degree of continuity in both estate structure and family ownership. For example, 100 years ago, less than 7% of England was held in estates larger than 8100 ha (20 000 acres), yet the figure for Scotland as a whole was then over 50% and is still over 30% today. Second, land ownership in Scotland is still legally defined as feudal. The retention of this complex system, which was dismantled in England from 1293, has made title deeds a useful source of information and also produced a wealth of legal disputes. For example, detailed records exist of 18th century court cases over the pinewoods of upper Deeside and Glen Tanar.

Estate records from the Highlands do not merely provide source material. In addition, the size and distribution of estates and the frequency with which areas changed hands have been important variables affecting native woodlands. At present, there is no published research on the relationship between the patterns of native woodlands and land ownership. This relationship may have been particularly important in the 17–19th centuries, when there was a rapid decline in the number of landowners. The number of large estates in upper Deeside (>100 kha) fell from 58 to 7 in 150 years.

The most critical relationship to study now is that between native woodlands and forestry management. McKenzie's (1975) short study suggested a 2-edged relationship where forestry can both contribute to maintaining a local population of native woods and also pose the greatest threat to it. His results showed that this relationship has existed since the start of plantation forestry, and that native woodlands have, in this sense, always been a part of forestry. The need now is to bring native woodlands under controlled management if the present development of forestry is not to result in a decline in native woodlands, and if proposals to allow native species to regenerate within plantations are to. be integrated with the dynamics of the wider pattern of native woodlands in the Highlands.

4 Summary

The paper considers the contribution of historical information to the management of native woodlands in the Scottish Highlands.

These native woods have a different ecological character from those in the the rest of Britain. Historical sources can be the only means of identifying woods of native origin in the Highlands and of explaining their changing patterns, so that their total area and local distributions can be managed. Historical sources can also be used to explain the extent, age structure and species composition of individual native woodlands and to allow their condition to be assessed for management.

The Highlands also have the most distinctive woodland history of any region in Britain, yet not much is known about this in detail. The dominant influences on native woodlands since large-scale exploitation in the 17th and 18th centuries have been extensive sheep, cattle and deer grazing, plantation forestry and commercial sport. These land uses, together with the pattern of land ownership associated with them, offer good potential for research aimed at understanding the basis of the present distribution and condition of native woodlands.

Without local studies of the relationships between native woodlands and these land uses, it will not be possible to manage the changing pattern of native woodlands or to assess the priority to be given in individual native woodlands to nature conservation, timber production or other management objectives.

5 References

Anderson, M.L. 1967. *A history of Scottish forestry.* 2 vols. London: Nelson.

Callander, R.F. 1985. *History in Birse.* Finzean: Callander.

Carlisle, A. 1975. The impact of man on the native pinewoods of Scotland. In: *Native pinewoods of Scotland,* edited by R.G.H. Bunce & J.N.R. Jeffers, 70–77. Cambridge: Institute of Terrestrial Ecology.

Darling, F.F. 1955. *West Highland survey.* Oxford: Oxford University Press.

Darling, F.F. & Boyd, J.M. 1964. *The Highlands and Islands.* (New naturalist no. 6.) London: Collins.

Diack, F.C. (n.d.) *History of Glen Tanar.* Glen Tanar Estate Papers.

Gilbert, J. 1979. *Hunting and hunting reserves in mediaeval Scotland.* Edinburgh: John Donald.

Grigor, J. 1839. Report on the native pine forests of Scotland. *Trans. R. Highld agric. Soc. Scotl.,* **6,** 122.

Hechter, M. 1975. Internal colonialism: the Celtic fringe in British national development, 1536–1966. London: Routledge & Kegan Paul.

James, N. 1981. *A history of English forestry.* Oxford: Blackwell Scientific.

Kirby, K.J. 1986. The management of native woods for wildlife. In: *Trees and wildlife in the Scottish uplands,* edited by D. Jenkins, 166–176. (ITE symposium no.17.) Abbots Ripton: Institute of Terrestrial Ecology.

Kirby, K.J., Peterken, G.F., Spencer, J.W. & Walker, G.J. 1984. *Inventories of ancient semi-natural woodland.* (Focus on nature conservation no. 6.) Peterborough: Nature Conservancy Council.

Lindsay, J.M. 1974. *The use of woodland in Argyllshire and Perthshire between 1650–1850.* PhD thesis, University of Edinburgh.

Lindsay, J.M. 1975. *Land use history and tenure of Glasdrum National Nature Reserve.* Report to Nature Conservancy Council. (Unpublished.)

McKenzie, N.A. 1975. *The management and utilization of birch in an upland Aberdeenshire parish.* MSc thesis, University of Edinburgh.

McVean, D.N. & Ratcliffe, D.A. 1962. *Plant communities of the Scottish Highlands.* (Nature Conservancy monograph no. 1.) London: HMSO.

Nicholson, R. 1974. *Scotland: the later middle ages.* Edinburgh: Oliver & Boyd.

Peterken, G.F. 1981. *Woodland conservation and management.* London: Chapman & Hall.

Peterken, G.F. 1986. The status of native woods in the Scottish uplands. In: *Trees and wildlife in the Scottish uplands,* edited by D. Jenkins, 14–19. (ITE symposium no. 17.) Abbots Ripton: Institute of Terrestrial Ecology.

Rackham, O. 1976. *Trees and woodland in the British landscape.* London: J.M. Dent.

Rackham, O. 1980. *Ancient woodlands.* London: Edward Arnold.

Ritchie, J. 1920. *Animal life in Scotland.* Cambridge: Cambridge University Press.

Roy, General. 1750. *The military survey of Scotland 1747–1755.* Edinburgh: National Library of Scotland. (Unpublished.)

Rymer, L. 1980. Recent woodland history of north Knapdale, Argyllshire. *Scott. For.,* **34,** 244–256.

Scott, H. 1974. *A study of the history, structure and status of Dinnet Oakwood, Aberdeenshire.* MSc thesis, University of Aberdeen.

Shaw, J. 1984. *Water power in Scotland.* Edinburgh: John Donald.

Stell, G.P. & Hay, G.D. 1984. *Bonawe iron furnace.* Edinburgh: HMSO.

Steven, H.M. & Carlisle, A. 1959. *The native pinewoods of Scotland.* Edinburgh: Oliver & Boyd.

Thompson, F. 1978. *A Scottish bestiary.* Glasgow: Molendinar Press.

Tittensor, R. M. 1970. History of Loch Lomond oakwoods. *Scott. For.,* **24,** 100–118.

Tivy, J. 1973. *The organic resources of Scotland.* Newton Abbot: David & Charles.

Watson, A. 1983. 18th century deer numbers and pine regeneration near Braemar. *Biol. Conserv.,* **25,** 289–305.

The effects of afforestation on the wildlife of open habitats

D A RATCLIFFE
Nature Conservancy Council, Peterborough

1 Introduction

When treeless ground is afforested, the impact on its wildlife is profound. Despite early work by Lack (1933, 1939) on the East Anglian Breckland new forests and by Goddard (1935) on predator/prey relationships in the Scottish border forests, this effect of afforestation is a neglected subject. Recent interest gives more attention to the gains than to the losses which the new forests bring to wildlife, mainly birds (Chard 1972; Williamson 1974; Moss 1978; Moss *et al.* 1979; Leslie 1981; Harris 1983; Garfitt 1983; Royal Forestry Society 1983; Newton 1984). The portents for further substantial expansion of new afforestation in Britain, affecting the principal remaining areas of semi-natural habitat, underline the urgent need for information about the losses to wildlife from such operations. This paper attempts a summary of such changes, but only briefly points to their implications for nature conservation. Fuller evaluation of conservation needs in relation to new afforestation is being made by the Nature Conservancy Council (NCC).

2 The character of the plantable habitats

This paper deals with the planting of open ground that has only negligible existing tree cover. During the present (Sub-Atlantic) climatic period, woodland was, and potentially still is, the climatic climax formation over most of Britain. It can thus be re-established on a wide range of open ground habitats, excluding only those which are too wet, wind-exposed, elevated, rocky or saline. Human manipulation expands this former range by draining wet ground, improving soil fertility, and breeding new genetic forms of trees which grow better under marginal conditions.

Afforestation is restricted to the sub-montane zone (ie below the potential tree-line, varying from 650 m to 300 m in the far north-west), and mainly to poorer soils with semi-natural vegetation. Agricultural policy has resisted the planting of fertile lowland farmland and also, to a large extent, areas of calcareous upland grazing where sheep farming is relatively productive. In Scotland, afforestation has been mainly on acidic, base-deficient substrata. In the lowlands, these are especially podzolized sands and gravels with dwarf shrub heaths, but also the deep peat of raised bogs. Planted coastal sand dune systems vary from calcareous to acidic. Planted upland soils range from acidic brown earths and podzols with dry grassland or dwarf shrub heath to peaty podzols and gleys with damp grassland and heath or flush bogs, and deeper blanket bog peats with more hydrophilous moorland vegetation.

Much of this range of habitats was derived by woodland clearance, but some areas were only sparsely covered with trees, and many wetter raised and blanket bogs have not carried significant tree cover during the period of their formation which began by overwhelming original forest. Some areas show intercalated tree layers, suggesting temporary drying followed again by wetter conditions (Birks 1975), and some (notably in Caithness, Orkney and Shetland) developed on ground lacking any appreciable woodland cover since the end of the last (Devensian) glaciation (Peglar 1979).

The vegetation and, hence, the animal communities of deforested ground vary greatly in degree of subsequent modification. Many open dwarf shrub heaths are evidently the little-modified communities of the original woodland, for they occur in present-day remnants of such woodland, notably in native Highland pinewoods. Repeated burning causes some, though variable, floristic impoverishment, but species-rich dwarf shrub heaths occur locally, especially in Scotland. Where grazing by sheep, deer, goats or cattle has increased, dwarf shrubs show progressive replacement by grasses, and fire accelerates the process. On drier ground, there is often also extensive invasion by bracken.

On base-rich soils, woodland field communities usually become converted to herb-rich grassland. The communities of former alderwoods (*Alnus glutinosa*) and damp willow (*Salix* spp.) scrubs persist as valley bogs or flush bogs on wet gleys. Vegetation on deeper ombrogenous peat becomes modified by burning and draining, with vascular plants increasing in cover at the expense of *Sphagnum*. Pools deepen and become less vegetated, and at higher levels peat erosion often becomes pronounced.

The afforestable open ground plant communities are thus largely *semi-natural,* ie though modified, they are composed of native species and have a structure approximating to that of original types. The abiotic environmental conditions are also usually little modified. Undisturbed raised bogs and blanket bogs are, however, as close to the truly natural as any vegetation now occurring in Britain. Many of these plant communities have been reclaimed to give various types of improved grassland or arable crops, which are artificial vegetation types but mostly unavailable for afforestation (see above).

The flora of plantable habitats consists mainly of dwarf

shrubs and herbs (including grasses), pteridophytes, mosses, liverworts and lichens. Many of the characteristic species are widespread in Britain, and the rarer species belong especially to the lowland heaths and coastal dunes. The peatlands support many localized species and are especially productive habitats for the bog mosses (*Sphagna*). Flush bogs and flushes often have a more varied flora than the surrounding, more extensive, vegetation types, and are important sedge (*Carex*) habitats.

Distinctive animal communities of open ground are also recognized. Fuller (1982) has described those of breeding birds. The dwarf shrub heaths tend to be richer for both vertebrates (especially birds) and invertebrates than the grassland, but some of the sheepwalks have a notable group of predatory birds. Perhaps the most important bird community is that of the Caithness blanket bogs, with up to 12 wader species and several other northern birds, forming the nearest equivalent in western Europe to the avifauna of the northern Eurasian tundras. The mammal fauna is rather limited and less notable than that of the other groups.

3 The impact of afforestation on open ground
The NCC has recently conducted or commissioned relevant studies, and other parties have also been working in parallel. The amount of available information is now considerable, but some studies are unpublished or still in progess, and there are many gaps which prevent a comprehensive and quantitative picture from being drawn. The account presented here is necessarily brief and qualitative, but draws attention to the main issues. The NCC's main efforts of late have concentrated on a survey of northern moorlands likely to be regarded as afforestable land, to identify the most important areas which should be safeguarded in their present condition in the interests of nature conservation. This survey has given much information on bird populations, and the effects of afforestation on them.

The general picture, drawn from observations at a large number of sites well distributed throughout Britain, is that modern practices of afforestation cause an ecological transformation, in which open ground habitats and their wildlife largely disappear and are replaced by a woodland ecosystem. The process is mitigated as follows.

i. Some open ground species are adapted to forest edge, scrub or open woodland and occupy an ecotonal or seral position between the 2 habitats. As a result, they may exist in both phases.

ii. Not all the open ground within a newly afforested area is actually planted, so that, depending on the extent and type of such habitats left, a variable representation of their flora and fauna will remain.

iii. Death or poor growth of young trees leaves patches of open ground or pre-thicket stage which are not later replanted.

iv. Management of the forest, with clearfelling of stands followed by replanting, gives a controlled succession, in which open ground phases are periodically but temporarily restored. Windthrow locally makes an unplanned contribution to the same process.

Modern afforestation differs from natural establishment or regeneration of woodland by involving cultivation, eg ploughing, fertilizer application, planting of nursery-grown seedlings of exotic conifers and, sometimes, pesticide treatments. There are effects on the abiotic environment (hydrology , chemical composition of waters and soils), which may affect ground not actually planted and sometimes beyond the forests. These effects can be considered only briefly here, as factors affecting the biological component of the ecosystem.

4 Affected habitats, vegetation types and flora
The vegetation types concerned have mostly been described in detail by Tansley (1939) and more briefly by Ratcliffe (1977), while those in Scotland have received phytosociological treatments (McVean & Ratcliffe 1962; Birse 1980). They are being more comprehensively defined and described in the National Vegetation Classification funded by the NCC (Rodwell unpubl.). Table 1 lists the main vegetation types which have been afforested in Britain, but there is no accurate information on the actual extent of any type affected.

The first change is a marked increase in luxuriance of the existing vegetation in response to cessation of burning and the reduction or removal of grazing by sheep, cattle and deer. The grasses grow tall and tussocky and produce a deep litter layer, whilst heather (*Calluna vulgaris*) and bilberry (*Vaccinium myrtillus*) become more bushy and conspicuous. Where these dwarf shrubs had previously declined but still persisted, they increase in cover and may reassume dominance. Grazed-down growths of taller shrubs, such as gorse (*Ulex europaeus*), bog myrtle (*Myrica gale*) and willow, begin to recover and may form thickets, while seedlings of rowan (*Sorbus aucuparia*) and birch (*Betula* spp.) sometimes establish quite rapidly. Deep ploughing dries the ground considerably, so that the moisture-loving peatland species dwindle and may even disappear quite quickly after tree planting. Herbaceous plants susceptible to grazing, which had persisted in rosette form previously, often shoot up and flower well, and lush vegetative patches may be established, eg devil's-bit scabious (*Succisa pratensis*), water avens (*Geum rivale*), globeflower (*Trollius europaeus*), goldenrod (*Solidago virgaurea*), green-ribbed sedge (*Carex binervis*), great wood-rush (*Luzula sylvatica*) and tufted hair-grass (*Deschampsia caespitosa*). Some ferns, such as *Blechnum spicant*, *Athyrium filix-femina* and *Polystichum*

Table 1. Vegetation types subject to afforestation in Scotland

Lowland dwarf shrub heaths, including wet heaths (Tansley 1939, pp 724–741)

Lowland acidic grasslands, including bracken and gorse communities (Tansley 1939, pp 499–506)

Lowland raised bog
    Erica tetralix – Sphagnum papillosum community
    Sphagnum magellanicum – Andromeda polifolia sub-community
    (Rodwell unpubl.)

Sub-montane dwarf shrub heaths
    Callunetum vulgaris (McVean & Ratcliffe 1962, pp 28–30)
    Vaccineto – Callunetum (McVean & Ratcliffe 1962, pp 31–33)
    Arctostaphyleto – Callunetum (McVean & Ratcliffe 1962, pp 30–31)
    Vaccinietum myrtilli (Tansley 1939, pp 758–762)

Sub-montane acidic grasslands
    Species-poor Agrosto – Festucetum (McVean & Ratcliffe 1962, p 52)
    Nardetum sub-alpinum (McVean & Ratcliffe 1962, pp 58–59)
    Juncetum squarrosi sub-alpinum (McVean & Ratcliffe 1962, pp 59–61)
    Molinietum caeruleae (Tansley 1939, pp 518–523)

Sub-montane basic grasslands
    Species-rich Agrosto – Festucetum (McVean & Ratcliffe 1962, pp 54–57)

Sub-montane wet heath
    Trichophoreto – Callunetum (McVean & Ratcliffe 1962, pp 106–108)
    Molinieto – Callunetum (McVean & Ratcliffe 1962, pp 108–109)

Sub-montane blanket bog
    Trichophoreto – Eriophoretum typicum (McVean & Ratcliffe 1962, pp 101–102)
    Calluneto – Eriophoretum (McVean & Ratcliffe 1962, pp 103–105)

Sub-montane flush bog
    Trichophoreto – Eriophoretum caricetosum (McVean & Ratcliffe 1962, p 112)
    Molinia – Myrica nodum (McVean & Ratcliffe 1962, p 112)
    Sphagneto – Juncetum effusi (McVean & Ratcliffe 1962, p 113)
    Sphagneto – Caricetum sub-alpinum (McVean & Ratcliffe 1962, p 114)
    Juncus acutiflorus – Acrocladium cuspidatum nodum (McVean & Ratcliffe 1962, p 117)
    Hypno – Caricetum alpinum (McVean & Ratcliffe 1962, p 118)
    Carex rostrata – Sphagnum warnstorfianum (McVean & Ratcliffe 1962, p 119)

The detailed floristics of these communities can be found from lists in the references given. Many of the rarer or more local species are, however, not represented in these lists

lobatum, also become more robust. Some small herbs may soon be overwhelmed by the vigorous growth of grasses and shrubs. In general, the floristic composition of the vegetation does not change much but the competitive balance and relative cover between species show a readjustment.

For a time, the young trees exert little influence on the other vegetation, but, after a few years, their rapidly expanding radial growth begins to shade out the adjoining plants. By the age of 10–12 years, the spreading trees coalesce to form an increasingly dense thicket which suppresses all the original open ground vegetation (Hill 1983). The possibilities for redevelopment of vegetation within the forest *per se*

then depend on the subsequent management regime. In many western and northern districts, current silvicultural practice aims to minimize the severe windthrow hazards and generally maintains thicket plantations. Light thinning may allow the development of an incomplete field layer, but stands are commonly felled while they are almost devoid of other vegetation. Sparse growths of bilberry, creeping bent (*Agrostis stolonifera*), bracken (*Pteridium aquilinum*) and mosses such as *Pleurozium schreberi* and *Hypnum cupressiforme* maintain a common link with the floristics of the previous, open ground vegetation. The increased light penetration of heavier thinning in lowland forests is, however, usually marked by the more copious growth of broad buckler-fern (*Dryopteris dilatata*) and the heathland mosses (common also to woodland) under spruce, and of bramble (*Rubus fruticosus* agg.) and bracken under pine (Hill 1983).

4.1 Roadsides, rides, stream and lake edges

During this main phase of forest growth, the opportunities for survival of open ground vegetation and flora thus depend almost entirely on the existence of unplanted areas within the forest (see Goldsmith 1981). These areas are always present in the form of roadsides and rides, forming linear networks of open ground habitats, though they can never represent the original diversity or completeness of vegetational pattern. On wet ground, especially, deep ploughing of all the adjoining areas usually lowers water tables, so that only the drier facies of bog communities persist, the more hydrophilous plant species being lost. Flush bog, flush and spring communities usually depend on the maintenance of a concentrated water flow at or near the ground surface, and are so vulnerable to hydrological disturbance that they are seldom represented in anything approaching original form within these linear habitats. Some rides are also mown or otherwise treated to reduce the luxuriance of vegetation, and hence the fire risk.

While rides and roadsides retain remnants of the open ground vegetation, they are thus usually impoverished in terms of both community and species variety. Some species are represented in more vigorous and freely flowering form here, but their populations are often much reduced, and the spatial pattern of their communities is truncated to a highly unnatural configuration. Most forests also contain other more natural but more localized linear habitats in the form of streams and their banks, and sometimes there are lake margins. Persistence of stream and bank and lake edge vegetation depends on silvicultural practice. The tendency has been to plant trees to the edge of smaller streams and rills, which then lose virtually the whole of their vegetation through shading and litterfall. Recent practice has tended increasingly to keep the forest edge back from the stream banks, especially of the larger watercourses, and from lake margins. This practice is beneficial, permitting a luxuriant recovery of stream edge and bank vegetation from grazing, and a free flowering of the usually numerous herbs associated with the richer soil conditions. Similar benefits occur along unplanted lake edges. Possible changes in the aquatic flora have not been studied but must be vulnerable to abiotic changes involving stream flows, erosion and sedimentation, acidification through the 'scavenging' by the forest of atmospheric acidity, and eutrophication through the application of fertilizers to promote tree growth.

Areas of failed tree growth are commonly replanted, but sometimes they are left as open or sparsely wooded ground. Other unplanted areas vary greatly in size and fall into the following main habitat categories.

4.2 Cliffs and screes
The vegetation of these open rock habitats within forest may benefit by protection from fires, which can sweep up even steep faces and devastate shrub and lichen communities. Scree plants may also sometimes benefit from the restrictions on grazing, and mosses and liverworts may become more luxuriant in places where the trees give moderate shade and shelter from the wind. The growths of some lichens also become more robust in places where forest edges or open tree growth appear to give some form of protection.

4.3 Heaths and grasslands on dry, thin and rocky soils
These are often associated with rock habitats: examples occur in Galloway, where the rocky crests of certain low hills (eg Fell of Fleet) have been left unplanted. In general, there is an increase in luxuriance of vegetation as described for rides and roadsides but, apart from rowan and birch, there appears to be little invasion of species not already present in the unplanted habitat. The change in vegetation is thus almost entirely an increase in stature and shift in proportional cover between those species which had survived the previous grazing and burning regime. There is hardly any increase in species diversity, and there may, indeed, be a reduction in small, competition-intolerant species, eg heath bedstraw (*Galium saxatile*), heath milkwort (*Polygala serpyllifolia*) and wild thyme (*Thymus drucei*). The same applies to the bryophytes and lichens. On ground where heavy grazing and burning had previously eradicated the dwarf shrubs, these plants do not return: there develops instead a dense, rather tussocky grass sward over a deep litter layer, which remains highly resistant to the entry of new species.

4.4 Peatlands
During recent years, afforestation has extended increasingly on to blanket bogs, which become plantable when ploughing lowers the water table. Here and there, especially within the border forests, patches of particularly spongy bog have been left as enclaves within the forest, usually not exceeding 50 ha in size, but certain summit plateau blanket bogs at a higher elevation have been left unplanted too. In northern Scotland, patches of patterned bog with pool systems have also been left as open ground within new forest.

There is a general increase in luxuriance of the vegetation, but again an absence of new colonists. Protection from fire allows previously damaged *Sphagnum* carpets and hummocks to rejuvenate, giving a more natural appearance to the vegetation. This kind of benefit can extend to bogs immediately adjoining but beyond the forest limits, such as the Silver Flowe in Galloway, which now has a less disturbed appearance than when it was first surveyed in 1951. Light grazing may nevertheless be beneficial to bog vegetation, and it is the natural condition on most open ground vegetation. Possible adverse factors affecting isolated bogs within forest are alteration in microclimate (especially evapotranspiration) and vulnerability to drift of aerially applied fertilizer. A usual problem is that the forest edge to such bogs forms a highly artificial boundary, determined by the cutting of drains, and quite unrelated to any previous natural limits to peat development. Plateau blanket bogs that are left unplanted may become more natural, provided that marginal drainage is not increased, but they have not been studied.

5 The second rotation
Current practice usually involves clearfelling large blocks of trees, sometimes whole compartments, and replanting the same ground. Clearance of windthrown areas also gives an unplanned element of forest rotation locally. The 'slash' from the cut trees is usually left as a patchy litter which helps to limit the regrowth of secondary vegetation that might compete with the new tree seedlings. Herbicides are often also used deliberately to suppress these 'weeds'. The opportunities for redevelopment of open ground vegetation before closure of the second generation tree canopy are thus rather limited. Hill (1983) has studied the recolonization of cleared ground by species other than the planted trees, and pointed to the importance of buried seed. Usually, it appears that only a limited number of species characteristic of the pre-afforestation open ground vegetation are able to reappear; they include heather, gorse, green-ribbed sedge, creeping bent, purple moor-grass (*Molinia caerulea*), tufted hair-grass and wavy hair-grass (*Deschampsia flexuosa*). Clearance typically produces an abundance of common, disturbed ground species such as foxglove (*Digitalis purpurea*), rosebay willowherb (*Chamaenerion angustifolium*), bramble and raspberry (*R. idaeus*). Bryophytes which occupy open or disturbed habitats increase, but again include many species which did not belong to the original plant communities.

The second and subsequent rotations are highly unlikely to give opportunities for the periodic re-establishment of the complete former open ground plant communities, at least of a northern and upland type. There is, in consequence, a permanent reduction in flora of these former habitats, especially of the smaller species and those of wet ground (Table 2). Hill (1983) has discussed the appearance of a new floristic component during the open ground phase of second rotation forests, but this aspect is beyond the scope of the present paper. The degree to which later rotation management may modify forest composition and structure is unknown, but is most likely to affect the specifically woodland component of the forest biota.

6 Affected animal communities and fauna

Faunal changes run somewhat parallel with those in vegetation. The first 10 years after afforestation can usually be regarded as a productive phase for animal wildlife (Ratcliffe 1980). Some species, especially certain moorland wading birds (Table 3), disappear at once or within a few years, but others increase in abundance, and there is colonization by species which need open scrub with good cover and scattered trees (Lack 1933; Reed 1982; Harris 1983; Newton 1984). In upland areas, population density of the short-tailed field vole (*Microtus agrestis*) usually rises in response to increased luxuriance of grass, and this attracts open ground predators such as short-eared owl (*Asio flammeus*), kestrel (*Falco tinnunculus*) and, locally, hen harrier (*Circus cyaneus*). Black grouse (*Tetrao tetrix*), stonechat (*Saxicola torquata*) and whinchat (*Saxicola rubetra*) typically increase and, at lower elevations, species such as tree pipit (*Anthus trivialis*), grasshopper warbler (*Locustella fluviatilis*) and willow warbler (*Phylloscopus trochilus*) often appear. Some predators, especially those dependent on sheep carrion and open moorland prey, nevertheless begin to disappear or show reduced breeding performance, though at varying rates; they include raven (*Corvus corax*), buzzard (*Buteo buteo*), golden eagle (*Aquila chrysaetos*) and merlin (*Falco columbarius*).

Mammals are probably mostly favoured during this stage by the abundance of food, though deer of various species are usually controlled to reduce

Table 2. Open ground vascular plants affected by afforestation in Scotland

A. Common species substantially reduced but remaining plentiful elsewhere

Thelypteris limbosperma	Plantago lanceolata	Trichophorum caespitosum
Viola riviniana	Campanula rotundifolia	Carex demissa
V. palustris	Galium verum	C. rostrata
Polygala serpyllifolia	G. saxatile	C. panicea
Potentilla erecta	Succisa pratensis	C. flacca
Drosera rotundifolia	Solidago virgaurea	C. pilulifera
Conopodium majus	Achillea millefolium	C. caryophyllea
Calluna vulgaris	Cirsium vulgare	C. nigra
Erica tetralix	C. palustre	C. echinata
E. cinerea	Leontodon autumnalis	C. pulicaris
Vaccinium myrtillus	Hieracium pilosella	Molinia caerulea
V. vitis-idaea	Narthecium ossifragum	Sieglingia decumbens
Empetrum nigrum	Juncus squarrosus	Festuca rubra
Veronica officinalis	J. effusus	F. ovina
V. chamaedrys	J. acutiflorus	Cynosurus cristatus
Pedicularis sylvatica	J. articulatus	Deschampsia caespitosa
Pinguicula vulgaris	Luzula sylvatica	D. flexuosa
Melampyrum pratense	L. campestris	Agrostis canina
Euphrasia officinalis agg.	L. multiflora	A. tenuis
Thymus drucei	Dactylorhiza ericetorum	A. stolonifera
Prunella vulgaris	Eriophorum angustifolium	Anthoxanthum odoratum
Teucrium scorodonia	E. vaginatum	Nardus stricta

At least another 46 species would qualify for addition to this list

B. Local species which have declined nationally due to afforestation

Lycopodium selago	Arctostaphylos uva-ursi	Dactylorhiza fuchsii
Selaginella selaginoides	Arctous alpinus	D. purpurella
Equisetum sylvaticum	Vaccinium oxycoccus	Orchis mascula
Dryopteris spinulosa	Pyrola media	Eleocharis multicaulis
Thelypteris phegopteris	Trientalis europea	Eriophorum latifolium
T. dryopteris	Menyanthes trifoliata	Schoenus nigricans
Botrychium lunaria	Pedicularis palustris	Rhynchospora alba
Juniperus communis	Pinguicula lusitanica	Carex hostiana
Trollius europaeus	Utricularia minor	C. lasiocarpa
Viola lutea	U. intermedia	C. lepidocarpa
Geranium sylvaticum	Valeriana dioica	C. pauciflora
Genista anglica	Crepis paludosa	C. curta
Parnassia palustris	Antennaria dioica	C. dioica
Drosera anglica	Cirsium heterophyllum	C. pallescens
D. intermedia	Listera cordata	C. limosa
Carum verticillatum	Gymnadenia conopsea	C. paupercula
Betula nana	Salix repens	Festuca vivipara

Sand dune species are not included

Table 3. Open ground vertebrate animals affected by afforestation in Scotland

A. Species permanently displaced or substantially reduced

Birds: Golden plover (*Pluvialis apricaria*), greenshank (*Tringa nebularia*), dunlin (*Calidris alpina*), curlew (*Numenius arquata*), snipe (*Capella gallinago*), redshank (*Tringa totanus*), lapwing (*Vanellus vanellus*), raven (*Corvus corax*), merlin (*Falco columbarius*), buzzard (*Buteo buteo*) (Galloway), red grouse (*Lagopus lagopus*), ring ouzel (*Turdus torquatus*), wheatear (*Oenanthe oenanthe*), skylark (*Alauda arvensis*)

Mammals: Mountain hare (*Lepus timidus*), rabbit (*Oryctolagus cuniculus*)

Amphibia: Frog (*Rana temporaria*)

B. Species at risk of decline through further expansion of afforestation

Birds: Golden eagle (*Aquila chrysaetos*) (Galloway and Kintyre), chough (*Pyrrhocorax pyrrhocorax*) (Islay), red-throated diver (*Gavia stellata*), Arctic skua (*Stercorarius parasiticus*) (Caithness), common gull (*Larus canus*), black-headed gull (*Larus ridibundus*), twite (*Acanthis flavirostris*), dipper (*Cinclus cinclus*)

C. Species which occupy open ground within new forests

Birds: Hen harrier (*Circus cyaneus*), kestrel (*Falco tinnunculus*), peregrine (*Falco peregrinus*) (may be at risk in areas with few homing pigeons), black grouse (*Tetrao tetrix*), cuckoo (*Cuculus canorus*), short-eared owl (*Asio flammeus*), nightjar (*Caprimulgus europaeus*), carrion and hooded crows (*Corvus corone*), stonechat (*Saxicola torquata*), whinchat (*Saxicola rubetra*), meadow pipit (*Anthus pratensis*)

Mammals: Red deer (*Cervus elaphus*), fox (*Vulpes vulpes*), short-tailed field vole (*Microtus agrestis*), bank vole (*Clethrionomys glareolus*), stoat (*Mustela erminea*), weasel (*Mustela nivalis*)

Reptiles: Adder (*Vipera berus*), common lizard (*Lacerta vivipara*)

The effects of afforestation on some moorland birds, especially those associated with open water, are unknown and need careful observation, eg greylag goose (*Anser anser*), teal (*Anas crecca*), wigeon (*Anas penelope*), common scoter (*Melanitta nigra*), black-throated diver (*Gavia arctica*), oystercatcher (*Haematopus ostralegus*), common sandpiper (*Tringa hypoleucos*) and grey wagtail (*Motacilla cinerea*).

browse damage to the young trees. Reptiles and amphibia are probably little affected, but few species occur in Scotland. There is little information on invertebrates but probably, except for species of wet ground, many open ground types survive well during the early stage of forest.

This varied animal community is, however, quite rapidly depleted and replaced as the trees close to form thicket forest, with rapid loss of most species which belong to open ground, and even of some which favour open scrub or woodland edges. The most characteristic group now is the canopy-dwelling woodland bird fauna consisting especially of song birds (Moss 1978; Moss *et al.* 1979). Foxes (*Vulpes vulpes*) find breeding refuges in dense young forest, as do some of the other carnivores, but the mammal fauna must become limited in population size and density by the ability of ancillary or adjoining unplanted habitats to provide a food supply. Those forests which grow to sufficient height and age to become well thinned and develop a field layer vegetation increase again in feeding value, but the thicket stands have to be complemented by the rides and roadsides, stream and lake margins, unplanted enclaves, and the land outside the forest.

Vole numbers may remain high in linear habitats, yet these areas are usually too narrow for upland nesting birds, except meadow pipits (*Anthus pratensis*), because the feeding area is too limited and the exposure to predators too great. The larger unplanted enclosures of open ground are of less value to birds than similar ground outside the forest. Some are again much too small to hold even single pairs of the larger bird predators, and the increased stature of the vegetation makes them unfavourable for waders such as the golden plover (*Pluvialis apricaria*). Mammal predators fare better, and the more agile species such as pine marten (*Martes martes*) are able to take tree-dwelling birds. They also become an adverse factor for the birds of open ground within the forest. It is indeed claimed that the predator force of foxes and crows which finds a breeding refuge within new forests has become an increasingly serious factor in depressing breeding performance, and even populations, of birds nesting on the surrounding moorlands, notably the red grouse (*Lagopus lagopus*). For similar reasons, red deer (*Cervus elaphus*) which use the forests for cover may have to forage largely outside, and the degree to which they become a management problem there may well depend on the long-term capacity of the forest to provide food. Roe deer (*Capreolus capreolus*) usually colonize new forests and become more self-contained within this ecosystem.

The value of unplanted habitats to invertebrates is high, and tree shelter is advantageous to winged species. Rides and roadsides are often productive for butterflies and moths, which feed as adults on the freely flowering herbs and shrubs, though some come from outside the forest. Even dragonflies, which may be adversely affected by draining of wet ground, benefit as adults from the shelter of the woodland edge, where they hunt and rest.

The importance of the second rotation open ground phase to animals has not yet been studied in depth. There is no reversal to the bird community of the area before afforestation, but a shift to a mixed type in which some of the original species return, but less numerously than those of open woodland, scrub or forest edge and glade (Leslie 1981; Bibby 1986). The nightjar (Caprimulgus europaeus) is one open ground species occurring very sparingly in restocked young forest in Scotland. Probably most of the mammals benefit from the increased food supply which results from a regeneration of other vegetation. Invertebrates are likely to have even greater advantage, though the number of original open ground species will most probably be depleted, especially phytophagous species through loss of food plants.

Adverse effects have been reported in stocks of game fish (salmon, sea trout and brown trout) in streams within afforested catchments, resulting from altered stream flows, erosion and siltation of spawning beds, shading and litterfall, and enhanced acidification (Graesser 1979; Drakeford 1982; Harriman & Morrison 1982; Smith 1980; Mills 1980). On the other hand, the increased trophic levels in water bodies resulting from fertilizer applications and runoff may benefit fish populations locally (Harriman 1978). Ormerod et al. (1985) connect a decline in dipper (Cinclus cinclus) numbers on the River Irfon with afforestation of the catchment, acting through the food chain. Table 3 summarizes effects of afforestation on open ground vertebrates, other than fish.

7 Implications for nature conservation

Afforestation causes a substantial reduction of the biota of the natural and semi-natural habitats affected. The remnants which persist cannot be regarded as adequately representing what has been lost, because of the scale of change. The open ground ecosystem is largely replaced by a forest ecosystem, and the previous variety of habitats and species, their extent, abundance, spatial pattern, and relationships with each other and with the abiotic environment cease to exist. Conservation of moorland, peatland and other open ground ecosystems thus requires that adequate areas of these formations be kept free of afforestation. As the national range of geographical and ecological variation in these ecosystems is wide, yet uneven in its importance, the overall programme for site safeguarding is based on the selection of a country-wide network of the most important examples. In addition, the wildlife conservation interest is best served by maintaining a reasonable balance between different land uses in any one district, as such a balance will tend to maintain habitat diversity, including an adequate extent of open ground. New afforestation should, by preference, be conducted on ground where the scientific interest of the native fauna and flora is low. The question of how far new forests can provide a compensatory substitution for the loss of open ground ecosystems is not regarded by nature conservationists as relevant to the above issues.

In Scotland, apart from certain coastal sand dune systems, nearly all major afforestation affects land which is upland or sub-montane in character, though it includes peatland 'flows' almost at sea level. Potentially plantable land thus covers a large part of the total area of uncultivated land which is also regarded by conservationists as the last extensive reservoir of wildlife and its habitat in Britain. Indeed, the Scottish Highlands were singled out in the World Conservation Strategy (International Union for the Conservation of Nature and Natural Resources 1980) as one of the 'priority biogeographical provinces of the land for the establishment of protected areas'. This reference was based not only on the importance of the region as a biogeographical province, but also on the inadequate representation within it of national parks or other protected areas. The rationale and principles for the selection of a countrywide series of the areas of national importance to biological conservation, and an actual list of the areas selected, were presented in *A nature conservation review* (NCR) (Ratcliffe 1977).

The basic need was to define a geographical network of 'key areas' sufficient in number and extent to represent adequately the total range of variation in natural and semi-natural ecosystems, with their characteristic environmental conditions, and plant and animal communities. Variations are related to gradients of climate, both on the regional scale and the local (mainly altitudinal) scale, to differences in geology with its effects on topography, drainage and soils, and to differences in past and present patterns of land use. The breadth of this environmental diversity gives an extremely wide range of plant and animal communities across Scotland. In outline, the most significant features in the present context are as follows.

Sand dunes Variations in physical structure (especially machair types), lime content of sand (from acidic to highly calcareous), and wetness of the ground (development of slack systems and machair lochs and marshes).

Peatlands Variations classifiable into 6 main topographic types, of which raised bogs, blanket bogs and some valley bogs are those relevant to afforestation. Raised bog is a very local, low-level type, and a north-to-south series, with a range of structural features, is desirable. Blanket bog occurs widely from nearly sea level to well over 1000 m, and is a particularly important British feature because of its world rarity (confined to a few hyper-oceanic regions). The Caithness–Sutherland flow country is probably the largest peatland system in Europe, and of great value for its birds. Both raised and blanket bogs are important structurally for the scientific interest of their peat deposits as a post-glacial record, and the small-scale micro-topography of their living surface. Patterned surfaces with networks of pools and hummocks are a special feature of these peatlands in Scotland, and from their variability according to situation and climate need a geographical series for their proper representation.

Upland grasslands and heaths Blanket bogs are associated with these habitats in many mountain and moorland areas, but the present category refers mainly to drier ground. There is an extremely wide range, but it is classifiable into: sheepwalks, especially on more base-rich ground, such as the southern uplands and Breadalbane hills; grouse moors, especially of heather and in the drier east; and deer forests, especially on rugged ground in the highlands and islands. Topography and soil fertility vary widely and the botanically rich areas are mainly on calcareous rocks. Many higher mountains are valued for the extent of their montane ('arctic–alpine') habitats, above the potential tree-line, but on these it is felt important to select whole topographic units for conservation, from the highest point down to the lowest adjoining valley bottom, so that the full altitudinal and aspect range of variation is included. Many of the widespread types of hill vegetation and associated animal communities in Scotland, and especially those in the sub-montane zone, have no exact equivalents anywhere in the world, and are thus internationally important. Oceanic dwarf shrub heath is an especially localized and declining type in other parts of Europe.

More specific statements of requirements for the national series are given in the NCR, Volume 1, under chapters on coastlands, peatlands and upland grasslands and heaths. This work identified the following key areas in Scotland containing afforestable land as having equivalent importance to that of existing National Nature Reserves (it included actual NNRs), and thus deserving a similar level of safeguard.

Formation type	Number of sites	Area of sites (ha)
Sand dunes (including machairs)	15	10 234
Peatlands (excluding fens)	28	38 340
Upland grasslands and heaths	67	336 161
TOTAL	110	384 735

Much of this land is too elevated, wet, rocky or maritime to be suitable for afforestation, but consultation with the Forestry Commission elicited the view that about half of it would be plantable. Since then, some further areas, mainly peatlands, have been identified as also having national quality for nature conservation, and they extend the total area by about 50 000 ha, probably most of which would be regarded as plantable. Under the Wildlife and Countryside Act 1981, NCC is bound to regard all of these sites as meeting the standards of Sites of Special Scientific Interest (SSSIs), and to notify the remainder of those which are not already thus formally designated. At least another 1.7 Mha of plantable land have been identified in Scotland (Centre for Agricultural Strategy 1980). In cases where there is conflict over private proposals for planting of SSSIs, the NCC has agreed to apply the principle of compensation for profit foregone in return for withdrawing a proposal. The conservation interests have yet to discuss with the Forestry Commission the interpretation of the latter's new duty to achieve a reasonable balance between the needs of afforestation and timber production, and the conservation of wildlife, including the native flora, and natural beauty. Conservationists hope that foresters will recognize both the need to avoid undesirable afforestation of SSSIs, and to maintain significant treeless areas in all upland districts.

8 Summary

Afforestation causes a transformation of open ground ecosystems, and this paper deals with the resulting wildlife losses. The main habitats subject to afforestation are lowland and sub-montane upland grasslands, heaths and bogs, and coastal sand dunes, with soils of generally low fertility and carrying semi-natural vegetation composed of herbs, dwarf shrubs, pteridophytes, mosses and lichens. Silvicultural methods, notably ploughing and fertilizer application, profoundly modify the abiotic environment and then, after an initial phase of increased luxuriance of pre-existing vegetation, closure of the tree canopy shades out virtually all other plants. The open ground fauna is also largely eradicated. Opportunities for survival of open ground biota within new forests depend on the extent and type of unplanted habitats remaining, and on rotational clearance phases. Afforestation causes an inevitable permanent depletion of open ground plant and animal communities and species, and a loss of ecosystem wholeness. Nature conservation concern about these wildlife losses has to be related to the portents for further expansion of afforestation, and the gains created by the new forests are considered to be a separate issue.

9 References

Bibby, C. 1986. Birds of restocked conifer plantations in Wales. *J. appl. Ecol.* In press.

Birks, H.H. 1975. Studies in the vegetational history of Scotland. IV. Pine stumps in Scottish blanket peats. *Phil. Trans. R. Soc. B,* **270,** 181.

Birse, E.L. 1980. *Plant communities in Scotland: a preliminary Phytocoenosia.* Aberdeen: Macaulay Institute for Soil Research.

Centre for Agricultural Strategy. 1980. *Strategy for the UK forest industry.* (CAS report no. 6.) Reading: CAS.

Chard, J.S.R. 1972. Forestry and wildlife. *Q. Jl For.,* **66,** 113–122.

Drakeford, T. 1982. Management of upland streams (an experimental fisheries management project on the afforested headwaters of the River Fleet, Kirkcudbrightshire). *Proc. Annual Study Course, 12th,* 86–92. Durham: Institute of Fisheries Management.

Fuller, R.J. 1982. *Bird habitats in Britain*. Calton: Poyser.

Garfitt, J.E. 1983. Afforestation and upland birds. *Q. Jl For.,* **77,** 253–254.

Goddard, T.R. 1935. A census of short-eared owl (*Asio f. flammeus*) at Newcastleton, Roxburghshire, 1934. *J. Anim. Ecol.,* **4,** 113-118, 289-290.

Goldsmith, B. 1981. *The afforestation of the uplands: the botanical interest of areas left unplanted.* (Discussion papers in conservation no. 35.) London: University College.

Graesser, N.W. 1979. Effect on salmon fisheries of afforestation, land drainage and road making in river catchment areas. *Salmon net,* **10,** 38–45.

Harriman, R. 1978. Nutrient leaching from fertilized forest watersheds in Scotland. *J. appl. Ecol.,* **15,** 933–942.

Harriman, R. & Morrison, B.R.S. 1982. Ecology of streams draining forested and non-forested catchments in an area of central Scotland subject to acid precipitation. *Hydrobiologia,* **88,** 251–263.

Harris, J. 1983. *Birds and coniferous plantations.* Tring: Royal Forestry Society.

Hill, M.O. 1983. Plants in woodlands. Session 3. *Centenary Conference on Forestry and Conservation.* Tring: Royal Forestry Society.

International Union for the Conservation of Nature and Natural Resources. 1980. *World conservation strategy. Living resource conservation for sustainable development.* Gland: IUCN.

Lack, D. 1933. Habitat selection in birds with special reference to the effects of afforestation on the Breckland avifauna. *J. Anim. Ecol.,* **2,** 239–262.

Lack, D. 1939. Further changes in the Breckland avifauna caused by afforestation. *J. Anim. Ecol.,* **8,** 277–285.

Leslie, R. 1981. The birds of north-east England forests. *Q. Jl For.,* **75,** 153-158.

McVean, D.N. & Ratcliffe, D.A. 1962. *Plant communities of the Scottish Highlands.* (Monographs of the Nature Conservancy, no. 1.) London: HMSO.

Mills, D. 1980. Scottish rivers and their future management. In: *Atlantic salmon: its future,* edited by A.E.J. Went, 70–81. Farnham: Fishing News Books Ltd.

Moss, D. 1978. Song bird populations in forestry plantations. *Q. Jl For.,* **72,** 5–14.

Moss, D., Taylor, P.N. & Easterbee, N. 1979. The effects on song bird populations of upland afforestation with spruce. *Forestry,* **52,** 129–150.

Newton, I. 1984. Upland forestry brings wildlife gains. *Econ. For. Group Mag.,* 8–10.

Ormerod, S.J., Tyler, S.J. & Lewis, J.M.S. 1985. Is the breeding distribution of dippers influenced by stream acidity? *Bird Study,* **32,** 32–39.

Peglar, S. 1979. A radio-carbon dated pollen diagram from Loch of Winless, Caithness, north-east Scotland. *New Phytol.,* **82,** 245–263.

Ratcliffe, D.A., ed. 1977. *A nature conservation review.* 2 vols. Cambridge: Cambridge University Press.

Ratcliffe, D.A. 1980. *Forestry in relation to nature conservation.* (Minutes of evidence, House of Lords Select Committee on Science & Technology, Sub-Committee I – Forestry.) Memorandum submitted by the Nature Conservancy Council. London: HMSO.

Reed, T.M. 1982. Birds and afforestation. *Ecos (Br. Assoc. Nat. Conserv.),* **3,** 8–10.

Royal Forestry Society. 1983. *Centenary conference on forestry and conservation.* Tring: Royal Forestry Society.

Smith, B.D. 1980. The effects of afforestation on the trout of a small stream in southern Scotland. *Fish. Manage.,* **11,** 39–57.

Tansley, A.G. 1939. *The British islands and their vegetation.* Cambridge: Cambridge University Press.

Williamson, K. 1974. Habitat changes in a young Forestry Commission plantation. *Bird Study,* **210,** 215–217.

What are the effects of trees on soils?

J MILES
Institute of Terrestrial Ecology, Banchory

1 Introduction

This paper discusses the tendency for conifers and hardwoods to cause contrasting changes in certain soil properties, and the consequences of these changes for tree growth and for the composition of the field layer, and points out where knowledge is lacking. Because of a dearth of studies in the Scottish uplands, most data quoted will be from sites with similar soils elsewhere in Europe.

All plants influence soil properties, but trees tend to have greater effects than other plant life forms because of their size and longevity. Trees have many direct and indirect effects on the physical, chemical and biological properties of soils. For example, root channels increase soil aeration and drainage, and allow downward mixing of soil particles, while the root mat as a whole inhibits particle erosion by wind and water, and downhill movements of soil. Plant litter and exudates, and animal wastes and corpses are incorporated, with at least two-thirds of the total litter input coming from death of fine roots and mycorrhizas (Persson 1978; Fogel 1980; Ulrich *et al.* 1981). These organic inputs are the energy and carbon source for a great variety of soil-living animals, fungi and microorganisms that *inter alia* mediate the recycling of mineral nutrients, and thus sustain soil productivity. The litter of different species can vary markedly in content of mineral nutrients and of organic chemicals that influence litter palatability and decomposability (Zonn 1954; Túszynski 1972; Swift *et al.* 1979). Such variations influence rates of nutrient cycling directly, and also indirectly by causing changes in the populations of decomposer organisms. Different tree species also vary in the degree to which they modify the chemical composition and acidity of rain dripping off their leaves or canalized as stemflow (Ernst 1978).

These and other effects of trees can produce marked changes in soil properties. This paper discusses certain of these changes, but consideration of the mechanisms of change is beyond its scope.

2 Effects on soil properties

There is a large but confused literature on the effects of trees on soils. Frequently, the reported effects of particular species are apparently contradicted by contrasting effects noted by other authors at other places. There are 2 main reasons for this confusion. First, many published studies, especially the earlier ones, are seriously flawed (Holmsgaard *et al.* 1961; Stone 1975). They were based on contemporaneous observations of soil under different forest patches, and depended on key assumptions that were never tested, in particular the supposition of inherent soil homogeneity under the different patches. Second, most studies have dealt with a few isolated examples, so that species, and also provenance, age of stand, soil conditions and past management, insofar as they are precisely stated, vary greatly. Direct comparison between different studies is therefore commonly invalid. However, despite the confusion, certain generalities can be inferred, in particular that effects vary with differing soil type and soil parent material, and vary during the life cycle of the tree stand. Also, there is a tendency for coniferous species to have contrasting effects to broadleaved species, especially on poorly buffered soils.

2.1 Effects of soil

The amount and rate of change of particular plant-dependent soil properties by particular species can vary greatly from site to site (Wittich 1972; Howard & Howard 1984), depending in particular on the nature and degree of weathering of the soil minerals (Saly 1965, 1980; Miles 1986). Freshly exposed surfaces weather rapidly. The surface pH of unvegetated avalanche debris on Mt Rainier fell from 8.7 to 6.7 in only 3 years (Bollen *et al.* 1969), while the surface pH of a glacial till in south-east Alaska fell in 20 years from 8.2 to 7.0 under a moss cover, and to 6.8 under grey alder (*Alnus incana*). In contrast, when Norway spruce (*Picea abies*) and Scots pine (*Pinus sylvestris*), both species commonly associated with soil acidification, were planted in place of natural stands of beech (*Fagus sylvatica*) and oak (*Quercus robur, Q. petraea*) on soils exposed for at least 10 000 years in Europe, pH reductions of only 0.1–1.0 unit occurred in up to 100 years (Miles 1978). Non-calcareous soils with little clay are poorly buffered, and change faster than well-buffered soils. For example, in nutrient-poor sands, the early signs of podzolization may be visible within 100–150 years (Tamm 1920; Ball & Williams 1974), whereas clay soils exposed 10 000 years ago in Britain show no visible signs, and would not be expected to do so.

In upland Scotland, poorly buffered, siliceous soils predominate. Those that are intrinsically freely drained are most susceptible to change. Those that are poorly drained, either intrinsically or because an ironpan (Bf horizon) has developed, show only superficial changes during the lifespan of a tree stand. Peat, which covers almost 11% of Scotland (Jowsey 1973) when defined as a surface organic layer more than 30–40 cm thick, changes most markedly in physical properties, at least during the first tree crop. After afforestation, blanket peat dries progressively and irreversibly, and large shrinkage cracks can occur (Binns 1959; Boggie & Miller 1976; Pyatt & Craven 1979). All these cases have been reported under lodgepole pine (*Pinus contorta*), which has been used as the pioneer crop, but it seems likely that other species would have similar effects if they could be established. Base saturation and pH have been shown to have decreased under stands of lodgepole pine from 16 to 47 years old (Williams *et al.* 1978), apparently as a result of greater decomposition of the peat as it dried out, leading to a higher cation exchange capacity, thus diluting the base cations present and lowering pH. Again, therefore, any tree species would be expected to have the same effect, provided that the peat dried to a similar degree.

2.2 Effects of conifers compared with broadleaved species

Many studies have now shown that, on susceptible soils, conifers tend to promote more surface organic matter accumulation, greater acidity, and a higher degree of podzolization than broadleaved species, with consequential decreases in base saturation and bulk density, an increase in infiltration capacity, and a repositioning within the profile of organically bound nitrogen and phosphorus. This tendency is well exemplified by Ovington's (1953, 1954) data from Abbotswood (Table 1). There, the amounts of surface organic matter and organically bound nitrogen accumulated under conifers 38 to 46 years old were up to 9 and 7 times greater respectively than under broadleaved species, and topsoil pH was up to 1.3 units less. There was, however, an overlap between the responses of the 2 classes, a feature found by Ovington under experimental planting at 2 other sites, and indeed by other workers generally.

Because of its importance as a timber tree in continental Europe, the effects of Norway spruce on the soil have been widely studied. Published reports from at least 10 countries have shown that on poorly buffered soils this species acidifies the surface soil (Table 2) and causes or accelerates podzolization (Miles 1985). However, these effects are only tendencies, albeit strong ones, and are not always found. Thus, Gennsler

Table 1. Dry weight and nitrogen content (t ha^{-1}) of surface organic matter, and pH in the top 5 cm of mineral soil in a coarse sandy loam, 38–46 years after planting a range of tree species on a former mixed oak/beech woodland site at Abbotswood, Forest of Dean (source: Ovington 1953, 1954)

	Dry weight	Nitrogen content	pH
European larch (*Larix decidua*)	0.59	35	4.1
Norway spruce (*Picea abies*)	0.44	26	4.0
Corsican pine (*Pinus nigra* var. maritima)	0.27	22	4.1
Scots pine (*Pinus sylvestris*)	0.19	13	4.0
Beech (*Fagus sylvatica*)	0.18	11	4.7
Douglas fir (*Pseudotsuga menziesii*)	0.12	8.3	4.6
Sweet chestnut (*Castanea sativa*)	0.08	4.1	5.2
Pedunculate oak (*Quercus robur*)	0.07	3.7	5.3

Table 2. Increased acidity of natural beech and oak woodland soils after planting Norway spruce and Scots pine (source: Miles 1978)

Country of observation	pH decrease after planting spruce or pine (increased acidity)
i. Norway spruce	
South Sweden	0.4
North-west Germany	0.2–0.5
South-west Germany	0.1–0.8
South-east Germany	0.3
Czechoslovakia	0 –0.9
Czechoslovakia	0.3–1.0
Czechoslovakia	0.2–0.5
West Yugoslavia	0.3–0.8
West Rumania	0.3–0.7
ii. Scots pine	
East Scotland	0.2–0.7
Czechoslovakia	0.5

(1959) found no signs of podzolization after 250 years of spruce culture in the Harz Mountains, though he did record surface acidification, while Saly and Obr (1965) recorded one instance where the pH of the surface soil under planted spruce in Czechoslovakia had increased to 4.2 from a value of 3.9 under the natural beechwood. Variations in these effects reflect varying degrees of soil buffering.

Conifers growing at similar rates to broadleaved species produce similar amounts of litter, at least above ground (Miller 1984). The tendency for greater surface accumulation of organic matter under conifers reflects different decomposition systems from those usual under broadleaves. Decomposition is often slower, but also results in a positional change of organic matter within the soil profile (Nihlgard 1971). Litter is typically comminuted very quickly by earthworms and other soil-living animals under broadleaved stands, and mixed into the mineral horizons (as 'mull' humus) where it continues to decay. Conifer litter, in contrast, tends to lie on the soil surface for many years (as 'mor' humus), being slowly degraded by microbial decay before comminution and soil mixing occurs. One reason is that conifer litter tends to be more acid and to have a higher tannin content, which makes it less palatable to earthworms and other consumers of litter (Satchell 1967).

The soil acidification, surface organic matter accumulations and other associated changes in labile soil properties caused by conifers, or similar changes caused by heather (*Calluna vulgaris*), can be reversed if the decomposition system switches to mull production following a change in the predominant plant cover. Such opposite changes can occur when the main cover is of 'warty' (*Betula pendula*) or 'downy' (*B. pubescens*) birch (Miles & Young 1980; Miles 1981), aspen (*Populus tremula*) (Frank & Borchgrevink 1982) or holly (*Ilex aquifolium*) (Dimbleby & Gill 1955; Malcolm 1957), or, in the absence of trees, under bracken (*Pteridium aquilinum*) and well-grazed bent/fescue (*Agrostis/Festuca*) grasslands (Miles 1985).

Many other broadleaved species would probably have similar effects to birch, aspen and holly, if they were established on soils where conifer- or heather-induced changes had occurred. They seem to have no features not also found in other broadleaved species, apart from their ability to establish abundantly on poor soils. However, other species that might do this are not planted in such sites, either because they would fail or grow only poorly (eg elms (*Ulmus* spp.) or limes (*Tilia* spp.)), or because they are negligible timber producers (eg rowan (*Sorbus aucuparia*)), or both (eg hazel (*Corylus avellana*)). Oak and beech probably cannot reverse soil changes induced by conifers, except perhaps on less base-poor soils. Although mull soils can be found under natural stands of both, so can mor soils and shallow podzols (Kubiena 1953; Dimbleby & Gill 1955; Mackney 1961; Bublinec 1973). The pedogenic influence of oak and beech seems to lie about midway between the contrasting effects of birch and Norway spruce. It is likely that the nature of the field layer under oak and beech often determines in which direction the soil develops. Herbaceous swards push the system towards mull formation, but abundant bilberry (*Vaccinium myrtillus*), cowberry (*V. vitis-idaea*) and, if the tree canopy is fairly open, heather, drive the system towards mor formation (ie

acidification, surface organic matter accumulation, etc). Indeed, Låg (1959, 1971) has suggested that, in Norwegian forests, the composition of the field layer is more important than that of the tree stand in determining the direction of soil development.

2.3 Influence of stand age

Soil properties which result from continued plant growth tend to change in a cyclic way during the life of a tree stand. This change was demonstrated graphically by Page (1968) for Sitka spruce (*Picea sitchensis*), Douglas fir (*Pseudotsuga menziesii*) and Japanese larch (*Larix leptolepis*) growing in north Wales. As stands developed, topsoil pH gradually decreased and surface organic matter increased. These changes peaked after canopy closure, when litter input was at a maximum, and when litter decay was slowest, because of relatively cool and dry conditions at the soil surface (because of the heat-insulating effects of the canopy, with maximal rainfall interception by the canopy and evapotranspiration losses). Later, as stands underwent management thinning (or natural self-thinning), and then selective or clearfelling (or ageing and death naturally), pH and organic matter at the surface tended to return to their original values (Figure 1). These cyclic trends have been confirmed elsewhere, notably in Newfoundland (Page 1974). The change in soil pH under birch shows exactly the opposite trend, reaching its peak when the input of readily decomposable birch litter is greatest, but when moisture and temperature conditions at the soil surface are still favourable for rapid decomposition because of the different canopy structure.

i.

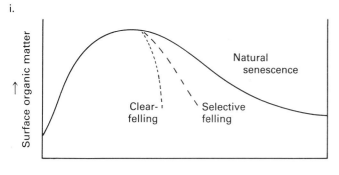

ii.

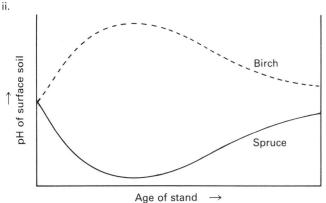

Age of stand →

Figure 1. Generalized sequence of change (i) in amounts of surface organic matter under spruce, and (ii) in topsoil pH under birch and spruce, on well-drained, poorly buffered soils (source: Page 1968; Miles 1981)

However, not all plant-dependent soil properties change cyclically during the life of a stand, in particular the horizon differentiation resulting from podzolization. Although the rate of podzolization is increased under many conifers on susceptible soils (Miles 1985), and probably changes cyclically, the results of podzolization are cumulative and stable. The depth of the eluviated horizon in podzols in north Wales planted with Sitka spruce increased steadily as the stands aged (Page 1968). Similar results were obtained from Swedish forests (Troedsson 1972).

Once a podzol profile has developed, it can only be obliterated by mechanical mixing of the horizons. The uprooting of trees in gales causes partial or complete inversion of the upper horizons (Stephens 1956; Stone 1975), and, in areas prone to windthrow, the uprooting will have retarded podzol profile differentiation (Armson & Fessenden 1973). Biological activity in soils constantly mixes particles (Hole 1981), with ants and earthworms being particularly important. When biological mixing is sufficiently intense, effective depodzolization can occur (Lyford 1963; Langmaid 1964). The reported depodzolization under birch (Tamm 1932; Dimbleby 1952; Miles 1981) and herbaceous vegetation (Miles 1985) was probably because of biological soil mixing.

3 Consequences for the field layer

Progressive changes in the composition of the field layer occur during the life of a forest stand, whether the stand arose after disturbance in old forest (Mac-Lean & Wein 1977; Brakenhielm & Persson 1980) or replaced moorland (Hill 1979; Miles 1981; Sakura *et al.* 1985), blanket peat (Doyle & Moore 1982) or farmland (Brakenhielm 1977). Table 3 summarizes the changes in species richness of the field layer between an old Scots pine plantation and part of it that was felled 20 years before and colonized by birch. Soil under the birch stand was significantly less acid (pH 4.4 compared with 3.8 under the pine) and had mull-like humus, whereas under the pine there was mor. Many more species grew under the birch than under the pine stands, while half those under the birchwood did not grow under the pine. The extent to which the changed

Table 3. Changing numbers of field layer species found under an old Scots pine plantation and an adjacent stand of silver birch, established naturally after felling of pine on Dinnet Moor, Aberdeenshire (source: original data)

	89-year-old Scots pine	18-year-old silver birch
Number of vascular species present as growing plants	14	20
*Total number of vascular species present	15	25
Number of pinewood species absent from the birchwood	5	—
Number of species present in the birchwood not occurring in the pinewood	—	11
Number of bryophytes present	5	12
Number of pinewood bryophytes absent from the birchwood	2	—
Number of birchwood bryophytes absent from the pinewood	—	9

*Includes species present only as buried viable seed, which is an important part of any flora

soil conditions were responsible for these differences in the field layer is unclear. Differential shading by tree canopies and competition, particularly for nutrients, do cause change in themselves (Miles 1979), but are confounded with the effects of changing soil conditions. However, soil changes of this order do facilitate the succession in the field layer. For example, Table 4 shows the result of experimentally sowing seeds of a variety of field layer species on moorland and in adjacent successional birch stands of different ages near Advie, Morayshire, where a gradient of soil conditions also existed (Miles 1981). It shows a sequence of species progressively able to establish as the soil changed towards mull conditions.

4 Consequences for the trees

The trends of soil change under conifers and under broadleaved species generally would, in an agricultural context, be considered as degradation and improvement respectively. Is there any evidence that such soil

Table 4. Presence of species established 2 years after sowing seed experimentally on bared ground in heather moorland and adjacent successional silver birch stands of different ages near Advie, Morayshire. Brackets indicate that young plants were weak and unhealthy-looking (source: original data)

	Heather	Birch 20 years	28 years	40 years
Calluna vulgaris	+	+	+	+
Deschampsia flexuosa	+	+	+	+
Luzula sylvatica	+	+	+	+
Festuca rubra	(+)	+	+	+
Holcus lanatus	(+)	(+)	+	+
Galium saxatile		(+)	+	+
Rumex acetosa		(+)	+	+
Ranunculus acris			(+)	+
Rubus idaeus			(+)	+
Geranium sylvaticum				+
Primula vulgaris				+
Prunella vulgaris				+
Viola riviniana				+

changes materially alter tree growth and actual or potential yields of timber? At present, the answer is a qualified 'no', although a more accurate response might be 'answer unknown' because little critical work has been done in this field.

It has often been claimed that deleterious soil changes under conifers cause losses in yield (eg Noirfalise 1968). Certainly, over large areas of Europe, conifers, especially Norway spruce in continental Europe and Sitka spruce in Britain, have been planted in the place of natural broadleaved forest (or, in Britain, on land formerly under broadleaved forest), and many of these soils are showing surface acidification and accelerated podzolization. For example, Marzhan (1959) has estimated that up to 400 kha are podzolizing in Czechoslovakia under Norway spruce and Scots pine. However, early claims about yield depletion as a result of soil change have been shown to be confounded with problems of disease, lack of wind-firmness on surface-water gley soils (an inherent soil property rather than one caused by conifers) and nutrient depletion from litter gathering and sod cutting by peasants (Jones 1965; Stone 1975). Critical studies of the growth and yield of second compared with first generation crops of Norway spruce in Germany and Denmark failed to detect any decreases in yield (Gennsler 1959; Holmsgaard *et al.* 1961; Hausser 1964). Indeed, Hausser (1964) found that the second generation stand grew better than the first. Conversely, tree ring analysis at the birch site near Advie discussed earlier showed that the birch stands there did not apparently grow better as the soils changed from mor- to mull-forming conditions.

The only other direct evidence for progressive yield decline in conifers is Siren's (1955) report that, when Norway spruce established after forest fire in northern Finland, soil changes occurred that slowed down growth of the next generation of trees. However, soil and climatic conditions there were poorer than at the natural broadleaved woodland sites discussed earlier. The site naturally bore spruce, and lies within the circumboreal zone in which periodic lightning fires are an intrinsic part of the ecosystem. There is evidence that under these conditions periodic fire is needed to maintain high rates of nutrient cycling (Viro 1974).

How do the Scottish uplands fit in the context of the central European situation, where evidence for an effect of conifer-induced soil changes on subsequent growth is lacking, and of the more plausible evidence from Finland that such feedback occurs there? Like Finland, the Highlands are naturally part of the fire-dependent circumboreal forest zone. They have soils mostly formed from base-poor Precambrian rocks, and may therefore be expected to behave similarly. The southern upland soils are derived from more base-rich Silurian and Ordovician sediments, and on freely drained ground are mostly unpodzolized (Muir 1956; Ragg 1960). They are probably more akin to those of central Europe, and feedback effects on tree growth are less likely.

The Finnish hypothesis is that nutrients become immobilized in the progressively thickening layer of surface organic matter, and that this mat inhibits seedling establishment, while growth of the existing trees slows down. A pronounced reduction in the growth of a second generation is unlikely to occur in Scotland because most coniferous forests are re-generated by ploughing and replanting. Ploughing breaks up the surface mat, accelerating its decay and the mobilization of the organically bound nutrients, and also brings relatively unweathered soil minerals to the surface. Only if the proportion of forests being restocked by natural regeneration without site prepara-tive treatments were to increase, might nutrient immobilization become more of a problem. Further, Sitka spruce, the main commercially grown species in the uplands, is adapted to growing on deep surface organic layers, and commonly regenerates on rotting logs within its natural range (Gregory 1960; Franklin & Dyrness 1969). It is thus likely to be relatively uninfluenced by changes in the mineral soil horizons.

Nevertheless, because podzols are normally associ-ated with poorer growth in volume of trees, even of species adapted to such conditions, than unpodzolized soils with mull humus (Låg 1962; Pyatt 1970; Page 1971), concern about the possible effects of podzoliz-ation and soil acidification is legitimate. In New England soil pH has been used as an indicator of potential tree growth (Stratton & Struchtemeyer 1968; Mader 1976), while soil pH is closely correlated with the growth of many apple varieties (Kotze & Joubert 1980; Hoyt & Nielsen 1985). However, a confounding factor in Scotland is that most forests have been established on land which was deforested centuries or even millennia ago, when soils were biologically and physically very different from the forest soils of today (Miles 1985).

Differences in many soil properties resulting from past land use can profoundly influence tree growth (Van Goor 1954; Armson 1959; Skinner & Attiwill 1981a, b). Most existing soils are therefore not valid baselines against which to judge change.

The faster rates of decomposition and nutrient release associated with mull-forming birch stands do increase the growth of herbaceous plants in bioassay trials. Table 5 gives an example from the old Scots pine stand and the succeeding birch stand discussed in Table 3. Although there is no evidence as yet that the

Table 5. Mean dry weight (mg) of 8-week-old test plants grown in a glasshouse in soil from an old Scots pine plantation and an adjacent stand of silver birch, established naturally after felling of pine, on Dinnet Moor, Aberdeenshire (source: original data)

	89-year-old Scots pine	18-year-old silver birch	LSD at 5% level
Rumex acetosa (shoots)	2.9	18	14
Luzula sylvatica (shoots)	7.4	26	13
Raphanus spp. (shoots)	10	43	15
(roots)	4.5	53	36

birches respond similarly, the question has often been put: 'would an admixture of birch or similarly behaving broadleaved species benefit the growth of conifers?' There have been claims to this effect (Shumakov 1958; Kovalev 1969; Blintsov 1971; Prudic 1972), but the supporting data are unconvincing. However, more recently, admixtures of Scots pine, lodgepole pine and Japanese larch with Sitka spruce have been shown to increase growth of the spruce (O'Carroll 1978; McIn-tosh & Tabbush 1981; McIntosh 1983), apparently by increasing nitrogen availability. Similarly, Brown and Harrison (1983) reported that the mean height of 25-year-old Norway spruce in an experiment in the Gisburn Forest in the north-west Pennines was 9 m in pure stands, 10 m with a 50% mixture of alder (Alnus glutinosa), and 11 m with a 50% mixture of Scots pine.

The processes underlying these effects are not known. The soils at Gisburn are surface-water gleys, and are thus not susceptible to major change to any depth. Brown and Harrison (1983) estimated that earthworm biomass was doubled under the spruce/alder mixture, and increased 5-fold under the spruce/Scots pine mixture, an unexpected and inexplicable result. Available nitrogen and phosphorus in the soil increased in proportion to the worm biomass, and Brown and Harrison (1983) suggested that increased earthworm activity under the mixtures increased mineralization of nitrogen and phosphorus, so leading to improved tree growth. Earthworms have long been associated with soil productivity (Russel 1910); their presence has stimulated tree growth in pot experi-ments (Marshall 1971) and forage yield in field experiments (Hopp & Slater 1948; Stockdill 1966, 1982). Unfortunately, the earthworm populations at

Gisburn were estimated using baited traps, so that densities cannot be calculated. However, if it were assumed that each trap attracted only worms within a radius of 1 m, then the worm population under the spruce/Scots pine mixture might consume only 8–12% of the annual litterfall of needles. On this basis, the increased earthworm numbers under the mixtures are more likely to be a result of the increased availability of soil nitrogen and phosphorus than the cause.

One pointer to possible mechanisms is the finding that there was greater exploitation of the soil profile by roots in the spruce/pine mixture at Gisburn, with pine roots occurring below the mainly surface root mat of the spruces (Brown 1986). This phenomenon might lead to a slight lowering of the water table, and hence to higher mineralization rates of nitrogen and phosphorus, and it could also stimulate nitrogen fixation (Richards 1964, 1973; Fisher & Stone 1969).

5 Conclusions

There is good evidence that both conifers and broadleaved tree species can change many soil properties, sometimes markedly, especially on well-drained, poorly buffered sandy soils. Many conifers, especially spruces, seem to accelerate podzolization, and *inter alia* cause surface acidification and organic matter accumulation, though the latter trends reverse to some extent during the life of a stand. In contrast, birch, aspen and probably some other broadleaved species are associated with reduced soil acidity, mull formation and a different soil fauna which may tend to depodzolize soils by physically intermixing the A and B horizons. Soil changes induced by trees significantly affect the composition of the field layer, but as yet there is little evidence that they materially affect the growth of the trees that brought about the changes. There are, however, grounds for suspecting that tree performance of naturally regenerated conifer stands might be affected by acidification and podzolization in the Scottish Highlands, though perhaps not in the usually more base-rich soils of the southern uplands. If there is ever a swing to restocking forests by natural regeneration without ploughing the soil, then this point should be further investigated.

At a more fundamental level, there is still little detailed information about the extent to which different species, and perhaps different genotypes, can alter soil properties when growing on different soil types. Is there a threshold level of soil base status below which mull soils undergo acidification, mor formation and perhaps podzolization, and how does this threshold vary for different species? What is the role of the field layer in promoting mull or mor soils, and what are the pedogenic effects of different field layers in relation to different tree canopies? A degree of acidification can occur by a dilution effect, when increasing surface organic matter increases cation exchange capacity. Profound acidification (excluding pollution effects) occurs only when the leaching of soil bases exceeds the supply from mineral weathering and from atmospheric inputs. The answers to the questions posed above can only be found through studies of nutrient fluxes.

The old debate about the yield of mixtures compared to that of pure stands has recently been given new emphasis by the finding from various experiments that the growth of Sitka and Norway spruce can be markedly improved by admixtures of other species, conifers as well as hardwoods. This increased growth seems to result from increased availability of nitrogen and phosphorus, but the underlying mechanisms are unknown.

6 Summary

On the poorly buffered, sandy soils that predominate in the Scottish Highlands, conifers tend to promote soil acidification, podzolization, and surface accumulations of mor humus. In contrast, broadleaved species tend to reduce soil acidity, to form mull humus, and to have a soil fauna which may depodzolize soils by intermixing the surface horizons. Some of these changes reverse, at least in part, as the tree stands senesce.

Any role of the field layer in helping to bring about such changes is only conjectural, as are the threshold levels of soil base status that permit gross change to occur. Soil changes induced by trees can significantly affect the composition of the field layer. They would be expected to influence the growth of the trees themselves, especially if sites were restocked by natural regeneration without ploughing the soil. Increased growth of spruces grown in mixture with various other species, apparently because of increased availability of nitrogen and phosphorus, has recently been noted in several experiments, but the underlying mechanisms are unknown.

7 References

Armson, K.A. 1959. An example of the effects of past land use on fertility levels and growth of Norway spruce (*Picea abies* (L.) Karst). *Univ. Tor. Fac. For. Tech. Rep.* no. 1.

Armson, K.A. & Fessenden, R.J. 1973. Forest wind throws and their influence on soil morphology. *Proc. Soil Sci. Soc. Am.,* **37,** 781–783.

Ball, D.F. & Williams, W.M. 1974. Soil development on coastal dunes at Holkham, Norfolk, England. *Trans. int. Congr. Soil Sci., 10th,* **6,** 380–396.

Binns, W.O. 1959. *The physical and chemical properties of deep peat in relation to afforestation.* PhD thesis, University of Aberdeen.

Blintsov, I.K. 1971. The effect of spruce and birch on soddy-podzolic (pale yellow) silty-loam soils. *Izv. vyssh. ucheb. Zaved. Les. Zh.,* **14,** (6), 28–33. (In Russian.)

Boggie, R. & Miller, H.G. 1976. The growth of *Pinus contorta* at different water-table levels in deep blanket peat. *Forestry,* **49,** 123–131.

Bollen, W.B., Lu, K.C., Trappe, J.M. & Tarrant, R.F. 1969. Influence of Sitka and alder on soil formation and microbiological succession on a landside of alpine origin at Mount Rainier. *U.S. Dept Agric. For. Serv. Res. Note,* PNW-103.

Brakenhielm, S. 1977. Vegetation dynamics of afforested farmland in a district of south-eastern Sweden. *Acta phytogeogr. Suec.*, no. 63.

Brakenhielm, S. & Persson, H. 1980. Vegetation dynamics in developing Scots pine stands in central Sweden. In: *Structure and function of northern coniferous forests – an ecosystem study*, edited by T. Persson, 139–152. (Ecological bulletin no. 32.) Stockholm: Swedish Natural Sciences Research Council.

Brown, A.H.F. 1986. The use of cotton strip assay as a discriminator of forest and grassland management effects. 1. Pine versus mixed stands at Gisburn Forest. In: *Cotton strip assay of cellulose decomposition in soil*, edited by A.F. Harrison, P.M. Latter & D.W.H. Walton. Abbots Ripton: Institute of Terrestrial Ecology. In press.

Brown, A.H.F. & Harrison, A.F. 1983. Effects of tree mixtures on earthworm populations and nitrogen and phosphorus status in Norway spruce (*Picea abies*) stands. In: *New trends in soil biology*, edited by P. Lebrun, H.M. Andre, A. de Nedts, C. Gregoire-Wibo & G. Wauthy, 101–108. Ottignies-Louvain-la-Neuve: Dieu-Brichart.

Bublinec, E. 1973. Effects of Scots pine stands on the soil in the Zahorie region and the advisability of biological soil amelioration by broadleaved trees. *Lesnictvi*, **19**, 139–146. (In Slovakian.)

Dimbleby, G.W. 1952. Soil regeneration in the north-east Yorkshire moors. *J. Ecol.*, **40**, 331–341.

Dimbleby, G.W. & Gill, J.M. 1955. The occurrence of podzols under deciduous woodland in the New Forest. *New Phytol.*, **28**, 95–106.

Doyle, G.J. & Moore, J.J. 1982. Floristic changes in developing conifer plantations growing on blanket peat in the west of Ireland. In: *Struktur und Dynamik von Wälden*, edited by H. Dierschke, 699–716. Vaduz: Cramer.

Ernst, W. 1978. Chemical soil factors determining plant growth. In: *The structure and functioning of plant populations*, edited by A.H.J. Freyson & J.W. Woldendorp, 155–187. Amsterdam: North-Holland.

Fisher, R.F. & Stone, E.L. 1969. Increased availability of nitrogen and phosphorus in the root zone of conifers. *Proc. Soil Sci. Soc. Am.*, **33**, 955–961.

Fogel, R. 1980. Mycorrhizal and nutrient cycling in natural forest ecosystems. *New Phytol.*, **63**, 199–212.

Frank, J. & Borchgrevink, I. 1982. The soil development under Norway spruce (*Picea abies*) and aspen (*Populus tremula*) stands at As. *Meld. Norg. LandbrHøisk.*, **61**, no. 19.

Franklin, J.F. & Dyrness, C.T. 1969. Vegetation of Oregon and Washington. *U.S. Dept Agric. For. Serv. Res. Pap.*, PNW-80.

Gennsler, H. 1959. *Veränderungen von Boden und Vegetation nach generationsweisem Fichtenanbau.* Dissertation, Georg-August University, Göttingen.

Gregory, R.A. 1960. The development of forest soil organic layers in relation to time in southeast Alaska. *U.S. Dept Agric. For. Serv. Res. Cent. Tech. Note,* no. 47.

Hausser, K. 1964. Wachstumsgang und Ertragsleistung der Fichte auf den vorherrschenden Standorten einiger Wuchsbezirke der Altmoränen- und Schotterlandschaft des Württembergischen Oberschwabens. In: *Standort, Wald und Waldwirtschaft in Oberschwaben*, 149–177. Stuttgart: Der Verein für forstliche Standortskunde und Forstpflanzenzüchtung.

Hill, M.O. 1979. The development of a flora in even-aged plantations. In: *The ecology of even-aged plantations*, edited by E.D. Ford, D.C. Malcolm & J. Atterson, 175–192. Cambridge: Institute of Terrestrial Ecology.

Hole, F.D. 1981. Effects of animals on soil. *Geoderma*, **25**, 75–112.

Holmsgaard, E., Holstener-Jorgensen, H. & Yde-Anderson, A. 1961. Bodenbildung, Zuwachs und Gesundheitszustand von Fichtenbeständen erster und zweiter Generation. I. Nord-Seeland. *Forst. ForsVaes Danm.*, **27**, 1–167.

Hopp, H. & Slater, C.S. 1948. Influence of earthworms on soil productivity. *Soil Sci.*, **66**, 421–428.

Howard, P.J. & Howard, D. 1984. Soil changes through afforestation. *Annu. Rep. Inst. terr. Ecol. 1983*, 86–89.

Hoyt, P.B. & Neilsen, G.H. 1985. Effects of soil pH and associated cations on growth of apple trees planted in old orchard soil. *Pl. Soil,* **86**, 395–401.

Jones, E.W. 1965. Pure conifers in central Europe - a review of some old and new work. *J. Oxf. Univ. Forest Soc.*, **13**, 3–15.

Jowsey, P.C. 1973. Peatlands. In: *The organic resources of Scotland: their nature and evaluation*, edited by J. Tivy, 109–121. Edinburgh: Oliver & Boyd.

Kotze, W.A.G. & Joubert, M. 1980. Effect of soil reaction and liming on the growth and mineral situation of apple trees. *Agrochemophysica*, **12**, 15–20.

Kovalev, L.S. 1969. Effect of the admixture of birch and caragana on the breakdown of forest litter and the growth of pine in plantations in the forest-steppe of the central chernozern regions. *Izv. vyssh. ucheb. Zaved. Les. Zh.*, **12**, 166–168. (In Russian.)

Kubiena, W. 1953. *The soils of Europe.* London: Thomas Murby.

Låg, J. 1959. Influence of forest stand and ground cover vegetation on soil formation. *Agrochimica*, **4**, 72–77.

Låg, J. 1962. Studies on the influence of some edaphic growth factors on the distribution of various forest vegetation in Norway. *Adv. Front. Plant Sci.*, **1**, 87–96.

Låg, J. 1971. Some relationships between soil conditions and distribution of different forest vegetation. *Suom. maatal. Seur. Julk. (Acta agral. fenn.)*, **123**, 118–125.

Langmaid, K.K. 1964. Some effects of earthworm invasion in virgin podzols. *Can. J. Soil Sci.*, **44**, 34–37.

Lyford, W.H. 1963. Importance of ants to brown podzolic soil genesis in New England. *Harv. Forest Pap.*, no. 7.

Mackney, D. 1961. A podzol development sequence in oakwoods and heath in central England . *J. Soil Sci.*, **12**, 23–40.

MacLean, D.A. & Wein, R.W. 1977. Changes in understorey vegetation with increasing stand age in New Brunswick forests: species composition, biomass and nutrients. *Can. J. Bot.*, **55**, 2818–2831.

Mader, D.L. 1976. Soil-site productivity for natural stands of white pine in Massachusetts. *Proc. Soil Sci. Soc. Am.*, **40**, 112–115.

Malcolm, D.C. 1957. Site degradation in stands of natural pine in Scotland. *Bull. For. Dep. Univ. Edinb.*, no. 4.

Marshall, V.G. 1971. Effects of soil arthropods and earthworms on the growth of black spruce. *Ann. Zool., Ecol. Anim. Special Publ.*, no. 4.

Marzhan, B. 1959. Degradation of forest soils in Czechoslovakia. *Vestnik. Sel' khoz. Nauki*, 1959, 87–98. (In Czechoslovakian.)

McIntosh, R. 1983. Nitrogen deficiency in establishment phase Sitka spruce in upland Britain. *Scott. For.*, **37**, 185–193.

McIntosh, R. & Tabbush, P. 1981. Nutrition. *Rep. Forest Res. 1981*, 21–22.

Miles, J. 1978. The influence of trees on soil properties. *Annu. Rep. Inst. terr. Ecol. 1977*, 7–11.

Miles, J. 1979. *Vegetation dynamics.* London: Chapman & Hall.

Miles, J. 1981. *Effects of birch on moorlands.* Cambridge: Institute of Terrestrial Ecology.

Miles, J. 1985. The pedogenic effects of different species and vegetation types and the implications of succession. *J. Soil Sci.*, **36**, 571–584.

Miles, J. & Young, W.F. 1980. The effects of heathland and moorland soils in Scotland and northern England following colonization by birch (*Betula* spp.). *Bull. Ecol.*, **11**, 233–242.

Miller, H.G. 1984. Nutrient cycles in birchwoods. *Proc. R. Soc. Edinb.*, **85B**, 83–96.

Muir, J.W. 1956. *The soils of the country around Jedburgh and Morebattle.* Edinburgh: HMSO.

Nihlgard, B. 1971. Pedological influence of spruce planted on former beech forest soils in Scania, south Sweden. *Oikos,* **22,** 302–314.

Noirfalise, A. 1968. *Aspects of forest management.* Strasburg: Council of Europe.

O'Carroll, N. 1978. The nursing of Sitka spruce. 1. Japanese larch. *Irish For.,* **35,** 60–65.

Ovington, J.D. 1953. Studies on the development of woodland conditions under different trees. I. Soils pH. *J. Ecol.,* **41,** 13–34.

Ovington, J.D. 1954. Studies of the development of woodland conditions under different trees. II. The forest floor. *J. Ecol.,* **42,** 71–80.

Page, G. 1968. Some effects of conifer crops on soil properties. *Commonw. Forest. Rev.,* **47,** 52–62.

Page, G. 1971. Properties of some common Newfoundland forest soils and their relation to forest growth. *Can. J. For. Res.,* **1,** 174–192.

Page, G. 1974. Effects of forest cover on the properties of some Newfoundland forest soils. *Can. For. Serv. Publ.,* no. 1332.

Persson, H. 1978. Root dynamics in a young Scots pine stand in central Sweden. *Oikos,* **30,** 508–519.

Prudic, Z. 1972. The effect of hornbeam on the soil and on the yield of Scots pine stands in the Moravian Carpathian foothills. *Lesnictvi,* **18,** 689–698. (In Czechoslovakian.)

Pyatt, D.G. 1970. *Soil groups of upland forests.* (Forestry Commission forest record no. 71.) London: HMSO.

Pyatt, D.G. & Craven, M.M. 1979. Soil changes under even-aged plantations. In: *The ecology of even-aged plantations,* edited by E.D. Ford, D.C. Malcolm & J. Atterson, 369–386. Cambridge: Institute of Terrestrial Ecology.

Ragg, J.M. 1960. *The soils of the country round Kelso and Lauder.* Edinburgh: HMSO.

Richards, B.N. 1964. Fixation of atmospheric nitrogen in coniferous forests. *Aust. For.,* **28,** 68–74.

Richards, B.N. 1973. Nitrogen fixation in the rhizosphere of conifers. *Soil Biol. Biochem.,* **5,** 149–152.

Russel, E.J. 1910. The effect of earthworms on soil productiveness. *J. agric. Sci.,* **2,** 246–257.

Sakura, T., Gimingham, C.H. & Miller, C.S. 1985. Effect of tree density on ground vegetation in a Japanese larch population. *Scott. For.,* **39,** 191–198.

Saly, R. 1965. Notes on the influence of Norway spruce on the soil. *Les. Bratisl.,* **21,** 4–7. (In Slovakian.)

Saly, R. 1980. Soils of spruce forests in the Slovak Socialist Republic. In: *Stability of spruce forest ecosystems,* edited by E. Klimo, 355–362. Brno: University of Agriculture.

Saly, R. & Obr, F. 1965. Notes on the conversion of copses and the problem of spruce–fir monocultures in the Czechoslovakian People's Republic. *Lesn. Cas.,* **1,** 1–16. (In Slovakian.)

Satchell, J.E. 1967. Lumbricidae. In: *Soil biology,* edited by A. Burges & F. Raw, 259–322. London: Academic Press.

Shumakov, V.S. 1958. The question of the influence exerted by species rotation on the fertility of the soil. *Sb. Rab. les Khoz.,* **34,** 126–134. (In Russian.)

Siren, G. 1955. The development of spruce forest on raw humus sites in northern Finland and its ecology. *Acta for. fenn.,* **62,** no. 4.

Skinner, M.F. & Attiwill, P.M. 1981a. The productivity of pine plantations in relation to previous land use. I. Growth responses in agricultural and forest soils. *Pl. Soil,* **60,** 161–176.

Skinner, M.F. & Attiwill, P.M. 1981b. The productivity of pine plantations in relation to previous land use. II. Phosphorus adsorption isotherms and the growth of pine seedlings. *Pl. Soil,* **60,** 329–339.

Stephens, E.P. 1956. The uprooting of trees: a forest process. *Proc. Soil Sci. Soc. Am.,* **20,** 113–116.

Stockdill, S.M.J. 1966. The effect of earthworms on pasture. *Proc. N.Z. ecol. Soc.,* **13,** 68–75.

Stockdill, S.M.J. 1982. Effects of introduced earthworms on the productivity of New Zealand pastures. *Pedobiologia,* **24,** 29–35.

Stone, E.L. 1975. Windthrow influences on spatial heterogeneity in a forest soil. *Mitt. schweiz. Anst. forstl. VersWes.,* **51,** 77–87.

Stone, E.L. 1975. Effects of species on nutrient cycles and soil change. *Phil. Trans. R. Soc. Lond.,* **271B,** 149–162.

Stratton, K.G. & Struchtemeyer, R.A. 1968. Evaluation of soil sites for white pine in Maine. *Tech. Bull. Maine Agric. Exp. Sta.,* no. 32.

Swift, M.J., Heal, O.W. & Anderson, J.M. 1979. *Decomposition in terrestrial ecosystems.* Oxford: Blackwell Scientific.

Tamm, O. 1920. Bodenstudien in der Nordschwedischen Nadelregion. *Meddn St. Skogsförsk Inst.,* **17,** 49–300.

Tamm, O. 1932. Die Braune Waldboden in Schweden. *Proc. int. Congr. Soil Sci., 2nd,* **5,** 178–187.

Troedsson, T. 1972. The importance of soil properties in modern town and country planning. *K. Skogs- o. LantbrAkad. Tidskr.,* **111,** 250–262. (In Swedish.)

Tuszynski, M. 1972. Chemical properties of forest litters. *Pr. badaw. Inst. badaw. Lesn.,* **1972,** 90–108. (In Polish.)

Ulrich, B., Benecke, P., Harris, W.F., Khanna, P.K. & Mayer, R. 1981. Soil processes. In: *Dynamic properties of forest ecosystems,* edited by D.E. Reichle, 265–339. Cambridge: Cambridge University Press.

Van Goor, C.P. 1954. The influence of tillage on some properties of dry sandy soils in the Netherlands. *Landbouwk. Tijdschr., 's-Grav.,* **66,** 175–181.

Viro, P.J. 1974. Effects of forest fire on soil. In: *Fire and ecosystems,* edited by T.T. Kozlowski & C.E. Ahlgren, 7–45. New York: Academic Press.

Williams, B.L., Cooper, J.M. & Pyatt, D.G. 1978. Effects of afforestation with *Pinus contorta* on nutrient content, acidity and exchangeable cations in peat. *Forestry,* **51,** 29–35.

Wittich, W. 1972. Die Bodenfleglichkeit der Buche. *Forst- u. Holzwirt,* **27,** 52–54.

Zonn, S.V. 1954. *The influence of forests on the soil.* Moscow: Akademiya Nauk (In Russian.)

Are the occurrences of sheathing mycorrhizal fungi in new and regenerating forests and woodlands in Scotland predictable?

P A MASON and F T LAST
Institute of Terrestrial Ecology, Edinburgh

1 Introduction

To many people, the names 'deceiver', 'brown rim roll' and 'blusher' may suggest varieties of butterflies, but in the event they, like 'poison pie', 'blewit', and 'fly agaric', refer to ground fungi that develop in woodlands and forests. Poison pie (*Hebeloma crustuliniforme*) is usually associated with young trees, while blewits (*Tricholoma* spp.) and fly agaric (*Amanita muscaria*) are linked with older trees. The bolete *Suillus luteus* is strongly associated with pines, while other fungi are less restricted in their choice of hosts. There is, therefore, evidence to suggest that toadstools within forests and woodlands do not occur at random. What are the 'rules' governing their occurrence? Are they the same in natural/semi-natural woodlands and man-made plantations? Are they the same in second rotations as in first rotations, remembering that soils in the former will have been ameliorated by the preceding stand. These are matters of interest in the Highlands of Scotland where afforested areas are likely to increase and where existing plantations will be felled and replanted.

It is now recognized that 'soil fungi' have an important role to play in the cycling of nutrients and energy in terrestrial ecosystems (Harley 1971). Many species of soil fungi are decomposers that can actively break down moribund tissues of both plants and animals, with the release of carbon dioxide and a variety of soluble compounds, many of which are absorbed by later generations of plants and animals in addition to other microbes. Plant litter, twigs, wood and/or roots are colonized by ordered sequences of saprotrophic fungi. These early colonizers, the primary decomposers, are being replaced by an array of secondary decomposers, including many basidiomycetes. This sequence of microbes with different capabilities ensures that even the lignin and cellulose components of plant material are degraded to soluble substances (Harley & Waid 1955; Harley 1971; Frankland 1981). Fungal successions would, therefore, seem to be commonplace within forest ecosystems.

In addition to decomposers, the reservoir of soil microbes includes many fungi that can colonize roots of trees and subsequently form mycorrhizas. Within the UK, trees in the Rosaceae (eg species of apple (*Malus*), cherry (*Prunus*) and pear (*Pyrus*)) and Aceraceae (sycamore (*Acer pseudoplatanus*)) develop, like most herbs and shrubs, vesicular–arbuscular (endo-)mycorrhizas with members of the Endogonaceae, whereas the majority of trees including pine (*Pinus* spp.), spruce (*Picea* spp.), larch (*Larix* spp.), fir (*Abies* spp.), willow (*Salix* spp.), lime (*Tilia* spp.), oak (*Quercus* spp.), beech (*Fagus* spp.) and birch (*Betula* spp.) develop sheathing (ecto-)mycorrhizas with an array of mostly basidiomycetous and ascomycetous fungi. Interestingly, the genera of mycorrhizal fungi listed for Scotland (Table 1) are similar to those recorded for high-altitude locations in southern India (Last & Fleming 1985).

Table 1. Genera of fungi that have been recorded in woodlands and forests in Scotland (source: Watling 1984a,b)

Agaricus	*Gomphidius	Oudemansiella
*Amanita	*Hebeloma	*Paxillus
*Amphinema	Hygrophorus	Peziza
*Boletus	Hypholoma	Pholiota
*Cantharellus	*Inocybe	Psathyrella
*Cenococcum	*Laccaria	*Rhizopogon
Clitocybe	*Lactarius	*Russula
Collybia	*Leccinum	*Scleroderma
*Chroogomonophus	Lepiota	*Suillus
*Cortinarius	Lepista	*Thelephora
Cystoderma	Marasmius	*Tomentella
*Elaphomyces	Mycena	*Tricholoma
Entoloma	*Naucoria	*Tuber
Galerina	Nolanea	

*Genera with species proven or suspected of being able to form sheathing mycorrhizas with roots of trees

Mycorrhizas facilitate the uptake of nutrients which may otherwise remain unavailable to their hosts; they can also produce growth stimulatory substances which may enhance the growth and longevity of roots (Slankis 1973). In return, mycorrhizal fungi, to a greater or lesser extent, depend on their hosts for supplies of energy. If they are deprived of access to their hosts' current assimilates, either by root severance or defoliation, sheathing mycorrhizal fungi appear unable to produce fruitbodies (Last *et al.* 1979). Although sheathing mycorrhizas seem essential for sustained growth in forests, surprisingly little is known about the factors controlling their occurrence. Do they, like decomposers, occur in ordered sequences? Bearing in mind the changes that occur among non-parasitic microbes which colonize living leaves and roots, it would, by analogy, be surprising if the fungi forming sheathing mycorrhizas with trees 40 years old were the same as those colonizing the roots of saplings. If there are differences, can they be explained and predicted, and how should they influence our approach to the future management of forests in the Highlands?

2 Occurrence of mycorrhizal fungi in 'primary' woodlands and forests

Mycorrhizal fungi which develop in stands of trees growing on sites that have been treeless for many years ('primary' woodlands) are likely to be substantially different from those in 'secondary' woodlands where seedlings grow either among mature trees or on sites where mature trees have only recently been clearfelled.

2.1 From establishment to canopy closure

Trappe (1962, 1977) estimated that more than 2000 species of fungi have the potential to form mycorrhizas. Most of these fungi form readily identifiable fruitbodies, including toadstools, earth balls, earth fans and elf cups, which have formed the focus of attention of innumerable fungal forays. While recording the presence of these often colourful fungi, however, mycologists have rarely added detailed habitat data such as the state of woodland development (before or after canopy closure), or the soil type.

While it has long been recognized that species of birch (*Betula*), major components of the Scottish countryside, are able to invade open ground and colonize gaps within established woodlands (Kirby 1984), it is only during the last few years that it has become clear that the fungi forming sheathing mycorrhizas on pioneer sapling birch are likely to differ from those associated with mature birch. By studying the sequence of fruitbodies associated with silver birch (*Betula pendula*) and downy birch (*B. pubescens*) during the first 10 years after outplanting at the Bush Estate, Midlothian (lat. 55°52'N), Mason *et al.* (1982, 1983) identified an ordered array, in time and space, of mycorrhizal fungi. During the second to fourth year after planting, they recorded species of *Hebeloma*, *Inocybe*, *Laccaria* and *Thelephora*, which are not usually associated with mature birches: in years 6–10, fruitbodies of species of *Cortinarius*, *Leccinum* and *Russula* appeared (Table 2). Paralleling these changes in types of fungi, there were also changes in numbers of different species associated, at any one time, with ageing trees. Numbers increased from 4 per tree in year 3 to nearly 30 in year 10 (Last *et al.* 1983), with a consistently greater variety of fungi associated with silver birch than with downy birch (Mason *et al.* 1982).

The fruitbodies of fungi associated with 3-year-old lodgepole pine (*Pinus contorta*), growing in the same field as the birches already mentioned, included *Rhizopogon luteolus*, *Suillus luteus* and *Amphinema byssoides*, in addition to species of *Hebeloma* (*H. fragilipes*) and *Thelephora* (*T. terrestris*) (J H Warcup pers. comm.). Species of *Hebeloma* are thought to be pioneer fungi colonizing the roots of young saplings (eg *Hebeloma fragilipes* with pine, *H. populinum* with Sitka spruce (*Picea sitchensis*), and *H. versipelle* with lime (*Tilia cordata*) (Watling 1981)).

The fruitbodies associated with stands of lodgepole

pine and Sitka spruce, growing in peat in Northumberland, changed from *Laccaria* spp. and *Paxillus involutus* when trees were 3–4 years old to species of *Inocybe*, *Lactarius*, *Cortinarius* and *Russula* when the trees were older (Dighton *et al.* 1986). Although Dighton's study did not detail the first appearance of each fungus, the available evidence suggests that *Laccaria* was followed by *Lactarius rufus*, to be joined, in turn, by *Inocybe longicystis*, *Cortinarius croceofolius* and *Russula emetica* before canopy closure. A nearly identical sequence was observed in conjunction with stands of Sitka spruce, namely *Laccaria* spp. → *Inocybe longicystis* → *Lactarius rufus* → *Cortinarius croceofolius*.

From the occurrence of fruitbodies, it is apparent that similar sequences of mycorrhizal fungi were associated with lodgepole pine and Sitka spruce in peaty soils in northern Britain. The differences between these sequences were less than those between 2 stands of the same species (lodgepole pine) growing at different locations (*vide* Dighton and Warcup). It, therefore, seems that fungi occurring early in mycorrhizal successions are not host-specific. Furthermore, lodgepole pine, at different locations, can associate with a variety of early-stage mycorrhizal fungi. This capability probably helps the establishment of pioneer trees in a variety of habitats. Kropp and Trappe (1982)

Table 2. Succession of fruitbodies of proven or suspected sheathing mycorrhizal fungi appearing in a stand of birches planted at Bush Estate, near Edinburgh (source: Last *et al.* 1983)

Years after planting	Fungi whose fruitbodies occurred for the first time
1	Nil
2	*Hebeloma crustuliniforme* (Bull.: St. Amans) Quelet
	Laccaria proxima (Boud.) Pat.
3	*Laccaria tortilis* (｛Bolt.｝ S. F. Gray) Cooke
	Thelephora terrestris Ehrenb.: Fr.
4	*Hebeloma fragilipes* Romagnesi
	H. sacchariolens Quelet
	H. mesophaeum (Pers.: Fr.) Quelet
	Inocybe lanuginella (Schroet.) Konrad and Maublanc
	Lactarius pubescens (Fr.: Krombh.) Fr.
6	*Cortinarius* sp.
	Hebeloma leucosarx P. D. Orton
	Hymenogaster tener Berkeley and Broom
	Inocybe petiginosa (Fr.: Fr.) Gillet
	Leccinum roseofracta Watling
	L. scabrum (Bull.: Fr.) S. F. Gray
	L. versipelle (Fries and Hök) Snell
	Peziza badia Persoon ex Merat
	Ramaria sp.
7	Other *Cortinarius* spp.
	Other *Hebeloma* spp.
	Lactarius glyciosmus (Fr.: Fr.) Fr.
	Leccinum subleucophaeum Dick and Snell
10	*Hebeloma vaccinum* Romagnesi
	Russula betularum Hora
	R. grisea (Pers.: Secr.) Fr.
	R. versicolor J. Schaeff
14	*Laccaria laccata* (Scop.: Fr.) Cooke
	Lactarius spinosulus Quelet
	Russula atropurpurea (Krombh.) Britz.

also noted that western hemlock (*Tsuga heterophylla*), which in nature grows in mixed stands, usually associates with mycorrhizal fungi that are not host-specific. In contrast, 'early' fungi associated with red alder (*Alnus rubra*) tend to be host-specific, so possibly helping to explain why this tree grows in pure stands.

Sequences of mycorrhizal fungi similar to those occurring in the northern hemisphere have been found in association with young conifers growing in New Zealand (Chu-Chou 1979; Chu-Chou & Grace 1981). As with young stands of lodgepole pine in Scotland, species of *Hebeloma* and *Rhizopogon* were found in association with Monterey pine (*Pinus radiata*) growing in New Zealand (Chu-Chou 1979). *Hebeloma crustuliniforme* was soon replaced by *Laccaria* spp. and 2 species of *Inocybe* and *Suillus*. Taken together, these observations in temperate regions of the world suggest that some mycorrhizal fungi (eg *Hebeloma, Laccaria, Inocybe* and *Thelephora*) are characteristic of young stands of trees growing at 'primary' sites.

Support for the concept of mycorrhizal succession in birch has been provided by J H Warcup (pers. comm.) and Deacon *et al.* (1983) at Bush Estate. They found that the above-ground fruitbodies were associated with their own distinctive types of below-ground mycorrhizas (Plate 10). Additional evidence, however, indicates that the range of early-stage fungi forming mycorrhizas on young trees can be modified by soil type and genotypic differences within species of trees (Last *et al.* 1984). While all seedlings within a seed lot would associate with early-stage fungi, one might be linked with *Hebeloma* spp., whereas another might form mycorrhizas with *Inocybe* spp. The effects of soil type were highlighted in inoculation experiments with *Hebeloma sacchariolens* (Last *et al.* 1985). While *H. sacchariolens* continued to dominate root systems of inoculated birch seedlings when growing in mineral soils and sedge peat, it was completely replaced by naturally occurring fungi in a more acidic *Sphagnum* peat. In the USA, there is a suggestion of a broader environmental effect. While the mycorrhizal fungus *Pisolithus tinctorius* facilitated the establishment of pine seedlings in south-eastern USA (Marx 1980), it seems to have been of little value in cooler more northerly areas (Grossnickle & Reid 1983), where species of *Laccaria* appear to be more successful (Molina & Trappe 1982).

2.2 From canopy closure to maturity

As the canopies of trees begin to overlap, forest environments change, with temperatures and moisture conditions at ground level becoming less favourable for litter breakdown and nutrient mobilization by saprotrophic fungi (Swift *et al.* 1979; Vogt *et al.* 1983a).

With changes in the activities of saprotrophic fungi, it would be logical to expect corresponding changes in the activities of mycorrhizal species. After canopy closure, Vogt *et al.* (1983b) recorded that the biomasses of mycorrhizal fungi (which were not identified) associated with conifers in nutrient-poor sites were significantly larger than those associated with conifers at nutrient-rich sites. In contrast, instead of measuring fungal biomass, Watling (1984a) has concentrated on the identification of woodland macrofungi. After repeatedly visiting 19 woodland sites near the Kindrogan Field Centre, Perthshire, he established that 27% of the 540 recorded species of agarics were attributable to 4 genera of mycorrhizal fungi (*Cortinarius* (45 species), *Lactarius* (38 species), *Russula* (57 species) and *Amanita* (7 species)).

More recently, Dighton *et al.* (1986), who counted numbers of fruitbodies, found that the diversity of mycorrhizal fungi in stands of lodgepole pine decreased after canopy closure, and *Russula emetica* became dominant. This decrease in diversity in stands of mature conifers parallels the observations of Harvey *et al.* (1976), who indicated that root systems of Douglas fir (*Pseudotsuga menziesii*) and western larch (*Larix occidentalis*) were dominated by *Russula brevipes* and *Suillus cavipes* respectively. Richardson (1970), like Dighton, found that populations of toadstools attributable to mycorrhizal fungi in a mature (55-year-old) plantation of Scots pine (*Pinus sylvestris*) were dominated by *Russula emetica*, but with significant numbers of *Amanita* (*A. inaurata, A. rubescens, A. vaginata*) and *Lactarius* (*L. rufus, L. turpis*).

These observations show that the mycorrhizal fungi occurring in Scottish birchwoods are similar to those found in Scandinavia (Watling 1984b), to the extent that the 2 colour 'forms' of *Lactarius vietus* in Scotland have their counterparts in Scandinavia. Of the small group of *Amanita* species found in European birchwoods, *A. muscaria* is the best known. It has been recorded in the northern and southern hemispheres in association with mature stands of several tree species, although in southern India it appears in association with much younger trees, possibly because forests develop canopies more rapidly there than in temperate areas (Last *et al.* 1981). *Amanita crocea*, in contrast to *A. muscaria*, is usually found in troops (groups) in Scottish birchwoods (Watling 1984b). Species of *Russula* and *Lactarius* are also common in birchwoods, excepting *R. aquosa* (which has only recently been added to the British list) and the rare agaric *R. scotica* which is confined to Scotland (Watling 1984b).

Together, the data indicate that mature woodlands and forests in Scotland have mycorrhizal floras distinct from those associated with young stands of trees. Mature woods are characterized by species of *Amanita, Cortinarius, Lactarius, Russula* and *Tricholoma*. There is, however, a suggestion that the diversity of mycorrhizal fungi peaks at, or about, the time of canopy closure. Nevertheless, knowledge of the temporal changes occurring after canopy closure is at present fragmentary. Miles (1985), when observing stands of silver birch of different ages at Kerrow, Inverness-shire, found that most fruitbodies in a stand 20 years old were attributable to *Cortinarius* spp. and *Lactarius pubescens,* whereas in a stand 72 years old fruitbodies of *Amanita muscaria, Tricholoma columbetta, Laccaria amethystea* and *Lactarius tabidus* were the most numerous.

3 Occurrence of mycorrhizal fungi in 'secondary' woodlands and forests

Our knowledge of the ecology of mycorrhizal fungi in 'primary' woodlands and forests has steadily increased, but what happens when clearfelled areas are replanted or when seedlings regenerate naturally within established woodlands?

3.1 Naturally regenerating woodlands

Present evidence, although scant, suggests that mycorrhizal sequences on seedlings regenerating naturally within natural woodlands or forests may differ from those on seedlings establishing at 'primary' sites. Although soils within natural woodlands throughout Great Britain are likely to possess spores of wind-dispersed early-stage fungi, most roots of regenerating tree seedlings seem to be colonized by late-stage fungi. For example, 73% of a naturally occurring population of birch seedlings growing in a sweet chestnut (*Castanea sativa*) coppice in southern England were found at the end of the first year to have mycorrhizas attributable to late-stage boletes (Fleming 1983). In an attempt to explain this 'anomaly', Fleming planted birch seedlings (which had been propagated in sterile (axenic) conditions and were therefore without mycorrhizas) among the roots of ageing birch trees (Fleming 1983; Fleming *et al.* 1986). In one instance, the roots of the mature trees were left undisturbed, while in another they were severed by coring and trenching.

These treatments were tested at 2 sites: Bush Estate, with a stand of birch newly developing on former agricultural land, and Struan Wood, Perthshire, with a long-established mature birchwood. Irrespective of site, seedlings planted among undisturbed roots developed late-stage mycorrhizas. However, where they were planted among severed roots, there was a strong site effect. At Bush, most of the mycorrhizas that developed on the experimental seedlings were attributable to early-stage fungi, whereas at Struan many mycorrhizas were formed by species of the late-stage *Lactarius* and *Leccinum.*

Severing roots and depriving inocula (strands) of *Lactarius* and *Leccinum* of their sources of host assimilates prevented them from forming mycorrhizas on seedlings planted at Bush but not at Struan. The ability of late-stage fungi to outcompete early-stage fungi in naturally regenerating woodlands seems to reflect their ability to form strands and/or their responses to changing soil conditions, the most important aspect of which may be the accumulations of organic matter which occurred at Struan but not at Bush.

3.2 Second rotation plantations

Compared with naturally regenerating woodlands, even less is known of the fungi which colonize seedlings on sites being afforested for a second time. For how long does the inoculum (largely of late-stage fungi) present on roots of clearfelled stumps remain viable and able to colonize roots of seedlings, in the absence of currently produced host assimilates? How long does this capability persist, compared with the viability of propagules, probably mostly spores of early-stage fungi? Should the fate of cut stumps, and their associated mycorrhizas, be a consideration when planning the preparation of sites for second rotations? The answers will, of course, depend upon the early- or late-stage fungi which seem most appropriate for second and subsequent rotations. First, however, it is necessary to ascertain the sequence of mycorrhizal fungi, and their roles, on young seedlings planted at second rotation sites.

4 Factors influencing mycorrhizal distribution

Early- and late-stage mycorrhizal fungi seem able to form mycorrhizas with equal facility in sterile, axenic conditions (Mason 1980). However, results of controlled inoculation experiments indicate that late-stage fungi, unlike early-stage fungi, are unable to form mycorrhizas, because of their lack of competitiveness, on seedlings growing in first rotation unsterile forest soils (Table 3). In corroboration, laboratory experi-

Table 3. Factors possibly influencing the sequence of fungi forming sheathing mycorrhizas with tree roots (source: Dighton & Mason 1985)

Factors affecting the ability of mycorrhizal fungi to colonize roots	Occurrences of different fungi in mycorrhizal succession*	
	Early	Late
Energy demand (as judged by growth on artificial media)	Small	Large
Conjectured ability to supply nutrients to trees	Capable of supplying hosts with nutrients from labile inorganic pool	Capable of supplying hosts with nutrients from labile inorganic pool also, because of the possession of appropriate extracellular enzymes, from the organic pool
Competitive ability: Ability of fungi to form mycorrhizas on tree seedlings growing in first rotation soils which were		
i. partly sterilized	+	+
ii. untreated (not partially sterilized)	+	−

*Mycorrhizal succession *sensu* Mason *et al.* 1982; Deacon *et al.* 1983; Last *et al.* 1983

ments with artificial substrates showed that early-stage fungi are less glucose-demanding than late-stage fungi (Dighton & Mason 1985). It has also been suggested that early-stage mycorrhizal fungi are better suited to the colonization of seedlings growing in mineral soils than in organic soils (Alvarez *et al.* 1979), whereas late-stage mycorrhizal fungi prefer organic substrates (Harvey *et al.* 1976). On a mining site, Gardner and Malajczuk (1985) found that the early-stage fungus *Laccaria* fruited on the unaltered ridges, whereas the late-stage *Cortinarius* fruited in the litter-filled troughs associated with the planting of 5 species of eucalypts (*Eucalyptus* spp.).

However, because early-stage *Laccaria* spp. are able to colonize seedlings growing in peat, an organic substrate (Last *et al.* 1985), the suggestions made by Alvarez *et al.* (1979) and Harvey *et al.* (1976) need qualification. Accepting that the effects of organic matter on the formation of mycorrhizas and the production of fruitbodies may differ, it seems that late-stage fungi can colonize roots in soils which have been amended by plant litter, but not in soils, mineral and organic, which have not been altered in this way. Tyler (1984) found that the production of fruitbodies in beech woodlands by the late-stage *Russula mairei* and *R. fellea* was directly related to amounts of organic matter in surface soils (Figure 1).

The ability of late-stage fungi, in preference to early-stage fungi, to colonize and form mycorrhizas on seedlings growing in soils modified by the deposition and subsequent decomposition of litter may be a reflection of the ability of the fungi to produce extracellular enzymes. This characteristic might be particularly important because soil environment changes occurring at, or after, canopy closure seem likely to restrict litter decomposition and mobilization by other soil microbes (Vogt *et al.* 1983a). Bartlett and Lewis (1973) detected phosphatase and phytase in mycorrhizal roots collected from mature beech trees, whereas Giltrap (1982) found that a number of mycorrhizal fungi were able to produce polyphenol-oxidases, and Linkins and Antibus (1981) detected appreciable cellulase activity in the mycorrhizal roots of 'least' willow (*Salix rotundifolia*). Interestingly, exocell-ulase and β-glucosidase activities were 60 and 140 times greater in soil-permeating hyphal strands of mycorrhizal fungi than in the mantles of their myco-rrhizas. Much remains to be learnt. The mechanisms controlling mycorrhizal development in 'primary' and 'secondary' woodlands need to be clarified so as to ensure that the correct fungi are inoculated to saplings being planted in 'primary' and 'secondary' sites.

5 Conclusions

During the development of 'natural' and man-made forests, soil properties change, especially in the surface horizons where mycorrhizas are active. It is therefore not surprising that observations of the production of fruitbodies and the occurrence of myco-

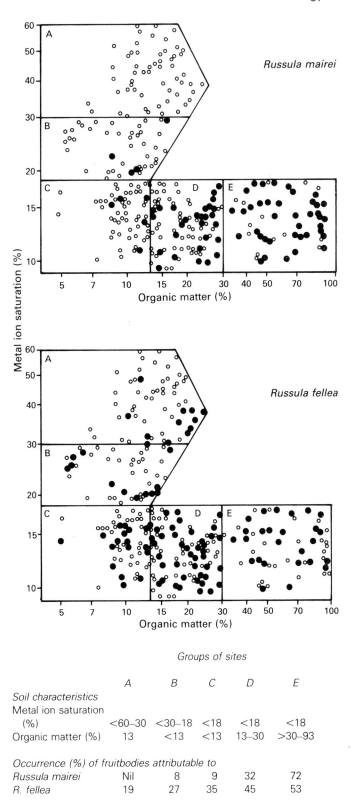

	Groups of sites				
	A	*B*	*C*	*D*	*E*
Soil characteristics					
Metal ion saturation (%)	<60–30	<30–18	<18	<18	<18
Organic matter (%)	13	<13	<13	13–30	>30–93
Occurrence (%) of fruitbodies attributable to					
Russula mairei	Nil	8	9	32	72
R. fellea	19	27	35	45	53

Figure 1. Autumn occurrence (%) of fruitbodies of 2 mycorrhizal fungi, Russula mairei *and* R. fellea, *found in association with stands of beech growing at a range of sites with different soils in southern Sweden. Soil data refer to top 5 cm after removing superficial litter (●, sites with fruitbodies; ○, sites without fruitbodies) (source: Tyler 1984).*

rrhizas have lent support to the concept of mycorrhizal succession. While these changes seem clear-cut in 'primary' woodlands in Scotland and other temperate areas, the data, as yet fragmentary, suggest that mycorrhizal development in 'secondary' woodlands is restricted to late-stage fungi.

The mechanisms controlling mycorrhizal development are far from obvious, although it is already apparent that several factors are involved. Possibly because they need few carbohydrates for rapid growth, early-stage fungi initially outcompete late-stage fungi when trees colonize or are planted on sites which were previously unafforested. However, with the accumulation, decomposition and incorporation of litter into the upper soil horizons, the conjectured ability of late-stage fungi, with the help of exoenzymes, to derive augmented sources of energy from the organic matter enriching the surface horizons seems to swing the balance in favour of late-stage fungi. This advantage could be magnified by the formation of mycelial strands which many late-stage fungi are able to form.

After becoming established in 'primary' woodlands, late-stage mycorrhizal fungi thereafter seem to hold sway, unless soil properties change in intervals between successive stands of trees and/or if the propagules (strands/spores) of late-stage fungi lose viability sooner than those of early-stage fungi. Interestingly, Read et al. (1985) have indicated that strands of mycorrhizas may transfer carbohydrates from mature trees to seedlings, thus giving tree seedlings in dense forests an advantage when they attempt to maintain themselves in suboptimal light conditions. This may be a good reason for using late-stage fungi in managing secondary woodlands.

These ideas now need to be examined experimentally, recognizing that they may help elucidate (i) the balance of factors determining the survival and fruitbody production of different fungi, and (ii) the benefits that may accrue to their 'tree' hosts. At the same time, they may guide the rational choices of mycorrhizal fungi for the controlled inoculation of saplings to be planted in 'primary' and 'secondary' sites. The choices may differ.

At the present time, no discussion of the dynamics of forests in western Europe can be complete without reference to the possible influences of atmospheric pollutants, regrettably encompassed by the umbrella term 'acid rain'. Recently, as a result of monitoring the occurrence of fruitbodies at intervals since 1912, colleagues have inferred that the production of toadstools by many agarics has appreciably decreased in the Netherlands, the decreases being particularly notable among mycorrhizal fungi in woodlands at acidic, sandy sites (Arnolds 1985). However, are events in sandy soils mirrored by those in other, equally acid, types of soil? Are inverse associations with atmospheric pollutants indicators of causal relationships? Are there other plausible explanations of the decreases? Even if the production of fruitbodies has decreased, have the ameliorating effects of mycorrhizal fungi on tree growth been adversely affected? Whatever the answers to these questions, it is perhaps appropriate to develop a more rational and objective approach to the conservation of fungi. They play a vital role in the cycling of nutrients, both as 'decomposers' and, as discussed in this paper, in facilitating the uptake and movement of nutrients through mycorrhizal associations.

6 Summary

Many fungi produce fruitbodies in forests and woodlands. Some are plant pathogens, while others either decompose moribund tissues or form sheathing (ecto-)mycorrhizas.

Gradually accumulating evidence suggests that sheathing mycorrhizal fungi associated with tree seedlings on new, primary, sites differ from those colonizing seedlings regenerating within mature woods or planted into secondary areas that have recently been clearfelled.

In the former, many of the sheathing mycorrhizas are attributable to species of *Hebeloma*, *Laccaria* and *Inocybe* (early-stage fungi), whereas in the latter they may be formed by species of *Amanita*, *Cortinarius*, *Lactarius*, *Russula* and *Tricholoma*, a fungal group found to be associated with ageing trees on primary sites where they have been designated late-stage fungi.

Why are seedlings in primary sites colonized by early-stage mycorrhizal fungi, whereas those in secondary sites seem to associate with late-stage fungi? The answer to this question is needed to ensure that seedlings planted into primary and secondary sites, which are abundant in the uplands, are inoculated with the appropriate fungi if and when controlled inoculations, during or immediately after propagation, are adopted. To date, evidence suggests that late-stage fungi are unable to compete in newly established primary woodlands. In contrast, they are able to monopolize roots (whether of ageing trees in 'primary' woods or of seedlings in 'secondary' loccations) growing in soils which were modified during earlier tree growth, possibly by the incorporation of decomposing litter. It is suggested that the production of pectolytic and cellulytic enzymes by late-stage fungi may favour them in modified soils at the expense of early-stage fungi.

7 References

Alvarez, I.F., Rowney, D.L. & Cobb, F.W. Jr. 1979. Mycorrhizae and growth of white fir seedlings in mineral soil with and without organic layers in a California forest. *Can. J. For. Res.*, **9**, 311–315.

Arnolds, E., ed. 1985. Veranderingen in de paddestoel–flora (mycoflora). *Wet. Meded. K. ned. natuurh. Veren.*, no. 167.

Bartlett, E.M. & Lewis, D.H. 1973. Surface phosphatase activity of mycorrhizal roots of birch. *Soil Biol. Biochem.*, **5**, 249–257.

Chu-Chou, M. 1979. Mycorrhizal fungi of *Pinus radiata* in New Zealand. *Soil Biol. Biochem.*, **11**, 557–562.

Chu-Chou, M. & Grace, L.J. 1981. Mycorrhizal fungi of *Pseudotsuga menziesii* in the north island of New Zealand. *Soil Biol. Biochem.*, **13**, 247–249.

Deacon, J.W., Donaldson, S.J. & Last, F.T. 1983. Sequences and interactions of mycorrhizal fungi on birch. *Pl. Soil*, **71**, 257–262.

Dighton, J. & Mason, P.A. 1985. Mycorrhizal dynamics during forest tree development. In: *Developmental biology of higher fungi*, edited by D. Moore, L.A. Casselton, D.A. Wood & J.C. Frankland, 117–139. Cambridge: Cambridge University Press.

Dighton, J., Poskitt, J.M. & Howard, D.M. 1986. Changes in occurrence of basidiomycete fruitbodies during forest stand development: with specific reference to mycorrhizal species. *Trans. Br. mycol. Soc.* In press.

Fleming, L.V. 1983. Succession of mycorrhizal fungi on birch: infection of seedlings planted around mature trees. *Pl. Soil*, **71**, 263–267.

Fleming, L.V., Deacon, J.W. & Last. F.T. 1986. Ectomycorrhizal succession in a Scottish birch wood. *Proc. European Symposium on Mycorrhizae, 1st*. Dijon: Institut National de Recherches Agronomiques. In press.

Frankland, J.C. 1981. Mechanisms in fungal successions. In: *The fungal community: its organisation and role in the ecosystem*, edited by D.T. Wicklow & G.C. Carroll, 403–426. New York: Marcel Dekker.

Gardner, J.N. & Malajczuk, N. 1985. Succession of ectomycorrhizal fungi associated with eucalypts on rehabilitated bauxite mines in South Western Australia. In: *Proc. N. American Conference Mycorrhizae, 6th*, edited by R. Molina, 265. Corvallis, OR: Oregon State University Press.

Giltrap, N.J. 1982. Production of polyphenol oxidases by ectomycorrhizal fungi with special reference to *Lactarius* spp. *Trans. Br. mycol. Soc.*, **78**, 75–81.

Grossnickle, S.C. & Reid, C.P.P. 1983. Ectomycorrhiza formation and root development of conifer seedlings on a high-elevation mine site. *Can. J. For. Res.*, **13**, 1145–1158.

Harley, J.L. 1971. Fungi in ecosystems. *J. Ecol.*, **59**, 653–668.

Harley, J.L. & Waid, J.S. 1955. A method of studying active mycelia on living roots and other surfaces in the soil. *Trans. Br. mycol. Soc.*, **38**, 104–118.

Harvey, A.E., Larsen, M.J. & Jurgensen, M.F. 1976. Distribution of ectomycorrhizae in a mature Douglas fir-larch forest soil in western Montana. *Forest Sci.*, **22**, 393–398.

Kirby, K.J. 1984. Scottish birchwoods and their conservation - a review. *Trans. bot. Soc. Edinb.*, **44**, 205–218.

Kropp, B.R. & Trappe, J.M. 1982. Ectomycorrhizal fungi of *Tsuga heterophylla*. *Mycologia*, **74**, 479–488.

Last, F.T. & Fleming, L.V. 1985. Factors affecting the occurrence of fruitbodies of fungi forming sheathing (ecto-) mycorrhizas with roots of trees. *Proc. Indian Acad. Sci. (Plant Sci.)*, **94**, 111–127.

Last, F.T., Pelham, J., Mason, P.A. & Ingleby, K. 1979. Influence of leaves on sporophore production by fungi forming sheathing mycorrhizas with *Betula* spp. *Nature, Lond.*, **280**, 168–169.

Last, F.T., Mason, P.A., Smith, R.I., Pelham, J., Bhoja Shetty, K.A. & Mahmood Hussain, A.M. 1981. Factors affecting the production of fruitbodies of *Amanita muscaria* in plantations of *Pinus patula*. *Proc. Indian Acad. Sci. (Plant Sci.)*, **90**, 91–98.

Last, F.T., Mason, P.A., Wilson, J. & Deacon, J.W. 1983. Fine roots and sheathing mycorrhizas: their form, function and dynamics. *Pl. Soil*, **71**, 9–21.

Last, F.T., Mason, P.A., Pelham, J. & Ingleby, K. 1984. Fruitbody production by sheathing mycorrhizal fungi: effects of 'host' genotypes and propagating soils. *For. Ecol. Manage.*, **9**, 221–227.

Last, F.T., Mason, P.A., Wilson, J., Ingleby, K., Munro, R.C., Fleming, L.V. & Deacon, J.W. 1985. 'Epidemiology' of sheathing (ecto-) mycorrhizas in unsterile soils: a case study of *Betula pendula*. *Proc. R. Soc. Edinb.*, **85B**, 299–315.

Linkins, A.E. & Antibus, R.K. 1981. Mycorrhizae of *Salix rotundifolia* in coastal arctic tundra. In: *Arctic and alpine mycology*, edited by G.A. Laursen & J. F. Ammirati, 507–531. Washington: University of Washington Press.

Marx, D. H. 1980. Ectomycorrhizal fungus inoculation: a tool for improving forestation practices. In: *Tropical mycorrhiza research*, edited by P. Mikola, 13–17. Oxford: Clarendon.

Mason, P.A. 1980. Aseptic synthesis of sheathing (ecto-) mycorrhizas. In: *Tissue culture methods for plant pathologists*, edited by D.S. Ingram & J.P. Helgeson, 173–178. Oxford: Blackwell Scientific.

Mason, P.A., Last, F.T., Pelham, J. & Ingleby, K. 1982. Ecology of some fungi associated with an ageing stand of birches (*Betula pendula* and *B. pubescens*). *For. Ecol. Manage.*, **4**, 19–39.

Mason, P.A., Wilson, J., Last, F.T. & Walker, C. 1983. The concept of succession in relation to the spread of sheathing mycorrhizal fungi on inoculated tree seedlings growing in unsterile soils. *Pl. Soil*, **71**, 247–256.

Miles, J. 1985. Soil in the ecosystem. In: *Ecological interactions in soil: plants, microbes and animals*, edited by A.H. Fitter, D. Atkinson, D.J. Read & M.B. Usher, 407–427. (British Ecological Society special publication 4.) Oxford: Blackwell Scientific.

Molina, R. & Trappe, J.M. 1982. Applied aspects of ectomycorrhizae. In: *Advances in agricultural microbiology*, edited by N.S. Subba Rao, 305–324. London: Butterworth Scientific.

Read, D.J., Francis, R. & Finlay, R.D. 1985. Mycorrhizal mycelia and nutrient cycling in plant communities. In: *Ecological interactions in soil: plants, microbes and animals*, edited by A.H. Fitter, D. Atkinson, D.J. Read & M.B. Usher, 193–217. (British Ecological Society special publication 4.) Oxford: Blackwell Scientific.

Richardson, M.J. 1970. Studies on *Russula emetica* and other agarics in a Scots pine plantation. *Trans. Br. mycol. Soc.*, **55**, 217–229.

Slankis, V. 1973. Hormonal relationships in mycorrhizal development. In: *Ectomycorrhizae: their ecology and physiology*, edited by G.C. Marks & T.T. Kozlowski, 232–298. New York: Academic Press.

Swift, M. J., Heal, O.W. & Anderson, J.M. 1979. *Decomposition in terrestrial ecosystems*. Oxford: Blackwell Scientific.

Trappe, J.M. 1962. Fungus associates of ecotrophic mycorrhizae. *Bot. Rev.*, **28**, 538–606.

Trappe, J.M. 1977. Selection of fungi for ectomycorrhizal inoculation in nurseries. *A. Rev. Phytopathol.*, **15**, 203–222.

Tyler, G. 1984. *Macrofungi of Swedish beech forest*. University of Lund.

Vogt, K.A., Grier, C.C., Meier, C.E. & Keyes, M.R. 1983a. Organic matter and nutrient dynamics in forest floor of young and mature *Abies amabilis* stands in western Washington, as affected by fine-root input. *Ecol. Monogr.*, **53**, 139–157.

Vogt, K.A., Moore, E.E., Vogt, D.J., Redlin, M.J. & Edmonds, R.L. 1983b. Conifer fine root and mycorrhizal root biomass within the forest floors of Douglas fir stands of different ages and site productivities. *Can. J. For. Res.*, **13**, 429–437.

Watling, R. 1981. Relationships between macromycetes and the development of higher plant communities. In: *The fungal community: its organisation and role in the ecosystem*, edited by D.T. Wicklow & G.C. Carroll, 427–458. New York: Marcel Dekker.

Watling, R. 1984a. Larger fungi around Kindrogan, Perthshire. *Trans. bot. Soc. Edinb.*, **44**, 237–259.

Watling, R. 1984b. Macrofungi of birchwoods. *Proc. R. Soc. Edinb.*, **85B**, 129–140.

Appendix 1. Specific names, including authorities, of all fungi
included in text (excluding those listed in Table 2)

Amanita crocea (Quel.) Kühn. and Romagn.
A. inaurata Secr.
A. muscaria (L. : Fr.) Hooker
A. rubescens ((Pers.) Fr.) S. F. Gray
A. vaginata (Bull. : Fr.) Vitt.
Amphinema byssoides (Pers. : Fr.) J. Erikss.
Cortinarius croceofolius Peck
Hebeloma populinum Romagnesi
H. versipelle (Fr.) Kumm.
Inocybe longicystis Atk.
Laccaria amethystea (Bull. : Merat) Murill
Lactarius rufus (Scop. : Fr.) Fr.
L. tabidus Fr.

L. turpis (Weinm.) Fr.
L. vietus (Fr.) Fr.
Paxillus involutus (Batsch. : Fr.) Fr.
Pisolithus tinctorius (Pers.) Coker and Couch
Rhizopogon luteolus Fr. & Nordh.
Russula aquosa Leclair
R. brevipes Pk.
R. emetica (Schaeff. : Fr.) S. F. Gray
R. fellea (Fr.) Fr.
R. mairei Sing.
R. scotica Pearson
Suillus cavipes (Opat.) Smith and Thiers
S. luteus (Fr.) S. F. Gray
Tricholoma columbetta (Fr.) Kummer

Ground flora and succession in commercial forests

M O HILL
Institute of Terrestrial Ecology, Bangor

1 Introduction

This paper describes the changes in ground flora induced by forestry in the uplands, emphasizing the long timescales and large spatial variations that are involved. Management options by means of which the forest manager may influence ground vegetation are outlined, considering both planted blocks and marginal habitats. Gaps in our knowledge are identified, and topics for further research are suggested.

Commercial forestry in Scotland generally starts with unplanted moorland, bog, heathland or heathy grassland. There are interesting exceptions to this generalization, such as afforestation of sand dunes and under-planting of uneconomic broadleaved woodlands; but the exceptions are almost all in the lowlands, and need not concern us here.

We are all aware that afforestation of unplanted ground is opposed, though not always simultaneously, by nature conservationists, landscape enthusiasts, hill walkers, grouse shooters and fishermen. Many of the arguments put forward by these people are based on a relatively narrow view of forestry, narrow both in time and in space. It is the business of the scientist to broaden the scope of the argument by putting the matter into a proper perspective.

2 Sources of data

In order to predict how vegetation will respond to various management options, the best source of information is direct experience based on long-term observation. For vegetation of planted forests in Britain, we are lacking in sources of such data from before 1940. From then on, there are a small number of long-term series of data, eg from Caeo Forest, south Wales, where observations date from 1944 (Hill & Jones 1978), J D Ovington's plots in southern England, where observations started in 1952 (Anderson 1979), and the Gisburn block of the Bowland Forest, a joint species trial started by the Forestry Commission (FC) and the Institute of Terrestrial Ecology (ITE), in 1955. A particularly notable series of observations is that started by ITE at Stonechest, just south of the Scottish border, in 1972 (Sykes *et al.* 1985).

In spite of these studies, we are seriously short of data based on long-term observation of particular sites. An alternative that can yield useful results is that of the chronosequence. When applied to Scottish forest vegetation, a chronosequence consists of a series of observations from supposedly similar sites that were planted at different dates. By comparing these sites and noting differences, patterns of vegetation change may be inferred. The method of the chronosequence is the classic one for documenting changes resulting from catastrophic events (fire, hurricane, landslip, etc) in natural vegetation. In the British context, the method has been applied with some success to succession in Sitka spruce (*Picea sitchensis*) plantations (Hill 1979) and to regeneration of birch (*Betula* spp.) scrub on moorland (Miles 1981).

The main difficulty with chronosequences is that they demand that the investigator has sound judgement as to what are, indeed, similar sites. Fortunately, various checks can be made. Detailed observations can be made on critical phases of vegetation change, for example on the phase immediately after clearfelling (Hill *et al.* 1984). It is also possible to check some of the theories that are derived by observation. Hill and Stevens (1981) had observed that many seeds germinating in forests after clearfelling are of species that seem unlikely to immigrate after the trees are cut down. This idea was confirmed by the observation that wind-borne seeds are largely confined to the superficial layer of conifer litter on the soil, whereas seeds of most other species are found in layers of the soil that were present before conifer litter started to accumulate (Figure 1).

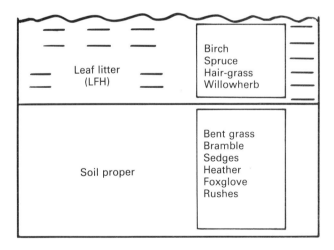

Figure 1. Position of buried viable seed in relation to the soil surface

Another kind of check that can be made is to see whether the pieces of information can be fitted together to make a coherent story. Such a story is sometimes called a word model, and it can be backed up by more quantitative models of particular aspects of the vegetation process. In particular, given a knowledge of certain species' power of spread and of their longevity as seed, it should be possible to predict the effects of various management practices on their abundance.

3 Vegetation changes in planted blocks

The vegetation changes that follow upland afforestation have been described at length elsewhere (Hill 1979, 1982). Some knowledge of these changes is necessary in order to evaluate the possible effects of differing management options. The long-term effect varies markedly from species to species (Table 1).

the west of Scotland in this habitat, and is very scarce or absent from other habitats in the west.

Fertilizer produces almost no qualitative effect on ground vegetation at this stage. It promotes the growth of plants that are already established, but does not lead to short-term changes, except in the presence of liming and heavy grazing (Milton 1940). Young forests are normally neither limed nor heavily grazed, so that fertilizer only helps to promote the growth of tussock grasses and dwarf shrubs that would increase anyway.

Table 1. Persistence of selected plant species in planted blocks of commercial forests (source: Hill 1978b)

	Scientific name	English name	Persistence in forest
	Agrostis capillaris	Common bent	Often abundant in clearcuts
	A. vinealis	Brown bent	Often abundant in clearcuts
D	Anthoxanthum odoratum	Sweet vernal-grass	Vanishes
I	Betula spp.	Birch	Generally increasing
D	Calluna vulgaris	Heather	Copious germination in clearcuts
	Carex binervis, C. pipulifera	Sedges	Locally abundant in clearcuts
I	Deschampsia flexuosa	Wavy-hair-grass	Often abundant in clearcuts
I	Digitalis purpurea	Foxglove	Locally abundant in clearcuts
I	Dryopteris dilatata	Broad buckler-fern	Abundant colonist after thinning
I	Epilobium angustifolium	Rosebay willowherb	Clearcuts on better soils
D	Erica tetralix	Cross-leaved heath	Scattered seedlings in clearcuts
D	Eriophorum angustifolium	Common cottongrass	Vanishes
D	E. vaginatum	Hare's-tail cottongrass	Scattered seedlings in clearcuts
D	Festuca ovina	Sheep's-fescue	Vanishes
	Galium saxatile	Heath bedstraw	Often abundant in clearcuts
	Juncus effusus	Soft rush	Copious regeneration in clearcuts
D	J. squarrosus	Heath rush	Scattered seelings in clearcuts
D	Molinia caerulea	Purple moor-grass	Dying out in planted blocks
D	Nardus stricta	Mat-grass	Vanishes
	Pteridium aquilinum	Bracken	Vanishes under Sitka spruce
I	Rubus fruticosus	Bramble	Rapid increase on better soils
I	Sorbus aucuparia	Rowan	Seedlings germinate in clearcuts
D	Scirpus cespitosus	Deergrass	Vanishes
	Vacinium myrtillus	Bilberry	Frequent to abundant

I increasing
D decreasing

3.1 Establishment to canopy closure (0–14 years)

The first major effects of afforestation are site preparation and cessation of sheep grazing. In Galloway, the usual result is a large increase of heather (Calluna vulgaris) and purple moor-grass (Molinia caerulea). Indeed, by the time that the trees are 5 years old, these species are normally dominant throughout the young forest. The same response is doubtless found elsewhere, though with a tendency for heather to be relatively more important in the east. Several common species of plant, such as deergrass (Scirpus cespitosus), heath rush (Juncus squarrosus) and mat-grass (Nardus stricta), rapidly decline.

Drainage and cessation of grazing are the main causes of the early increase in tussocky and shrubby species. Ploughing produces much less effect. Indeed, ground that is exposed by deep ploughing often remains bare for 5 years, becoming colonized by lichens and mosses. One species of moss, the rather attractive Polytrichum longisetum, has become widespread in

3.2 Canopy closure to clearfelling (14–55 years)

The effect of canopy closure depends strongly on the species that has been planted. Under Sitka spruce, all ground vegetation except mosses normally disappears; even mosses persist only in small amounts. A similar elimination can normally be observed under all species of conifer that cast a heavy shade, notably Norway spruce (Picea abies), Douglas fir (Pseudotsuga menziesii) and western hemlock (Tsuga heterophylla). Under pines (Pinus spp.) and larches (Larix spp.), the effect of canopy closure is harder to predict. There can sometimes be quite appreciable survival of ground vegetation, but, equally, there can often be almost no survival. Bracken (Pteridium aquilinum) is an interesting plant to observe at this stage. If it can survive the thicket stage under larch, it then becomes abundant in mature plantations, but it is quite often eliminated by larch thickets. On the other hand, small amounts of bracken almost always survive under pines, to increase again after thinning when more light reaches the forest floor.

The differences between the ground vegetation found under differing crop species are greatest shortly after canopy closure. For example, Ovington (1955) found very large differences between the vegetation under broadleaves and shade-casting conifers at 22 years. However, when the same plots were re-observed by Anderson (1979), 44 years after planting, the vegetation under all crop species resembled that which might be found in a native oakwood, and included bramble (*Rubus fruticosus*), bracken, creeping soft-grass (*Holcus mollis*) and bluebell (*Endymion non-scriptus*).

There were still marked effects of differing crop species. Bluebell was most plentiful under deciduous crops; wood-sorrel (*Oxalis acetosella*) was most plentiful under crops with thin litter; bracken and bramble were particularly abundant under Corsican pine (*Pinus nigra* var. *maritima*). Nevertheless, it was the similarity of the ground flora under differing crop species at this stage that was most impressive, not the differences.

Ovington's plots were on mineral soils in the English lowlands. The vegetation response to differing crop species on moors and in the uplands is more distinctive. Under densely shading crops such as Sitka spruce, there is often no appreciable ground vegetation at the time of clearfelling. In the lowlands, on the other hand, mature and fully thinned stands of Sitka spruce can support quite a rich ground vegetation. Upland plantations of pine and larch normally admit sufficient light to the forest floor to permit appreciable development of ground vegetation, with grasses (*Agrostis* spp., *Deschampsia* spp.), heather, broad buckler-fern (*Dryopteris dilatata*), bramble and bilberry (*Vaccinium myrtillus*) prominent, especially on extraction racks.

3.3 Clearfelling and replanting

Events following clearfelling depend rather precisely on the condition of the crop. If the stand was of good Sitka spruce, with no ground vegetation and little windthrow, then early regrowth of vegetation may be dominated by species that have lain dormant for a long time in the soil, notably heather, foxglove (*Digitalis purpurea*), rushes (*Juncus* spp.), sedges (*Carex* spp.) and gorse (*Ulex* spp.). Seeds of all these species can survive as buried seed throughout the dark phase of the rotation. Evidence from experiments (Kivilaan & Bandurski 1973; Toole & Brown 1946) and chronosequences (Peter 1893, 1894) suggests that buried seeds do not survive much beyond 80 years, so that, although they may persist through one rotation, they will not survive for 2 (Figure 2).

For other species which lack the potential to survive as buried seed, the presence or absence of a few vegetative individuals may be critical. Bracken, for example, commonly survives only along roads and rides, and may spread some way back into planted blocks from there. Wavy hair-grass (*Deschampsia flexuosa*), often notably abundant in areas that have been clearcut, has seeds which do not survive beyond one year. Unless a small population is already established at the time of clearfelling, the grass will be unlikely to spread extensively before canopy closure.

Seeds of conifers and birch are commonly present in large numbers in conifer litter at the time of clearfelling. They then germinate in the spring and early summer after clearance. Sitka spruce seed is shed irregularly between October and March (Brown & Neustein 1972), so that some seed is likely to be present on the forest floor if the stand is felled at any time except late summer. Neither birch seed nor spruce seed survives for more than a year once shed.

Intermediate between the types of seed with long and short longevity are those that appear not to survive through a rotation, but which can survive for about 20 years. The 2 common species of bent, *Agrostis capillaris* and *A. vinealis*, are in this category, having large persistent seed banks (Thompson & Grime 1979) but not apparently surviving through to the end of a full forest rotation (Hill & Stevens 1981). Probably also belonging to this intermediate category are bird-dispersed species such as bilberry, bramble, raspberry (*Rubus idaeus*) and rowan (*Sorbus aucuparia*). These seeds are gradually introduced to the forest floor by defecation of birds roosting in the tree tops. Inference of their longevity is therefore difficult. Analogy with the bird-dispersed pin cherry (*Prunus pensylvanica*), which was studied in North America by Marks (1974), suggests that potential survival for about 40 years is likely.

Events following clearfelling depend, therefore, on a complex interplay of factors, of which one of the most important is whether populations can establish in the short window of time, say 15 years, before the canopy closes again. Also of great importance is the type of soil. On poorer upland soils, coarse weedy species such as bramble and rosebay willowherb (*Epilobium angustifolium*) make relatively poor growth. Grasses, heather, sedges and rushes then predominate, even when seed sources for the coarse weeds are present. The level of grazing also has a large effect. In Beddgelert Forest, north Wales, exclusion of sheep resulted in a much more rapid spread of wavy hair-grass than in places where sheep could nibble off the inflorescences.

4 Vegetation changes outside planted blocks

Although planted blocks occupy most of the land area in forests, other types of habitat are more important for survival of interesting species. Hill (1978a) examined the occurrence of plant species throughout the area of 2 completely forested 1 km squares in north Wales, and came to the conclusion that roadsides were the most important habitat for survival of plant species. Bogs, streamsides and unplanted blocks made a significant additional contribution, but rides contributed little because they were occupied by heather and tussocky coarse grasses.

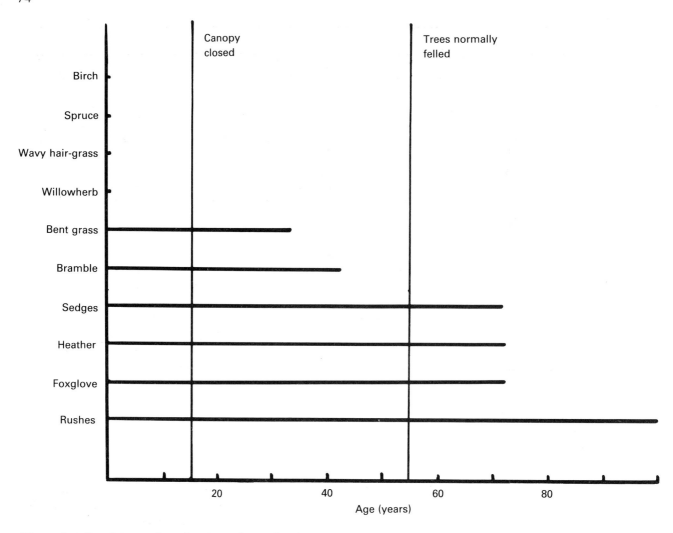

Figure 2. Seed longevity of selected species in relation to the length of a typical forest rotation

Roads do not, in fact, occupy a particularly large proportion of the total area in forests. Evans (1978) studied 5 Forestry Commission forests and estimated that 5% of their area was occupied by roads. Most of the interesting plant species grew on the verges, which accounted for only 1.6% of the forest area. The remaining 3.4% was occupied by banks, ditches and the road surface itself.

Streams and lakes can also contribute to the floristic diversity of forested areas, and the value of leaving unplanted margins is now generally appreciated. Goldsmith (1981) studied streams and lakes in a forested part of Galloway, and showed that, if the unplanted zone beside a stream is less than 3 m wide, very few species survived. Full floristic diversity was achieved with a 6 m margin, and marginal zones greater than 10 m wide could provide useful grazing for deer and other animals.

Unplanted areas within large forested blocks arise from various causes. Some are hilltops too high to plant, others are bogs where drainage would be costly, scree slopes where trees would grow too poorly, or smallholdings with a few fields. These areas often provide habitats for interesting plants or a supply of berries for birds. They are, however, unlikely to have much influence on the forest proper, unless they contain invasive and readily dispersed species such as birch, bramble and rowan.

5 Management options in relation to vegetation
5.1 Management of areas planted with trees
The vegetation of planted blocks generally has little intrinsic interest, even during the light phase between clearfelling and canopy closure. In this respect, it resembles the vegetation of the moors and grassland that had occupied the ground before afforestation. It follows that forest management of planted blocks should be directed not towards influencing vegetation as such, but towards primary objectives whose achievement may be affected by vegetation. The most notable of these objectives are crop establishment in the presence of weeds, maintenance of site fertility, creation of suitable habitats for ruminants and birds, and improvement of the visual impact of felling coupes and restocked areas.

The weed problem varies enormously from site to site. On poorer soils, heather is likely to be the only serious

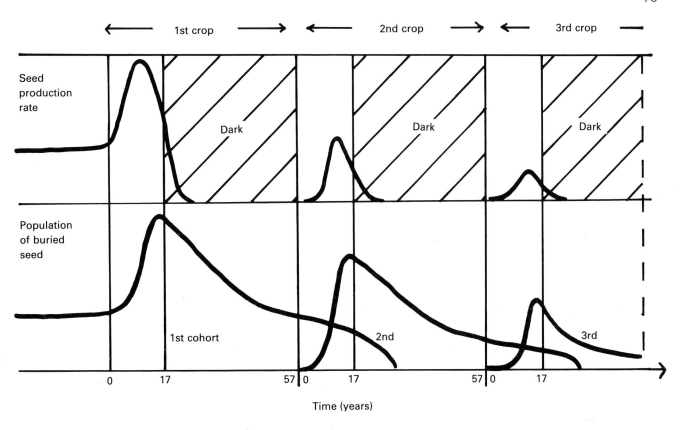

Figure 3. *Hypothetical pattern of decline in heather population over 3 crop rotations*

weed. In the first rotation, it is generally controlled by herbicide. The effect on the appearance of the site is dismal, but the trees fairly quickly close their canopy thereafter. It is interesting to speculate as to whether there will be an appreciable heather problem in later rotations (Figure 3). At the beginning of a first rotation on heathland, the soil contains buried viable seed from several decades of heather growth. Depending on the longevity of heather seed (currently unknown but probably more than 50 years), much more heather may germinate when the first crop is clearfelled than when the second crop is cleared. Indeed, with a timely herbicide application, very little heather seed may be shed between the end of the first rotation and closure of the canopy of the successor crop.

On fertile lowland sites, it is necessary to replant as quickly as possible after clearfelling, if weeds are not to make tree establishment difficult. On upland sites, there is much more flexibility, and there is a possibility that delayed replanting could serve some purpose in wildlife management. Some years ago, I was told by a forest manager working for Buccleuch Estates that delayed replanting could help in reducing damage to young trees by roe deer.

On the question of whether ground vegetation can have a significant effect in maintaining site fertility, there is little information. In some contexts, it could serve a useful purpose in retaining nitrogen in the ecosystem, as suggested by Marks (1974). For phosphorus retention, it is probably irrelevant, because

mineralized phosphorus is adsorbed in the top layers of the soil. If so, then ground vegetation is of little advantage to the forester in upland Britain, where nutrient limitation of crop growth is generally due to shortage of phosphorus, not nitrogen.

One of the major management options that can affect vegetation is the choice between whole-tree harvesting, with lop and top removed from the site, and conventional methods of felling, in which lop and top, often called 'brash', is left on the site to decompose. Brash is certainly ugly, and it delays regrowth of ground vegetation. Furthermore, it hinders replanting. If visual amenity is considered to be of high priority at a site, then whole-tree harvesting is to be preferred. At present, there is no market for chipped branches, so that even with whole-tree harvesting, the brash must be disposed of at the roadside. This creates a further blot on the landscape, and one which is all too apparent to visitors, because it is beside the roads along which they will walk. The best policy would be to burn this superfluous material. In many other countries it is burnt; why not in Britain?

The smothering effect of brash is less with species other than Sitka spruce, so that 'greening up' of clearfelled sites is quicker. Hardwood twigs decompose much faster than conifer brash. Anecdotal evidence suggests that Sitka spruce brash is not only the most copious but also the least readily decomposed of all the conifer residues that one normally encounters in Britain. If the greening-up of the site after a short rotation is deemed to be desirable, Sitka spruce should be either avoided or harvested as whole trees.

5.2 Management of whole forests

We are still remarkably ignorant about the survival and spread of plant species at the landscape scale. Many animals, by contrast, are well known to range over the landscape, so that this is the natural scale at which to consider them, but the landscape scale is undoubtedly relevant also to some plant species. Birch seeds can be carried over several hundred metres by strong winds. However, in a cleared Sitka spruce plantation with a row of standing birches along the road, birch regeneration may be much reduced at a distance of only 100 m from the road.

Afforested areas are necessarily different from the rangelands that they have replaced. Fire is eliminated, grazing reduced and water supplies to marshes diverted. These influences are inimical to small and specialized wild plants of open ground. In lowland forests on sandy ground, vegetation along forest edges is commonly kept open by harrowing. Such semi-open communities are of great floristic interest. Similar effects can be achieved in the uplands by mowing verges and by occasional, but not too frequent, regrading of roads.

Nevertheless, the forest environment is generally one that favours development of scrub, ericoid shrubs and tall grasses. Interesting small plants will survive chiefly where there are either special topographic features, such as rivers or rocky bluffs, or where there is active management.

Is scrub development desirable? Steele and Balfour (1979) have suggested planting 10–20 ha nature conservation blocks along watercourses, using birch, hazel (*Corylus avellana*) and alder (*Alnus glutinosa*). These blocks would be left as permanent features, and would occupy 5% of the forest area. Such a policy, although interesting, would be costly. Broadleaved plantations would get some of the best ground. On the other hand, the worst ground often has greatest topographic variation, so that the best gains in natural history interest may result from leaving the worst ground unplanted.

Miles and Kinnaird (1979a, b) have described methods of promoting scrub regeneration on moorland, but there is no necessity to confine this activity to the first rotation. In most cleared forest plantations, regeneration of trees occurs naturally. It would ordinarily be sufficient not to replant selected areas for their second rotation and to leave nature to take its course.

Unfortunately, there is one important respect in which naturally regenerating vegetation can no longer be trusted. This is because of the spread of rhododendron (*Rhododendron ponticum*). In western Britain, rho-

dodendron can be expected soon to occupy large areas of woodland, moorland and poor grassland (Shaw 1984). Traditional land use is incapable of excluding it, and it threatens to reduce large areas to an impenetrable thicket.

The rhododendron problem is potentially most serious in woodlands and wooded ravines in the west. Western ravines are notable as a habitat for bryophytes, especially for the rare Atlantic hepatics that are a unique feature of the British and Irish flora (Ratcliffe 1968). There can be no doubt that dense rhododendron along ravine-sides would shade out many of the best bryophyte habitats. Forestry could serve as a valuable adjunct to management for conservation in such places. Provided that the forest manager maintains a policy of rhododendron exclusion, interesting broadleaved woodlands and ravines can be conserved within a matrix of commercial plantations. However, if the matrix is moorland or open hill, and if rhododendron is starting to invade, then exclusion of rhododendron from woodlands and ravines will be almost impossible.

6 Conclusions and recommendations for research

Most of the management recommendations that are made above are non-controversial, and agree with the Forestry Commission's recent recommendations on wildlife conservation in restocked areas (Low 1985). At the present time, these ideas are beginning to be put into practice in upland north Wales, and doubtless also in parts of Scotland. For example, in Beddgelert Forest, north Wales, the Commission have drawn up a restocking plan which assigns 6% of the land area to 'long-term forest structure'. This long-term structure includes natural scrub, planted hardwoods, mature conifers and open water.

While it is gratifying to see the results of conservation-orientated research from the past decade being put into practice so rapidly, some important questions remain unanswered. Particularly interesting is the question of the overall survival and spread of plant populations in forested areas. Forests are far more dynamic than the grasslands and shrublands that they have replaced. In grasslands, individual clones may persist for centuries or millenia. In forest plantations, plant populations must constantly be on the move. So we need an understanding of the dynamics of plant populations at the landscape scale. How far do plants spread from refuges by roads, by streams and in hardwood clumps? How significant are such landscape features in the maintenance of plant populations in the longer term? To answer these questions, we require a combination of observations on permanently marked and repeated surveys of a few selected forests.

At a more practical level, we still need better documentation of the response of vegetation to differing crop species and site types, especially in the period after clearfelling. Events after clearfelling depend not only on the vegetation present under the crop when it was felled, but also on the rate of litter breakdown and nutrient release from the forest floor, and on the rate of disappearance of woody harvesting residues. All of these factors depend on the preceding species of crop.

Finally, it is worth giving serious consideration to the question of whether conifer plantations might be used by nature conservationists to provide *cordon sanitaire* against invasion by rhododendron. Does the spread of rhododendron adversely affect Atlantic bryophtes? If it does, can rhododendron be excluded from sensitive areas by suitably managed conifer forests?

7 Summary
Commercial forest plantations are large in area and take about a century to attain a pattern of age classes approximating to a normal forest. Effects of forest management on the non-crop vegetation need to be considered over commensurate areas and timescales. Within planted blocks, all vascular plants are eliminated during the thicket stage by Sitka spruce, and also by other spruces, firs and western hemlock. Survival of some vascular plants under larch and pine is normal. In mature upland plantations, there is often quite appreciable vegetation cover under larch and pine, but almost none under the crop species that cast heavier shade. After clearfelling, vegetation regrowth can be rapid, especially if the amount of brash is not excessive. Depending on the state of the ground vegetation at the time of clearfelling, the source of propagules may be existing vegetation or buried viable seed.

Vegetation within planted blocks is of little intrinsic value and its management should be considered in relation to crop establishment, wildlife and visual amenity. Most of the more interesting vegetation in forests is found along roads and streams. The value of leaving good unplanted margins has now been widely appreciated. There is a general tendency for scrub to develop in afforested areas. Such scrub should be encouraged. Parts of the forest that will not yield a commercial return of timber should be allowed to develop naturally.

Spread of rhododendron is a serious threat to good botanical habitats in western Scotland. The possibility of using forestry as a means of excluding rhododendron from threatened areas deserves consideration from nature conservationists.

8 Acknowledgements
I am grateful to the Nature Conservancy Council for funding much of the fieldwork on which this paper is based (NERC/NCC contract no. F3/03/78).

9 References
Anderson, M.A. 1979. The development of plant habitats under exotic forest crops. In: *Ecology and design in amenity land management*, edited by S.E. Wright & G.P. Buckley, 87–108. (Proceedings of conference held at Wye College). Wye: Wye College.

Brown, J.M.B. & Neustein, S.A. 1972. Natural regeneration of conifers in the British Isles. In: *Conifers in the British Isles*, 29–39. London: Royal Horticultural Society.

Evans, D.F. 1978. *Roads as a habitat for wild plants in coniferous plantations*. (CST report no. 170.) Banbury: Nature Conservancy Council.

Goldsmith, F.B., ed. 1981. *The afforestation of the uplands: the botanical interest of areas left unplanted*. (Discussion Papers in Conservation no. 35.) London: University College.

Hill, M.O. 1978a. *Comparison of the flora of forested and un-afforested kilometre squares on the Hiraethog Moors, Clwyd*. (CST report no. 168.) Banbury: Nature Conservancy Council.

Hill, M.O. 1978b. *Notes on plant species and their habitats in British upland forests*. (CST report no. 169.) Banbury: Nature Conservancy Council.

Hill, M.O. 1979. The development of a flora in even-aged plantations. In: *The ecology of even-aged forest plantations*, edited by E.D. Ford, D.C. Malcolm & J. Atterson, 175–192. Cambridge: Institute of Terrestrial Ecology.

Hill, M.O. 1982. Plants in woodlands. In: *Forestry and conservation*, edited by E.H.M. Harris, 56–68. Tring: Royal Forestry Society.

Hill, M.O. & Jones, E.W. 1978. Vegetation changes resulting from afforestation of rough grazings in Caeo Forest, south Wales. *J. Ecol.*, **66,** 433–456.

Hill, M.O. & Stevens, P.A. 1981. The density of viable seed in soils of forest plantations in upland Britain. *J. Ecol.*, **69,** 693–709.

Hill, M.O., Hornung, M., Evans, D.F., Stevens, P.A., Adamson, J.K. & Bell, S.A. 1984. The effects of clear-felling plantation forests. *Annu. Rep. Inst. terr. Ecol. 1983*, 9–11.

Kivilaan, A. & Bandurski, R.S. 1973. The ninety-year period for Dr. Beal's seed viability experiment. *Am. J. Bot.*, **60,** 140–145.

Low, A.J. 1985. *Guide to upland restocking practice*. (Forestry Commission leaflet no. 84.) London: HMSO.

Marks, P.L. 1974. The role of pin cherry (*Prunus pensylvanica* L.) in the maintenance of stability in northern hardwood ecosystems. *Ecol. Monogr.*, **44,** 73–88.

Miles, J. 1981. *Effect of birch on moorlands*. Cambridge: Institute of Terrestrial Ecology.

Miles, J. & Kinnaird, J.W. 1979a. The establishment and regeneration of birch, juniper and Scots pine in the Scottish Highlands. *Scott. For.*, **33,** 102–119.

Miles, J. & Kinnaird, J.W. 1979b. Grazing: with particular reference to birch, juniper and Scots pine in the Scottish Highlands. *Scott. For.*, **33,** 280–289.

Milton, W.E.J. 1940. The effect of manuring, grazing and cutting on the yield, botanical and chemical composition of natural hill pastures. *J. Ecol.*, **28,** 326–356.

Ovington, J.D. 1955. Studies of the development of woodland conditions under different trees. III. The ground flora. *J. Ecol.*, **43,** 1–21.

Peter, A. 1893. Kulturversuche mit 'ruhenden' Samen. *Nachr. Ges. Wiss. Göttingen*, **17,** 673–691.

Peter, A. 1894. Kulturversuche mit 'ruhenden' Samen. II. Mittheilung. *Nachr. Ges. Wiss. Göttingen, math-phys. Klasse*, **4,** 373–393.

Ratcliffe, D.A. 1968. An ecological account of Atlantic bryophytes in the British Isles. *New Phytol.*, **67,** 365–439.

Shaw, M.W. 1984. *Rhododendron ponticum* – ecological reasons for the success of an alien species in Britain and features that may assist in its control. *Asp. appl. Biol.*, **5,** 231–242.

Steele, R.C. & Balfour, J. 1979. Nature conservation in upland forestry – objectives and strategy. In: *Forestry and farming in upland Britain*, compiled by J.M.M. Cunningham & D.T. Seal, 161–192. (Forestry Commission occasional paper no. 6.) Penicuik: Hill Farming Research Organisation.

Sykes, J.M., Lowe, V.P.W. & Briggs, D.R. 1985. Changes in plants and animals in the first 10 years after upland afforestation. *Annu. Rep. Inst. terr. Ecol. 1984*, 16–21.

Thompson, K. & Grime, J.P. 1979. Seasonal variation in the seed banks of herbaceous species in ten contrasting habitats. *J. Ecol.*, **67**, 893–921.

Toole, E.H. & Brown, E. 1946. Final results of the Duvel buried seed experiment. *J. agric. Res.*, **72**, 201–210.

The ecology of the pine beauty moth in commercial woods in Scotland

A D WATT
Institute of Terrestrial Ecology, Edinburgh

1 Introduction

The pine beauty moth (*Panolis flammea*) is a noctuid which occurs throughout the UK, Scandinavia and the rest of Europe. Scots pine (*Pinus sylvestris*) is its natural host and outbreaks of the moth occur on Scots pine on the continent. In Scotland, it is a pest of lodgepole pine (*Pinus contorta*), but no outbreaks have been recorded there on Scots pine. This paper is concerned with the factors which influence the temporal and spatial population dynamics of the pine beauty moth in commercial pinewoods in Scotland, and discusses conclusions reached from research in progress.

2 Temporal dynamics of pine beauty moth

In 1976, 120 ha of lodgepole pine were defoliated and killed by the pine beauty moth (Stoakley 1979, 1981). In the next 5 years, another 200 ha were destroyed and 10 000 ha were sprayed with insecticide. Outbreaks occurred in areas as far apart as Naver Forest (Highland Region) and Bareagle Forest (Dumfries and Galloway Region). Between 1982 and 1983, no further control measures were needed, but 2 serious outbreaks occurred in Highland Region in 1984. In 1985, 4700 ha were sprayed and there were firm indications from population assessments in 1985 that further control would be necessary in 1986. It is now clear that the moth poses a serious threat to the successful growing of lodgepole pine in Scotland. Indeed, it is probable that outbreaks did not occur earlier only because lodgepole pine was not widely planted in Scotland until the late 1950s and early 1960s (Lines 1976) and was not susceptible before the early 1970s.

The numbers of pupae at one site, the Elchies block of Speyside Forest, over a 9-year period are shown in Figure 1. This population was sprayed with fenitrothion in 1979 (Stoakley 1981) but started to increase in size immediately thereafter. However, the population trend since 1979 has been rather erratic; numbers increased by varying degrees in 4 years but declined in 2 years, most notably in 1985. Elsewhere, as mentioned above, the pine beauty increased rapidly after control operations in 1977–79 to outbreak levels in 1984–85.

The variability in the moth's performance from one year to the next is demonstrated by the survivorship curves shown in Figure 2. In 1984, the population in a study plot in the North Dalchork block of Shin Forest (Highland Region) showed a fecundity of 123 eggs per female and the mortality in the successive stages was low at 56.5% (Barbour 1985). However, in Elchies in 1985, the fecundity was only 35 eggs per female, and the mortality in the subsequent stages was much higher at 99.3%. A number of factors could be responsible for these different patterns of fecundity and mortality. These factors include host plant condition, natural enemies, competition, and weather acting directly or indirectly through other factors. They are discussed below, using North Dalchork 1984 and Elchies 1985 as examples.

2.1 Host plant condition

Host plant condition may be defined as the level of nitrogen and other indicators of the nutrient content of plant foliage, and tannins or other chemicals which are known to be detrimental to some insect herbivores. Changes in host plant condition are thought to be responsible for different temporal patterns of population behaviour, from irregular eruptions to regular cycles (Rhoades 1983; White 1984). White (1969, 1974), for example, postulated that when plants are stressed they become a better source of food for insect herbivores because stress, usually caused by water shortage or waterlogging, results in an increase

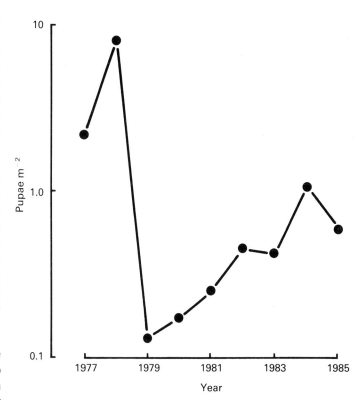

Figure 1. The number of pine beauty moth pupae m^{-2} *in the Elchies block of Speyside Forest (an insecticidal spraying operation was done in 1979) (source: D A Barbour & J T Stoakley pers. comm.)*

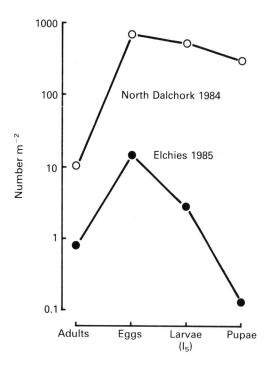

Figure 2. *Survival of 2 contrasting generations of the pine beauty moth at North Dalchork (Shin) 1984 and Elchies (Speyside) 1985 (source: Barbour 1985; original data)*

in the amount of nitrogen available for immature herbivorous insects. White (1974) found that certain insect populations fluctuated in accordance with a stress index which was a measure of winter waterlogging and summer drought. When a similar exercise was done for the pine beauty population in Elchies, population growth was not found to be correlated with January–March waterlogging and April–June drought when these 2 factors were considered together (Watt 1986). However, a much better correlation was found between population growth and late spring–early summer drought alone (Figure 3): population growth was highest in years when rainfall amounts were low. Is this correlation due to the effect of drought stress on plant nitrogen, and hence on insect survival?

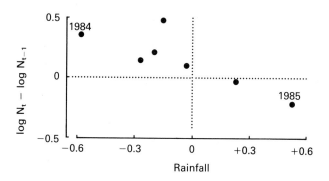

Figure 3. *The relationship between the population rate of increase of pine beauty moth in Elchies (R = log N_t-log N_{t-1}) and the deviation from average of rainfall in April, May and June at Glenlivet (source: original data)*

To examine the role of plant condition further, chemical analyses of pine foliage were done in Elchies during the feeding period of larvae from 1983 to 1985. Also, in 1984 and 1985, the effects of host plant condition and natural enemies were examined by using cages to exclude natural enemies. The results show that nitrogen levels in the current year's needles did not vary significantly even between years such as 1983, when the 'stress index' was low, and 1984, when it was high (Figure 4).

Larval mortality in the absence of natural enemies was measured in 2 contrasting years, ie 1984 and 1985, which had even higher rainfall than 1983 in April, May and June. Larval mortality was 32% in 1984 and 29% in 1985. From this evidence, it may be concluded that host plant condition plays no significant role in the temporal dynamics of the pine beauty moth. One possible exception is that sublethal levels of insect damage may cause a reduction in host plant quality (as found elsewhere, eg Rhoades 1983). Although herbivore-induced plant defences (or merely reactions) cannot prevent moth outbreaks, it is possible that they may extend the time between outbreaks.

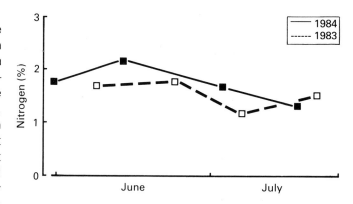

Figure 4. *The nitrogen content of the current year's growth of lodgepole pine in Elchies, 1983 and 1984 (source: original data)*

2.2 Natural enemies

A variety of natural enemies feed on the different stages of the pine beauty moth (Table 1). Parasitism by ichneumonid and braconid wasps and tachinid flies has been recorded at both low and outbreak densities. However, the proportion of moth larvae parasitized each year does not appear to increase as moth numbers rise. At North Dalchork, for example, parasitism between 1981 and 1984 never exceeded 7%, and was only 2.7% in 1984 when the average number of larvae per tree was 1700 (Barbour 1985). In contrast, parasitism in Elchies in 1984 and 1985 was 48% and 50% when larval numbers were 42.8 and 9.4 per tree respectively. It is as yet unclear whether these differences were site-related or whether parasites are generally more effective at low densities of the pine beauty moth.

Table 1. Natural enemies of pine beauty moth recorded, up to 1985, in Scotland (source: Barbour 1985; Stoakley 1979; H Crick pers. comm.; R H Dennis pers. comm.; original observations)

i. Parasites

    Aphanistes xanthopus (Ichneumonid, pupal parasite)
    Banchus hastator (Ichneumonid, pupal parasite)
    Zele albiditarsus (Braconid, pupal parasite)
    Ichneumon septentrionalis (Ichneumonid, pupal parasite)
    Therion circumflexum (Ichneumonid, pupal parasite)
    Meteorus spp. (Braconid, larval parasites)
    Ernestia spp. (Tachinid, pupal parasites)

ii. Predators

    Redwing (*Turdus iliacus*) (pupal predator)
    Fieldfare (*Turdus pilaris*) (pupal predator)
    Robin (*Erithacus rubecula*) (pupal predator)
    Raven (*Corvus corax*) (pupal predator)
    Great tit (*Parus major*) (adult & larval predator)
    Coal tit (*Parus ater*) (adult & larval predator)

iii. Fungi

    Isaria farinosa

iv. Viruses

    Panolis flammea NPV (nuclear polyhedrosis virus)

Unlike the effect of parasitism, the mortality caused by fungal and viral diseases has been found to be directly proportional to the density of the moth. For example, the number of diseased pupae at North Dalchork rose steadily from 3% in 1981 when there were 100.6 larvae per tree to 46% in 1984 when 1700 larvae per tree were found (Barbour 1985). Disease mortality was clearly density-dependent. However, it has never been found to reach a level high enough to prevent the moth from destroying its host plant.

The role of specific predators in the population dynamics of the pine beauty is poorly understood. However, life table and predator exclusion studies have given an indication of the level of predation at different stages of the life cycle. Predation during the egg and early larval instars, for example, has been studied with the aid of predator exclusion cages placed over individual branches. During the egg laying period, eggs were taken from heavily infested trees and placed, at known densities, within these cages. The cages were later examined and the development, growth and mortality of the larvae within each cage noted. In 1985, 60 cages were placed on lodgepole pine in Elchies. The mean level of survival to the third instar was 71%.

Precisely comparable figures for natural populations could not be obtained because it is difficult to assess density in the first 3 larval instars. The mean level of survival to the start of the fourth instar in the natural population in 1985 was 52%. Therefore, predation during the egg and larval stages in that year was less than 20%. Predation in subsequent stages could only be assessed by natural population counts. While most mortality in the late larval stages may be attributable to predation, some caution is needed in interpretation because there are few causes of mortality whose impact can be separately assessed by population counts alone. Two such causes of mortality are larval starvation and failure to find a suitable pupation site. Returning to the 1985 example, it was found that, although mortality due to predation was less than 20% in the egg and early larval instars, it reached 61% in the fourth instar alone and then soared to 96% in the fifth instar and pre-pupal stage. Such high losses of older larvae are unusual but they have been encountered before, at Borgie (Naver Forest) in 1981 (Barbour 1985). A contrasting example is shown in Figure 2, North Dalchork 1984, where the egg to pupal mortality was 56.5% compared to 99.3% at Elchies in 1985. It is notable that, unlike disease but like parasitism, the level of predation has not been found to be density-dependent.

2.3 Intraspecific competition

Intraspecific competition clearly plays an important role in unsprayed outbreaks through larval starvation. However, there is no indication that competition exerts any significant effect on reproduction and survival in the years prior to an outbreak. In one of the examples given above, North Dalchork 1984, when there were on average 1700 larvae per tree, mortality attributable to both predation and starvation was only 56.5%. Similarly, there appears to be no reduction in the fecundity of the moth as its population density increases, at least until widespread defoliation occurs. Even then, the number of eggs laid in a defoliated area appears to be largely determined by moth dispersal (see below).

2.4 Weather

It may be concluded from recent research that the numbers of pine beauty moths are limited by the availability of its food resource, and that this limitation is only felt when there is substantial damage to the host plant. There is considerable variation in fecundity and mortality at different stages of the life cycle between different years, but little of this variation is related to the density of the moth. So, although pine beauty moth outbreaks are not everywhere as frequent as might be expected, density-dependent regulation does not appear to be the reason.

The remaining possibilities are that populations behave in an endemic/epidemic manner or that density-independent factors act to prevent or delay outbreaks. The density-independent action of weather in particular is now known to play a major role in pine beauty moth population dynamics. The phenology of the moth is such that critical parts of its life cycle occur when the year-to-year variation in the weather is large. In particular, adult emergence and egg laying are vulnerable to the weather in March, April and early May.

Adult emergence is dependent on temperature. Figure 5 shows the emergence of adults at North Dalchork in 1985. Emergence started in early April but was interrupted by cold weather on 10–15 April. Interrup-

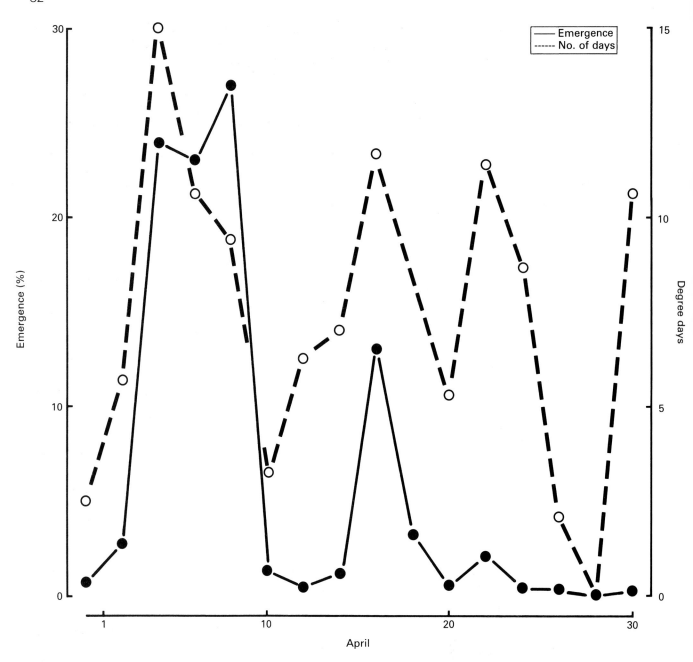

Figure 5. *The emergence of pine beauty moth adults at one site in North Dalchork in 1985 and the number of degree days accumulated over 7°C at Lairg (each point is the sum of 2 consecutive nights' catches or day degrees (source: S R Leather & A D Watt unpubl.)*

tions in emergence, and cold weather after emergence are both likely to cause a delay in mating, and this delay in turn is known to affect the pattern of egg production and the fertility of the eggs laid (Leather *et al.* 1986). Poor weather is also likely to affect adult mortality, and any decrease in adult longevity will result in a disproportionate effect on moths which have experienced a delay in mating (because of their different pattern of egg laying). The result is that the moth's fecundity is lower in cool springs than in warm springs (Figure 6).

Very little is known as yet about the effect of weather at other stages of the life cycle. The levels of parasitism and disease, for example, appear to be unrelated to weather conditions, even though correlations have been noted in other studies. However, it may be that predation of older larvae and pre-pupae is more severe during cool summers because such weather causes larval development to be extended, and therefore makes the insect vulnerable to predation for a protracted period. This possibility is supported by the fact that the unusually high level of predation of older larvae and pre-pupae in Elchies 1985 occurred during an unusually cool summer.

The pine beauty moth has now been shown to be capable of rapid population growth, so rapid that in some forests control measures have been required twice in the last 7–8 years. Elsewhere, on the other

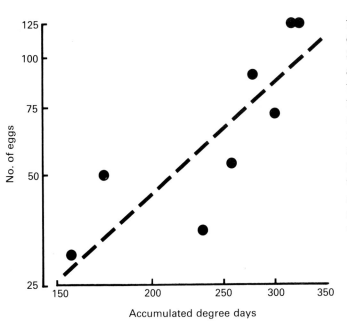

Figure 6. The relationship between the fecundity of pine beauty moth and day degrees accumulated above 7°C at North Dalchork (1981–85) and Elchies (1983–85) (source: Leather et al. 1986; original data)

hand, its density has remained below outbreak levels. Some understanding of this species' population dynamics has been gained by looking at temporal patterns of abundance but, given the differences in population behaviour between, and even within, forest blocks, it is also appropriate that spatial patterns of abundance should be studied.

3 Spatial dynamics of pine beauty moth
Two aspects of the spatial dynamics of a forest pest are important. First, are outbreaks more likely to start in some places than in others and, if so, can we explain why and then predict which sites are at risk? Second, when an outbreak has started, how far and how fast is it likely to spread?

3.1 Soil type
Forest entomologists have often tried to identify areas at risk from pest attack. 'Site hazard rating' systems have been developed for coleopterous, hemipterous and lepidopterous pests (eg Berryman & Stark 1985). It was quickly noted that outbreaks of the pine beauty moth in the early stages were associated with lodgepole pine growing on deep unflushed peat (Stoakley 1977). Moreover, it was suggested that this association was because trees growing on deep peat are 'stressed', and therefore are a better food source for the larvae. This suggestion was largely prompted by White's (1974) convincing evidence for the effect of soil conditions and plant stress on the population dynamics of the looper *Selidosema suavis* on Monterey pine (*Pinus radiata*) in New Zealand.

Therefore, in 1983, a series of experiments was started to see whether soil type had any influence on

the population biology of the pine beauty moth. These experiments were set up in the Elchies block of Speyside Forest because an outbreak developed in an area of deep unflushed peat in that block in 1978. Two techniques were used: (i) population monitoring and the construction of life tables, and (ii) predator exclusion experiments. For both these approaches, treatments were set up in areas of deep peat and ironpan soils. In 1983 and 1984, populations were monitored on artificially infested trees, but in 1985 observations were made on the natural population. The predator exclusion experiments were done with single branch cages placed within the top 5 whorls of trees 23–26 years old.

No significant differences were found in the population development of pine beauty moth on lodgepole pine growing in different soils between 1983 and 1985, either in exposed or caged populations (Watt 1985, 1986). Therefore, the observed outbreak behaviour of the moth in areas of deep unflushed peat does not appear to be the result of any improvement in pine foliage quality associated with deep peat. The tendency for outbreaks to develop on deep peat must be due to some other factor. It may be that pupal survival is greater in deep peat. Leather (1984) found that soil and peat were equally good pupal substrates, but that lodgepole pine needle litter was significantly better than either. As the needle litter layer is deeper and more persistent on deep peats than on sandy mineral soils (Blatchford 1978), and because pupation occurs at the needle litter/soil interface, pupal survival is likely to be greater in deep peat areas.

Alternatively, adult emergence from deep soils may be better synchronized with the development of the host plant, or adult moths may lay their eggs preferentially on trees growing on deep peat. A further possibility is that some trees in deep peat act as a 'sink', 'collecting' moths from surrounding areas because of their topography, associated temperature profiles and the wind patterns they experience. Greenbank *et al.* (1980) described one way how this may occur for the spruce budworm (*Choristoneura fumiferana*) in Canada. Moth dispersal in New Brunswick mainly follows the south-west to north-east direction of the prevailing wind. Moths tend to collect in the north central highlands of New Brunswick where decreasing night temperatures limit both the emigration of local moths and the re-emigration of invading individuals. There is, unfortunately, very little evidence concerning any of these possibilities for the pine beauty moth.

At present, then, certain areas of lodgepole pine can be said to be more at risk from pine beauty moth attack than others, but there is no clear reason why.

3.2 Host plant species
To try to explain why pine beauty outbreaks are frequent on lodgepole pine, which is a North American species, yet absent from Scots pine (Barbour 1986a),

which is a native host, natural and caged (from which natural enemies were excluded) populations of the moth were monitored in Scots pine as well as in lodgepole pine in 1984 and 1985. The exclusion experiments clearly showed that the survival of caterpillars was slightly (though not significantly) higher on Scots pine than on lodgepole pine, and that larval growth and development were better on Scots pine (Watt 1985). The monitoring of natural populations, however, showed that the species survived less well on Scots pine than on lodgepole pine, at least during the egg and early larval stages (Watt 1986). Thereafter, the difference disappeared. Mortality in the late larval and pre-pupal stages was as high on lodgepole as on Scots pine. This particular study is in its early stages, but it is already evident that the observed lack of outbreaks on Scots pine in Scotland is not due to the nutritional quality of Scots pine as a host plant. In fact, Scots pine appears to be a better host than (at least some provenances of) lodgepole pine in terms of larval growth and development, and perhaps for larval survival also.

A number of other possibilities may explain the absence of outbreaks on Scots pine. First, the phenology of Scots pine may be such that Scots pine shoots are likely to be at an unfavourable stage of development at the time of egg hatch. This was not the case in either 1984 or 1985. It is nonetheless a matter requiring attention as the development of shoots of Scots pine lags behind that of lodgepole pine, and the survival of young larvae could be poorer on Scots pine in years when the eggs hatch early in relation to shoot development. A second possibility is that the structure of Scots pine is such that newly hatched larvae have more difficulty in finding suitable feeding sites on Scots pine than they do on lodgepole pine. In 1984, sticky traps were placed under both lodgepole and Scots pine trees to see how many larvae fell from the canopy during the early instars. This experiment showed that only a small percentage of larvae was lost from the canopy during the early instars, but that significantly fewer were lost from Scots pine than from lodgepole pine (Table 2). There is no evidence that Scots pine is a poorer host for the moth than lodgepole pine: at present, the reverse appears to be true.

A third possibility is that the soil or litter, or both, is less suitable for pupae under Scots pine than under lodgepole pine. There is no information on this

hypothesis to date, but it obviously requires investigation, given that Scots pine tends to be planted in different soils from lodgepole pine. A fourth possible reason why outbreaks of pine beauty do not occur in Scots pine plantations is that natural enemies may be causing greater mortality on Scots pine than on lodgepole pine. The life table and exclusion cage studies referred to earlier indicate that the moth suffers heavier mortality on Scots than on lodgepole pine during the egg and early larval stages, but that the reverse may be true for the late larval and pre-pupal stages. In 1984 and 1985, the difference between the mortality of the early stages on the 2 host plants was not large and was, in any case, masked by the mortality acting upon the later stages. However, as pointed out earlier, this late larval mortality was exceptionally high in 1985 and the technique used in 1984 may itself have exaggerated late larval mortality.

The significance of mortality of eggs and early larvae of pine beauty moth on Scots pine has yet to be assessed fully. In both 1984 and 1985, the mortality of late larvae was higher on lodgepole pine than on Scots pine. This was in contrast to the mortality of eggs and early larvae, perhaps because of the faster development of pine beauty larvae on Scots pine which would leave them vulnerable to predation for less time than on lodgepole pine.

It may be concluded that, although it is known where pine beauty moth outbreaks start, ie on lodgepole pine rather than on Scots pine and on unflushed peats rather than other soils, the reasons are only just beginning to be understood. Consequently, population monitoring should be restricted to these 'at risk' sites with caution. Experience of pine beauty moth is still fairly limited, so that the observed associations between outbreak behaviour and site characteristics may be misleading. Moreover, until the reason why outbreaks are centred on certain areas are discovered, there will be no basis for pest management other than by chemical, viral or bacterial spraying.

Two examples are relevant to current research into the pine beauty moth. First, if the association between outbreaks and deep peat had been found to be nutritional, fertilizer application or thinning might have been tried in order to make the foliage less suitable for the caterpillars. Second, if outbreaks of pine beauty moth are absent from Scots pine because natural enemies are more effective on Scots pine than on lodgepole pine, the planting of the 2 species in mixture might lead to the prevention of outbreaks, or a reduction in their frequency. If, on the other hand, pine beauty outbreaks centre on certain areas because the soil conditions there are more suited to pupal survival, both these control practices will be ineffective.

3.3 Spread of pine beauty moth outbreaks

Although outbreaks of pine beauty moth tend to start in relatively small areas within forest blocks, they

Table 2. Number of young pine beauty moth larvae caught under lodgepole and Scots pine on sticky traps (Elchies block, Speyside, 1984) (source: original data)

	Eggs m^{-2} (artificially infested)	Larvae trapped m^{-2}	Larvae trapped as % of eggs
Lodgepole pine	264.2	20.0	7.6
Scots pine	282.7	11.3	4.0

spread rapidly to larger areas. For example, in 1984 an outbreak occurred in the North Dalchork block of Shin Forest, killing trees over 30 ha. By the following year, however, 1550 ha had to be sprayed. The development of such an outbreak is the sum of 2 processes. First, insect populations grow and decline at slightly different rates in different parts of a forest (ie what might appear to be a spreading outbreak is really a population reaching damaging levels at different times in different parts of the forest). Second, moths disperse from areas of high densities into surrounding parts of the forest.

Both these processes occurred in the development of the pine beauty moth population in North Dalchork, where annual surveys of pupae have been done by the Forestry Commission (FC) since 1977. In 1985, a joint ITE/FC study was undertaken on adult emergence and egg laying in different parts of the forest. In 1979, an insecticide spraying operation was carried out in the older parts of the forest block where densities had risen to a maximum of 40 pupae m^{-2}. In all parts of the forest, pupal densities declined or remained at low levels until (after no counts were done in 1981) an appreciable rise was noted in 1982. During 1983, a small increase in pupal density occurred in most areas, but a marked increase in numbers occurred throughout the forest in 1984. The high densities found in 1984 were, as already mentioned, only great enough to cause substantial defoliation in one part of the forest. However, the rate of population increase in that part of the block in 1984 was only marginally greater than that found in other areas. Moreover, the annual rate of increase in previous years was not consistently higher in the area defoliated in 1984 than in other areas. The reason why an outbreak centred on this part of the forest in 1984 seems to have been mainly because the numbers of pine beauty moths did not drop to such low levels there in 1979 and 1980 as elsewhere. Thereafter, with the rate of population increase being more or less the same throughout the block, the next outbreak was almost inevitably going to be centred in the place where the numbers of moths were high initially.

In the autumn of 1984, the pupal survey in North Dalchork showed that almost the whole block was at risk from defoliation by the pine beauty moth in 1985. In spring 1985, a study was done to see whether dispersal by moths out of the area defoliated in 1984 would lead to an even greater risk of damage in the surrounding parts of the block.

There was substantial pupal mortality during the winter of 1984–85 but the average number of moths which emerged in April 1985 was 29.4 m^{-2}, almost double the damage threshold of 15 m^{-2}. In the defoliated area, 181.5 moths m^{-2} emerged but average densities in 7 sites 1–3 km distant ranged from 12.4 to 21.9 moths m^{-2}. Later, there was much less variation in the numbers of eggs laid (1202–5496 eggs per tree), but the number of eggs laid per emerged female ranged from 18 to 163. Only 18 eggs per female were laid on the defoliated trees, but 57 to 163 eggs per female were laid at the other 7 sites. The greatest numbers of eggs per female were found at the 3 sites nearest the area defoliated in 1984. Apparently moths emigrated from the defoliated area, laying the equivalent of at least two-thirds of their eggs elsewhere, so that the number of eggs laid on trees surrounding the defoliated area was approximately twice as great as expected.

The 'spread' of the outbreaks of pine beauty moth in North Dalchork in 1984–85 was therefore the sum of 2 processes, ie the slightly different population trends over a number of years in different parts of the block, and the dispersal of moths from the severely defoliated area in the spring of 1985. It would be wrong, however, to conclude that the only moth movement of any significance occurs after severe defoliation. Barbour (1986b) showed that adult pine beauty moths in the Elchies block of Speyside (then Craigellachie) Forest in 1979 underwent significant dispersal so that there was a large difference between the distributions of pupae, adults and eggs. This redistribution was not a response by adult moths to defoliation but could be explained by the direction of the wind during the flight period.

4 Discussion

A number of factors is now known to affect the temporal and spatial dynamics of the pine beauty moth. The most notable effects on temporal dynamics are by natural enemies, intraspecific competition and weather. There is good evidence that parasites and predators are more effective at low densities of the pine beauty moth. Fungal and viral diseases cause significant mortality at high densities but their impact is not great enough to prevent complete defoliation of host plants, and sharp population declines result from intense intraspecific competition. At this stage of research, the population dynamics of the pine beauty moth can be described either completely by a resource limitation model or, because of the possibly greater role of natural enemies at low densities, by an endemic/epidemic model. Whichever of these models is a truer representation of pine beauty moth dynamics, the role of weather must not be underestimated. Its effect on moth fecundity is particularly marked, but its effects on other stages of the life cycle are yet to be evaluated.

Although outbreaks of the pine beauty moth appear to be cyclical, a number of factors can be seen to be acting to make it very difficult to predict the length of time between successive outbreaks. This prediction was attempted by Watt et al. (1986), who used a simple simulation model incorporating the relationship between fecundity and weather together with the frequency of different patterns of spring weather found in northern Scotland. The model was used primarily to assess the susceptibility of different provenances of lodgepole pine. It did not, however, include the large variability in larval mortality which was seen particularly in 1984 and 1985. Further research will be needed before the impact of late larval mortality and other factors can be satisfactorily included in a population simulation model. As such models are necessary for the strategic planning of pest control (Leather *et al.* 1986; Watt *et al.* 1986), a further commitment to the study of pine beauty moth populations through the life table approach is clearly needed.

The spatial aspects of the population dynamics of the pine beauty moth also require further attention. Outbreaks seem to be limited to lodgepole pine growing on certain soils, but the reason or reasons are unclear. The extensive approach to studying this pest must therefore continue to accompany the intensive approach, and future research must include the effect of crop age and further work on plant species mixtures.

Are there any wider implications from current research into the population ecology of the pine beauty moth? First, it has been confirmed that the pine beauty moth has become an integral part of the lodgepole pine ecosystem. The numbers of the moth are determined in part by several other organisms, and the abundance of these organisms is also certain to be affected by fluctuations in the density of the pine beauty moth. The same is likely to be true of other pests so that it would be wrong to consider the ecology of many of the other fauna of forests in isolation from forest pests.

Second, the prospect for the control of the pine beauty moth is, at present, limited to the use of insecticides, whose side-effects on other organisms are giving cause for concern. Further research should be done to develop less harmful pest control techniques and to improve the tactic of chemical control so that it is used as efficiently as possible. An important example is the timing of chemical application. A joint ITE/FC programme of research is attempting to predict pine beauty moth emergence, egg laying and egg hatch so that insecticidal application can be timed more easily and more effectively. This technique has been used for the control of a number of other pests, with the emphasis on trying to apply insecticides when the pest is most vulnerable. In future, the emphasis might be placed on trying to avoid harming the vulnerable stages of butterflies, dragonflies and other insects which are worth preserving within woodlands. This aspect would, however, require a far greater knowledge of the population ecology and behaviour of these insects.

Third, forest management practices designed for ensuring the conservation of wildlife within woodland or promoting the amenity value of woodland are extremely unlikely to have no effect on the population dynamics of the pine beauty moth and other insect pests. For example, mixtures of tree species will promote insect diversity but may also decrease the abundance of certain pests. The mixed planting of different pines may be an effective management strategy against pine beauty moth, but more research is needed on its population ecology on Scots pine before this strategy is seriously considered.

Other mixed planting combinations such as pine/spruce, pine/birch and conifer/broadleaf combinations will, in general, lead to greater diversity among insects and probably other wildlife. There is, perhaps, a feeling that such diversity will lead inevitably to decreased pest problems. However, it must not be forgotten that the reason for fewer pest problems in some polycultures is not diversity *per se*, but some factor such as greater mortality during dispersal, or enhanced natural enemy action due to a predator or parasite being particularly associated with one of the plant species in the polyculture. These factors are not necessarily present in a species mixture which is chosen for conservation or amenity reasons.

Indeed, there is a risk that pest problems could be increased by mixed planting, because a number of serious forest pests are both polyphagous and phenological specialists. That is, they can feed on a number of plant species but they must hatch from the egg stage at a certain stage of the host plant's development: individuals hatching early and late may fail to become established. For example, if 2 or more host plant species are available with different phenologies, they will present the pest with a longer period during which it can successfully appear. One example is pine beauty moth on lodgepole and Scots pine which flush at different times. Two other examples are winter moth (*Operophtera brumata*) and vapourer moth (*Orgyia antiqua*), which have extremely wide host ranges including both broadleaved and coniferous trees. These examples provide a further reason why research into the management of forests for wildlife must include an assessment of how particular species mixtures, and indeed any other aspect of forest structure, will affect the incidence of insect pests. Moreover, this aspect and any other work done on insects for conservation or amenity reasons must be done rigorously. In particular, population surveys of insects must take note of the fact that insect abundance varies greatly from year to year, from month to month and, indeed, between superficially similar areas at the same time.

There are, therefore, good reasons why mixed planting would lead to both increased and decreased pest problems. A programme of research is urgently needed to find species mixtures which have fewer pest outbreaks.

Fourth, and finally, it should not be forgotten that the

exotic tree species which form so much of plantation forestry in the UK have been shown to be vulnerable to hitherto harmless indigenous insects which can become pests serious enough to jeopardize not just the economic value of forestry, but its wildlife and amenity values as well. At present, we do not even have complete records of which insect species currently feed on trees in commercial plantations. This basic gap must be filled, but a species list will not enable us to predict which insects will be pests in the future. Some indigenous insects can rapidly achieve pest status on exotic conifers, as in the case of the pine beauty moth. Other insects may adapt over a number of years before becoming pests. We therefore need to monitor and try to understand the population fluctuations of insects in woodlands.

5 Summary

The temporal and spatial population dynamics of the pine beauty moth are affected by host plant condition, natural enemies, competition, weather and dispersal. Natural enemies and weather are the principal factors affecting the sub-outbreak dynamics of the pine beauty moth, but their roles are still poorly understood so that adequate medium- and long-term prediction is as yet impossible. Unsprayed outbreaks are terminated by competition in the face of extreme food shortage. Fungal and viral diseases do not prevent complete host plant defoliation. Outbreaks of pine beauty moth are restricted to certain areas for reasons that are unclear, so that the classification of sites at risk still requires a firm scientific basis. The spread of outbreaks of the pine beauty moth is caused by slight differences in dynamics between different parts of forest blocks (apparent spread) and also by dispersal from heavily defoliated areas (actual spread).

The pine beauty moth forms an integral part of the pine ecosystem. Any forest management plan for whatever purpose (timber production, wildlife conservation, amenity) must take into account the fact that this and indeed many other pests are likely to be affected incidentally in ways that cannot yet be predicted.

6 Acknowledgements

Valuable advice and assistance have been given by D A Barbour, S Heritage, S R Leather, J T Stoakley and A Thompson (all of the Forestry Commission). Assistance in the laboratory and the field was given by D Roberts (and others, ITE Chemical Analytical Section), C Beetham, J Clarke, S Collins, R Evans and H McKay; and the Edinburgh Meteorological Office provided weather data.

7 References

Barbour, D.A. 1985. Panolis *life-table study*. Report to the Forestry Commission. (Unpublished.)

Barbour, D.A. 1986a. Pine beauty moth population dynamics: general considerations and the life table work. In: *Population biology and control of the pine beauty moth* (Panolis flammea), edited by J.T. Stoakley & S.R. Leather. (Research and development paper no. 139.) Edinburgh: Forestry Commission. In press.

Barbour, D.A. 1986b. Monitoring the moth population by means of pheromone traps: the effect of moth dispersal. In: *Population biology and control of the pine beauty moth* (Panolis flammea), edited by J.T. Stoakley & S.R. Leather. (Research and development paper no. 139.) Edinburgh: Forestry Commission. In press.

Blatchford, O.N. 1978. *Forestry practice*. (Forestry Commission bulletin no. 14.) London: HMSO.

Berryman, A.A. & Stark, R.W. 1985. Assessing the risk of forest insect outbreaks. *Z. angew. Entomol.*, **99**, 199–298.

Greenbank, D.O., Schaefer, G.W. & Rainey, R.C. 1980. Spruce budworm (Lepidoptera: Tortricidae) moth flight and dispersal: new understanding from canopy observations, radar and aircraft. *Mem. Entomol. Soc. Can.*, **110**, 1–49.

Leather, S.R. 1984. Factors affecting pupal survival and eclosion in the pine beauty moth, *Panolis flammea* (D. & S.). *Oecologia*, **63**, 75–79.

Leather, S.R., Watt, A.D. & Barbour, D.A. 1986. The effect of host plant and delayed mating on the fecundity and lifespan of the pine beauty moth, *Panolis flammea* (Denis and Schiffermüller) (Lepidoptera: Noctuidae): their influence on population dynamics and relevance to pest management. *Bull. Ent. Res.*, **75**. In press.

Lines, R. 1976. The development of forestry in Scotland in relation to the use of *Pinus contorta*. In: Pinus contorta *provenance studies*, edited by R. Lines, 2–5. (Research and development paper no. 114.) Edinburgh: Forestry Commission.

Rhoades, D.F. 1983. Herbivore population dynamics and plant chemistry. In: *Variable plants and herbivores in natural and managed systems*, edited by R.F. Denno & M.S. McClure, 155–220. London: Academic Press.

Stoakley, J.T. 1977. A severe outbreak of the pine beauty moth on lodgepole pine in Sutherland. *Scott. For.*, **31**, 113–125.

Stoakley, J.T. 1979. *Pine beauty moth*. (Forestry Commission forest record no. 120.) London: HMSO.

Stoakley, J.T. 1981. Control of the pine beauty moth, *Panolis flammea*, by aerial application of fenitrothion. In: *Aerial application of insecticide against pine beauty moth*, edited by A.V. Holden & D. Bevan, 9–14. Edinburgh: Forestry Commission.

Watt, A.D. 1985. The influence of host plant species and soil type on the population ecology of the pine beauty moth. *Annu. Rep. Inst. terr. Ecol. 1984*, 28–30.

Watt, A.D. 1986. Pine beauty moth outbreaks: the influence of host species, plant phenology, soil type, water stress and natural enemies. In: *Population biology and control of the pine beauty moth* (Panolis flammea), edited by J.T. Stoakley & S.R. Leather. (Research and development paper no. 139.) Edinburgh: Forestry Commission. In press.

Watt, A.D. & Leather, S.R. 1986. Pine beauty moth population dynamics synthesis, simulation and prediction. In: *Population biology and control of the pine beauty moth* (Panolis flammea), edited by J.T. Stoakley & S.R. Leather. (Research and development paper no. 139.) Edinburgh: Forestry Commission. In press.

White, T.C.R. 1969. An index to measure weather-induced stress of trees associated with outbreaks of psyllids in Australia. *Ecology*, **50**, 905–909.

White, T.C.R. 1974. A hypothesis to explain outbreaks of looper caterpillars, with special reference to populations of *Selidosema suavis* in a plantation of *Pinus radiata* in New Zealand. *Oecologia*, **16**, 279–301.

White, T.C.R. 1984. The abundance of invertebrate herbivores in relation to the availability of nitrogen in stressed food plants. *Oecologia*, **63**, 90–105.

The effects of commercial forestry on woodland Lepidoptera

M R YOUNG

Department of Zoology, University of Aberdeen, Aberdeen

1 Introduction

This paper considers current knowledge of the habitat requirements of woodland Lepidoptera, the habitat changes which different commercial operations might entail in relation to these requirements, and some of the few data available which illustrate actual effects. It concludes with some suggestions for managing commercial woodlands for the benefit of Lepidoptera.

Very little reliable information exists on the effects of commercial forestry on woodland Lepidoptera in Scotland (especially upland Scotland), and so to draw realistic conclusions it has been necessary to refer occasionally to English or Scandinavian studies, although the emphasis remains Scottish.

The reasons for this lack of data are varied and, at first sight, surprising, in view of the general popularity of the Lepidoptera. First, commercial forest entomologists, such as those employed by the Forestry Commission, are rightly preoccupied with species which have an economic impact, such as the pine beauty moth (*Panolis flammea*) or the pine shoot moth (*Rhyacionia buoliana*). Second, those academic entomologists who have studied woodland species have concentrated on individual species which illustrate particular principles, such as the classic work on 'k' factor analysis and life tables using the winter moth (*Operophtera brumata*) (as reviewed by Varley *et al.* 1973). Third, most of the references to the impact of forestry operations on woodland insects in general have been by amateur lepidopterists and, unfortunately, their data have mostly been circumstantial or unpublished.

The scale of commercial management can vary enormously, from small amounts of extraction, leaving a woodland largely unchanged, to extensive areas of clearfelling or widespread planting of open ground, when the woodland environment is altered dramatically; the consequences for the Lepidoptera mirror the scale of the changes involved.

2 The habitat requirements of woodland Lepidoptera

Woodland plants provide a direct resource for some species of Lepidoptera, ie the actual tree species themselves may be the larval food plants, but, equally important, the woods can provide a varied and distinctive micro-climate favourable to insects and markedly different from that of more open habitats. Shade and shelter are just as characteristic and influential factors in woodlands as are the tree species present as food resources.

2.1 Insects associated with different tree species

Non-commercial woodlands in Britain are generally composed of native trees and shrubs. For various reasons, these have many more Lepidoptera feeding on them than do non-native species. Table 1 records the numbers of species of Scottish butterflies and

Table 1. The number of Lepidoptera which specialize in feeding as larvae on various tree species in Scotland (source: Allan 1949; Emmet 1979)

Native Scottish tree species		Introduced tree species	
Tree species	Number of associated Lepidoptera	Tree species	Number of associated Lepidoptera
Birch (*Betula* spp.)	79	*Beech (*Fagus sylvatica*)	10
Oak (*Quercus* spp.)	59	Spruce (*Picea* spp.)	9
Sallow (*Salix* spp.)	54	Fir (*Abies* spp.)	5
Hawthorn (*Crataegus monogyna*)	32	Larch (*Larix* spp.)	5
Scots pine (*Pinus sylvestris*)	23	Sycamore (*Acer pseudoplatanus*)	4
Alder (*Alnus glutinosa*)	23	Lime (*Tilia europaea*)	3
Aspen (*Populus tremula*)	23		
Blackthorn (*Prunus spinosa*)	17		
Rowan (*Sorbus aucuparia*)	13		
Wych elm (*Ulmus glabra*)	13		
Hazel (*Corylus avellana*)	12		
Juniper (*Juniperus communis*)	9		
Ash (*Fraxinus excelsior*)	8		
Cherry (*Prunus* spp.)	5		
Holly (*Ilex aquifolium*)	1		

*Native to England
Polyphagous species of Lepidoptera are excluded

moths associated with a variety of tree species, and it is obvious that widespread and abundant native trees, such as birch (*Betula* spp.), have the richest fauna, closely followed by oak (*Quercus* spp.) and sallow (*Salix* spp.), whereas even the widespread non-native commercial species such as spruce (*Picea* spp.) or larch (*Larix* spp.) have very few. Widely polyphagous moths have been excluded from Table 1 because some of these feed on both native and non-native trees, but the overall figures illustrate the correct general situation. The reasons why native trees harbour so many more insects than introduced species are discussed in detail by Strong (1979) and by Kennedy and Southwood (1984), amongst others. The reasons include important factors such as the extent of a tree's distribution and abundance, and therefore the ease of colonization, the length of time a tree species has been present in Britain, and therefore the time available for insects to find it and adapt to it, its palatability, and other factors which go to make up its 'apparency' to herbivores. As commercial species have become more common and widespread, and because they have now been in this country for a considerable period (measured in terms of insect generations), it is be expected that their associated fauna should be increasing. This is certainly so, as shown by Winter (1974), Welch (1981) and Carter (1983), for example.

A further point is that, in general, commercial woodlands consist of a restricted number of tree species, when compared with semi-natural woodlands, often with very few individuals remaining of the native species, and these tend to be localized around the edges of the commercial blocks or in such features as stream gullies. Table 2 provides examples of comparable woodland sites. At Tillyfoure on Donside, an apparently semi-natural oakwood Site of Special Scientific Interest (SSSI) exists immediately adjacent to a commercial wood with which it can be compared, and in Glen Tanar National Nature Reserve (NNR) a comparison is made between a largely unmanaged stand of Caledonian Scots pine (*Pinus sylvestris*) at Allachy and a nearby 40-year-old planted stand at the Strone. In both cases, the semi-natural woodland has a higher diversity of tree and shrub species present.

It might be argued that the retention of native tree species at the margins of woods will allow their insect fauna to survive, but an exposed position would certainly not be suitable for some insects, and, in any case, too few specimens of the tree species may remain to maintain viable insect populations. Apparently, no studies have yet quantified the insect communities of the deciduous margins of commercial forests, in contrast to those in comparable semi-natural woodlands. On the one hand, some studies have noted the continued survival of some insect populations on very small stands of trees (for example, Thomas (1974) showed that this survival is possible for the black hairstreak butterfly (*Strymonidia pruni*) in

Table 2. Comparison of the numbers of tree species present in stands within semi-natural and commercial woodlands in Aberdeenshire (source: original data)

Semi-natural woodlands	Commercial woodlands
i. *Tillyfoure oakwood SSSI* NJ 668194	ii. *Tillyfoure commercial woodland* NJ 670194
Oak*	Scots pine
Scots pine	Sitka spruce
Birch	Larch
Rowan	(Rowan)
Sallow	(Birch)
Alder	(Sallow)
Gean (*Prunus avium*)	(Alder)
Wych elm	
Hazel	
(Bird cherry) (*Prunus padus*)	
(Hawthorn)	
(Holly)	
(Sycamore)	
ii. *Glen Tanar NNR Allachy* NO 485921	ii. *Glen Tanar NNR Strone plantation* NO 472942
Scots pine	Scots pine
Juniper	
(Rowan)	
(Aspen)	
(Holly)	
(Birch)	

*Latin names are given in Table 1
( ) Rare species

England), whereas there are numerous other circumstantial accounts of the loss of species from woodlands as these have been reduced in size.

In general, it is obviously reasonable to conclude that semi-natural woodlands, rich in tree species, will have a more diverse insect fauna than otherwise comparable commercial woodlands. This point is substantiated by Heliovaara and Vaisanen (1984), who review the data available for Scandinavian forests.

2.2 The food plants of Lepidoptera in woodland

So far, it has been assumed that woodland Lepidoptera depend on the trees for food, but this assumption is misleading for 2 reasons. First, many butterflies and moths, which only inhabit woodland, feed as larvae on herbs, grasses or other miscellaneous food resources (such as fungi), rather than on the trees, and many of these butterflies and moths favour plants growing in clearings, rides or woodland margins. Table 3 illustrates this preference in Tillyfoure oakwood SSSI.

Second, even for species which use trees as their larval food plant, it is common for the adults to require nectar or honeydew as a food resource, and so these species may also depend upon flowers within the wood. For example, Kelly (1983) studied the chequered skipper butterfly (*Carterocephalus palaemon*), which occurs in open woodlands in western Scotland, and noted that adults feed on a succession of flowers, including bluebell (*Endymion non-scriptus*), bugle

Table 3. The larval food sources of the Lepidoptera known to breed in Tillyfoure oakwood SSSI, Aberdeenshire (source: original data)

	Trees	Shrubs	Categories of larval food resource	
			Herbs, grasses etc, under the canopy	Herbs, grasses etc, in clearings or margins
Number of species of Lepidoptera	100	44	42	146
Number of food 'items' involved	9	5	about 6	over 20

The numbers entered here are approximate because of the difficulty of placing polyphagous species correctly

(*Ajuga reptans*) and marsh thistle (*Cirsium palustre*), all of which occur only in clearings.

The significance of this point is that anything which reduces the abundance and diversity of the herbs, grasses and other food sources will adversely affect the insect community. However, it is the plants of clearings and margins that are the major resource and these may survive with appropriate management, even though those under the canopy are likely to be eliminated by the heavy shade of the early commercial forest.

2.3 Other woodland features which influence insects
Many woodland features which depend upon the diversity and architecture of the wood are important to Lepidoptera. For example, the speckled wood butterfly (*Pararge aegeria*) is known to have a behavioural 'need' for dappled shade, because it uses sun patches as territorial features (Davies 1978).

The major indirect effect of woodlands is undoubtedly their provison of a micro-climate which seems to suit many insects. Kelly (1983) found that the glades in woodland in Argyll were less windy, more humid and warmer than the nearby open hillsides, and he suggested that this situation favoured the chequered skipper butterfly. However, if clearings or rides are too narrow they remain shaded, and so cool, and if too straight they may act as 'wind tunnels'. These effects depend partly on the degree of shade provided, which will vary between commmercial and non-commercial woodlands, but also on the design of the plantings and form of the trees, and equivalent shelter could obviously occur in either woodland type.

2.4 Notable Scottish woodland lepidoptera and their requirements
Parsons (1984) lists the rarer British Microlepidoptera, including several species from Scottish woodland. Table 4 lists these species and equivalent Macrolepidoptera, and gives some indication of their food plants and preferences. Whilst the list is obviously incomplete and it is, in any case, inappropriate to concentrate on single species rather than insect communities, it nevertheless again makes the point that consideration of the effects of forestry operations must include topics other than the mere accounting of which tree species are present.

Table 4. Some notable Scottish woodland Lepidoptera and their food plants and requirements (source: Parsons 1984; original data)

Myrmecozela ochraceella Tengst.	A species living as a larva in nest of wood ants (*Formica* spp.)
Archinemapogon yildizae Kocak	Larva on rotting bracket fungi (*Piptoporus* spp. and *Fomes* spp.) on birch
Paraleucoptera sinuella Reutti	Larva on aspen; perhaps extinct
Choreutis diana Hubn.	Larva on birch leaves
Acrolepiopsis betulella Curtis	Larva on flowers and seeds of ramsons (*Allium ursinum*) in light woodland
Coleophora idaella Hofm. } *C. glitzella* Hofm. }	Larvae in cases on cowberry (*Vaccinium vitis-idaea*) in open woodland
Elachista orstadii Palm	Larva on grasses on woodland margin
Biselachista trapeziella Stt	Larva on wood-rush (*Luzula* spp.)
Exaeretia ciniflonella L. and Z.	Larva may live on birch leaves
Dichomeris juniperella Linn.	Larva on juniper (*Juniperus communis*)
Clepsis rurinana Linn.	Larva polyphagous on trees and shrubs
Acleris logiana Cl.	Larva on birch leaves
A. abietana Hb.	An introduced species feeding on various conifers, including grand fir (*Abies grandis*)
Olethreutes metallicana Hb.	Larva on bilberry in open woods
Pammene luedersiana Soer.	Larva on bog myrtle (*Myrica gale*) on moors and in open woods
P. obscurana Steph.	Larva on birch catkins
Carterocephalus palaemon Pallas	Larva on grasses in woodland rides and clearings
Endromis versicolora Linn.	Larva on young birches in regenerating woodland
Epione paralellaria Hufn.	Larva on aspen.
Paradiarsia sobrina Dup.	Larva on heather (*Calluna vulgaris*), bilberry and birch saplings in regenerating woodland
Brachionycha nubeculosa Esp.	Larva on well-grown birches

3 The effects of commercial management on woodlands

As indicated previously, commercial woodland management may take many forms, and so have correspondingly varied effects on the woodland environment and on the Lepidoptera.

3.1 The direct loss of tree and shrub species

In the past, especially in England, it was sometimes the practice to replace semi-natural woodland of native trees with exotic commercial species, which obviously changed the insect fauna of such woods dramatically, leading to a reduction in diversity and a change in species present. This practice seems to have been less common in Scotland, and in any case there is now a general presumption in favour of conserving semi-natural woodlands, as evidenced by the recent strengthening of the Forestry Commisssion's support for broadleaved woodland.

Nevertheless, commercial planting in Scotland, although mostly on open ground, may sometimes involve some loss of native tree species, especially when these are small or young, sparsely distributed, unconsidered remnant woodlands, or newly established.

3.2 The loss of shrubs, herbs, grasses and other food resources

The ground preparation needed for commercial afforestation, the use of herbicides, dense early shade and direct shrub removal are all known to reduce greatly the many food resources shown above to be so necessary to woodland insects (Heliovaara & Vaisanen 1984). Although the woodland may later mature and become suitable for some, at least, of these plants, the plants may not recolonize quickly, especially if the area is isolated from other semi-natural woodland. The break in continuity of even one year may prove vital to the survival of the insects, and this can apply not only to the plants and grasses but also to the over-mature trees and dead wood, which will not occur in young plantations.

3.3 The loss of clearings and rides

Although it is appreciated that some semi-natural woods may have few natural gaps, in general commercial plantations are more uniform and have fewer effective clearings. Furthermore, the access rides which are created are sometimes themselves too uniform or too neatly managed to provide the plants and micro-climates which are favoured by insects. Mature commercial woodlands of longer rotations may provide ample spaces, but the loss of their continuity in the early stages may be crucial. In any case, most forestry involves harvesting trees long before maturity is reached.

This effect is really one of the loss of favourable micro-climates. The area may become too exposed at clearfelling, only to become too shaded in early stages, before reverting to the favoured conditions at maturity.

This pattern will apply especially where conifers have replaced deciduous species, so changing the patterns of shade present, especially in the spring.

3.4 Positive effects of commercial forestry

Lepidoptera are rather feeble, cold-blooded creatures and, although there are many open area specialists, the majority favour warm, sheltered conditions. For this reason, woodland communities of butterflies and moths are generally rich. This statement can apply to mature, varied commercial forests, as well as to semi-natural areas, provided that they are managed in a way favourable to the insects.

It follows that an appropriately managed commercial woodland may benefit many Lepidoptera, resulting in a diverse fauna, when compared to agricultural land or impoverished open areas. Furthermore, even Britain's semi-natural woodlands usually require some management to remain optimal (largely because remaining fragments are so small and isolated), and so the opportunities for management provided by commercial operations may be beneficial. In England, some large commercial forests (such as Bernwood Forest) are considered to harbour very interesting and diverse insect communities, and the point has been made that the woodland structure and the tree spacing matter as much as the tree species present (Peachey 1980). Diversity does not necessarily correspond to 'value', however, and a rather uniform fauna of a few interesting species on open moorland may be of greater 'conservation value' than the more diverse woodland fauna that replaces it, following the establishment of the commercial woodland. It is not true to assert that the wildlife potential of forests is such that this generally compensates for the lost interest of the open ground it replaces. This assertion may be true when the open ground is of low conservation value, but in other cases the wildlife importance of the open ground is much greater than that of the forest replacing it. Each case must be judged on its own merits. Furthermore, the beneficial management practices (as detailed below) may be uneconomic and impractical, or the woodland may be too small or isolated to attract insect colonists.

The positive value of commercial woodlands depends on their size, position, layout and management, and on the plant and insect community that they displaced.

4 Examples of species and communities of Lepidoptera which have been influenced by woodland management

The best Scottish example of the effects of afforestation of open ground concerns not commercial plantings but the native woodland regeneration project on the island of Rhum. Wormell (1977) has monitored not only the progress of the woodland but also the re-establishment of characteristic insects, and the especially interesting feature of this study is the degree of isolation involved. Briefly, the island was denuded of trees in the decades leading up to the 1830s (although presumably a few survived in stream gullies), when a very small shelterbelt was planted at Kinloch. Later, at the turn of the century, 80 000 mixed conifers and deciduous trees were planted, again at Kinloch, and some woodland insects certainly reinvaded this area. The main plantings began in the 1960s and now several hundred hectares of woodland have been established.

The principal result of Wormell's (1977) study has been to show that Lepidoptera can be better colonists than was at first thought, even in a situation where they have to migrate across the sea to reach the woodland. At least 130 species of butterflies and moths which depend upon trees and shrubs directly have now re-established themselves on Rhum, and many others are present which use the woodland micro-climate or flora. A number of these invaded the original Kinloch planting, but each year more new arrivals are recorded. On the neighbouring island of Canna, J L Campbell (pers. comm.) has noted a similar arrival in his woodlands, most of which were planted from 1945 onwards. Whilst some species may have survived as relict populations on the few trees in gullies, the majority must have flown across from Rhum or the mainland. These species include such examples as the speckled wood butterfly (*P. aegeria*), the may highflyer moth (*Hydriomena impluviata*) and the yellow-horned moth (*Achyla flavicornis*). However, many other species found in woodlands on the nearest mainland have yet to arrive on these islands.

A second Scottish example is the chequered skipper butterfly (*C. palaemon*), which occurs naturally in sheltered clearings amongst native woodland on sunny slopes in western Inverness-shire and northern Argyll where it has recently spread slightly. It now also occurs along sheltered margins and rides in recent spruce plantations (Thomson 1980), although it seems probable that these areas will become more shaded and so unsuitable, once the trees have grown. This butterfly clearly responds to a favourable micro-climate and does not distinguish the tree species forming the woodland; furthermore, as might be expected of a species using transitory woodland clearings, it does have some colonizing ability.

A further, similar, example is that of the Rannoch looper moth (*Semiothisa brunneata*) which feeds as a larva on bilberry (*Vaccinium myrtillus*). This moth occurs naturally amongst open birch and pine woodland in the central Highland valleys, including Deeside and Donside, but now also occurs along the edges of rides in commercial woodland. It also responds to the micro-climate provided by the trees and manages to survive on the fringe of bilberry available to it.

Warren (1984) studied the wood white butterfly (*Leptidea sinapis*) in England. This butterfly feeds as a larva on various vetches (*Lathyrus* spp., *Vicia* spp. and *Lotus corniculatus*) and, although in some localities it lives in sheltered fields, it is found principally in rides and clearings in the deciduous woods of central, southern England. In several parts of its range, these woods have been planted with conifers, but the butterfly has often survived this process and now lives along the rides in the new plantations. The ride management is such that the vetches have remained, as has the shelter.

In contrast, several species of butterfly belonging to the group called fritillaries (*Boloria* spp. and *Argynnis* spp.) have declined, as their food plants, wild violets (*Viola* spp.), have been shaded out by the change to conifers and by the cessation of coppicing (Pollard 1981; Thomas 1984). The heath fritillary butterfly (*Mellicta athalia*), which feeds mainly on common cow-wheat (*Melampyrum pratense*), has been particularly affected. It is now Britain's most endangered butterfly, being found only in a handful of sites in Kent, Devon and Cornwall (Warren *et al.* 1981). The loss of coppice management has dramatically altered many English woods and, although not directly relevant to most Scottish situations, it does illustrate the subtle ways in which insects respond to woodland change. The decline in the fritillaries can be contrasted to the extension in range and abundance of the white admiral butterfly (*Ladoga camilla*). This species lays its eggs only on honeysuckle (*Lonicera periclymenum*) growing within woodland shade, and so has benefited from the reduction in coppicing (Pollard 1979).

A final English example illustrates the lack of mobility of a butterfly and stresses the point that recolonization following commercial management cannot be assumed, even for flying insects. Thomas (1974) noted the extreme localization of the black hairstreak butterfly (*S. pruni*) to discrete stands of mature blackthorn (*Prunus spinosa*) and its absence from other, apparently suitable, nearby stands. He also found that there were several examples of successful introductions, although these had remained as small colonies and had not spread far; he concluded that the butterfly was limited by a behavioural tendency to remain very faithful to its home and so would not survive a loss of site continuity, as recolonization would not occur unless other colonies were very close indeed.

These examples illustrate that some Lepidoptera are adversely affected by changes in woodland management whereas others are more adaptable. Furthermore, some recolonize areas quickly, as sites become available, whereas others cannot. Overall, it is obviously not possible to make generalizations about the possible effects of any commercial scheme.

5 Managing commercial woodlands for Lepidoptera
The examples and data discussed above suggest some principles of management which should favour the retention of woodland Lepidoptera in commercial forests. It must be stressed again, however, that for

almost all species the habitat requirements of even the adult stage are not fully known, and so these suggestions are largely empirical. If the conservation of Lepidoptera is considered desirable in any forest, then it will certainly be necessary to monitor their numbers effectively and to be prepared to modify practices according to what is noticed.

Entomologists must welcome the current, more sympathetic attitude towards including consideration for insect communities in commercial woodland management, and it is hoped that the suggestions outlined below will be helpful to woodland managers. Reassuringly to conservationists interested in other types of animals or plants, these management principles are very similar to those suggested previously for other groups.

5.1 Management practices and woodland features which generally favour Lepidoptera

5.1.1 Wherever possible, retain existing woodland communities rather than rely on recolonization after radical management.

5.1.2 Retain as many native trees, shrubs, herbs and grasses as possible, not only in thin belts around the edges, but especially in groups and along rides, around clearings, along streamsides and in other sheltered, sunny areas. Even a brief break in their continuity may be very detrimental.

5.1.3 Retain and create rides and clearings, especially those with a sheltered but sunny aspect, and manage these spaces to favour a wide variety of the plants referred to in 5.1.2. Avoid straight 'wind tunnel' rides. Provide 'linkage' between clearings.

5.1.4 Where possible, fell and replant in moderate coups, rather than clearfell large areas, and encourage as much variety in tree age and form as possible.

5.1.5 Tolerate some over-mature trees and dead wood, as well as 'untidy' corners.

5.1.6 Encourage the recording of Lepidoptera, but insist on the records being available, and try to monitor the effectiveness of the management schemes (using more than one 'indicator' species).

6 Summary

6.1 Although little is known about the habitat requirements of most Lepidoptera, it is clear that:

i. native tree and shrub species harbour substantially more Lepidoptera than do exotic tree species;

ii. many woodland Lepidoptera do not depend directly on the trees for food but rely on associated woodland plants and on the modified woodland micro-climate;

iii. the principal attribute of the woodland micro-climate is shelter, although an open, sunny aspect is also preferable.

6.2 Different commercial management practices will vary widely in their effects. Direct losses will follow the reduction in native trees and shrubs, with the associated lost ground flora; indirect losses will result from detrimental changes to the micro-climate.

6.3 Some Lepidoptera have proved adaptable and colonize commercial woodlands readily; others either cannot adapt to new conditions or food resources, or lack the ability to migrate to colonize them.

6.4 Management practices which should favour Lepidoptera are detailed in the paper, but generally include the principle of retaining as much as possible of the food resources and sheltered micro-climate of the existing woodland, with tolerance of some non-commercial features, rather than relying on re-creation of the woodland habitat followed by reinvasion by the Lepidoptera.

6.5 Appropriately managed commercial forests can be acceptable to Lepidoptera and can harbour diverse communities, whereas inappropriately managed areas have only an impoverished fauna.

7 Acknowledgements
I have benefited from the generous advice and help I have received from various colleagues, and especially from Huw Parry of Aberdeen University Forestry Department and from David Barbour of the Forestry Commission. I am most grateful to all these people.

8 References
Allan, P.B.M. 1949. *Larval foodplants*. London: Watkins & Doncaster.

Carter, C.I. 1983. Some new aphid arrivals to Britain's forests. *Proc. Trans. Br. entomol. natur. Hist. Soc.*, **16**, 81–86.

Davies, N.B. 1978. Territorial defence in the speckled wood butterfly (*Pararge aegeria*): the resident always wins. *Anim. Behav.*, **26**, 138–147.

Emmet, A.M., ed. 1979. *A field guide to the smaller British Lepidoptera*. London: British Entomological and Natural History Society.

Heliovaara, K. & Vaisanen, R. 1984. Effects of modern forestry on north-western European forest invertebrates: a synthesis. *Acta for. fenn.*, **189**, 1–29.

Kelly, P.G. 1983. *The ecology of the chequered skipper (*Carterocephalus palaemon *Pallas) in Scotland*. Report to the Nature Conservancy Council. (Unpublished.)

Kennedy, C.E.J. & Southwood, T.R.E. 1984. The number of species of insect associated with British trees: a re-analysis. *J. Anim. Ecol.*, **53**, 455–478.

Parsons, M. 1984. *Invertebrate site register. Report no. 53. A provisional national review of the status of British Microlepidoptera*. Banbury: Nature Conservancy Council.

Peachey, C. 1980. *The conservation of butterflies in Bernwood Forest*. Report to the Nature Conservancy Council. (Unpublished.)

Pollard, E. 1979. Population ecology and change in range of the white admiral butterfly *Ladoga camilla* L. in England. *Ecol. Entomol.*, **4**, 61–74.

Pollard, E. 1981. Population studies of woodland butterflies. In: *Forest and woodland ecology,* edited by F.T. Last & A.S. Gardiner, 120–124. (ITE symposium no. 8.) Cambridge: Institute of Terrestrial Ecology.

Strong, D.R. 1979. Biogeographic dynamics of insect–host plant communities. *A. Rev. Entomol.,* **24,** 89–119.

Thomas, J.A. 1974. *Ecological studies of hairstreak butterflies.* PhD thesis, University of Leicester.

Thomas, J.A. 1984. The conservation of butterflies in temperate countries: past efforts and lessons for the future. In: *The biology of butterflies,* edited by R.I. Vane-Wright & P.R. Ackery, 333–353. (Symposium no. 11.) London: Royal Entomological Society.

Thomson, G. 1980. *The butterflies of Scotland: a natural history.* London: Croom Helm.

Varley, G.C., Gradwell, G.R. & Hassell, M.P. 1973. *Insect population ecology.* Oxford: Blackwell Scientific.

Warren, M.S. 1984. The biology and status of the wood white butterfly, *Leptidea sinapis* (L.) (Lepidoptera: Pieridae), in the British Isles. *Entomologist's Gaz.,* **35,** 207–223.

Warren, M.S. et al. 1981. *The heath fritillary: survey and conservation report.* London: Joint Committee for the Conservation of British Insects.

Welch, R.C. 1981. Insects on exotic broad-leaved trees of the Fagaceae, namely *Quercus borealis* and species of *Nothofagus.* In: *Forest and woodland ecology,* edited by F.T. Last & A. S. Gardiner, 110–115. (ITE symposium no. 8.) Cambridge: Institute of Terrestrial Ecology.

Winter, T.G. 1974. New host plant records of Lepidoptera associated with conifer afforestation in Britain. *Entomologists's Gaz.,* **25,** 247–258.

Wormell, P. 1977. Woodland insect population changes in the Isle of Rhum in relation to forest history and woodland restoration. *Scott. For.,* **31,** 13–36.

What do we know about insects in Scottish woods?

R C WELCH
Institute of Terrestrial Ecology, Huntingdon

1 Introduction

Although this symposium is primarily concerned with woodlands in the Scottish uplands, I have, by necessity, had to take a wider overview of insects in Scottish woodlands as a whole. However, information from the Forestry Commission (FC) (1985) and from Davies (1985) shows that over the past 65 years the land under trees in Scotland has risen from 3% to 14%, mostly in the uplands, which is a loosely defined area comprising about 42% of Scotland. Almost without exception, this planting has involved conifers. Indeed, broadleaved woodlands probably occupy no more than 10% of the 1 Mha of commercial and 'unproductive' woodland in Scotland. Clearly, in any examination of the insects occurring in Scottish woodlands, those of the conifer plantations should take precedence. Although rides, streamsides and clearings within forests are refuges for many insect species, these sites have been discussed elsewhere during this symposium (Young 1986), and I shall not consider them further.

Apart from the small band of dedicated FC staff, most entomologists visiting or resident in Scotland have largely ignored the coniferous plantations. Instead, they seek out the relict areas of 'Caledonian' pine forest or concentrate on the deciduous woodlands, especially the birchwoods (*Betula* spp.) of the Highlands. In both these ecotypes, their quest is for species of insects with distributions in Britain restricted to the Highland forests. Such species may have an arctic–alpine distribution in continental Europe. Most entomologists give only a cursory inspection of the outer margins of the dark serried ranks of Sitka spruce (*Picea sitchensis*) and lodgepole pine (*Pinus contorta*) plantations, whilst the attention of the FC entomologists is usually only attracted when a particular insect species reaches epidemic proportions. It will, therefore, come as no surprise to learn that our knowledge of the entomology of Scottish upland forests is somewhat scanty. That which does exist is largely scattered through the literature and is difficult to find and abstract. My intention here is to provide an introduction to the major sources of information in this field, without too much specific detail.

2 Broadleaved woodlands

In Scotland, broadleaved woodlands are typical of the central lowlands and the coastal fringe, especially on the west coast. Crowson (1962, 1964) made a particular study of the Coleoptera of oakwoods (*Quercus* spp.) within easy reach from Glasgow, and recorded a number of species with a very restricted distribution in Scotland. In the 1960s and early 1970s, teams of entomologists, funded by the Nature Conservancy and Shell Chemical Company, surveyed several areas of Scotland, paying particular attention to National Nature Reserves (NNRs). The resulting lengthy species lists are not suitable for publication and most now reside in various Nature Conservancy Council files. However, accounts of one such survey have been published for the Isle of Rhum (Steel & Woodroffe 1969; Wormell 1982). Despite the small size and recent origin of woodland of both deciduous and coniferous species, the accounts contain reference to many woodland insects. Woodroffe (1974) also compared Hemiptera found on Rhum with those collected in other surveys based on Speyside, Deeside, and at Invernaver, but interpretation of the species list requires a previous knowledge of the biology of this group of insects.

Regrettably, most insects found in Scottish broadleaved woodlands are, with very few exceptions, much more abundant in the woods of England and Wales. Many species of insect appear to have spread into Scotland along the milder coastal regions, so that broadleaved trees in Caithness, Sutherland and even on the Orkneys have what can be regarded as a diluted southern fauna, with the addition of a few northern elements. However, our present knowledge of the insect fauna of the western oak/birch woodlands is very limited, and many such woods are either totally unknown entomologically or such information as does exist resides in private collections and notebooks. It is mainly in the central Highlands where the insect fauna differs markedly. I have previously described typical examples from a wide range of habitats (Welch 1974, 1981) and will not consider Scottish broadleaved woodlands further here.

3 Coniferous woodlands

In 1974, the Nature Conservancy set up a Native Pinewoods Discussion Group as a forum for owners, managers and scientists concerned with the conservation and study of native pinewoods (*Pinus* spp.) in Scotland. This initiative culminated in a symposium volume in which Hunter (1977) provided an excellent review of the 'ecology of pinewood beetles'. He lists 129 species of Coleoptera associated with pine, of which 4 are of doubtful status. Of the remainder, 105 are known to occur in Scotland, and 44 of these have a geographic range lying mainly within the relict Caledonian forests. Hunter mentions an additional 6 species which occur both in pine and in association with other trees. Although relying heavily on published records, much of this account is based on his own experience in the field. Not only is this the most comprehensive record of any group of pine insects in Britain, but it is rare among published accounts in distinguishing the Scottish element of the fauna. Speight (1985) argues the absence of Caledonian pine insects in Ireland as evidence for the extinction there of Scots pine (*Pinus sylvestris*), and for its present fauna having been acquired since its reintroduction by man.

The Lepidoptera of the Cairngorms NNR were surveyed by MacAlpine (1979a, b) and most of his trapping sites were in pine forest. His published lists contain 393 species but, unfortunately, for most he provides only locality and date of collection. For only 4 species is pine mentioned as the host plant, although the knowledgeable reader will recognize a number of other species associated with pine, and a few known to feed on species of spruce (*Picea* spp.). Many other lists of Lepidoptera have been published for Scottish counties or localities but, often for brevity, data on habitat or host plant are lacking. Such lists usually presume that the reader possesses that information. It will always be the case that the 'expert' can read more into a simple list than the novice, which is no help to the latter.

It can be seen that even for the 2 best studied insect groups, the Lepidoptera and Coleoptera, data are poor. Information on the other Orders is even more sparse. Crooke (1957) reviewed 27 species of conifer-feeding sawflies (Hymenoptera: Symphyta), and, in recent years, Liston has published on Scottish species but, although several are pests of conifers, very few of his papers concern this element of the fauna (Liston 1981). Among a list of 66 conifer forest insects, Speight (1985) included 35 species of Symphyta. Of these, the larvae of 4 species of wood wasp in the family Siricidae are recorded feeding on a wide range of tree hosts. Eleven species in the families Diprionidae, Pamphilidae and Xyelidae have foliage-feeding larvae which prefer pine as their plant host. A further 11 species, almost exclusively Tenthredinidae, feed on spruce, but 9 of these also feed on fir (*Abies* spp.). Eight species are recorded from larch (*Larix* spp.). Published accounts of other groups such as Homoptera and Diptera are few and far between. However, in his list of conifer insects, Speight includes 20 species of hoverfly (Diptera: Syrphidae), 3 of which have saproxylic larvae, whilst the remainder feed on aphids and related plant bugs. Eight species are listed exclusively from pine, but such predators generally have less specific relationships with their host plants.

3.1 Colonization of conifers by native and introduced insects

Hunter (1977) comments that 'it would be difficult to assemble separate British lists of beetles for species of *Pinus*, and it is doubtful if such lists would differ'. However, Speight (1985) considers that 'in Great Britain it is possible to differentiate between the faunas of indigenous *P. sylvestris* forest ("Caledonian" pine forest) and commercial *Pinus* plantations (includ-

ing plantations of *P. sylvestris*)' (cf Welch 1974, 1981). He further remarks that, although the saproxylic species associated with European pines are well represented in Britain, those species 'exclusive to one or another of the introduced genera of conifers are generally lacking'. The inference is that colonization by those insects which feed on the foliage and shoots is much more rapid than colonization by species feeding on the woody tissues and associated saprophytic fungi. This hypothesis is supported by the fact that most of the 'Urwaldtiere', or ancient forest indicator species, fall into this latter group. One would expect, therefore, that the colonization of introduced conifers will be by the true phytophages. The primary hindrance to the accumulation of such data is the reluctance, or inability, of most entomologists to record the host tree beyond the generic level. This reluctance is true for both coniferous and broadleaved species, but is particularly true for introduced conifers. Not surprisingly, such information as does exist stems almost entirely from publications by FC staff, not least because they can identify the tree species concerned.

Crooke (1957) listed 9 species of sawfly feeding on spruce and 7 on larch. He noted that, like their hosts, all were introductions into Britain. Furthermore, Japanese larch (*Larix leptolepis*) and hybrid larch (*L. eurolepis*) appeared to be more attractive to the larch sawflies than European larch (*L. decidua*), and *Neodiprion sertifer* readily transferred from its usual host, Scots pine, to lodgepole pine. When present in high densities, this insect was also capable of feeding on Sitka spruce.

Winter (1983) provides data for several species of lepidopterous larvae feeding on both native and introduced conifers. Under pine, he distinguishes Scots pine, lodgepole pine, Corsican pine, (*P. nigra*) and Monterey pine (*P. radiata*), whilst under spruce he includes Norway and Sitka spruce, together with 2 records for oriental spruce (*P. orientalis*) and one for Serbian spruce (*P. omorika*). In an FC Booklet, presently in preparation, Bevan gives some information on the preferred or alternative hosts of a number of insect species. However, it is among the Homoptera, with their more intimate relationship with their host plant, that specific differences are best observed. Carter (1983) provides a useful summary of the occurrence of 13 adelgid and 35 aphid species on 18 species of conifer in Britain. He comments that only one adelgid is native to Britain, and among the aphids it is probable that only 4 of the 22 species of *Cinara* (Lachnidae) are native. Parthogenetic, winged, female aphids are among the first phytophagous insects to colonize exotic tree species. Most have spread to Britain from Europe, although 2 polyphagous species, one the ubiquitous bean aphid (*Aphis fabae*), now feed on young seedling conifers throughout Britain. Adelgids are more catholic in their choice of host. Those of European origin may form galls on Asiatic and American spruces, but adelgids introduced from North

Plate 1. Cultivation of deep peat moorland by double mouldboard plough at Naver Forest, Sutherland (Photograph Forestry Commission)

Plate 2. Shrub layer of juniper and well-developed ground layer of tussocky heather and bilberry in an opening of the old, native pine forest of Glen Tanar (Photograph N Picozzi)

Plate 3. Fifth instar pine beauty moth larva (Photograph R Parks)

Plate 4. Defoliation caused by pine beauty moth larvae at Rimsdale, near Tongue, Sutherland (Photograph R Parks)

Plate 5. Birchwood at Dunbeath, Caithness. Stable core on cliff, with some expansion over old pasture (Photograph G F Peterken)

Plate 6. Rassel Ashwood showing the dramatic regeneration within an enclosure. c1973 (Photograph G F Peterken)

Plate 7. Management of native pinewoods must be carefully planned to benefit wildlife such as capercaillie and these golden eagles (Photograph N Picozzi)

Plate 8. A family group of red deer in pre-thicket Sitka spruce. Red deer are now resident, often at high densities, in most forestry plantations in Scotland (Photograph M D C Hinge

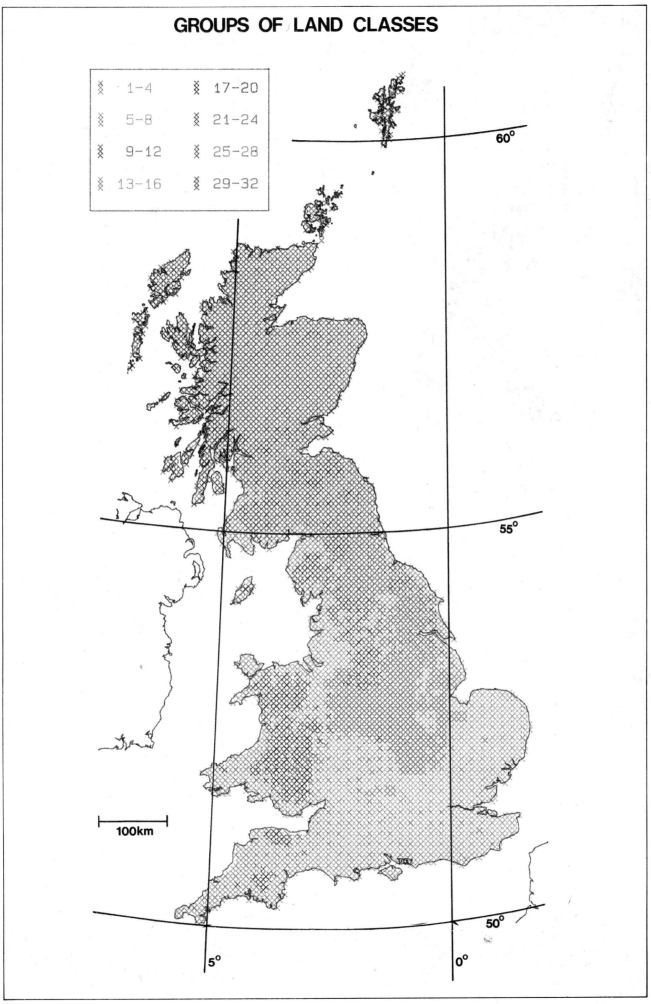

GROUPS OF LAND CLASSES

⁂	1–4	⁂	17–20
⁂	5–8	⁂	21–24
⁂	9–12	⁂	25–28
⁂	13–16	⁂	29–32

60°

55°

50°

5°   0°

100km

Plate 9. Map showing the distribution in the UK of 32 land classes characterized by Bunce *et al.* (1982) (source: Bunce & Last 1981)

A1

B1

A2

B2

Plate 10. Fruitbodies and mycorrhizas formed by species of Laccaria (early state) and *Leccinum* (late-stage) with birch (A1 *Laccaria proxima* and A2 *Laccaria*-type; B1 *Leccinum roseofracta* and B2 *Leccinum*-type) (Photograph A1 A2, A Crossley; B1 B2, V Fleming)

America almost exclusively gall only American species of spruce.

Perhaps the most interesting tree colonists are those insects which have previously not had a conifer as a host plant. As early as 1933, larvae of the bilberry tortrix (*Aphelia viburnana*) and the narrow-winged pug (*Eupethecia nanata*) had been recorded severely damaging young plantations of various conifers after exhausting their normal food plants, bilberry (*Vaccinium*), heath (*Erica*) and heather (*Calluna vulgaris*) in Cornwall and parts of Wales (Crystal 1937). Styles (1959, 1961) was the first to compile lists of Lepidoptera reared on unusual food plants based on FC field survey notes and record cards. As more and more previously treeless upland areas were being planted, mainly with introduced conifers, so such unusual records increased. Several species of Lepidoptera appear to have found the young succulent shoots of these conifers a readily acceptable alternative to the grasses, heather and other moorland plants on which they normally fed. Between 1968 and 1970, Winter (1974) investigated the causes of post-planting losses in recently afforested areas, including 18 forests in Scotland. He provided the first records for 24 species of lepidopterous larvae feeding on conifers, of which Sitka spruce was the most common new host. Some woodland species such as the winter moth (*Operophtera brumata*) and dotted border (*Agriopis marginaria*) were being increasingly found adapting to moorland conditions, feeding on heather (Wormell 1977). These events were unusual enough in that both species have flightless females and rely for dispersal upon aeronauting first instar larvae. However, once established in such areas, remote from deciduous woodland, the winter moth proved capable of a further change of food plant and became a pest of young Sitka spruce. More recently in south-east Scotland, and in the absence of heather and bog myrtle (*Myrica gale*), winter moth is behaving as a primary pest of plantations 8–12 years old (Stoakley 1985). Early plantings of larch on areas of purple moor-grass (*Molinia caerulea*) have suffered ring-barking by the clay-coloured weevil (*Otiorhynchus singularis*).

Foresters have always kept a watchful eye on the dangers of introduced pests. The large larch bark beetle (*Ips cembrae*), which was first recorded on larch in northern Scotland in 1955, has since spread south as far as Peebles and has been found on windblown Sitka spruce. Another long-expected arrival from northern Europe was the great spruce bark beetle (*Dendroctonus micans*), albeit at present confined to England and Wales. Although only discovered in 1982, by counting the annual rings of the tissues occluded following attack, it was clear that this beetle had been in the UK since about 1973 (Bevan & King 1983). Bevan (1986), aware of such dangers, regards the white pine weevil (*Pissodes strobi*) and 3 species each of the scolytids *Dendroctonus* and *Ips* as having a 'high quarantine hazard risk'. One of these species is the 8-toothed spruce bark beetle (*Ips typographus*). Although it has been recorded regularly since 1849, breeding in Britain is not proven (Winter 1985). Winter (1983) also lists some Scolytidae and Cerambycidae known only as non-breeding introductions in spruce and pine.

Many species of Lepidoptera are widespread and of common occurrence in low numbers on pines in Britain, but only rarely reach pest proportions. However, lodgepole pine has proved to be unusually susceptible to attack by species such as the pine shoot moth (*Rhyacionia buoliana*), larch bud moth (*Zeiraphera diniana*), pine looper (*Bupalus piniaria*), and the pine beauty moth (*Panolis flammea*). An intensive study of the pine beauty moth has revealed differences in larval behaviour from that reported for this species on the continent (Bevan 1986). This is quite a common, although not well-documented, phenomenon. Many species of phytophagous insect may behave differently on the same host plants in Britain and on the continent. Even pest species, which have been the subjects of prolonged research in continental Europe, may behave quite differently in Britain. Hunter (1977) points out that 77 of the species of beetle which he lists for Scots pine are considered in Finland to be associated with spruce. In 17 of these species, this association is thought to be especially close. He mentions 6 pine species which have been found on spruce in Britain and states 'no doubt many others are capable of the same transition'.

3.2 Numbers of insect species on 4 conifer genera

Southwood (1961) was the first person to assemble data concerning the number of insect species associated with their host trees in Britain. Insect data were taken from only 3 Orders, Hemiptera, Lepidoptera and Coleoptera. In addition to the native Scots pine and European larch, an introduction since 1629, Southwood included Norway spruce (*Picea abies*) and species of fir (*Abies* spp. (*alba*)) on the strength of there having been native trees in Britain before the last glacial phase, noting their reintroduction in the 16th and 17th centuries respectively. However, in updating this information (Kennedy & Southwood 1984), he retains spruce but inexplicably drops fir; otherwise, the same tree hosts are used but coverage of insect orders is greatly improved, with the resulting increase in numbers of associated insect species.

Exactly what comprises an 'associated insect' is still a matter for considerable discussion, and even personal interpretation. In Table 1, I have attempted to compile lists of the numbers of insects attributed to 4 conifer genera by various authors. Comparison of the 2 lists by Southwood and Kennedy shows how the data have been improved since the much-quoted 1961 paper. In each case, the records are referable to a single host species. I have included Hunter's comprehensive Coleoptera list for Scots pine for comparison, and the list prepared for Carlisle and Brown (1968) by O W

Table 1. Numbers of insect and mite species associated with 4 genera of conifers in Britain

Host	Pinus							Picea					Abies				Larix				
Reference* (author's initials & date)	TRES 1961	CEJK & TRES 1984	AC & AHFB 1968	FAH 1977	TGW 1978–83 JHS 1959–61	DB 1985	PIDB 1985	TRES 1961	CEJK & TRES 1984	TGW 1979–83 JHS 1959–61	DB 1985	PIDB 1985	TRES 1961	TGW 1979–83 JHS 1959–61	DB 1985	PIDB 1985	TRES 1961	CEJK & TRES 1984	TGW 1979–83 JHS 1959–61	DB 1985	PIDB 1985
Acarina	0	1	0	—	1	1	2	0	0	2	3	2	0	0	0	2	0	1	0	0	2
Heteroptera	15	15	10	—	1	—	23	9	9	0	—	14	5	0	—	8	3	3	0	0	7
Homoptera	3	10	8	—	16	8	21	1	14	18	10	22	0	7	3	9	0	6	7	3	6
Thysanoptera	0	5	0	—	0	—	5	0	1	1	—	0	0	0	—	0	0	0	0	0	0
Lepidoptera	38	41	28	—	41	12	56	19	22	58	7	36	3	17	0	25	12	16	39	3	28
Diptera	0	2	2	—	3	2	10	0	3	1	0	5	0	0	0	8	0	1	1	1	5
Hymenoptera	0	11	12	—	12	3	20	0	10	13	6	22	0	2	1	19	0	5	8	6	13
Coleoptera	35	87	32	131	30	16	126	8	11	15	12	77	8	5	1	52	2	6	4	2	39
Total	91	172	92	(131)	104	42	263	37	70	108	38	178	16	31	16	123	17	38	59	15	100

*DB 1985 = D Bevan's MS for Forestry Commission Booklet
PIDB = ITE's phytophagous insect data bank (see text)

Richards. When I compared the lists of Styles (1959, 1961) with that of Winter (1974, 1983), I found numerous inconsistencies. In his 1983 FC Booklet, Winter includes only some, but not all, of Styles' records and also omits some from his own earlier publication. I have, therefore, combined all these records into a single column entry for all 4 tree hosts. I have taken the liberty of abstracting details from Bevan's forthcoming Booklet as it is hoped that this will become widely used by practising foresters when available. His selection of insect species is based not only on those known to feed directly upon their host, but upon those species for which the Entomology Branch of the FC had received most enquiries over the years. It is, therefore, biased towards pests and the more obvious species. This and the remaining lists include the combined records of insects from a number of different tree species within each genus. For example, of the 94 insect species listed from spruce by Winter (1983), 19 were recorded from Norway spruce and 29 from Sitka spruce. Among those from non-specific spruces are 5 Coleoptera not yet known to breed in Britain. Similarly, a further 3 are included in his list for pines. I should remind you that Bevan's list also includes 5 spruce and 2 pine insects of similar status.

The last columns for each tree genus in Table 1 contain data from the Institute of Terrestrial Ecology's Phytophagous Insect Data Bank (PIDB). The data included here are a very small part of the mammoth undertaking by Dr Lena K Ward and D F Spalding to abstract important published literature containing references to the relationships between insects in Britain and their recorded plant hosts. Many of the records are taken from European sources which must be treated with caution when considering the British fauna. However, in many cases, although an insect may be well known from a particular host in Britain, the only published account so far abstracted (and possibly the only such reference) is from a continental reference. Table 1 provides the non-specialist with some indication of the range and accessibility of data on insects and their tree hosts. All numbers given in Table 1 relate to Britain as a whole, and many species included may not occur in Scotland.

4 Conclusions and recommendations

I hope that I have demonstrated the scattered nature of the available published data on woodland and forest insects. Much more information may exist in an unpublished form, so that the combined personal knowledge of various specialist entomologists, foresters and ecologists will vastly exceed this summary. In my opinion, the root of the problem lies in our lack of knowledge of the ecology of introduced tree species. This is true for broadleaved as well as coniferous species. There appear to be 3 major areas where more information is urgently needed and where future work could be directed. These are as follows.

4.1 Mapping introduced trees

Most county floras and plant mapping schemes ignore introduced trees, although occasionally they are included for counties where they regenerate naturally. We need to know more about their distribution in Britain. Jeffers (1972) provides some useful 10 km distribution maps for Scots pine, Corsican pine, lodgepole pine, Norway spruce and Douglas fir, but Sitka spruce is notable by its absence. If it has not already been done, a start could be made by bringing together planting records for this (and other) species from all the FC Conservancies. Hopefully, this compilation could include not only plantings on land owned by the FC, but also for grant-aided schemes in private woodlands. This information, in turn, could possibly be supplemented by data from the Kew Index of Living Collections, which already contains the computerized records of trees at Kew, Wakehurst Place, and 53 National Trust properties. Once such base maps are available, there will be an incentive for others to add to them.

4.2 Recording insects on introduced trees

There is nothing better guaranteed to promote a flow of information than the production of a 'definitive' list of insect species. We should consider publishing lists of those insects which are currently known to occur on such trees as Sitka spruce. We should not then just sit back and await the anticipated flood of 'additional' records, but should consider implementing an active survey programme in order to understand better which insects are able to utilize these vast new man-made habitats, and to encourage other people to do likewise.

4.3 Colonization from Caledonian pinewoods into plantations

Many of the native pinewood areas identified by Steven and Carlisle (1959) were small relict populations which had survived at the heads of glens or in locations which became isolated by adjacent felling and forest clearance. As a result, many of the rare insects associated with them have survived in isolated pockets throughout the Highlands. Increasingly, these areas have become caught up in the approaching legions of commercial plantations so that they may now be contiguous with, or relatively close to, young conifers of various species. I can only reiterate Hunter's (1977) comment that 'the ability of relict pinewood species to colonise plantations has (still) not yet received sufficient attention'. He also saw the need for monitoring the development of the beetle fauna in a number of new pine plantations within the Caledonian forest area. Ten years have passed since that symposium, and the plea for more detailed information in this field is as real today as it was then.

5 Summary

A brief background is given to our present state of knowledge of forest entomology in Scotland, which explains how entomologists have largely ignored recent conifer plantations in favour of relict 'Caledonian' pinewoods and broadleaved woodlands. The insect fauna of the latter is regarded as being essentially a diluted southern fauna with some additional northern elements.

Some examples are given of the types of insect species lists prepared by individuals and teams of entomologists. The acceptability of such lists for publication and the interpretation of their contents are discussed.

Introduced conifers are typically colonized by insects which have either transferred from a native tree, or have themselves become established by accidental introduction or natural immigration. Some immigrant pests from continental Europe and North America are considered, and the susceptibility of certain introduced tree hosts to native insects is discussed. Particular attention is also paid to the increasing ability of certain insects to transfer to conifers from unrelated native host plants.

Data on the numbers of insect species associated with 4 conifer genera, *Pinus*, *Picea*, *Abies* and *Larix*, are presented, combining records from various sources. Caution is stressed when continental insect host data are used.

Recommendations are made for the distributional mapping of introduced trees in Britain, and the recording of the insects associated with them. It is also suggested that the movement of insects between Caledonian pinewood relics and conifer plantations be investigated.

6 Acknowledgements

I am deeply grateful to my colleagues Dr Lena K Ward and D F Spalding for providing me with the available data in their Phytophagous Insect Data Bank, and for their time and assistance in ensuring that I understood the resulting coded printouts. It is a pleasure also to thank D Bevan for access to the manuscript of his Forestry Commission Booklet.

7 References

Bevan, D. 1986. *Forest insects.* (Forestry Commission booklet.) London: HMSO. In press.

Bevan, D. & King, C.J. 1983. *Dendroctonus micans* Kug. – a new pest of spruce in UK. *Commonw. Forest. Rev.,* **62,** 41–51.

Carlisle, A. & Brown, A.H.F. 1968. *Pinus sylvestris* L. (Biological flora of the British Isles, no. 109.) *J. Ecol.,* **56,** 269–307.

Carter, C.I. 1983. Some new aphid arrivals to Britain's forests. *Proc. Trans. Br. ent. nat. Hist. Soc.,* **16,** 81–87.

Carter, C.I. & Nichols, J.F.A. 1985. Host plant susceptibility and choice by conifer aphids. In: *Site characteristics and population dynamics of lepidoteran and hymenopteran forest pests,* edited by D. Bevan & J.T. Stoakley, 94–99. (Forestry Commission research and development paper no. 135.) London: HMSO.

Crooke, M. 1957. A brief review of the British conifer feeding sawflies. *Z. angew. Entomol.,* **41,** 179–183.

Crowson, R.A. 1962. Observations on Coleoptera in Scottish oak woods. *Glasg. Nat.,* **18,** 177–195.

Crowson, R.A. 1964. Additional records of Coleoptera from Scottish oak woods. *Glasg. Nat.,* **18,** 371–375.

Crystal, R.N. 1937. *Insects of the British woodlands.* London: Warne.

Davies, E.J.M. 1985. *Forestry in Scotland.* Edinburgh: Forestry Commission.

Forestry Commission. 1985. *Forestry facts and figures 1984–85.* Edinburgh: FC.

Hunter, F.A. 1977. Ecology of pinewood beetles. In: *Native pinewoods of Scotland,* edited by R.G.H. Bunce & J.N.R. Jeffers, 42–55. Cambridge: Institute of Terrestrial Ecology.

Jeffers, J.N.R. 1972. Conifers and nature conservation. In: *Conifers of the British Isles,* 59–73. London: Royal Horticultural Society.

Kennedy, C.E.J. & Southwood, T.R.E. 1984. The numbers of species of insects associated with British trees: a re-analysis. *J. Anim. Ecol.,* **53,** 455–478.

Liston, A.D. 1981. Notes on little known British *Pristophora* Lat. (Hym., Tenthredinidae) of the *abietina* group. *Entomologist's mon. Mag.,* **117,** 73–75.

100

MacAlpine, E.A.M. 1979a. The Lepidoptera of the Cairngorms National Nature Reserve. *Entomologist's Rec. J. Var.,* **91,** 1–6, 65–70, 213–216, 241–244.

MacAlpine, E.A.M. 1979b. The Macrolepidoptera of Inverness-shire – Newtonmore District, Supplement 10. *Entomologist's Rec. J. Var.,* **91,** 157.

Southwood, T.R.E. 1961. The number of species of insect associated with various trees. *J. Anim. Ecol.,* **30,** 1–8.

Speight, M.C.D. 1985. The extinction of indigenous *Pinus sylvestris* in Ireland: relevant faunal data. *Ir. Nat. J.,* **21,** 449–453.

Steel, W.O. & Woodroffe, G.E. 1969. The entomology of the Isle of Rhum National Nature Reserve. *Trans. Soc. Br. Ent.,* **18,** 91–167.

Steven, H.M. & Carlisle, A. 1959. *The native pinewoods of Scotland.* Edinburgh: Oliver & Boyd.

Stoakley, J.T. 1985. Outbreaks of winter moth, *Operophtera brumata* L. (Lep., Geometridae) in young plantations of Sitka spruce in Scotland. *Z. angew. Entomol.,* **99,** 153–160.

Styles, J.H. 1959. Notes on some Microlepidoptera. *Entomologist's Gaz.,* **10,** 43–44.

Styles, J.H. 1961. Additions to the list of foodplants of Lepidoptera larvae, not recorded in 'Larval food plants' by P.B.M. Allan, and 'The caterpillars of the British moths' by W.J. Stokoe. *Entomologist,* **94,** 86–88.

Welch, R.C. 1974. Insects and other invertebrates. In: *The Cairngorms, their natural history and scenery,* edited by D. Nethersole-Thompson & A. Watson, Appendix 2, 257–285. London: Collins.

Welch, R.C. 1981. The modern story – insects. In: *The Cairngorms, their natural history and scenery,* edited by D. Nethersole-Thompson & A. Watson, 281–283. 2nd ed. Perth: Melvin Press.

Winter, T.G. 1979. New host plant records of Lepidoptera associated with conifer afforestation in Britain. *Entomologist's Gaz.,* **25,** 247–258.

Winter, T.G. 1983. *A catalogue of phytophagous insects and mites on trees in Great Britain.* (Forestry Commission booklet no. 53.) Edinburgh: Forestry Commission.

Winter, T.G. 1985. Is *Ips typographus* (Linnaeus) (Coleoptera: Scolytidae) a British insect? *Entomologist's Gaz.,* **36,** 153–160.

Woodroffe, G.E. 1974. Hemiptera from Rhum, the Cairngorms, Deeside and Invernaver. *Glasg. Nat.,* **19,** 101–114.

Wormell, P. 1977. Woodland insect population changes on the Isle of Rhum in relation to forest history and woodland restoration. *Scott. For.,* **31,** 13–36.

Wormell, P. 1982. The entomology of the Isle of Rhum National Nature Reserve. *Biol. J. Linn. Soc.,* **18,** 291–401.

Young, M.R. 1986. The effects of commercial forestry on woodland Lepidoptera. In: *Trees and wildlife in the Scottish uplands,* edited by D. Jenkins, 88–94. (ITE symposium no. 17.) Abbots Ripton: Institute of Terrestrial Ecology.

The effects of fenitrothion applications to control pine beauty moth on non-target animals in Scotland

H Q P CRICK

Department of Zoology, Culterty Field Station, University of Aberdeen, Aberdeen

1 Introduction

The pine beauty moth (*Panolis flammea*) became a pest in Scotland in 1976 when it defoliated an area of 120 ha of lodgepole pine (*Pinus contorta*) in Sutherland (Stoakley 1979a). After a failed attempt at control using the bacterium *Bacillus thuringiensis* in 1977, nearly 5000 ha of lodgepole pine were sprayed in 1978 with the organophosphate pesticide fenitrothion to avoid serious defoliation by this pest. Since 1978, fenitrothion has been the main chemical used in pine beauty control in Scotland, although much research is currently being undertaken to understand its outbreaks and to develop less toxic methods of control (Leather & Stoakley 1986). Fenitrothion is potentially harmful to animals, and this paper reviews what is known about the impact of the Scottish spraying programme on wild animal populations.

2 The pest and the pesticide

2.1 The pine beauty moth

The life cycle and pest status of the pine beauty moth in Scotland have been fully described elsewhere (Stoakley 1979a, b, 1981a, b), and are briefly summarized below. Before 1973, the pine beauty was considered to be endemic to British plantations of Scots pine (*Pinus sylvestris*). Although it was often a major pest in central Europe (Leather 1984), no outbreaks had occurred in Britain. In 1973, pine beauty moths were found to occur in plantations of lodgepole pine in Caithness and Sutherland. The pest status of the pine beauty in Scottish lodgepole pine plantations is summarized chronologically in Table 1.

The lodgepole pine is an introduction from western North America and is particularly adapted to wet, acid and infertile soils. It has been planted commercially in Scotland mainly since the late 1950s, and there are indications that it is most susceptible to pine beauty outbreaks when 10–20 years old and growing on deep unflushed peats. In its larval stage, the pine beauty causes damage to lodgepole pines. The moths overwinter as pupae in the soil and emerge in northern Scotland in early April. The adults mate and females lay the majority of their eggs in rows along pine needles in the crowns of trees in April and May. The eggs hatch at the beginning of June and the larvae go through 5 instars before descending to the ground to pupate in early August. Larvae initially feed on the new shoots of a tree and later attack older needles. Totally defoliated trees die from the top downward in winter and early spring.

2.2 Fenitrothion

The Forestry Commission (FC) chose fenitrothion for its pine beauty control programme because of the chemical's high toxicity to lepidopterous larvae, low toxicity to mammals and fish, and fairly low persistence in the environment (Stoakley & Heritage 1979). Additionally, there was much published information about the use of fenitrothion over large areas of North America to control the spruce budworm (*Choristoneura fumiferana*) (eg National Research Council of Canada 1975; Roberts *et al.* 1977). Fenitrothion inhibits the action of acetylcholinesterase in the nervous system, causing a build-up of acetylcholine at synapses and the failure of nerves to repolarize after a period of continuous stimulation (Fleming & Grue 1981). It is derived from thiophosphoric acid and has the chemical name of 0,0-dimethyl 0-(4-nitro-m-tolyl) phosphorothioate (Hill *et al.* 1975).

3 The spraying regime

3.1 Timing

Spraying is timed to occur as soon as possible after 90% of pine beauty eggs have hatched (Stoakley 1981a). This timing exposes the majority of the larval population to the pesticide, but minimizes damage to lodgepole pines by reducing the effects of larval feeding on them. Fenitrothion has usually been applied in Scotland during the first 2 weeks of June.

3.2 Application method

In 1978, the FC compared low-volume (LV) and ultra-low-volume (ULV) application techniques for the pine beauty control programme (Holden & Bevan 1979). It was found that the ULV technique had several advantages over the more conventional LV applications. In particular, ULV applications deposited pro-

Table 1. History of pine beauty moth on lodgepole pine in Scotland (source: Stoakley 1979a, 1981a, b, pers. comm.)

1973	Pine beauty moth on lodgepole pine in Highland Region
1976	Outbreak in Sutherland; 120 ha of lodgepole pine killed
1977	540 ha treated with *Bacillus thuringiensis*. Failed. c60 ha lodgepole pine killed. Autumn pupal counts of 12 000 ha of lodgepole pine reveal 5020 ha with high pine beauty populations
1978	4800 ha of lodgepole pine sprayed with fenitrothion
1979	3200 ha of lodgepole pine sprayed with fenitrothion, including new outbreaks in Grampian Region and in Dumfries and Galloway Region
1980	1400 ha sprayed
1981	60 ha sprayed
1982–84	No areas at risk or sprayed
1985	4700 ha sprayed

portionally more insecticide on target larvae and needles, deposited less on the ground, and gave a more even coverage of insecticide over a forest (Spillman & Joyce 1979). From 1979 onwards, spraying has been done by ULV methods.

ULV applications are made using rotary atomizers which produce a droplet spectrum with a mean diameter of 50μ. To avoid excessive evaporation before hitting the target area, a formulation with low volatility is used. This is a mixture of fenitrothion (50% emulsifiable concentrate) and butyl dioxitol. It is sprayed at a dosage rate of 300 g AI ha^{-1} (AI = active ingredient) and at a volume rate of 1 l ha^{-1}. The ULV system of small droplets, small volumes and a concentrated formulation uses turbulent air over the forest to effect pesticide deposition on to the target area, and therefore requires a minimum windspeed of about 3–4 knots (Stoakley 1981a).

3.3 Fenitrothion deposition

Deposition of fenitrothion on the foliage of the upper third of lodgepole pines is predicted to be 375 ng cm^{-2} (Joyce & Spillman 1979); but it has not been measured during standard ULV applications in the Scottish programme. Joyce and Beaumont (1979) measured fenitrothion deposition from a non-standard sequential spraying operation in which half the spray was applied on 2 successive days at 100 m lane separation to produce an overall spray with 50 m lane separation; they measured fenitrothion at 19.7 ppm on fresh foliage from the top third of sample trees. In 1978, using fluorescent tracer particles added to the formulation, measurements of droplet deposition after ULV treatments were attempted. Unfortunately, some of the dyes were only partially visible when foliage was examined and the results have a low degree of accuracy (Spillman & Joyce 1979; Joyce & Beaumont 1979).

Fenitrothion deposition at ground level has been measured from the collection of droplets by 100 cm^2 glass plates coated with a thin layer of silica gel (Ruthven 1979; Hamilton & Ruthven 1981a; Ruthven unpubl.; Hunter unpubl.). Fenitrothion deposition under trees in 1978 and 1979 was not significantly different between years and had a combined median of 19 g ha^{-1} (n=95), or 6.3% of the applied dosage rate. Deposition on open forest rides or roads in 1978, 1979 and 1985 was not significantly different between years and had a combined median of 53 g ha^{-1} (n=176), or 17.7% of the applied dosage rate. An experimental spraying operation in 2 plots, each of 70 ha, in 1984 gave a median deposition of 98 g ha^{-1} (n=77), 32.7% of the applied dose. This deposition was significantly larger than that measured in other years on open rides (Mann-Whitney, W = 12 020, P<0.0001), probably due to spraying when the wind-speed was at the minimum required for ULV applications. Overall, the majority (>90%) of the fenitrothion is deposited on the trees of a forest, and there is

evidence for only minimal (5%) deposition outside target areas (Holden & Bevan 1981).

Peak fenitrothion concentration in stream water after ULV applications was recorded at 48 μg l^{-1} on one occasion, but was usually less than 10 μg l^{-1} in 1978 (Wells et al. 1979) and was 19 μg l^{-1} in 1979 (Morrisson & Wells 1981). These peaks occurred within a few hours of spraying, after which concentrations declined rapidly to <1 μg l^{-1} 1–5 days later. Rainfall after spraying only results in a slight increase in fenitrothion in stream water in Scotland (Wells et al. 1979), and in Canada (Symons 1977).

4 Degradation of fenitrothion

No measurements of the degradation of fenitrothion have been made in Scottish lodgepole pine plantations. Studies in Canada have shown that spruce (Picea spp.) and fir (Abies spp.) foliage sprayed at 275 g ha^{-1} collected 2–4 ppm of fenitrothion, of which 50% was lost in 4 days and 70–85% lost by 14 days (Yule & Duffy 1971); a later study measured a loss of 50% in 2 days and 95% in 10 days (Sundarem 1974a). These losses were not due to metabolic processes or to intra-plant transport, but occurred by volatilization, photodegradation and weathering (Sundarem 1974a; Sundarem et al. 1975). A small fraction (0.3 ppm) is stored in cuticular waxes in conifer foliage (Sundarem et al. 1975), where it may persist for at least one year (Yule & Duffy 1971; Sundarem 1974b).

Fenitrothion is undetectable in forest soils 32–64 days after application and has a half-life of 2–4 days in acidic ponds, becoming undetectable within 40 days (Sundarem 1974a; Symons 1977).

5 Effects on pine beauty moth larvae

Hamilton et al. (1981) measured fenitrothion residues of 1.3–2.7 ppm on pine beauty larvae after standard ULV applications. This figure is less than the LD90 of 24 ppm (after 6 h) found by Stoakley and Heritage (1979). However, measurements of larval mortality at 4 sites sprayed in 1979 show a 97% kill (Stoakley 1981a, b). This phenomenon can be explained by the observations of Joyce et al. (1981) that, within seconds of spraying, larvae become very active and collect a lethal dose initially by crawling over sprayed foliage and later by ingesting poisoned foliage. Deaths of larvae stop after 2–3 days.

6 Effects on non-target animals

6.1 Terrestrial invertebrates

The effects of fenitrothion applications on non-target terrestrial invertebrates in Scotland have not been studied in detail. Tilbrook (1979) observed that, after fenitrothion applications in 1978, pine sawfly larvae (Neodiprion sertifer), aphids and lepidopterans were killed; he also observed that there was a 50–100% drop in the numbers of 2 species of dragonfly observed flying in 2 small plots after spraying. Hamilton and Ruthven (1981b) analysed a few dipterans and lepidopterans found dead on the day of spraying and found substantial fenitrothion residues (0.48–24.7 ppm) on them; but insects found on subsequent days did not have detectable residues, although they exhibited symptoms consistent with poisoning. The numbers of flying insects, mainly dipterans, significantly decreased after spraying in 1984, as measured from the numbers caught on sticky traps attached to tree trunks (Spray *et al.* in prep.). However, casual observations have been made of geometrid moths, bumblebees, flies, mayflies, stoneflies and dragonflies flying in plantations shortly after spraying (Tilbrook 1979; Wells *et al.* 1979).

Additional information comes from the catches of terrestrial insects in drift net samples taken from streams in sprayed areas. (Drift nets are fine-meshed nets placed perpendicularly to the flow of water to catch invertebrates drifting downstream.) In 1978, one stream showed a very significant increase (>1000%) in terrestrial insects after spraying; but in another stream there was a large decrease (>50%), the most abundant insects being psocopterans, dipterans and plecopterans (Wells *et al.* 1979).

Information from North American studies has to be interpreted with care because of important differences in spraying regimes compared with Scotland (Crick & Spray 1986). Studies of the impact of fenitrothion applications at 280 g ha^{-1} or less have demonstrated (i) decreases in ground-dwelling insects 2–3 days after spraying, with populations recovering by the following year (Buckner 1974), (ii) decreases in predatory insects (NRCC 1975), (iii) increases in insects and spiders caught in drop cloths, decreases in carabid beetle and lycosid spider populations for at least a year, and decreases in spruce budworm predators and parasites (Symons 1977). Other studies have shown large mortalities of honey bee (*Apis mellifera*) and wild bee populations (Wood 1977; Plowright 1977), although Buckner (1974) showed that the numbers dying were a small proportion of the total population in a hive. One 10-year study has monitored the arthropod fauna of balsam fir (*Abies balsamea*) forests subject to intermittent or perennial fenitrothion applications (Varty 1977). Mortality of non-target arthropods occurred in a patchy pattern, both spatially and temporally, and population recuperation was usually rapid. It was concluded that forest arthropod communities were resilient to certain types of pesticide usage.

6.2 Freshwater invertebrates

The median 24 h LC50 for aquatic insects is 66 μg l^{-1}, with a range of 0.5–40 474 μg l^{-1} (Symons 1977). The majority of LC50s were greater than the maximum fenitrothion concentration found in Scottish forests (48 μg l^{-1}, see above), and the time course of fenitrothion in Scottish streams shows that aquatic invertebrates will be subject to a much lower average concentration over 24 hours. It can be expected that there will be little mortality in streams after standard ULV spraying.

The effects of fenitrothion applications on freshwater invertebrates in Scotland have been studied using drift nets in 1978 and 1979. In 1978, the numbers of ephemeropteran, plecopteran, trichopteran and dipteran nymphs or larvae caught in drift nets increased rapidly within a few hours of spraying. The numbers caught then decreased rapidly as fenitrothion concentrations in the streams fell (Wells *et al.* 1979). Kick samples taken one month after spraying showed qualitatively that representatives of many freshwater invertebrates were still living in affected streams. Similar increases in invertebrate drift have been found in Canada after fenitrothion applications (Flannagan 1973; NRCC 1975; Lockhart *et al.* 1977). Such downstream drift can decrease insect biomass in streams by 15% (Symons 1977).

In a further Scottish study in 1979, Morrisson and Wells (1981) found that, although a significant increase in the drift of invertebrates downstream occurred after a fenitrothion application, a high percentage of each drift net sample was alive and very active when caught. Caged invertebrates, such as nymphal or larval ephemeropterans, plecopterans, trichopterans and adult coleopterans all survived in the contaminated stream, juvenile forms even changing successfully into the winged stage. Sampling of the bottom fauna showed no overall change in numbers of animals following spraying.

6.3 Fish

The 24 h or 48 h LC50s recorded for freshwater fish are about 100 times greater than the maximum fenitrothion concentration found in Scottish streams (Symons 1977, see above). Wells *et al.* (1979) made detailed observations in 1978 in Scotland. They found that caged rainbow trout (*Salmo gairdneri*) held in a stream in an area sprayed with fenitrothion showed no stress or abnormal behaviour. Fenitrothion uptake by fish was rapid, with maximum concentrations of 0.97–1.91 mg kg^{-1} within 6–12 h of spraying; its loss occurred over the next 5 days and followed the concentration profile of the stream water. Among 36 caged salmon fry at 3 sites, 2 died, their deaths not ascribed to fenitrothion poisoning, and the concentration of fenitrothion in those surviving to 5 days after spraying was 3–6 ng g^{-1}. The concentrations of fenitrothion in wild fish caught 2 days after spraying in 2 streams were 0.78–1.48 μg g^{-1} (n=6) in brown trout (*Salmo trutta*) and 0.03–0.59 μg g^{-1} (n=12) in eels (*Anguilla anguilla*); no fenitrothion was detectable in fish caught one month later.

In 1979 in Scotland, Morrisson and Wells (1981) observed no mortalities among juvenile salmon or trout caged in a stream inside a sprayed forest during 5 days after spraying. No movements of wild fish were observed after spraying. Fenitrothion concentration in fish (unnamed species) taken from a contaminated stream followed the concentration profile in the water. Maximum concentrations were: in the skin

0.25 mg kg^{-1}, in the stomach and its contents 0.22 mg kg^{-1}, in muscle 0.16 mg kg^{-1}, and in the liver 0.08 mg kg^{-1}; the concentrations in each of the 4 tissues fell to 0.02 mg kg^{-1} after 24 hours (all measurements refer to wet weight of tissue).

Canadian studies confirm the lack of effect (reviewed above) of fenitrothion on fish in sprayed areas. Although fenitrothion residues have been found in the fish shortly after spraying, no mortalities have been observed (Symons 1977), or any reductions in plasma or brain acetylcholinesterase (Lockhart et al. 1977). The only reported effect has been that fish may grow more slowly because of reduced invertebrate food supply (Symons 1977).

6.4 Amphibians

The effect of fenitrothion on amphibians in the Scottish spraying programme has not been investigated. However, Canadian studies have shown that amphibians have a high tolerance to fenitrothion, and no effects on their populations have been observed in forest ponds sprayed with up to 800 g ha^{-1} (Buckner 1974).

6.5 Birds

The effect of fenitrothion in Scotland on forest birds has been the subject of a detailed 3-year investigation (Spray et al. in prep.), and has been reviewed in detail by Crick and Spray (1986). A brief summary of their conclusions is given below.

Birds tend to be more sensitive to the toxic effects of pesticides (including organophosphates) than mammals due to a number of physiological attributes (Walker 1983). Also, sensitivity to the effects of organophosphates increases as species body mass decreases (Hill et al. 1975) and as age decreases within a species (Ross & Sherman 1960; Hudson et al. 1972). Spray et al. (in prep.) concentrated their studies on the 5 commonest passerine species in lodgepole pine plantations, and especially upon the small-bodied, canopy-living coal tit (Parus ater). Larger forest species, such as capercaillie (Tetrao urogallus), have not been studied because of their low population densities and secretive habits.

There is no evidence that ULV fenitrothion applications cause any reduction in numbers of breeding passerines within forest plantations in Scotland, as measured from territory mapping and point count censuses or mortalities among adults or nestlings. Sublethal poisoning of adult birds has been measured after commercial fenitrothion applications (Hamilton et al. 1981), but spraying has not affected the breeding success of coal tits in nest boxes (Spray et al. in prep.). Sublethal effects on the growth of nestlings may occur, but confirmation of the results awaits the analysis of data obtained during spraying operations in 1985 (Crick in prep.).

6.6 Mammals

Small mammals were trapped in Scottish lodgepole pine plantations after fenitrothion applications in 1978 and 1979. No fenitrothion residues were detected in 3 woodmice (Apodemus sylvaticus), in 3 short-tailed voles (Microtus agrestis) or in 3 common shrews (Sorex araneus) collected within 24 h of ULV spraying (Tilbrook 1979). However, the duration of trapping may have been too short to detect fenitrothion accumulation by insectivorous shrews. In 1979, one common shrew was caught on the day after spraying, and fenitrothion residues (0.19 mg kg^{-1} whole body) were found only on its skin and fur (Hamilton & Ruthven 1981b). Thereafter, 2 common shrews were caught 2 days post-spray, 2 more were caught 4 days post-spray, then 8 common and 3 pygmy shrews (Sorex minutus) were caught 5 days post-spray; these contained between <0.02–0.08 mg kg^{-1} body weight, all on the skin and fur. The effects of such residues are unknown, but are probably not lethal. Reviews of laboratory toxicity studies reveal a variability in LD50 for mice of 870–1416 mg kg^{-1} (ingested) and 220 mg kg^{-1} (intravenous), and for rats of 200–740 mg kg^{-1} (ingested) and 33 mg kg^{-1} (intravenous) (NRCC 1975; Symons 1977).

In Canada, fenitrothion application rates of <413 g Al ha^{-1} did not measurably affect small forest mammals; at higher rates, populations of juvenile masked shrews (Sorex cinereus) were reduced such that, at 1238 g ha^{-1}, their mortality reached 100% (Buckner 1974). Laboratory studies of masked shrews, red-backed voles (Clethrionomys gapperi) and white-footed mice (Peromyscus maniculatus) showed that fenitrothion affects young animals more than old, females more than males, shrews more than voles, and voles more than mice (Buckner et al. 1977). At 275 g ha^{-1}, breeding was suppressed, animals missed oestrus, had stillbirths and regressed their foetuses. However, there was evidence for shrews learning to avoid injected mealworms, a factor which could be important in reducing the effects of fenitrothion applications on forest mammals. Repeated applications of fenitrothion at 275 g ha^{-1} may slightly reduce small mammal populations over 5 years (Buckner et al. 1977). Finally, a study in Japanese forests showed that fenitrothion sprayed at 1200 g ha^{-1} had no demonstrable effects on plasma or erythrocyte acetylcholinesterase concentrations or on the populations of the Japanese woodmouse (Apodemus speciosus) (Tabata & Kitahara 1980).

7 Discussion

7.1 What we know

ULV fenitrothion applications are a very successful short-term control method for pine beauty moth larvae in lodgepole pine plantations in Scotland. However, it is also clear that long-term control cannot be achieved by a single spraying, as areas treated in 1978–79 have had to be resprayed in 1985. This is a general feature of the chemical control of insect pests (Dahlsten 1983; Dahlsten & Rowney 1983; Pimental & Andow 1984).

The effects of fenitrothion applications on each class of non-target animal have been assessed in varying degrees of detail. The best studied group are the common small forest passerines which are not affected by spraying, except for apparently minor sublethal poisoning. Freshwater fish are not affected lethally or sublethally by the fenitrothion concentrations in streams flowing through sprayed forests, although there is the possibility that they could be affected by decreases in their invertebrate food supply. Freshwater invertebrates in streams become more active after forest spraying, thereby increasing their drift downstream; lethal effects are not usually observed, although some types of animal are theoretically at risk. Small forest ground-dwelling mammals are unlikely to be affected by fenitrothion applications, because (i) mammals have a relatively low sensitivity to fenitrothion, (ii) the concentrations of fenitrothion reaching the forest floor are low, and (iii) mammals show tendencies to avoid poisoned prey.

7.2 What we don't know

In Scottish lodgepole pine plantations, the least studied group of animals is probably the most at risk from fenitrothion. These are the terrestrial invertebrates. Amphibians have not been studied either, but they are known to have a low sensitivity to organophosphate poisoning (Hall & Kolbe 1980). Studies of mammals have concentrated on small ground-dwelling species and not on bats, carnivores or large herbivores. The freshwater ecosystem has been investigated over the short term, but long-term effects of large-scale invertebrate drift after fenitrothion spraying are unknown. The long-term effects of spraying on forest animals other than common passerines in Scotland have not been studied.

The faunal composition of lodgepole pine plantations in Scotland is largely undescribed, especially the terrestrial invertebrate, amphibian and mammalian fauna. The impact of fenitrothion applications on non-target animals cannot be assessed accurately if the pre-spray populations are unknown. The common passerines have been studied most thoroughly in the light of fenitrothion spraying, but even among birds the mainly coniferous-dwelling species such as capercaillie, redwing (*Turdus iliacus*), crossbill (*Loxia* spp.) and siskin (*Carduelis spinus*) have not been studied.

It is important to remember that the lodgepole pine plantation is a man-created habitat and that populations of animal species which are adapted to conifers would probably not be present there without the plantation. Afforestation in upland Scotland usually occurs on open moorland or hill farmland, and some animals are able to live both in open land and in woods (Harris 1983). However, species which make the transition between habitats may be less well adapted to living in plantations than in moorland, and, if they are adversely affected by fenitrothion applications, then local populations may become endangered. Unless comparative faunal surveys are made in lodgepole pine plantations and in the habitats they replace, the national importance of the effects of fenitrothion applications on animal populations cannot be assessed.

The biggest question mark over the spraying programme is whether fenitrothion applications will be required more frequently in future and in greater concentrations. Pesticide resistance and the destruction of natural enemies by pesticides are common phenomena (Pimental *et al.* 1980) and could pose problems in Scotland in the future. In a very different forest spraying programme in Canada, it has been suggested that the chemical control of spruce budworm outbreaks may prolong the duration of outbreaks and hasten their recurrence (Blais 1974). The consequences of repeated applications on wildlife populations may be different from those after one application. However, animals in high latitude areas tend to have relatively high reproductive rates (Lack 1954; Krebs 1972), and therefore their populations are probably capable of rapidly recovering any losses caused by fenitrothion applications. In Scotland, the populations of birds apparently most vulnerable to the effects of fenitrothion are not affected except in very minor ways (Spray *et al.* in prep.). In Canadian coniferous forests, the populations of terrestrial arthropods and birds have been resilient to the effects of large-scale, long-term, perennial fenitrothion spraying programmes (Varty 1977; Pearce & Peakall 1977); it seems reasonable to expect the same to be the case in the much smaller scale and less frequent spraying programme in Scotland.

9 Summary

The pine beauty moth has been a defoliating pest in lodgepole pine plantations in Scotland since 1976. The organophosphate pesticide fenitrothion has been used to control these outbreaks; it is applied at 300 g ha^{-1} and 1 l ha^{-1} using ultra-low-volume techniques. Canadian studies have shown that fenitrothion persists at high concentrations for only 10–14 d, but this fact has not been confirmed in Scotland. Commercial control kills 97% of pine beauty moth larvae. The full effects of fenitrothion on non-target terrestrial invertebrates are unknown in Scotland, but large numbers may be killed. Concentrations of fenitrothion in streams cause significant invertebrate drift, but are rarely at lethal levels. Freshwater fish are unaffected directly by fenitrothion in streams. Amphibians have not been studied but are unlikely to be affected by fenitrothion applications. Populations of small forest passerines are not affected by spraying, although minor sublethal poisoning of adults and nestlings occurs. The consequences of spraying on forest mammals have not been assessed. It is concluded that the impact of fenitrothion on non-target animals cannot be fully measured until faunal surveys are made which determine the national importance of the habitat for animals. Furthermore, the consequence of more frequent spraying in the future, if it becomes necessary, cannot be predicted from present information from Scotland, although Canadian studies have shown that some animal populations are resilient to the effects of repeated spraying.

10 References

Blais, J.R. 1974. The policy of keeping trees alive via spray operations may hasten the recurrence of spruce budworm outbreaks. *For. Chron.*, **50**, 19–21.

Buckner, C.H. 1974. *The biological side-effects of fenitrothion in forest ecosystems.* (Information report CC–X–67.) Ottawa: Chemical Control Research Institute.

Buckner, C.H., Sarazin, R. & McLeod, B.B. 1977. The effects of the fenitrothion spray programme on small mammals. In: *Fenitrothion: the long-term effects of its use in forest ecosystems – current status*, edited by J.R. Roberts, R. Greenhalgh & W.K. Marshall, 377–390. (NRCC publication no. 15389.) Ottawa: National Research Council of Canada.

Crick, H.Q.P. & Spray, C.J. 1986. The impact of aerial application of fenitrothion on forest bird populations. In: *Population biology and control of the pine beauty moth* (Panolis flammea), edited by S.R. Leather & J. T. Stoakley. (Research and development paper no. 139.) Edinburgh: Forestry Commission. In press.

Dahlsten, D.L. 1983. Pesticides in an era of integrated pest management. *Environment (Wash. D.C.)*, **25**, 45–54.

Dahlsten, D.L. & Rowney, D.L. 1983. Insect pest management in forest ecosystems. *Environ. Manage.*, **7**, 65–72.

Flannagan, J.F. 1973. Field and laboratory studies of the effect of exposure to fenitrothion on freshwater aquatic invertebrates. *Manit. Ent.*, **7**, 15–25.

Fleming, W.J. & Grue, C.E. 1981. Recovery of cholinesterase activity in five avian species exposed to dicrotophos, an organophosphate pesticide. *Pestic. Biochem. Physiol.*, **16**, 129–135.

Hall, R.J. & Kolbe, E. 1980. Bioconcentration of organophosphorus pesticides to hazardous levels by amphibians. *J. Toxicol. environ. Health*, **6**, 853–860.

Hamilton, G.A. & Ruthven, A.D. 1981a. Deposition of fenitrothion at ground level. In: *Aerial application of insecticide against pine beauty moth*, edited by A.V. Holden & D. Bevan, 77–84. (Occasional paper no. 11.) Edinburgh: Forestry Commission.

Hamilton, G.A. & Ruthven, A.D. 1981b. The effects of fenitrothion on some terrestrial wildlife. In: *Aerial application of insecticide against pine beauty moth*, edited by A.V. Holden & D. Bevan, 91–100. (Occasional paper no. 11.) Edinburgh: Forestry Commission.

Hamilton, G.A., Hunter, K. & Ruthven, A.D. 1981. Inhibition of brain acetylcholinesterase activity in songbirds exposed to fenitrothion during aerial spraying of forests. *Bull. environ. Contam. Toxicol.*, **27**, 856–863.

Harris, J.A. 1983. *Birds and coniferous plantations.* Tring: The Royal Forestry Society.

Hill, E.F., Heath, R.G., Spann, J.W. & Williams, J.D. 1975. Lethal dietary toxicities of environmental pollutants to birds. *Spec. scient. Rep. U.S. Fish. Wildl. Serv., Wildl.*, no. 191. Washington DC.

Holden, A.V. & Bevan, D., eds. 1979. *Control of pine beauty moth by fenitrothion in Scotland 1978.* (Occasional paper no. 4.) Edinburgh: Forestry Commission.

Holden, A.V. & Bevan, D., eds. 1981. *Aerial application of insecticide against pine beauty moth.* (Occasional paper no. 11.) Edinburgh: Forestry Commission.

Hudson, R.H., Tucker, R.K. & Haegele, M.A. 1972. Effect of age on sensitivity: acute oral toxicity of 14 pesticides to mallard ducks of several ages. *Toxicol. appl. Pharmacol.*, **22**, 556–561.

Joyce, R.J.V. & Beaumont, J. 1979. Collection of spray droplets and chemical by larvae, foliage and ground deposition. In: *Control of pine beauty moth by fenitrothion in Scotland 1978*, edited by A.V.

Holden & D. Bevan, 63–80. (Occasional paper no. 4.) Edinburgh: Forestry Commission.

Joyce, R.J.V. & Spillman, J.J. 1979. Discussion of aerial spraying techniques. In: *Control of pine beauty moth by fenitrothion in Scotland 1978*, edited by A.V. Holden & D. Bevan, 13–24. (Occasional paper no. 4.) Edinburgh: Forestry Commission.

Joyce, R.J.V., Schaefer, G.W. & Allsopp, K. 1981. Distribution of spray and assessment of larval mortality. In: *Aerial application of insecticide against pine beauty moth*, edited by A.V. Holden & D. Bevan, 15–46. (Occasional paper no. 11.) Edinburgh: Forestry Commission.

Krebs, C.J. 1972. *Ecology.* New York: Harper & Row.

Lack, D. 1954. *Natural regulation of animal numbers.* Oxford: Clarendon.

Leather, S.R. 1984. Factors affecting pupal survival and eclosion in the pine beauty moth, *Panolis flammea* (D&S). *Oecologia*, **63**, 75–79.

Leather, S.R. & Stoakley, J.T., eds. 1986. *Population biology and control of the pine beauty moth* (Panolis flammea). (Research and development paper no. 139.) Edinburgh: Forestry Commission. In press.

Lockhart, W.L., Flannagan, J.F., Moody, R.P., Weinberger, P. & Greenhalgh, R. 1977. Fenitrothion monitoring in southern Manitoba. In: *Fenitrothion: the long-term effects of its use in forest ecosystems – current status*, edited by J.R. Roberts, R. Greenhalgh & W.K. Marshall, 233–252. (NRCC publication no. 15389.) Ottawa: National Research Council of Canada.

Morrisson, B.R.S. & Wells, D.E. 1981. Assessment of the effect on the aquatic environment of aerial spraying with fenitrothion. In: *Aerial application of insecticide against pine beauty moth*, edited by A.V. Holden & D. Bevan, 85–90. (Occasional paper no. 11.) Edinburgh: Forestry Commission.

National Research Council of Canada. 1975. *Fenitrothion: the effect of its use on environmental quality and its chemistry.* (NRCC publication no. 14104.) Ottawa: NRCC.

Pearce, P.A. & Peakall, D.B. 1977. The impact of fenitrothion on bird populations in New Brunswick. In: *Fenitrothion: the long-term effects of its use in forest ecosystems – current status*, edited by J.R. Roberts, R. Greenhalgh & W.K. Marshall, 299–306. (NRCC publication no. 15389.) Ottawa: National Research Council of Canada.

Pimental, D. & Andow, D.A. 1984. Pest management and pesticide impacts. *Insect Sci. Applic.*, **5**, 141–149.

Pimental, D., Andow, D.A., Dyson-Hudson, R., Gallahan, D., Jacobson, S., Irish, M., Kroop, S., Moss, A., Schreiner, M., Thompson, T. & Vinzant, B. 1980. Environmental and social costs of pesticides: a preliminary assessment. *Oikos*, **34**, 126–140.

Plowright, R.C. 1977. The effect of fenitrothion on forest pollinators in New Brunswick. In: *Fenitrothion: the long-term effects of its use in forest ecosystems – current status*, edited by J.R. Roberts, R. Greenhalgh & W.K. Marshall, 335–342. (NRCC publication no. 15389.) Ottawa: National Research Council of Canada.

Roberts, J.R., Greenhalgh, R. & Marshall, W.K., eds. 1977. *Fenitrothion: the long-term effects of its use in forest ecosystems – current status.* (NRCC publication no. 15389.) Ottawa: National Research Council of Canada.

Ross, E. & Sherman, M. 1960. The effect of selected insecticides on growth and egg production when administered continuously in the feed. *Poultry Sci.*, **39**, 1203–1211.

Ruthven, A.D. 1979. Deposition of fenitrothion at ground level. In: *Control of pine beauty moth by fenitrothion in Scotland 1978*, edited by A.V. Holden & D. Bevan, 95–102. (Occasional paper no. 4.) Edinburgh: Forestry Commission.

Spillman, J.J. & Joyce, R.J.V. 1979. Low volume and ultra-low volume spray trials from aircraft over Thetford Forest. In: *Control of pine beauty moth by fenitrothion in Scotland 1978*, edited by A.V. Holden & D. Bevan, 31–51. (Occasional paper no 4.) Edinburgh: Forestry Commission.

Stoakley, J.T. 1979a. The pine beauty moth – its distribution, life-cycle and importance as a pest in Scottish forests. In: *Control of pine beauty moth by fenitrothion in Scotland 1978,* edited by A.V. Holden & D. Bevan, 7–12. (Occasional paper no. 4.) Edinburgh: Forestry Commission.

Stoakley, J.T. 1979b. *Pine beauty moth.* (Forestry Commission forest record no. 120.) London: HMSO.

Stoakley, J.T. 1981a. Control of the pine beauty moth, *Panolis flammea,* by aerial application of fenitrothion. In: *Aerial application of insecticide against pine beauty moth,* edited by A.V. Holden & D. Bevan, 9–14. (Occasional paper no. 11.) Edinburgh: Forestry Commission.

Stoakley, J.T. 1981b. 1979/80 spraying forecast and programme completed. In: *Aerial application of insecticide against pine beauty moth,* edited by A.V. Holden & D. Bevan, 111. (Occasional paper no. 11.) Edinburgh: Forestry Commission.

Stoakley, J.T. & Heritage, S.G. 1979. Selection of an insecticide for aerial application. In: *Control of pine beauty moth by fenitrothion in Scotland 1978,* edited by A.V. Holden & D. Bevan, 25–29. (Occasional paper no. 4.) Edinburgh: Forestry Commission.

Sundarem, K.M.S. 1974a. *Distribution and persistence of fenitrothion residues in foliage, soil and water in Larose Forest.* (Information report CC–X–64.) Ontario: Chemical Control Research Institute.

Sundarem, K.M.S. 1974b. *Persistence studies of insecticide: III. Accumulation of fenitrothion and its oxygen analog in foliage, soil and water in Larose Forest.* (Information report CC-X-65.) Ontario: Chemical Control Research Institute.

Sundarem, K.M.S., Yule, W.N. & Prasad, R. 1975. *Studies of foliar penetration, movement and persistence of C-14 labelled fenitrothion in spruce and fir trees.* (Information report CC-X-85.) Ontario: Chemical Control Research Institute.

Symons, P.E.K. 1977. Dispersal and toxicity of the insecticide fenitrothion; predicting hazards of forest spraying. *Residue Rev.,* **68,** 1–36.

Tabata, K. & Kitahara, E. 1980. Effects of fenitrothion (Sumithion) spraying on the population density and the blood cholinesterase activity of the Japanese wood mouse, *Apodemus speciosus* Temmink. *Appl. Entomol. Zool.,* **15,** 242–248.

Tilbrook, P.J. 1979. The effects on wildlife of fenitrothion application to Forestry Commission plantations in Sutherland. In: *Control of pine beauty moth by fenitrothion in Scotland 1978,* edited by A.V. Holden & D. Bevan, 133–141. (Occasional paper no. 4.) Edinburgh: Forestry Commission.

Varty, I.W. 1977. Long-term effects of fenitrothion spray programs on non-target terrestrial arthropods. In: *Fenitrothion: the long-term effects of its use in forest ecosystems – current status,* edited by J.R. Roberts, R. Greenhalgh & W.K. Marshall, 343–376. (Publication report no. 15389.) Ottawa: National Research Council of Canada.

Walker, C.H. 1983. Pesticides and birds–mechanisms of selective toxicity. *Agric. Ecosyst. Environ.,* **9,** 211–226.

Wells, D.E., Morrisson, B.R.S. & Cowan, A.A. 1979. Chemical and biological observations in streams following aerial spraying of forests with fenitrothion. In: *Control of pine beauty moth by fenitrothion in Scotland 1978,* edited by A.V. Holden & D. Bevan, 103–131. (Occasional paper no. 4.) Edinburgh: Forestry Commission.

Wood, G.W. 1977. The effects of the fenitrothion spray programme on bees and pollination. In: *Fenitrothion: the long-term effects of its use in forest ecosystems – current status,* edited by J.R. Roberts, R. Greenhalgh & W.K. Marshall, 321–334. (NRCC publication no. 15389.) Ottawa: National Research Council of Canada.

Yule, W.N. & Duffy, J.R. 1971. *The persistence and fate of fenitrothion insecticide in a forest environment.* (Information report CC-X-10.) Ottawa: Chemical Control Research Institute.

Protecting the timber resource

J T STOAKLEY
Forestry Commission, Northern Research Station, Edinburgh

1 Introduction
This paper deals with the protection of commercial forests against insect pests. It aims to discuss 3 questions:

i. What is the timber resource requiring protection?
ii. What are the insect species against which protection may be required?
iii. What is involved in providing that protection?

2 The timber resource requiring protection
This resource includes all existing woodland and plantations, from planting to rotation age, managed chiefly for timber production whether by the Forestry Commission or under private ownership. In Scotland, it amounts to 950 kha, of which a very high proportion can be taken as upland in character. The resource therefore includes new plantations formed by the restocking of older plantations as they come to maturity and are felled, currently at the rate of some 3700 ha yr^{-1}. Forestry in Scotland is still expanding by afforestation at the rate of about 19 kha yr^{-1}.

Much of our forest is planted on former hill grazings mostly on soils of poor quality, in agricultural terms, and some very poor indeed. However, a generally mild and moist climate results in good tree growth overall and rotations which are short by continental standards. Nevertheless, we still have a preponderance of plantations in the younger age classes as a result of the expansion occurring after the Second World War, with new ecological conditions still being created which may influence the occurrence of pest outbreaks. As with the forests, so with the pests: the situation is dynamic rather than static.

The tree species include a preponderance of conifers, with 91% in Scotland as a whole and a higher proportion in the uplands. There is very great emphasis on Sitka spruce (*Picea sitchensis*), and to a lesser extent on lodgepole pine (*Pinus contorta*), and the range of possible pest species in Scotland is correspondingly limited compared with those in southern Britain. Although fashionably deplored, the paucity of tree species can be justified by the primary objectives of timber production and lack of logical alternatives, and the large-scale use of Sitka spruce has yet to be contra-indicated by any really significant pest problems. In any case, lack of diversity in crop structure is, I suggest, a phase resulting from the short history of forestry on most sites. Extensive afforestation, particularly with exotics, can be seen as a large-scale ecological experiment in which the occurrence and distribution of insect pest outbreaks is just one of the many ways in which we learn where the limitations of site, species and silvicultural practice lie, prompting suitable adjustments as far as possible. In 3 instances over the past 30 years, the long-term solution to severe pest outbreaks has been a managerial decision to change the species, and this approach had the strong support of the entomologists involved.

3 Potential insect pests and the nature of the damage
The species of insects which feed on, and therefore cause some degree of harm to, trees are, of course, legion and give ample scope to the spanophilia of enthusiastic forest entomologists. This enthusiastic love of the rare should certainly not be deplored, because it is the background to the identification and evaluation of any pest problem which arises. However, the list of species which regularly or frequently cause damage regarded by forest managers, as well as by entomologists, as significant in terms of tree growth and crop value in the Scottish uplands is much more limited. This list contains fewer species than are pests in Britain as a whole, but it includes some species which represent problems for forestry in the Scottish uplands in particular. As already suggested, the pest status of species is likely to change with changing circumstances. For example, in the 1960s, such a list would almost certainly have included the larch sawfly (*Anoplonyx destructor*), which at that time caused considerable defoliation of larch (*Larix* spp.) plantations, particularly in Tayside Region, but which has not occurred in outbreak numbers since 1970. It would also have included the ambrosia beetle (*Trypodendron lineatam*), which was an important cause of timber degrade, particularly in the west Highlands, but is now less so due to hot logging. On the other hand, a 1960s list would certainly not have included the pine beauty moth (*Panolis flammea*). This species is perhaps our most important forest insect pest today, but it did not come to any prominence until the late 1970s, coincident with the arrival at thicket stage of the first extensive plantations of lodgepole pine, largely on acid peats, in the Highland Region of Scotland.

The pest species included in Table 1, which may be significant in the eyes of the resource manager, can be classified very simply according to the kind of damage which results from outbreak numbers.

3.1 Damage causing death of trees
Severe defoliation of tree crops understandably causes considerable alarm, but the number of pest species capable of causing death of trees in significant numbers is very small. Of course, it has often been pointed out that it is not in the interest of a

Table 1. Insect species responsible for severe damage to conifer plantations in the Scottish uplands (source: original information)

Outcome of severe attack	Species responsible
1. Death of trees due to: i. destruction of cambium	Pine weevil (*Hylobius abietis*) and black pine beetles (*Hylastes* spp.) Large larch bark beetle (*Ips cembrae*)
or ii. complete defoliation	Pine beauty moth (*Panolis flammea*) Pine looper moth (*Bupalus piniaria*)
2. Loss of apical dominance and stem form in addition to probable loss of volume increment, due to destruction of current shoots	Larch bud moth (*Zeiraphera diniana*) Winter moth (*Operophtera brumata*)
3. Loss of height and girth increment without more lasting damage, due to damage to older foliage	Green spruce aphid (*Elatobium abietinum*) Pine sawfly (*Neodiprion sertifer*)

well-adapted pest to destroy its host. In order to put forest insect pest problems into perspective, I will now outline the relevant characteristics of the current main pest species.

The so-called pine weevil (*Hylobius abietis*) and associated black pine beetles (*Hylastes* spp.), both of which breed in and attack all common conifer species, are almost invariably a real threat to young plants in restocking areas. Populations depend on the existence of stumps of the previous crop and other felling debris which they use as breeding material; and insecticidal protection of planting stock is a routine requirement. In its effect, this is spot treatment rather than overall application of insecticides to land.

Outbreaks of the pine beauty moth on lodgepole pine in the late 1970s have been followed by a further series of outbreaks in much the same areas, largely on the Moine Series, in 1984 and 1985, with further high populations confidently predicted for 1986. High numbers of larvae cause complete defoliation of both current and older needles. Infested trees, although they may be able to set buds, subsequently die in consequence without any apparent contribution from secondary factors. Aerial application of insecticide is essential if large-scale destruction of crops is to be prevented. There is now a considerable move towards planting Sitka spruce/lodgepole pine mixtures on sites which would have previously carried lodgepole pine only. This move has resulted from a reappraisal of the potential of Sitka spruce on such sites, and not solely from a desire to spread the risk from pine beauty moth.

Pine looper moth (*Bupalus piniaria*) also causes complete defoliation of pines, usually Scots pine (*Pinus sylvestris*), although on one occasion lodgepole pine has been severely at risk. Defoliation occurs late in the season, unlike that due to the pine beauty moth, and one season's heavy attack is probably not fatal. However, in Scots pine plantations, the *coup de grâce* is usually administered by pine shoot beetle (*Tomicus*

piniperda) the following spring. As with pine beauty, the threat of crop destruction calls for aerial application of insecticide.

The large larch bark beetle (*Ips cembrae*), a species introduced from Europe in the late 1940s or early 1950s, provides the only important example in the Scottish uplands of a bark beetle capable of killing trees. Circumstantial evidence suggests that some degree of stress is necessary to predispose the trees to attack, eg drought or sudden exposure. The insect breeds successfully in logs of most conifer species, but larches are the only live trees attacked. Outbreaks have been sporadic and of limited extent, perhaps reflecting the occurrence of larch, and control measures generally do not extend beyond the practice of good forest hygiene. Where logs cannot be removed quickly from the forest during the breeding season, some application of insecticide may be necessary.

3.2 Permanent damage from loss of apical dominance
In recent years, 2 insect species have been notable for causing a degree of permanent damage to crop trees. The so-called larch bud moth (*Zeiraphera diniana*) has so far been of very little significance on larch in Britain, but has occurred in the Scottish uplands and north-east England as a major pest of lodgepole pine and, to a lesser extent, Sitka spruce. Larval feeding takes place only on current shoots. In light attacks, only a small proportion of shoots are infested, with only one or 2 larvae per shoot, so that damage is unimportant and good terminal buds are set. However, heavy attacks with many larvae per shoot result in destruction of the shoots, consequent loss of tree form, and even permanent stunting; in severe outbreaks, occasional trees may be killed.

The winter moth (*Operophtera brumata*) is well known throughout Europe as a defoliator of a wide range of hardwood species. In Scotland, it has been recorded as a pest of Sitka spruce from time to time since the late 1950s, when an outbreak occurred in Rumster Forest (Caithness District of Highland Region). Recent extensive outbreaks in the Borders have shown that the existence of high populations does not depend on the immediate proximity of other food plants and the insect must now be regarded as a primary pest of Sitka spruce. The damage, which is confined to current shoots, is very similar to that caused by the larch bud moth.

So far, no detailed economic appreciation has been made of damage caused by these 2 insects. Any such appreciation would need to take account of possible reduction in timber quality, as well as lost increment. No attempt has so far been made to control the larch bud moth in Britain. One attempt, which was only partially successful, has been made to control winter moth on Sitka spruce; this attempt was carried out in the belief that the eventual unit value of potentially high-quality timber would be reduced. Both insects feed within the protection of needles spun together with webbing. As a result, control presents considerable technical difficulties.

3.3 Loss of height and girth increment

Again, there are 2 prominent examples, the attacks of which are largely confined to older needles so that damage to current growth, and consequent stem deformation, does not occur.

The green spruce aphid (*Elatobium abietinum*), although a sucking insect, is a well-known cause of defoliation of spruces, and particularly Sitka rather than Norway spruce (*Picea abies*). High populations may occur in both autumn and early spring but the insect, which continues to reproduce throughout the winter, is susceptible to winter cold. Widespread damage was last seen in the mid-1970s when there was a succession of uninterrupted mild winters. A very high monetary value has been placed on the estimated overall increment loss of one year of severe damage. Nevertheless, insecticidal control has never been considered necessary or practical on the forest scale.

The pine sawfly (*Neodiprion sertifer*) is familiar as a pest of both Scots and lodgepole pine. Although it also attacks older crops, it has attracted most notice as a problem in pre-thicket stage lodgepole pine in the Scottish uplands. Outbreaks lasting several years commonly delay suppression of competing heather (*Calluna*) and reduce the growth of the pine to a measurable degree. Epizootics of a naturally occurring nuclear polyhedrosis virus specific to this insect are a major factor in the eventual collapse of populations. The application of a formulation of this virus as a microbial insecticide earlier in the outbreak cycle can be used as an effective control measure. The virus was first applied from the air on a commercial scale in 1984 when 3000 ha were treated, and a similar programme was carried out in 1985. Prior to this, it was not considered necessary to use conventional insecticides against the insect, although the costs would be very similar to those involved in use of the virus. It is perhaps as well to remember that the availability of an environmentally safe treatment is not alone sufficient to justify its use. Although recent investigations do suggest that the cost of aerial application of Virox is justified when balanced against the increment loss due to a significant outbreak, the necessity for treatment deserves further critical appraisal.

4 What is involved in the protection of tree crops?

The foregoing has indicated some approaches to a protection philosophy. Bearing in mind that the growing of trees is a long-term business and the creation of forests even more so, there are inevitably 2 timescales involved. In an ideal world, all forests would, in the long term, be growing in healthy balance with their environment. In order to achieve this balance, the forests would consist of species mixtures and stand structures which, *inter alia*, minimized the opportunities for pests to reach outbreak numbers. However, it has to be recognized that a perfect balance is unlikely to be obtainable and that a very great amount of trial and error will be involved in any approach to such a balance. Furthermore, although the objective is laudable, it may in practice be difficult to reconcile with the economic needs of the real world of timber production. Nevertheless, it is a poor forester who does not respond to the ecological lessons of the forest. The fact that many insect outbreaks are site-related is well appreciated, even if not fully understood, and taking evasive action by changing the species has already been mentioned. In some cases, this change has been coupled with cultivation or drainage to improve the site. Recent investigations of pine beauty moth have shown that the south coastal provenance of lodgepole pine, which was most favoured in earlier plantings, is the most susceptible. Although the indications are that other suitable provenances are not immune, their use (which is, in any case, in train for other reasons), coupled with other measures, may be one way in which the risk of devastating outbreaks can be reduced.

However, in the short term, it is the duty of the forester, as of any resource manager, to protect his assets by the best means immediately available. In case of actual or anticipated outbreaks, there are 3 principal considerations.

i. Is the insect capable of causing economic damage?
ii. If so, are the numbers present or anticipated likely, on good evidence, to result in significant loss?
iii. If this is the case, what control measures are to be employed having due regard to environmental considerations?

It is fashionable in some quarters to berate foresters for carrying out necessary control measures. Such attacks sometimes arise apparently from a background of ignorance, wilful or otherwise, and often give no credit either to the professionalism of most foresters or to their feeling that it is their environment also. In addition, it must be stressed that the use of pesticides has been most stringently regulated under the Pesticides Safety Precautions Scheme, with the forest environment being recognized as one in which special care is needed; certainly, there is no reason to think that new arrangements about to be enforced will be more lenient.

While foresters will naturally tend to err on the safe side in making control decisions, they should, as already suggested, be able to back those decisions with population data and evidence that such populations, if unchecked, will cause real harm. In both state and private forests, the planning of control operations against pine beauty moth and pine looper is based on counts of overwintering pupae. Also, the need for treatment has always been checked by egg counts made shortly before spraying is due, and on occasion proposed programmes have been reduced in consequence. In 1984, an apparently small pine beauty outbreak with only moderate numbers of pupae found during the previous winter was deliberately left unsprayed as a check on our previous assumptions about the population levels at which unacceptable damage would occur. As it happens, these assumptions were broadly confirmed .

The control of both these insects, the only ones against which aerial spraying has proved unequivocally necessary on the basis of anticipated death of trees, depends to date on the use of chemical insecticides. For the pine looper moth, there has been a progression to safer insecticides, from DDT in the 1950s and 1963 to an organophosphorus insecticide, tetrachlorvinphos, in 1970 and 1977 and Dimilin (diflubenzuron) from 1979. Dimilin offers a real step forward as it is active only against the immature stages of invertebrates, and thus has no significant mammalian toxicity, does no direct harm to fish, and does not kill the adult stages of insect predators and parasitoids.

The first attempt to control pine beauty moth was made with a preparation of a bacterium (*Bacillus thuringiensis*) which is active only against the larvae of Lepidoptera. However, this substance proved disastrously ineffective, and subsequent commercial control operations have used the organophosphorus insecticide, fenitrothion. The use of this insecticide

was coupled with the introduction and further development of an ultra-low-volume (ULV) technique designed to maximize the number of spray droplets deposited on target foliage. Operations in 1978 and 1979 were extensively monitored without showing any significant problems, and further investigations of possible effects on upland bird populations have been made since.

Investigations on the ULV application of fenitrothion to forest trees have been the basis of research, by the Institute of Virology at Oxford, on the use of this same technique for treatment of pine sawfly and pine beauty moth with specific viruses. Pine beauty virus is likely to be used on a commercial scale in the near future. In 1985, Dimilin has also been applied very successfully at ULV against pine beauty moth in a field trial.

There are thus good grounds for saying that our most serious pests can be controlled, where necessary, with minimum harm to the environment, and there is a firm commitment to further development in this direction.

5 Summary
The current forest resource of Scotland is described briefly. It is emphasized that forest conditions and associated pest problems are found to change with time. Insects of real forest importance are distinguished from those which are mainly of entomological interest. The impact of the main pest species and the corresponding importance of control measures are described under 3 headings:

   i. damage causing death of trees;
  ii. permanent damage from loss of apical dominance; and
 iii. loss of height and girth increment.

Long- and short-term crop protection measures are discussed. The former are based on the achievement of a healthy balance between the forest and its environment; the latter depend mainly on the application of insecticides, following appraisal of the damaging potential of the pest and of the numbers occurring. Recent developments aimed at increasing the efficacy and environmental safety of aerial control measures are summarized, including the use of a more selective insecticide, diflubenzuron, and of host-specific viruses, and the introduction of an ultra-low-volume application technique.

Mammals of Scottish upland woods

B W STAINES

Institute of Terrestrial Ecology, Banchory

1 Introduction

In this paper I discuss the distribution and status of mammals in upland woods in Scotland, with particular reference to the effects of commercial forestry.

2 Status and distribution

There is little quantitative information about the status of most Scottish upland mammals, but generalized maps and biological accounts are found in Corbet and Southern (1977). Maps compiled by the Mammal Society (Corbet 1971) and the ITE Biological Records Centre (BRC) (Arnold 1984) (Table 1) largely rely on non-systematic records from observers and relate to a 10 km grid; absence can mean 'not present' or merely 'not looked for'. The response from observers in Scotland has generally been poor. The Wildlife Branch of the Forestry Commission (FC) has conducted and published 5-yearly wildlife surveys since 1973. These surveys are compatible with those of the BRC, but are restricted to species present on FC land, and do not include those found elsewhere in the same 10 km grid squares. The survey also refers to the one point in time and does not take into account whether or not a species had been present in the recent past. Hence, grey squirrels (*Sciurus carolinensis*) have been reported in the valley of the River Dee, Aberdeenshire, by FC staff, but they do not appear in their survey results as they were not actually seen on FC property.

The Clyde Area Branch of the Scottish Wildlife Trust has produced 'atlases' of wild vertebrates present in various parts of the Clyde area, and recently there have been systematic surveys of single species such as otters (*Lutra lutra*) (Green & Green 1980), pine martens (*Martes martes*) (Verlanders 1983) and wild cats (*Felis silvestris*) (Easterbee in progress), which give a much more objective idea of distribution and status than hitherto.

In any case, there are many problems of finding mammals, let alone enumerating them, compared, for example, with birds. Birds are more obvious, visually and vocally, and are mostly diurnal; they also attract greater public interest. Reasonable estimates of abundance can be made by counting the number of singing, territorial cocks in the spring (eg Moss 1978). Mammals, on the other hand, are more secretive, frequently nocturnal, and it is only in species such as moles (*Talpa europea*) and badgers (*Meles meles*) that leave obvious signs, that the problems are lessened somewhat. One important exception is the red deer (*Cervus elaphus*) living on open hill land. It is Britain's largest land mammal and is relatively easily seen and counted in open country. Sample counts have been made by the Red Deer Commission (RDC) since 1960, and these counts suggest a rise in total numbers from 180 000 in 1965 to 270 000 in 1984 (Stewart 1979, 1985). The counting technique is described by Stewart (1976), and the one test of consistency made from a population reconstruction using mortality data (Lowe 1969) suggested a level of precision for total numbers around 2%, although errors in classifying the sexes and different age classes were larger.

Other estimates of the population size of various mammals rely on intensive studies at particular sites or in specific habitats. The densities found in these studies are then extrapolated to similar habitats elsewhere and, too often, to dissimilar ones. Although this approach gives some idea of what densities might

Table 1. Recent sources for information on the distribution and status of mammals in upland Scotland

i. General	Biological Records Centre distribution maps	Arnold 1984
	Mammal Society distribution maps	Corbet 1971
	Generalized maps of distribution and general accounts	Corbet & Southern 1977
	Forestry Commission mammal/bird damage questionnaire	eg Tee *et al.* 1985
ii. Specific	Squirrels (*Sciurus* spp.)	Shorten 1954
		Lloyd 1983
	Deer	Whitehead 1964
	Red deer (*Cervus elaphus*)	Mitchell *et al.* 1977
	Sika deer (*Cervus nippon*)	Ratcliffe 1986
	Fallow deer (*Dama dama*)	Chapman & Chapman 1980
	Feral goat (*Capra* domestic)	Whitehead 1972
	Pine martin (*Martes martes*)	Lockie 1964
		Verlanders 1982
	Wild cat (*Felis silvestris*)	Taylor 1946
		Jenkins 1962
		Easterbee in progress
	Otter (*Lutra lutra*)	Green & Green 1980
	Mink (*Mustela vison*)	Cuthbert 1973

be expected in various habitat types, it is seldom tested over a wide area or in different habitats (cf MacDonald *et al.* 1981). For example, Loudon (1980) estimated the population densities of roe deer (*Capreolus capreolus*) in several forests in the Borders. He used a variety of methods, and his suggested densities are often used by forest managers to apply to their own areas, irrespective of the degree of similarity with the Border plantations. Charles (1981) estimated the numbers of short-tailed field voles (*Microtus agrestis*) in 2 first rotation forests, also the Borders, and related them to forest structure (see below). There are, however, no reliable estimates of vole densities from other parts of the country, or in older forests or second rotation crops. Considering the importance of this species as a prey item for carnivores and raptors, this is a serious gap in our knowledge.

3 Woodland type

Most British upland mammals are naturally animals of woodland or of the woodland edge. The forest provides not only food but also cover from predators and disturbance, shelter from weather, and sites for nesting and roosting. However, most upland mammals are very adaptable and are not obligate on particular woodland types, although their densities may be affected.

Woodmice (*Apodemus sylvaticus*) thrive best in broadleaved woods and hedgerows, and densities may reach up to 200 ha^{-1} in oak (*Quercus* spp.) forests after a good acorn crop (Gurnell 1979). Venables and Venables (1971) found that woodmice became less numerous in the older parts of a conifer plantation in Wales, and Birkan (1968) reports that they were abundant in pine (*Pinus* spp.) forests in France, especially in stands 10–12 years old. Woodmice densities are thought to be less than 30 ha^{-1} in northern conifer plantations (Flowerdew 1984) and may be restricted by the availability of seeds for food in winter, when they are known to migrate to nearby scrubland or broadleaved woods until more favourable conditions return (Gurnell 1979).

Bank voles (*Clethrionomys glareolus*) are also most abundant in broadleaved habitats, and in conifer plantations in France they are most numerous in stands 6–30 years old (Birkan 1968). S J Petty (pers. comm.), however, has found that both bank voles and woodmice were absent from young grassy restocked Sitka spruce (*Picea sitchensis*) sites in Northumberland and Argyll in spring and summer, and that numbers were very low in autumn. Such provisional findings are a cause for concern, and we need to know the shape, area and distribution of broadleaved woodland or scrub that may be necessary to maintain viable populations of these small rodents in conifer forests.

No British mammal depends entirely on conifers. Red squirrels (*Sciurus vulgaris*) are apparently most abundant in large Scots pine (*Pinus sylvestris*) woods (ie 80 100 ha^{-1} in Scotland (Tittensor 1970); 110 100 ha^{-1} in eastern England (Reynolds 1981); see Gurnell 1983). Red squirrels will also occupy pure broadleaved or mixed woods when available, and Purroy and Rey (1974, quoted in Gurnell 1983) give densities in Spanish woods varying from 31 100 ha^{-1} in mixed oak to 14 100 ha^{-1} in Scots pine and 3 100 ha^{-1} in beech/fir (*Fagus sylvatica/Abies* spp.) forests. The fruits and seeds of deciduous trees and shrubs are important food items for red squirrels at certain times of the year (Moller 1983). No quantitative information is available on the densities or the ecology of red squirrels in the extensive Sitka spruce forests in the Scottish uplands, although the squirrels do occur there and feed on the spruce seeds. Elsewhere in northern Europe, 'spruce woods' appear to be preferred over pine forests (Pulliainen 1973), and the seeds of spruces have a higher calorific value than those of pines (Danilov 1938). Provided that rotations are long enough to allow the trees to mature and produce good cone crops, Sitka spruce forests should make suitable habitat for red squirrels. It may be that small areas containing other tree species would enable red squirrels to survive in these plantations, if Sitka seed alone is insufficient to maintain them.

As few mammals are totally reliant on conifers for food but depend on them more for cover, it may be immaterial which species is planted. Nevertheless, Sitka spruce is clearly going to be the dominant tree in the uplands for the foreseeable future (Figure 1). Certainly, the undergrowth differs under various conifers or with different thinning or planting regimes (eg Sakura *et al.* 1985). Hill (1979), for example, found that the ground cover of vascular plants under pines and larches (*Larix* spp.) 20–60 years old was 20–30% and 25–60% respectively; under the denser canopies of Sitka spruce, cover was only 5%. One would imagine that a greater variety of insects would be found in habitats with a more diverse vegetation, but no comparative studies have been made on the insects associated with different conifer woods in the uplands (Welch 1986).

4 Effects of afforestation

The large-scale afforestation of the uplands since the 1920s has been beneficial to most mammals by starting to redress the balance between woodland and open ground habitats that has been upset since the forest clearances. On the other hand, re-creating forests must be at the expense of other habitats and those animals dependent on them.

Although planting large areas of moorland and sheepwalk has had detrimental effects on some species of wading birds and on some birds of prey (Newton 1983), the opposite appears to be true for mammals. Most mammals have profited from the increase in forest cover and the luxuriant ground vegetation found during the early forest stages due to ploughing, draining and fertilizing. Even mountain hares (*Lepus*

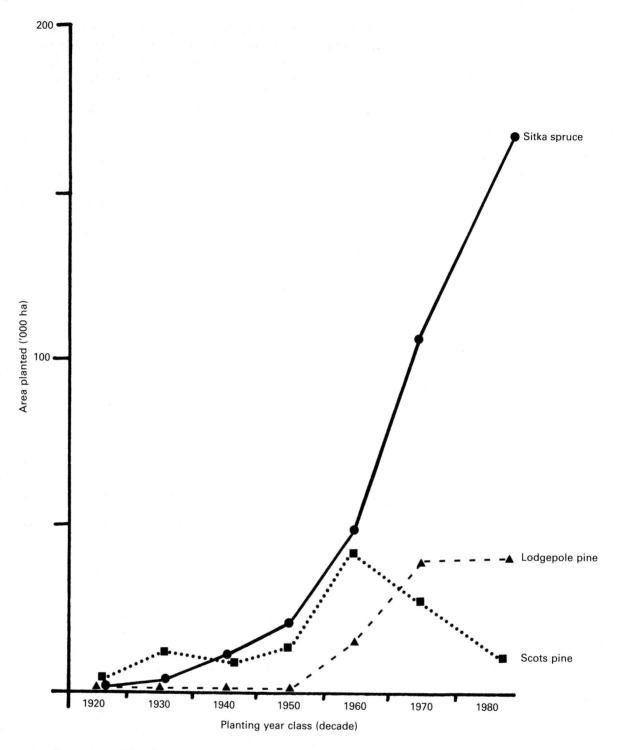

Figure 1. Area planted (kha) of Scots pine, lodgepole pine and Sitka spruce in Scotland per decade (source: Forestry Commission 1983)

timidus), which are most abundant on heather (*Calluna vulgaris*) moors in Britain, and particularly in the east and central Highlands (Watson & Hewson 1973), will use the cover of plantations and survive there, provided sufficient heather moorland is left above the tree-line. In many parts of the Highlands, a large area of moorland will be unplantable and should ensure their survival. Elsewhere in northern Europe, mountain hares are found in open woodland or scrub habitats (eg Pulliainen 1982) and not in very open country as in Britain. In fact, the FC wildlife survey (1983) shows

that mountain hares are present in around half of the 10 km squares where the FC has property in Scotland, and in most of these squares in the Scottish uplands.

Most concern should be over the loss of broadleaved woodland and of coppice and scrub through felling or through under-planting with more vigorous conifers. Although few mammals are obligate on such woodlands, mixed broadleaved/conifer stands should be better habitats for most mammals in the same way as they are for birds (Newton & Moss 1981; Newton

1983), the conifers providing good cover all year round and the deciduous parts a variety of food. Mixed woods also (i) allow a better development of the herb/shrub layer than pure conifer woods, (ii) contain many broadleaved species which are preferred foods for mammalian herbivores, eg brambles (*Rubus* spp.), rowan (*Sorbus aucuparia*), (iii) give a more diverse seed crop, (iv) contain a greater variety of insects, and (v) have more suitable roosting sites for bats.

In Scotland, Parr (1981) estimated that broadleaved woodland decreased by 50% and by as much as 80% in some counties between 1945 and 1979, and that this habitat now occupied less than 1% of the land area. He regarded the amount of coppice left as being 'negligible'.

5 Plantation structure

Following afforestation, the seral stages of the forest provide various combinations of food and cover which affect mammal species differently, but the young forest stages before canopy closure are the key habitats for nearly all mammals.

During the first few years of woodland establishment, there is abundant food, cover and nesting sites for short-tailed voles. Consequently, numbers of voles are higher in these young stages than in later ones. Charles (1981) found that population densities were also influenced by soil fertility and by ground vegetation, ranging from 23 100 ha^{-1} on blanket peat with heather to 280 100 ha^{-1} on mineral soils dominated by bent (*Agrostis*) grasses. In older stands, voles were restricted to rides and clearings, and densities of 5 100 ha^{-1} were similar to those found on open hill ground. During 'plague' years, such as in the Carron Valley, Stirlingshire, in 1952–53, exceptional densities of 2000–3000 voles ha^{-1} were recorded (Charles 1956). Likewise, common shrews (*Sorex araneus*) were found to be most numerous in the younger plantations, but they would occupy older stands when there was sufficient undergrowth (Middleton 1931). By contrast, red squirrels rely on mature forests for food and for their dreys, and bats such as the noctule (*Noctula noctula*) need dead trees or old hardwoods with holes for their roosts. A lack of old or dead trees is characteristic of the truncated successions found in commercial forestry systems throughout the world (eg Leopold 1978).

Whereas some mammals are more or less dependent on one seral stage, others such as the deer and carnivores use all stages, the young for food and the older ones for cover. In fact, these 2 groups of mammals have benefited more than most from afforestation.

Many of the larger Scottish Carnivora have increased their range since the turn of the century, eg pine martens (Lockie 1964; Verlanders 1983), wild cats (Jenkins 1962; Corbet 1971) and foxes (Lloyd 1981),

and more than one factor has been involved. Langley and Yalden (1977) reviewed the possible reasons for the decline of the rarer carnivores during the 19th century and for their subsequent recovery. They concluded that the revival was due mainly to less persecution because it coincided with a decrease in the number of gamekeepers (particularly during and immediately after the First World War) and occurred before large-scale afforestation from the 1920s. Hewson and Kolb (1974), on the other hand, associated the rise in the number of foxes (*Vulpes vulpes*) killed at Eskdalemuir forest with the increase in forestry there (Figure 2). They thought that the supply of field voles was more important than the protection from man given by thick plantations, for fox control was vigorous at Eskdalemuir. Although nowadays there is less persecution than formerly because there are fewer gamekeepers, there would seem little doubt that commercial forestry will favour most carnivores through the added protection afforded and the increased food supply from voles. Current restrictions on methods of control will also encourage carnivores throughout upland Scotland and elsewhere.

Less is known about the smaller mustelids such as stoat (*Mustela erminea*) and weasel (*M. nivalis*) in upland plantations. The increase in voles should assist both species, provided that they can hunt effectively in commercial forests where there has been much disturbance to the forest floor. This hypothesis also assumes that stoats, like foxes (Hewson & Leitch 1983), will be able to change from their dependence on rabbits for food. Both mustelids could, therefore, increase their range, especially in north and west Scotland where they are less common at present than in the south and east.

All 3 main deer species in the uplands, red, roe and sika (*Cervus nippon*), naturally live in open woodland or woodland edge and all have increased their range considerably with the advent of widespread afforestation.

Roe deer became extinct in the Scottish lowlands and in England and Wales by the end of the 17th century (Bewick 1800; Ritchie 1920), and were restricted to the 'highland fastnesses of Ross, Inverness, Argyll and Perth' (Ritchie 1920). They began to increase again following the planting of woodlands in the late 18th and early 19th centuries, and are now the most widespread deer species in Britain. They are even found in suitable habitats in suburban areas such as in and around the city of Aberdeen. Roe reach their highest densities in young plantations or in the early stages of restocked forests (Loudon 1980; Staines & Welch 1984) and may reach 25 100 ha^{-1} in spruce forests 5–15 years old. Population densities drop to around 10 100 ha^{-1} once the canopy has closed.

Red deer are no longer restricted to open hill ground, but have colonized most large coniferous plantations in

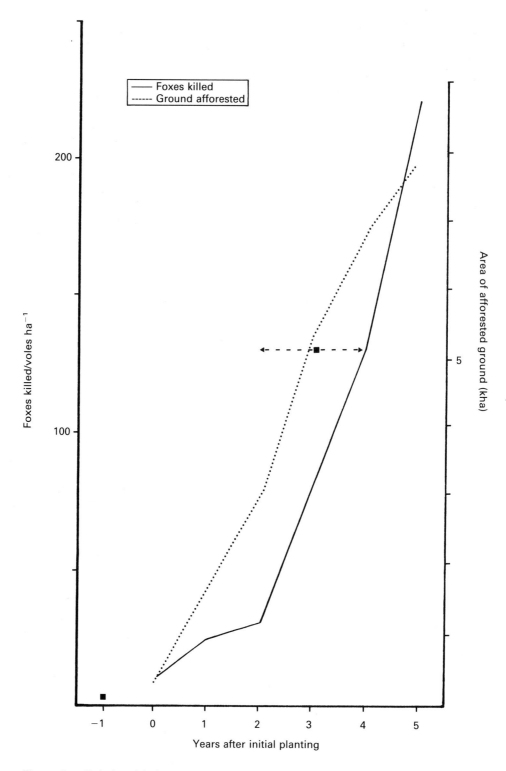

Figure 2.   Relationship between the number of foxes killed and ground afforested at Eskdalemuir, with densities of voles (■) (source: Hewson & Kolb 1974; Charles 1981)

the uplands except, so far, some in the Borders. These deer are not seasonal intruders but are resident in the woods throughout the year. Population densities of woodland red deer are similar to those found on open hill ground (see Stewart 1985) and generally range between 5 and 15 100 ha^{-1}, with up to 40 100 ha^{-1} recorded in better habitats (Ratcliffe 1984). Like roe, they are found mostly in parts of the forest where food and cover are mixed, but red deer tend to prefer older thickets for cover, especially when these are checked

and with an understorey of heather (Staines & Welch 1984). Body weights and reproductive rates are frequently higher in woodland populations (compare Mitchell et al. 1977 with Mitchell et al. 1981 and with Ratcliffe 1984). In woods, puberty in red deer is usually earlier than on the open hill and adult females breed every year, resulting in a very high population turnover.

Sika deer were introduced into the British Isles from 1860. They are now feral and widespread throughout much of north and west Scotland, and are particularly abundant in the Great Glen, in Knapdale (Argyll), and in parts of Sutherland, Inverness-shire and Peeblesshire. Their origins and current status are reviewed by Ratcliffe (1986), who estimates their current rate of spread at between 3–5 km yr^{-1}. Sika deer were present in 89 10 km squares in the FC 1983 survey, compared with only 36 squares a decade earlier. Little is known of their habitat preferences in conifer forests, but these are likely to be similar to those of red deer. In addition to the damage that sika deer do to forestry, they hybridize with red deer and cause concern for the genetic integrity of the native species.

6 Second rotation forests
Most studies of mammals in commercial forests have been done in first rotation crops. As a result, many of the findings already described have been from plantations of different planting age (eg Loudon 1980). In second and subsequent rotations, however, plantations will be structurally more diverse, the extent of this diversity depending on such factors as the size of felling coup, on problems of restocking and achieving silviculturally acceptable densities, on differential growth rates and on windthrow. There will be a greater amount of forest edge habitats and, more importantly, a greater area of young forest, because the proportion of a plantation before the canopy closes is related to the length of the rotation (König & Gossow 1979; Ratcliffe *et al.* 1986). The short rotations of 45–55 years predicted for many spruce forests in Scotland (Ratcliffe & Petty 1986) will result in about 40% of the forest being in these younger stages; in a wood with a 100-year rotation, as is common in continental Europe, this proportion drops to about 10%. British upland forests should, therefore, continue to provide good habitats for most mammals.

However, this conclusion assumes that the relationships between animal abundance and habitat types will be similar in the later rotations to those in the first. Few studies have been made in restocked forests and more knowledge is needed about the habitat preferences of mammals in this important habitat type. For example, supposing that vole numbers in restocked areas are similar to those found in afforested sites of similar age, will mammalian or avian predators still be able to hunt as effectively with the large amount of brash, other debris and ground disturbance caused by felling and extraction? The relationships between prey abundance and predator density are likely to be different.

7 Impact
Perpetuating high densities of mammals will lead to problems of management as many conflict with other land use interests. These conflicts have been reviewed by Staines (1980, 1983a) and for deer specifically by Mitchell *et al.* (1977), Staines & Welch (1981) and Staines (1983b). Briefly, carnivores can, or are thought to, influence game and farming interests and

herbivores can damage woodlands by affecting the establishment, growth, and composition of woods and by competing with livestock.

It is impractical to construct a 'hit list' of wild mammalian pests for the UK because these vary regionally and seasonally, but it is worth noting that more is spent on forest protection from sheep than from any wild herbivore. Also, some species may be a pest in one area and an asset in another (eg red squirrels), or both an asset and a pest in the same area (eg deer). Voles, rabbits and feral goats may be locally important, but foxes and deer cause the most widespread concern in the uplands. All these wild mammals are encouraged by modern forestry practices, so the management problems will continue. In addition, conservation measures aimed at habitat improvement may also further the pest species.

The control of carnivores in woodlands is usually done as part of a 'good neighbour' policy towards game and farming interests, and not specifically for the management of the woodland or for the conservation of species living there.

Herbivores, on the other hand, can have very marked effects on woodlands throughout the forest cycle. Seed eating by squirrels and woodmice is not generally thought to be of great significance in preventing woodland regeneration in broadleaved woods in the lowlands. Indeed, caching is thought to be beneficial through dispersing and burying seed (Mellanby 1968; Gurnell 1981). Miles and Kinnaird (1979a), however, found losses of up to 100% of experimentally sown Scots pine seeds in Glenfeshie, Inverness-shire. They also reported heavy grazing by small rodents and slugs on Scots pine seedlings, although Edwards (1980) thought that slugs were the most important predator of regenerating trees in the native pinewood at Glen Tanar, Aberdeenshire. Field voles can also have serious effects on both commercial and natural woodlands, especially during 'plague' years (eg Charles 1956; Miles & Kinnaird 1979b). However, these plagues are usually short-lived, and excessive damage is frequently localized.

Once saplings reach the height of the surrounding vegetation, and in the case of commercial trees this often means soon after being planted, they become susceptible to browsing by deer and other larger herbivores. This browsing is the most widespread form of damage. It is well established that large numbers of red deer can inhibit the establishment of certain herbaceous species and the regeneration of the native Caledonian pine forest; they can also severely damage commercial crops (Mitchell *et al.* 1977; Staines & Welch 1981). In simple terms, in natural woodlands the ratio of seedlings : deer needs to be increased, either by decreasing the deer population or by increasing the density of seedlings, as well as by fencing or other protection (for fuller discussions, see Mitchell *et al.* 1977; Miles & Kinnaird 1979b; Staines 1983b; Booth 1984).

Although the growth of Norway spruce (*Picea abies*) is often retarded by heavy browsing, Sitka spruce on fertile sites may be little affected. However, browsing on Sitka spruce can cause multiple stemming which reduces timber value (Welch *et al.* 1983; Staines & Welch 1984). There is no quantitative information on the long-term effects of browsing on the growth of other commercially grown conifers in this country, but many other conifer and broadleaved species are more susceptible and less resilient to browsing than Sitka spruce. It will be difficult, therefore, to have the diversity of tree species which is desirable from both silvicultural and conservation viewpoints, without adequate protection from the large deer populations.

In addition to the damage done by browsing, red and sika deer also eat the bark of many trees. The incidence and the effects of bark-stripping vary with the species of tree, but it is most prevalent on willows (*Salix* spp.) and aspen (*Populus tremula*) amongst hardwoods, and on Norway spruce and lodgepole pine (*Pinus contorta*) amongst the conifers (Mitchell *et al.* 1977). Bark-stripping is perhaps more of a problem in commercial than in natural forests, and damage can be extensive. If the trunk is completely girdled, the tree will die, but there is little evidence so far that the removal of smaller areas of bark has any appreciable effect on growth rates. However, such wounding means that the tree is more susceptible to attack from fungi and other pathogens, and the timber can be further degraded through staining and resin inclusion. Sitka spruce appears to be more resilient to this form of damage than other species, such as Norway spruce, but the long-term effects of bark-stripping are not yet adequately known.

Because of the good habitat provided by plantations and the difficulty of controlling deer there, deer populations will increase and the conflicts with other land uses will continue. More quantitative studies are needed on the long-term impact of deer and other herbivores on natural and commercial woodlands and, more importantly, specifically on the ways to resolve these land use problems.

8 Conclusions

Most upland mammals are increasing in Scotland and present-day systems of commercial forestry encourage them. Whereas no species of mammal is threatened by afforestation, more diverse habitats created through planting mixtures of trees will benefit most wildlife; more diverse habitats also have landscaping and amenity value and are silviculturally desirable. However, we need to know more about the extent, shape, distribution and size of hardwood 'islands' to encourage particular species of mammals, and about the consequences of these habitat improvements on others, including pests.

Most studies of the ecology of woodland mammals have been done either in broadleaved woods in the lowlands or in first rotation conifer crops in the Borders. There is a need for more studies which relate specifically to the major forest types in northern Britain and to the second rotation crops which will be the predominant woodland habitats in Britain in the future.

9 Summary

The status, distribution and impact of mammals are discussed, with particular reference to upland conifer plantations.

Most British mammals are naturally woodland dwellers, but few depend entirely on either broadleaved or coniferous woods. Plantation structure is regarded as having a more important effect on the numbers and distribution of most mammals than woodland type.

Overall, most mammals have benefited from the afforestation of open hill land, but concern is expressed over the loss of broadleaved woodlands.

Second rotation forests will be structurally more diverse and, because of short rotations, will have a large proportion of young, open canopy forest. These forests should make ideal habitats for most mammals, including pests.

More research is needed on the ecology of mammals in northern Scotland, and specifically in second rotation crops as these will become the predominant forest types in the future.

10 References

Arnold, H.R., ed. 1984. *Distribution of the mammals of the British Isles. (Provisional.)* Abbots Ripton: Institute of Terrestrial Ecology.

Bewick, T. 1800. *A general history of quadrupeds.* Newcastle-on-Tyne.

Birkan, M. 1968. Repartition écologique et dynamique des populations d'*Apodemus sylvaticus* et *Clethrionomys glareolus* en pinnède à Rambouillet. *Terre Vie*, **3**, 231–273.

Booth, T.C. 1984. Natural regeneration in the native pinewoods of Scotland. A review of principles and practice. *Scott. For.*, **38**, 33–42.

Chapman, N.G. & Chapman, D.I. 1980. The distribution of fallow deer: a world wide review. *Mammal Rev.*, **10**, 61–138.

Charles, W.N. 1956. The effect of a vole plague in the Carron Valley, Stirlingshire. *Scott. For.*, **33**, 280–288.

Charles, W.N. 1981. Abundance of field voles (*Microtus agrestis*) in conifer plantations. In: *Forest and woodland ecology*, edited by F.T. Last & A.S. Gardiner, 135–137. Cambridge: Institute of Terrestrial Ecology.

Corbet, G.B. 1971. Provisional distribution maps of British mammals. *Mammal Rev.*, **1**, 95–142.

Corbet, G.B. & Southern, H.N. 1977. *Handbook of British mammals.* 2nd ed. Oxford: Blackwell Scientific.

Cuthbert, J.H. 1973. The origins and distribution of feral mink in Scotland. *Mammal Rev.*, **3**, 97–103.

Danilov, D.N. 1938. The calorific value of main food-stuffs of the squirrel. *Zool. Zh.*, **17**, 734–738.

Edwards, I.D. 1980. *The conservation of the Glen Tanar native pinewood near Aboyne, Aberdeenshire.* PhD thesis, University of Aberdeen.

Flowerdew, J. 1984. *Woodmice*. Oswestry: Anthony Nelson.

Forestry Commission. 1983. *Census of woodlands and trees 1979–1982*. Edinburgh: FC.

Green, J. & Green, R. 1980. *Otter survey of Scotland 1977–79*. London: Vincent Wildlife Trust.

Gurnell, J. 1979. *Woodland mice*. (Forestry Commission forest record no. 118.) London: HMSO.

Gurnell, J. 1981. Woodland rodents and tree seed supplies. In: *Proc. Conf. Worldwide Furbearers*, edited by J.A. Chapman & D. Pursley, 1091–1124. Falls Chard: R.R. Donelly & Sons Co.

Gurnell, J. 1983. Squirrel numbers and the abundance of tree seeds. *Mammal Rev.*, **13**, 133–148.

Hewson, R. & Kolb, H. 1974. The control of foxes in Scottish forests. *Scott. For.*, **28**, 272–282.

Hewson, R. & Leitch, A.F. 1983. The food of foxes in forests and on the open hill. *Scott. For.*, **37**, 39–50.

Hill, M.O. 1979. The development of a flora in even-aged plantations. In: *The ecology of even-aged forest plantations*, edited by E.D. Ford, D.C. Malcolm & J. Atterson, 175–192. Cambridge: Institute of Terrestrial Ecology.

Jenkins, D. 1962. The present status of the wild cat *Felis silvestris* in Scotland. *Scott. Nat.*, **70**, 126–138.

König, E. & Gossow, H. 1979. Even-aged stands as habitat for deer in central Europe. In: *The ecology of even-aged forest plantations*, edited by E.D. Ford, D.C. Malcolm & J. Atterson, 429–451. Cambridge: Institute of Terrestrial Ecology.

Langley, P.J.W. & Yalden, D.W. 1977. The decline of the rarer carnivores in Great Britain during the nineteenth century. *Mammal Rev.*, **7**, 95–116.

Leopold, A.S. 1978. Wildlife and forest practice. In: *Wildlife and America*, edited by H.P. Brokaw, 108–120. U.S. Forestry & Wildlife Service. Forestry Service.

Lloyd, H.G. 1981. *The red fox*. London: Batsford.

Lloyd, H.G. 1983. Past and present distribution of red and grey squirrels. *Mammal Rev.*, **13**, 69–80.

Lockie, J.D. 1964. Distribution and fluctuations of the pine marten *Martes martes* (L.) in Scotland. *J. Anim. Ecol.*, **33**, 349–356.

Loudon, A.S. 1980. *The biology and management of roe deer in commercial forests*. University of Edinburgh.

Lowe, V.P.W. 1969. Population dynamics of red deer (*Cervus elaphus* L.) on Rhum. *J. Anim. Ecol.*, **38**, 425–457.

MacDonald, D.W., Bunce, R.G.H. & Bacon, P.J. 1981. Fox populations, habitat characterization and rabies control. *J. Biogeogr.*, **8**, 145–151.

Mellanby, K. 1968. The effects of some mammals and birds on the regeneration of oak. *J. appl. Ecol.*, **5**, 359–366.

Middleton, A.D. 1931. A contribution to the biology of the common shrew *Sorex araneus* Linnaeus. *Trans. zool. Soc. Lond.*, **133**, 133–143.

Miles, J. & Kinnaird, J.W. 1979a. The establishment and regeneration of birch, juniper and Scots pine in the Scottish Highlands. *Scott. For.*, **33**, 102–119.

Miles, J. & Kinnaird, J.W. 1979b. Grazing: with particular reference to birch, juniper and Scots pine in the Scottish Highlands. *Scott. For.*, **33**, 280–288.

Mitchell, B., Staines, B. W. & Welch, D. 1977. *Ecology of red deer: a research review relevant to their management in Scotland*. Cambridge: Institute of Terrestrial Ecology.

Mitchell, B., Grant, W. & Cubby, J. 1981. Notes on the performance of red deer *Cervus elaphus* in a woodland habitat. *J. Zool.*, **194**, 279–284.

Moller, H. 1983. Foods and foraging behaviour of red (*Sciurus vulgaris*) and grey (*Sciurus carolinensis*) squirrels. *Mammal Rev.*, **13**, 81–98.

Moss, D. 1978. Diversity of woodland song-bird populations. *J. Anim. Ecol.*, **47**, 521–527.

Newton, I. 1983. Birds and forestry. In: *Forestry and conservation*, edited by E.H.M. Harris, 21–36. Tring: Royal Forestry Society.

Newton, I. & Moss, D. 1981. Factors affecting the breeding of sparrowhawks and the occurrence of their song-bird prey in woodlands. In: *Forest and woodland ecology*, edited by F.T. Last & A.S.Gardiner, 125–131. (ITE symposium no. 8.) Cambridge: Institute of Terrestrial Ecology.

Parr, T. 1981. Scottish deciduous woodlands: a cause for concern? In: *Forest and woodland ecology*, edited by F.T. Last & A.S. Gardiner, 12–15. (ITE symposium no. 8.) Cambridge: Institute of Terrestrial Ecology.

Pulliainen, E. 1973. Winter ecology of the red squirrel (*Sciurus vulgaris* L.) in northeastern Lapland. *Ann. zool. fenn.*, **10**, 487–494.

Pulliainen, E. 1982. Habitat selection and fluctuations in numbers in a population of the arctic hare (*Lepus timidus*) on a subarctic fell in Finnish Forest Lapland. *Z. Säugetierk.*, **47**, 168–174.

Purroy, F.J. & Rey, J.M. 1974. Estudio ecologico y systematico de l'ardilla (*Sciurus vulgaris*) en navarra distribicion, densidad de poblaciones, alimentacion actividad diana y anual. *Bul. Estac. Cent. Ecol.*, **3**, 71–82.

Ratcliffe, P.R. 1984. Population dynamics of red deer (*Cervus elaphus* L.) in Scottish commercial forests. *Proc. R. Soc. Edinb.*, **82B**, 291–302.

Ratcliffe, P.R. 1986. The distribution and current status of sika deer, *Cervus nippon*, in Great Britain. *Mammal Rev.* In press.

Ratcliffe, P.R. & Petty, S.J. 1986. The management of commercial forests for wildlife. In: *Trees and wildlife in the Scottish uplands*, edited by D. Jenkins, 177–187. (ITE symposium no. 17.) Abbots Ripton: Institute of Terrestrial Ecology.

Ratcliffe, P.R., Hall, J. & Allen, J. 1986. Computer predictions of sequential growth changes in commercial forests as an aid to wildlife management, with reference to red deer. *Scott. For.* In press.

Reynolds, J.C. 1981. *The interaction of red and grey squirrels*. PhD thesis, University of East Anglia.

Ritchie, J. 1920. *The influence of man on animal life in Scotland: a study of faunal evolution*. Cambridge: Cambridge University Press.

Sakura, T., Gimingham, C.H. & Millar, C.S. 1985. Effect of tree density on ground vegetation in a Japanese larch population. *Scott For.*, **39**, 191–198.

Shorten, M. 1954. *Squirrels*. (New naturalist no. M12.) London: Collins.

Staines, B.W. 1980. The management of mammals in forestry plantations and research strategies. In: *Research strategy for silviculture*, edited by D.C. Malcolm, 100–105. Edinburgh: Institute of Foresters of Great Britain.

Staines, B.W. 1983a. The conservation and management of mammals in commercial plantations with special reference to the uplands. In: *Forestry and conservation*, edited by E.H.M. Harris, 38–55. Tring: Royal Forestry Society.

Staines, B.W. 1983b. Studies of growth, reproduction and food of red deer and their relevance to management. In: *Some research on deer and its relevance to management*, 25–30. Warminster: British Deer Society.

Staines, B.W. & Welch, D. 1981. Deer and their woodland habitats. In: *Forest and woodland ecology*, edited by F.T. Last & A.S. Gardiner, 138–142. (ITE symposium no. 8.) Cambridge: Institute of Terrestrial Ecology.

Staines, B.W. & Welch, D. 1984. Habitat selection and impact of red (*Cervus elaphus* L.) and roe (*Capreolus capreolus* L.) deer in a Sitka spruce plantation. *Proc. R. Soc. Edinb.*, **82B**, 303–319.

Stewart, L.K. 1976. The Scottish red deer census. *Deer*, **3**, 529–532.

Stewart, L.K. 1979. The present position: the red deer population. In: *The next twenty years*, 4–5. Inverness: Red Deer Commission.

Stewart, L.K. 1985. Red deer. In: *Vegetation management in northern Britain*, edited by R.B. Murray, 45–50. Croydon: British Crop Protection Council.

Taylor, W.L. 1946. The wild cat (*Felis silvestris*) in Great Britain. *J. Anim. Ecol.,* **15,** 130–133.

Tee, L.A., Rowe, J.J. & Pepper, H.W. 1985. *Mammal/bird damage questionnaire 1983.* (Research and development paper no. 137.) Edinburgh: Forestry Commission.

Tittensor, A.M. 1970. *The red squirrel* (Sciurus vulgaris *L.) in relation to its food resource.* PhD thesis, University of Edinburgh.

Venables, L.S.V. & Venables, U.M. 1971. Mammal population changes in a young conifer plantation 1960–1970. Newborough Warren, Anglesey. *Nature Wales,* **12,** 159–163.

Verlanders, K.A. 1983. *Pine marten survey of Scotland, England and Wales.* London: Vincent Wildlife Trust.

Watson, A. & Hewson, R. 1973. Population densities of mountain hares (*Lepus timidus*) on western Scottish and Irish moors and on Scottish hills. *J. Zool.,* **170,** 151–159.

Welch, D., Staines, B.W., Scott, D. & Catt, D.C. 1983. Browsing damage done by red deer to young stands of Sitka spruce. *Annu. Rep. Inst. terr. Ecol. 1982,* 10–12.

Welch, R.C. 1986. What do we know about insects in Scottish woods? In: *Trees and wildlife in the Scottish uplands,* edited by D. Jenkins, 95–100. (ITE symposium no. 17.) Abbots Ripton: Institute of Terrestrial Ecology.

Whitehead, G.K.W. 1964. *The deer of Great Britain and Ireland.* London: Routledge & Kegan Paul.

Whitehead, G.K.W. 1972. *The wild goats of Great Britain and Ireland.* Newton Abbot: David & Charles.

Principles underlying bird numbers in Scottish woodlands

I NEWTON
Institute of Terrestrial Ecology, Huntingdon

1 Introduction

In this paper, I will discuss the factors which influence bird numbers in woodland. I will be concerned primarily with generalizations which can be made from previous census work in various parts of the world, but will also mention some aspects, related to commercial forestry, which are especially relevant to the Scottish scene. The original pine and broadleaved forests, which formerly covered most of Scotland, have been so devastated by human impact as to remain only as scattered remnants in a greatly modified state. The bulk of existing woodland was planted in the last 50 years, chiefly in the form of commercial softwood monocultures. Although some native Scots pine (*Pinus sylvestris*) has been used, the plantings have included mainly the introduced spruces (*Picea* spp.) and larches (*Larix* spp.), lodgepole pine (*Pinus contorta*) and Douglas fir (*Pseudotsuga menziesii*).

Associated with its location, forming the cold northern part of an island off a large continental land mass, Scotland has fewer woodland bird species than have nearby parts of Europe. Britain as a whole has 75 woodland bird species, compared with 86 at similar latitudes in Europe. Within Britain, Scotland has about 68 species, but at least 25 of these depend on openings within the forest or on nearby open land. Another 13 species, dependent on water, are not considered here.

In most Scottish woods where censuses have been made, the chaffinch (*Fringilla coelebs*) and wren (*Troglodytes troglodytes*) were the commonest species, together with the goldcrest (*Regulus regulus*) and coal tit (*Parus ater*) in conifer areas and the willow warbler (*Phylloscopus trochilus*) in birch (*Betula* spp.). Total densities in spring have varied from less than 150 pairs km^{-2} in upland pine plantations to more than 1500 pairs km^{-2} in some lowland broadleaved woods with undergrowth (see later). In general, the greater numbers of individuals in a wood are associated with greater numbers of species.

2 Bird census methods

Various methods have been used to count woodland birds, and results are not always comparable between them. Most early work used the *'transect method'*, in which the observer takes a set course and notes all the birds encountered. The abundance of each species is expressed in relation to all the others as a 'relative abundance'. This method is biased towards conspicuous species, and does not readily give densities. It was used in Scottish woods by Yapp (1962) and Simms (1971).

The *area count* entails a line of observers walking through a wood, on a broad front, counting all the birds that fly back through the line. The method is probably biased towards conspicuous species and underestimates densities because some birds leave undetected. It was used in Scottish pinewoods by Watson (1969).

The *point count* entails noting all the birds detected in a set time period, say 10 min, at each of several randomly selected points within a wood. If the counts are restricted to a set radius, say 30 m from the observer, results can be extrapolated to give densities. However, the method is best used for broad comparisons, as it can give results from many woods in a short time. It was used in Scottish woods by Newton *et al.* (1986).

The *mapping method* entails marking on a gridded map the position of all birds encountered on each of 8–10 visits over several weeks to a census plot and, from the distribution of points, estimating the number of territories involved (Enemar 1959; Williamson 1964). This method is most appropriate for song birds, giving approximate densities of each species, as well as their relative abundance. It has been used in Scottish woods by Williamson (1969), Moss (1978a, b) and others. All song bird densities quoted in this paper were obtained by this method, and all trends have been established by methods which are comparable within themselves.

3 The birds

The 68 bird species which breed regularly in Scottish woodland are listed in Table 1. Of the 6 corvids, several are widespread, while magpies (*Pica pica*) and jays (*Garrulus glandarius*) are local, but all would be commoner in certain areas if they were persecuted less by gamekeepers. Among the seed eaters, the chaffinch is common everywhere, the greenfinch (*Carduelis chloris*) near farmland, and the bullfinch (*Pyrrhula pyrrhula*) in areas of young growth and scrub, but the hawfinch (*Coccothraustes coccothraustes*) is extremely local, found only in southern areas of mature broadleaved trees. The numbers of crossbills (*Loxia* spp.) and siskins (*Carduelis spinus*) fluctuate greatly from year to year, according to the size of conifer seed crops, and the numbers of redpolls (*C. flammea*) according to the birch crop in the preceding

Table 1. Breeding birds of Scottish woodlands
O – dependent on openings or nearby open land; B – dependent on broadleaved trees; C – dependent on conifers; N – found only in the north; S – found only in the south; E – found only in the east

Corvids (6)	Raven (*Corvus corax*) (O), carrion/hooded crow (*C. corone*) (O), rook (*C. frugilegus*) (O), jackdaw (*C. monedula*) (O), magpie (*Pica pica*) (O), jay (*Garrulus glandarius*)
Seed-eating song birds (8)	Hawfinch (*Coccothraustes coccothraustes*) (B,S), common crossbill (*Loxia curvirostra*) (C), Scottish crossbill (*L.c. scotica*) (C,N), greenfinch (*Carduelis chloris*) (O,S), siskin (*C. spinus*) (C), redpoll (*C. flammea*) (B), bullfinch (*Pyrrhula pyrrhula*), chaffinch (*Fringilla coelebs*)
Insect-eating song birds (30)	Tree pipit (*Anthus trivialis*) (O), nuthatch (*Sitta sitta*) (B,S), tree creeper (*Certhia familiaris*), wren (*Troglodytes troglodytes*), mistle thrush (*Turdus viscivorus*) (O), fieldfare (*T. pilaris*) (O,N), song thrush (*T. philomelos*), redwing (*T. musicus*) (N), blackbird (*T. merula*), redstart (*Phoenicurus phoenicurus*), robin (*Erithacus rubecula*), goldcrest (*Regulus regulus*) (C), blackcap (*Sylvia atricapilla*) (B), garden warbler (*Sylvia borin*) (B), whitethroat (*Sylvia communis*) (B), lesser whitethroat (*S. curruca*) (B,S), willow warbler (*Phylloscopus trochilus*), chiffchaff (*P. collybita*) (B), wood warbler (*P. sibilatrix*) (B), spotted flycatcher (*Muscicapa striata*) (B), pied flycatcher (*Ficedula hypoleuca*) (B), dunnock (*Prunella modularis*), starling (*Sturnus vulgaris*) (O), great tit (*Parus major*) (B), blue tit (*P. caeruleus*) (B), coal tit (*P. ater*) (C), crested tit (*P. cristatus*) (C,N), marsh tit (*P. palustris*) (B,S,E), willow tit (*P. montanus*) (S), long-tailed tit (*Aegithalos caudatus*) (B)
Near passerines (5)	Green woodpecker (*Picus viridis*) (B,O), great-spotted woodpecker (*Dendrocopus major*), wryneck (*Jynx torquilla*) (B,E), nightjar (*Caprimulgus europaeus*) (O), cuckoo (*Cuculus canorus*) (O)
Doves and game birds (6)	Wood pigeon (*Columba palumbus*) (O), stock dove (*C. oenas*) (O,E), turtle dove (*Streptopelia turtur*) (O,S), red grouse (*Lagopus lagopus*) (O), black grouse (*Tetrao tetrix*) (O), capercaillie (*Tetrao urogallus*) (N,C)
Owls and raptors (10)	Long-eared owl (*Asio otus*), tawny owl (*Strix aluco*), golden eagle (*Aquila chrysaetos*) (O), sparrowhawk (*Accipiter nisus*), goshawk (*A. gentilis*), buzzard (*Buteo buteo*) (O), honey buzzard (*Pernis apivorus*), kestrel (*Falco tinnunculus*) (O), merlin (*F. columbarius*) (O)
Waders (3)	Woodcock (*Scolopax rusticola*), wood sandpiper (*Tringa glareola*) (O,N), greenshank (*T. nebularia*) (O,N)

Of the above, Scottish crossbill, crested tit, wood sandpiper, greenshank and golden eagle do not breed in southern England, whereas woodlark (*Lullula arborea*), golden oriole (*Oriolus oriolus*), nightingale (*Luscinia megarhynchos*), firecrest (*Regulus ignicapillus*) and lesser-spotted woodpecker (*Dendrocopos minor*) breed in England, but not Scotland

winter (Newton 1972). In years when seeds are locally plentiful, any of these 3 species can outnumber all the other birds in a wood. The crossbills of northern Scotland form a distinct race (*L. c. scotica*), feeding primarily on seeds from pine cones; they are larger, with heavier bills, than the nominate *L. c. curvirostra* of northern Europe, which feeds largely on seeds from softer spruce cones. This crossbill is now found over most of Scotland, following the widespread planting of spruce.

Of 30 insectivorous song birds, the commonest are the wren, willow warbler (a summer visitor), goldcrest and coal tit. In general, the coal tit outnumbers the crested tit *(Parus cristatus)* in pinewoods by 3–4 to one (Nethersole-Thompson & Watson 1974) and, while the former can nest in holes in the ground, the latter requires soft, rotten tree stumps, and is thus largely absent from plantations which lack dead trees. In Britain, the crested tit is found only in north-east Scotland, but it has a wide distribution in conifer woods abroad. Great tits (*Parus major*) and blue tits (*P. caeruleus*) are found only near deciduous trees, while long-tailed tits (*Aegithalos caudatus*) and dunnocks (*Prunella modularis*) nest chiefly in low bushes. The pied flycatcher (*Ficedula hypoleuca*), which breeds in pinewoods in northern Europe, is scarce in such woods in Britain, but breeds locally in broadleaved woods. The willow warbler is the commonest warbler, followed by the chiffchaff (*Phylloscopus collybita*), while the various *Sylvia* species are all rather scarce.

Redwings (*Turdus musicus*) and fieldfares (*T. pilaris*) have colonized Scotland in recent years, and breed in a wide variety of sites, chiefly in association with birch. Wrynecks (*Jynx torquilla*) have also bred regularly in small numbers since about 1950, and in the same period the green woodpecker (*Picus viridis*) has spread into south and central Scotland from England. The great-spotted woodpecker (*Dendrocopus major*) became almost extinct during the last century, but has since re-established itself widely. The nightjar (*Caprimulgus europaeus*) has declined in the last 100 years, and is now extremely scarce in many of its former haunts. The cuckoo (*Cuculus canorus*) is common in openings and lays its eggs mainly in the nests of pipits. Wood pigeons (*Columba palumbus*) and stock doves (*C. oenas*) use woodland mainly for nesting, and are commonest close to farmland where they feed.

Broadly speaking, the 3 game birds occupy different stages of forest succession: the red grouse (*Lagopus lagopus*) occurs in large openings, where heather (*Calluna vulgaris*) prevails; the black grouse (*Tetrao tetrix*) is most numerous in young forests, with some birch and pine, and the capercaillie (*Tetrao urogallus*) prefers mature forests. This last species was extinct in Britain by 1770, but, after abortive attempts to reintroduce it from Sweden to Deeside in 1827–29, it was successfully re-established near Taymouth in 1837–38. Twenty-five years later there were thought to be 1000–2000 birds in the area (Ritchie 1920). Birds from Taymouth and fresh importations from Sweden were then released in various parts of Scotland from where birds spread naturally to other areas, though they are still absent from the south and west.

The woodcock (*Scolopax rusticola*) occurs in damp woodland throughout Scotland, but the other forest waders depend on extensive bogs, and are found only in the north. The wood sandpiper (*Tringa glareola*) may have colonized Scotland only in recent decades, and is still extremely scarce. Among the predators, the tawny (*Strix aluco*) and long-eared owls (*Asio otus*), sparrowhawk (*Accipiter nisus*), kestrel (*Falco tinnunculus*) and buzzard (*Buteo buteo*) are widespread; the golden eagle (*Aquila chrysaetos*) and merlin (*Falco columbarius*) breed only near the altitudinal tree limit (or lower on deforested ground), while the red kite (*Milvus milvus*) and honey buzzard (*Pernis apivorus*) were exterminated last century. The goshawk (*Accipiter gentilis*) was similarly exterminated, but has re-established itself in recent years, as a result of falconry escapes, and now breeds in some of the largest forests.

At least 4 of the species mentioned, the Scottish crossbill, siskin, crested tit and capercaillie, were formerly more or less restricted to northern Scotland, but all have spread with the planting of conifers. The Scottish crossbill and crested tit have spread only within the north, whereas the others have spread further, and the siskin now breeds in all parts of Britain with large plantations of conifers.

4 Factors influencing bird numbers

The importance of the dominant tree species in influencing the numbers and variety of birds in a forest is at once apparent to any ornithologist. But the same type of forest may grow in one region or another, on high or low ground, on rich or poor soil, and may vary in structure according to age and management. All these factors affect the bird life. The main questions are what determines, for any one forest: (i) the number of species, (ii) which species they will be, and (iii) at what densities they will occur. These aspects are best considered together, because the same factors influence all 3. Most bird censuses have been done in birch and oak (*Quercus* spp.), or in spruce and pine. Discussion will be limited to these types, as the main types available in Scotland. Reference will also be made to Finnish forests, where spruce, pine and birch dominate, and where much more census work has been done than in Scotland (Palmgren 1930; Merikallio 1946; Haapanen 1965, 1966).

4.1 Tree species

The obvious division is between broadleaved and coniferous trees. Most woodland birds in Britain live in both types, but a few species are almost entirely restricted to one or other type (Table 1). Thus, hawfinch, marsh tit (*Parus palustris*), garden warbler (*Sylvia borin*), blackcap (*Sylvia atricapilla*), wood warbler (*Phylloscopus sibilatrix*), chiffchaff, pied flycatcher and green woodpecker are more or less confined to broadleaved woods in Scotland, while capercaillie, crested tit and crossbill are restricted to conifers; in addition, goldcrest, coal tit and siskin are much commoner in conifers than in broadleaved woods. The tree species also influence bird density. Comparing forests with similar soils and field layers, breeding birds are more abundant in birch/oak than in spruce, and more abundant in spruce than in pine. Among mixed forests, bird densities in spruce/pine are nearer to pine than to spruce, whereas densities in birch/spruce are as high, or higher, than those in birch, and much higher than in spruce (Palmgren 1930; Merikallio 1946; Haapanen 1965). It is not clear why pine supports only low densities, but it has less foliage per unit area than the other trees, and hence less habitat for insects. It also offers less good nesting sites for birds than does spruce (von Haartman 1971), and has cones which are difficult for most birds to open. It is less clear whether consistent differences in song bird densities occur between different types of broadleaved woods, but few censuses have yet been made and further work is needed (see Massey 1974 for Wales). In Deeside woods, oak held more species and individuals than birch, which in this area held fewer birds even than conifers (French *et al.* 1986).

Mixtures of conifer and broadleaved trees increase bird species partly by improving structural diversity, but mainly by providing habitat for species tied to one or other tree type. Maximum bird densities are achieved if the ratio of conifer to broadleaf species lies between 1:3 and 1:5 in either direction, and if the subdominant tree type is present as clumps up to 1 ha in area, rather than intermixed. This was the conclusion of French *et al.* (1986) who compared bird life in various woods in north-east Scotland. The advantage of having the secondary tree type in clumps was that it then formed a discrete habitat, able to hold complete territories of type-specific birds which might be lacking in uniform mixtures.

4.2 Regional trends

In Europe as a whole, the numbers of bird species found in woodlands decrease from south to north, and from east to west across the continent. Similar trends are found in other animals and in plants. The reasons are not clear, but may depend on rates of spread from glacial refuges. Within Scotland, 8 species are found only in the south; 5 species are found only in the north; and 3 species are found in the east but not the west (Table 1). In addition, several other species become more local in the north and west, compared with the south and east (Sharrock 1976). Fuller (1983) presented a map showing the number of bird species which could be found in a standard '50 ha wood' in different parts of Scotland. This number varied from 45–55 in the south-east to 15–25 in the north-west. As a result of this and other survey work organized by the British Trust for Ornithology, regional aspects of bird distribution have been well studied, and no longer form a major research need.

4.3 Altitude

Within similar types of woodland, bird densities generally decline with increasing elevation (Newton *et al.* 1986). The reasons are not clear, but may link with climate (as in the south–north trend mentioned above) or with soil productivity, discussed below. Species changes with altitude usually link with vegetation changes.

4.4 Soil fertility

Soil productivity can be judged directly, or more readily from the ground vegetation. Arranged according to decreasing productivity, the following main vegetation types are distinguished in north European woods: grass/herb (several types), *Oxalis/Myrtilus*, *Myrtilus*, *Vaccinium* and *Calluna* (Cajander 1925). When other factors are constant, birds in Finnish woods were 3–6 times more numerous on the most productive than on the least productive soils (von Haartman 1971). In those species that were examined individually, this variation resulted from birds taking smaller territories in the good than in the poor areas (von Haartman 1971; Newton 1972). This trend is explicable in terms of organic production, for all types of productivity are better on better soils, including not only wood and foliage, but also various other crops, from flowers and fruits to earthworms (von Haartman 1971). Our knowledge of this aspect is based mainly on findings in Fennoscandia, and some similar work in Scotland is desirable.

4.5 Area

Another pattern found repeatedly is that the larger the area of uniform woodland, the lower the overall density of birds (Oelke 1968). This rule is mysterious but widespread; oceanic islands often have astonishingly high densities of birds, as do small islands of habitat in mainland situations (MacArthur 1971). It is unlikely that this effect can be explained in terms of productivity. One factor involved in woodland is the so-called 'edge effect' (Odum 1959), in which birds are found at much greater density at the boundary between 2 habitats than within either one of them. As small woods have relatively more edge than large ones, this effect contributes to increased bird densities. The edge effect is apparent at the junction between different tree communities, but especially where a wood adjoins an open area. In this last situation, some species nest on the forest edge, but do not penetrate the forest interior. They may obtain part (or all) of their food from nearby open land, so that the density of birds that nest in the wood is greater than could be sustained by the wood itself. Such species include crow (*Corvus corone*), wood pigeon and kestrel.

While the overall density of birds is greater in a small wood than in an equivalent area of a large wood, the number of species in a small wood is often less. Comparing various British woods, Moore and Hooper (1975) found that the number of species became fewer with decreasing area and also with increasing distance from other woods. This situation presents another parallel with oceanic islands, where size and degree of isolation influence the numbers of bird species present. One reason for this relationship in woodlands is that the smallest woods may be too small to accommodate even a single territory of certain bird species. Another reason is that larger woods tend to be more diverse, with rides and other openings which provide habitat for extra species. There may also be a chance element, with rare species more likely to be encountered in a large wood than in a small one.

The relationship between the area and isolation of a wood and its bird fauna needs further quantification in the British context. This aspect forms one of the most obvious research needs at present.

4.6 Structure

As a forest grows, its bird fauna changes from an initial predominance of field-dwelling species, through scrub and thicket species, to woodland species proper (Lack 1933; Moss *et al.* 1979). The overall density of birds may also increase, as may be expected from the increase in structural complexity of the habitat. In a well-grown forest, a many-layered stand containing trees and shrubs of varying height holds more bird species than a uniform stand in which all the trees are the same height. In a mature forest, structural diversity is apparently more important than the number of tree species in influencing the number of bird species present (MacArthur & MacArthur 1961; Moss 1978b; O'Connor 1981; Orians 1969; Recher 1969). Scottish pinewoods with a shrub layer hold slightly more species, and about double the density of birds, as do even-age stands with no shrub layer (Newton & Moss 1977).

The main reason why the complexity of the habitat has such a great influence on the bird community is that many woodland birds show a distinct vertical zonation in their feeding. Long ago, Colquhoun and Morley (1943) distinguished 3 separate classes: the upper canopy birds, the tree and shrub species, and the ground feeders. Among the tits, for example, in oakwoods, the blue tit feeds mainly in the canopy, the marsh tit on the lower branches and the shrub layer, and the great tit largely on the ground. If the shrub layer is lacking, then so too is a whole element of the bird fauna.

Complexity in structure has a horizontal, as well as a vertical, component, and many typical woodland birds are associated with openings of one sort or another. Some species, such as willow warbler, prefer a broken canopy, while others, such as tree pipit (*Anthus trivialis*), prefer glades devoid of trees, while yet others, such as whitethroats (*Sylvia communis*), require areas of low scrub. As a wood opens out, other bird species, more typical of open land, move in, and no clear boundary between communities can be drawn.

In a range of Deeside woods, bird species diversity was greatest where gaps occupied some 10–35% of the total woodland area, and had a mean diameter of 20–35 m (French *et al.* 1986). The distribution of gap sizes was skewed, however, and, with a mean of 20–35 m, some gaps exceeded 100 m. These areas still excluded certain species, such as short-eared owl (*Asio flammeus*), which require even larger open areas.

4.7 Micro-habitat

An important aspect of forest structure concerns the availability of nest sites. In managed forests, where dead timber and scrub may be absent, the densities of hole- and shrub-nesting birds may be limited by shortage of nest sites. This has been shown repeatedly by experiments in which the provision of nest boxes or bunches of branches (tied and stuck up to look like bushes) in managed woods was followed by marked increases (up to 10 times or more) in the density of hole-nesting and shrub-nesting birds (Pfeifer 1953, 1963). The main hole-nesting species involved were various tits, pied flycatchers and redstarts (*Phoenicurus phoenicurus*). The increase in breeding density usually followed immediately, but in some woods pied flycatchers invaded only after several years. In certain places in Europe, provision of nest boxes has resulted in densities of pied flycatchers equivalent to 2000 pairs km^{-2}, more than the total density of all birds so far found in any forest in Europe without nest boxes (Udvardy 1957; von Haartman 1971). Moreover, such increases were achieved over areas up to 25 ha (Pfeifer 1963). Given nest boxes, pied flycatchers will breed in pure conifer woods, lacking natural holes, if these woods also have an open structure.

Dead trees also provide feeding sites for woodpeckers, which extract insects from the rotten wood. Almost absent in commercial plantations, these birds can form a dominant element of the bird fauna in neglected woods, where large numbers of dead trees occur. One has to travel abroad to appreciate the devastating impact of forestry procedures on woodpeckers in Britain.

To summarize, the number of bird species breeding in a wood may be influenced by tree species, geographical location, altitude, forest structure and area;

the type of bird species by tree species, geographical location, altitude, forest structure and area; and bird density by tree species, altitude, forest structure, area and soil fertility. In any one region, irregular forests on good soil with a mixture of hardwoods and conifers contain significantly more bird species at a higher density than do regular, intensively managed, uniform stands on poor soil. Thus stated, it is clear that the planting of trees on open ground leads to an increase in the number and diversity of birds, but modern forestry practice, involving even-age monocultures, acts against high density and variety of birds in the mature wood.

5 Bird communities in winter

These generalizations apply to summer communities of breeding birds. They probably hold in winter too, but at this season high-altitude woods may be largely deserted, nest sites are no longer constraining, and the actual species of tree is of greater significance, especially to seed eaters. Thus, redpolls are dependent on birch seed, siskins on birch, alder (*Alnus glutinosa*) and conifers, while chaffinches, bramblings (*Fringilla montifringilla*) and several tit species gather in beechwoods (*Fagus sylvatica*) in years when mast is plentiful. In Swedish woods, Ulfstrand (1975) found a general correlation between the number of tree and shrub species present and the number of song bird species in winter feeding flocks, because the birds showed different preferences for feeding in certain trees. Little work of this type has been done in Scottish woods and the winter bird communities are in need of study.

6 Commercial forests

New forests have usually been planted on open land, which for hundreds of years previously has been grazed by sheep or burned for grouse. Each forest passes through a number of stages during its growth (Ratcliffe & Petty 1986). Ornithologically, the important divisions are as follows.

i. The establishment stage, a grassy or heathery landscape with young trees dotted through it. At this stage, the habitat is at once more structurally diverse than the sheepwalk, and not surprisingly holds more bird species.
ii. The pre-thicket stage, at which stage the open country birds have gone and the scrub-dwelling birds move in.
iii. The thicket stage, when most woodland species move in.
iv. Relatively mature-looking woodland, which develops as the trees grow, and the forest is thinned out.

These trends are illustrated in Table 2 from counts in south Scotland (Moss 1978b; Moss *et al.* 1979). The open land in this region holds only 2–3 species of song birds, mostly at densities of less than 100 pairs km^{-2}, but the well-grown plantation holds about 5 times as

Table 2. Numbers of breeding song birds in open upland and forests at different stages of growth, from counts in south Scotland

	Number of sites (and censuses)	Number of species	Number of pairs (range) km^{-2}
Unplanted heather moor	2 (3)	2	51 (38–72)
Unplanted grassland	3 (7)	4	93 (72–130)
Establishment	5 (8)	10	115 (54–203)
Pre-thicket	2 (3)	11	257 (231–289)
Thicket	3 (7)	15	347 (302–443)
Post-thinned	4 (8)	15	377 (318–425)

many species and 5 times as many individual birds. The same changes occur in birds other than song birds, but are less marked. So, at least in terms of species numbers and densities, the forests are considerably richer in birds than the open sheepwalk they replace. This finding reflects a general trend, found elsewhere, for both density and species numbers to increase with maturity of woodland (Jones 1972; Rose 1979; Yapp 1955).

Commercial forestry, by providing new habitat, has also led to a spread in the distribution of certain birds. Notable examples are the crossbill and siskin, 2 small finches which eat conifer seeds. Earlier this century, these species bred in only a small part of Britain, but they are now common throughout the uplands of Scotland, northern England and Wales, wherever large-scale areas of conifers are grown.

Other birds have spread with commercial forestry, but for different reasons. They include some raptors, such as the hen harrier (*Circus cyaneus*). For these species, afforestation has provided large areas free from gamekeeper predation. Owing to persecution, the hen harrier at the turn of the century was restricted to islands of north and western Scotland, and its return to the mainland from the 1930s coincided with the expansion of forestry, and with its being allowed to nest undisturbed in the young forests. The species now breeds regularly again in the uplands of the north and west. For such species, it is not the trees themselves which are important, but the sanctuary that the trees provide.

The early stages of tree growth are especially interesting to the naturalist, mainly because of the short-tailed vole (*Microtus agrestis*). The removal of sheep from grassland allows the grass to grow tall. This grass provides food and cover for other herbivores, including voles, which in 2–3 years reach densities that can be 100–200 times greater than on the original sheepwalk. The voles undergo cycles of abundance, with peaks about every 4 years. The initial increase usually leads to an influx of vole predators, particularly various kinds of owl. The short-eared owl, being a ground nester, can best exploit this situation in the open hills (Goddard 1935; Lockie 1955). At peak vole densities, these owls can reach densities of 7 pairs km^{-2}. They

start breeding in early spring, lay 7–9 eggs, and raise up to 2 broods in a year. At lower vole densities, they breed in lesser numbers and produce fewer young per pair. This abundance of voles lasts only 10–12 years, however, by which time the young trees have grown to shade out the grass on which the voles depend. At that stage, the owls leave.

Other avian predators benefit from high vole numbers, but, as they are not ground nesters, in the open hills they are often limited by a shortage of nest sites. They include barn owls (*Tyto alba*), which breed in abandoned buildings, long-eared owls, occupying any shelterbelts which already exist when the land is planted, and kestrels, which nest in tree holes, old crow nests or crag ledges (Village 1981, 1982, 1983). During peak vole conditions, all these species reach densities higher than those recorded anywhere else in Britain, but all must move on as the trees grow, and the grass which supports the voles disappears. These events are not repeated so spectacularly at the next rotation, in the gap between the felling of one tree crop and the growth of the next. A clearfelled area is covered initially by branches from the preceding crop, but vegetation soon grows through. This vegetation differs from that on the original sheepwalk, however, and voles occur but in unknown numbers. Vole predators also occur, but much less numerously. Tawny owls and kestrels frequently hunt on clearfelled areas, but short-eared owls occur only on the larger ones. So the extreme abundance of voles and vole predators is a once-only event in the history of any commercial forest.

The vegetation that prevails between the felling of one crop and the growth of the next depends on soil type, deer grazing and seed availability from birch and other non-commercial trees. In north Wales, in the absence of deer, rich soils were soon colonized by broadleaved seedlings and forbs, which in turn supported a diverse scrub-dwelling bird fauna, including blackcap, whitethroat and garden warbler (Currie & Bamford 1981). In Northumbria, on the other hand, where deer grazing resulted in grassy vegetation, the bird community was similar to that on newly planted land, with the meadow pipit (*Anthus pratensis*) the most abundant species (Leslie 1981).

The main conservation problems associated with commercial forestry have resulted from the sheer scale of planting in certain areas, such as Galloway. This afforestation has led to marked regional declines in open country birds, particularly certain predators such as ravens (*Corvus corax*), which are considered of high conservation value (Marquiss *et al.* 1978). In other parts of Scotland, populations of rare wading birds have also been affected, either by the trees themselves or by the lowering of water tables which precedes planting. As these aspects are considered by D A Ratcliffe in this volume, they will not be discussed further here.

Another problem, which has only recently come to the fore, is the enhanced acidification of soils and waters, which widespread conifer planting promotes (Harriman & Morrison 1982; Stoner *et al.* 1984). The effect is most marked in areas, such as Galloway, which are of mainly low base status anyway. It may have contributed to the recent decline (or disappearance) of fish and certain birds (such as dippers (*Cinclus cinclus*)) in many waters (eg Ormerod *et al.* 1985).

These broader problems can only be tackled by greater planning control over forestry, or by changes in incentive schemes. However, from what is known of birds in woodland, guidelines are readily available for foresters who wish to improve their individual holdings for wildlife. In a nutshell, the best advice would be to diversify, and in particular to grow more native hardwoods such as birch. The maintenance of long rotations, of ponds and other features, a varied age structure, islands of broadleaved shrubs and trees, and a tolerance of scrub and dead timber would all help to enhance the local bird fauna. Many of the procedures which foresters regard as good, clean silvicultural practice are, in fact, highly inimical to wildlife. Parallels occur in agriculture.

7 Summary

7.1 At least 68 bird species breed regularly in Scottish forests, but 24 depend on openings within the forest or on nearby open land. The bird fauna is distinctive and contains the crested tit, Scottish crossbill and capercaillie, which are absent elsewhere in Britain. The siskin was also formerly restricted to northern Scotland, but has recently spread, following the widespread planting of conifers. The common crossbill has also become widespread.

7.2 Within Scotland, 7 woodland bird species are found only in the south, 6 species only in the north, and 3 in the east but not the west.

7.3 The commonest birds in Scottish woods include the chaffinch and wren, together with the goldcrest and coal tit in conifers, and the willow warbler in broadleaved areas.

7.4 In any one region, the variety of birds is greater in woods (i) of birch and other broadleaved trees than of conifers, (ii) which are large rather than small, (iii) which have much rather than little undergrowth, and (iv) which have many rather than few nest holes. The same is true for bird densities, except that these tend to be highest in small woods, especially adjoining farmland. Densities also tend to be higher in woods on rich rather than poor soils.

7.5 A new forest passes through a number of stages during its growth, each of which has a distinct bird fauna. Because commercial forests are grown as single-aged monocultures, they are poor in birds compared with more natural woods, which contain a greater range of tree species, especially hardwoods, and a greater variety of

structure. An interesting feature of young forests planted on grassland is the high densities of short-eared owls and other vole predators, which occur in response to temporary increases in the numbers of field voles.

7.6 Main research needs include further study of the relationship between woodland area, isolation and bird population, and study of winter bird communities and factors influencing them.

8 References

Cajander, A.K. 1925. The theory of forest types. *Acta for. fenn.,* **29,** 1–108.

Colquhoun, M.K. & Morley, A. 1943. Vertical zonation in woodland bird communities. *J. Anim. Ecol.,* **12,** 75–81.

Currie, F.A. & Bamford, R. 1981. Bird populations of sample pre-thicket forest plantations. *Q. Jl For.,* **75,** 75–82.

Enemar, A. 1959. On the determination of the size and composition of a passerine bird population during the breeding season. *Vår Fågelvärld,* **18,** (Supplement 2), 1–114.

French, D.D., Jenkins, D. & Conroy, J.W.H. 1986. Guidelines for managing woods in Aberdeenshire for song birds. In: *Trees and wildlife in the Scottish uplands,* edited by D. Jenkins, 129–143. (ITE symposium no. 17.) Abbots Ripton: Institute of Terrestrial Ecology.

Fuller, R.J. 1983. *Bird habitats in Britain.* Calton: Poyser.

Goddard, T.R. 1935. A census of short-eared owls (*Asio f. flammeus*) at Newcastleton, Roxburghshire, 1934. *J. Anim. Ecol.,* **4,** 113–118.

Haapanen, A. 1965, 1966. Bird fauna of the Finnish forests in relation to forest succession. 1 and 2. *Ann. zool. fenn.,* **2,** 153–196; **3,** 176–200.

Harriman, R. & Morrison, B.R.S. 1982. Ecology of streams draining forested and non-forested catchments in an area of central Scotland subject to acid precipitation. *Hydrobiologia,* **88,** 251–263.

Jones, P.H. 1972. Succession in breeding bird populations of sample Welsh oakwoods. *Br. Birds,* **65,** 291–299.

Lack, D. 1933. Habitat selection in birds. With special reference to the effects of afforestation on the Breckland avifauna. *J. Anim. Ecol.,* **2,** 239–262.

Leslie, R. 1981. Birds of north-east England forests. *Q. Jl For.,* **75,** 153–158.

Lockie, J.D. 1955. The breeding habits and food of short-eared owls after a vole plague. *Bird Study,* **2,** 53–69.

MacArthur, R. 1971. Patterns of terrestrial bird communities. In: *Avian biology,* edited by D.S. Farner & J.R. King, Vol. 1, 189–221. London: Academic Press.

MacArthur, R. & MacArthur, J.W. 1961. On bird species diversity. *Ecology,* **42,** 594–598.

Marquiss, M., Newton, I. & Ratcliffe, D.A. 1978. The decline of the raven *Corvus corax* in relation to afforestation in southern Scotland and northern England. *J. appl. Ecol.,* **15,** 129–144.

Massey, M.E. 1974. The effect of woodland structure on breeding bird communities in sample woods in south-central Wales. *Nature Wales,* **14,** 95–105.

Merikallio, E. 1946. Über regionale Verbreitung und Anzahl der Landvögel in Süd- und Mittelfinnland, besonders in deren östlichen Teilen, im Lichte von quantitativen Untersuchungen. *Ann. zool. Soc. zool.-bot. fenn. Vanamo,* **12,** 1–140.

Moore, N.W. & Hooper, M.D. 1975. On the number of bird species in British woods. *Biol. Conserv.,* **8,** 239–250.

Moss, D. 1978a. Diversity of woodland songbird populations. *J. Anim. Ecol.,* **47,** 521–527.

Moss, D. 1978b. Song-bird populations in forestry plantations. *Q. Jl For.,* **72,** 4–14.

Moss, D., Taylor, P.N. & Easterbee, N. 1979. The effects on song-bird populations of upland afforestation with spruce. *Forestry,* **52,** 129–150.

Nethersole-Thompson, D. & Watson, A. 1974. *The Cairngorms: their natural history and scenery.* London: Collins.

128

Newton, I. 1972. *Finches.* (New naturalist no. 55.) London: Collins.

Newton, I. & Moss, D. 1977. Breeding birds of Scottish pinewoods. In: *Native pinewoods of Scotland,* edited by R.G.H. Bunce & J.N.R. Jeffers, 26–34. Cambridge: Institute of Terrestrial Ecology.

Newton, I., Wyllie, I. & Mearns, R. 1986. Spacing of sparrowhawks in relation to food-supply. *J. Anim. Ecol.,* **55,** 361–370.

O'Connor, R.J. 1981. Habitat correlates of bird distribution on British census plots. In: *Estimating the numbers of terrestrial birds,* edited by C.J. Ralph & J.M. Scott, 533–537. (Studies in avian biology no. 6.) Lawrence, KS: Allen Press.

Odum, E.P. 1959. *Fundamentals of ecology.* Philadelphia; London: Saunders.

Oelke, H. 1968. Ökologisch-siedlungsbiologische Untersuchungen der Vogelwelt einer nordwestdeutschen Kulturlandschaft. *Mitt. flor. -soz. ArbGemein., n.s.,* **13,** 126–171.

Orians, G.H. 1969. The number of bird species in some tropical forests. *Ecology,* **50,** 783–801.

Ormerod, S.J., Tyler, S.J. & Lewis, J.M.S. 1985. Is the breeding distribution of dippers influenced by stream acidity? *Bird Study,* **32,** 32–39.

Palmgren, P. 1930. Quantitative Untersuchungen über die Vogelfauna in den Wäldern Südfinnlands. *Acta zool. fenn.,* **7,** 1–218.

Pfeifer, S. 1953. Vorläufige Bericht über Versuche zur Steigerung der Siedlungsdichte höhlen- und buschbrütender Vogelarten auf forstlicher Kleinflache. *Biol. Abh.,* **6,** 1–20.

Pfeifer, S. 1963. Dichte und Dynamik von Brutpopulationen zweier deutscher Waldgebiete 1949–61. *Proc. Int. orn. Congr.,* **13,** 754–763.

Ratcliffe, P.R. & Petty, S.J. 1986. The management of commercial forests for wildlife. In: *Trees and wildlife in the Scottish uplands,* edited by D. Jenkins, 177–187. (ITE symposium no. 17.) Abbots Ripton: Institute of Terrestrial Ecology.

Recher, H. 1969. Bird species diversity and habitat diversity in Australia and North America. *Am. Nat.,* **103,** 75–80.

Ritchie, J. 1920. *The influence of man on animal life in Scotland.* Cambridge: Cambridge University Press.

Rose, C.I. 1979. Observations on the ecology and conservation value of native and introduced tree species. *Q. Jl For.,* **73,** 219–229.

Sharrock, J.T.R. 1976. *The atlas of breeding birds in Britain and Ireland.* Berkhamsted: Poyser.

Simms, E. 1971. *Woodland birds.* (New naturalist no. 52.) London: Collins.

Stoner, J.H., Gee, A.S. & Wade, K.R. 1984. The effects of acidification on the ecology of streams in the upper Tywi catchment in West Wales. *Environ. Pollut. A,* **35,** 125–157.

Udvardy, N. 1957. An evaluation of quantitative studies of birds. *Cold Spring Harb. Symp. quant. Biol.,* **22,** 301–311.

Ulfstrand, S. 1975. Bird flocks in relation to vegetation diversification in a south Swedish coniferous plantation during winter. *Oikos,* **26,** 65–73.

Village, A. 1981. The diet and breeding of long-eared owls in relation to vole numbers. *Bird Study,* **8,** 215–224.

Village, A. 1982. The home range and density of kestrels in relation to vole numbers. *Bird Study,* **28,** 215–224.

Village, A. 1983. The role of nest-site availability and territorial behaviour in limiting the breeding density of kestrels. *J. Anim. Ecol.,* **52,** 635–645.

Von Haartman, L. 1971. Population dynamics. In: *Avian biology,* vol. 1, edited by D.S. Farner & J.R. King, 391–459. London: Academic Press.

Watson, A. 1969. Preliminary counts of birds in central Highland pinewoods. *Bird Study,* **16,** 158–163.

Williamson, K. 1964. Bird census work in woodlands. *Bird Study,* **11,** 1–22.

Williamson, K. 1969. Bird communities in woodland habitats in Wester Ross, Scotland. *Q. Jl For.,* **63,** 305–328.

Yapp, W. B. 1955. The succession of birds in developing *Quercetum petraeae. NWest. Nat.,* **26,** 58–67.

Yapp, W.B. 1962. *Birds and woods.* London: Oxford University Press.

Guidelines for managing woods in Aberdeenshire for song birds

D D FRENCH, D JENKINS and J W H CONROY
Institute of Terrestrial Ecology, Banchory

1 Introduction

This paper uses data on song bird populations and habitat features from woods in Deeside, Aberdeenshire, to define some forest management practices that are likely to enhance the richness of the song bird populations in these woods in spring and summer. We analyse the relationships between song bird populations and the structural characteristics of the woods to test the ways in which forest structure and tree type affect song bird populations. We then derive from these relationships our recommendations for woodland management.

Our main emphasis is on the whole song bird population, especially numbers of birds, numbers of species, and species diversity, and secondarily on groups of species which occupy similar habitat types. We do not consider in detail the needs of most individual bird species, as these are not often likely to be catered for by simple adaptations of normal forest management.

Our results are most relevant to the management of established woods, rather than the early stages of a new wood. We do not, therefore, consider new plantings, except to the extent that the pattern of planting will affect the eventual structure of the established (mature) wood. Our sample does, however, include a young (<c40 yr maximum age) conifer plantation and an area of young birch (*Betula* spp.) of similar maximum age colonizing a former heather (*Calluna vulgaris*) moor.

2 Methods

We initially surveyed a number of semi-natural woods to test the general idea that forest structure and tree type both affected song bird populations. Later, we took selective samples, mainly in plantations, to test in more detail the effects of mixed tree species and the presence of a tall-shrub layer on numbers of birds and species. We have also monitored changes in bird populations following changes in forest management.

2.1 Study areas (sites)

Single census plots, mostly about 10 ha, were established in 14 woods during 1980–84 (Figure 1, Table 1) as our basic sampling units. A further 2 plots were set up in 1985, partly to test our ability to predict their song bird populations, so data from these plots are omitted from most of the more general analyses. Including these 2 woods, there were 6 conifer stands, 3 birch/aspen (*Populus tremula*), 1 oak (*Quercus* spp.)/ birch and 6 mixed broadleaf/conifer stands, of which one was mainly conifer, 2 mainly broadleaf trees, and 3 approaching equal proportions of the 2 tree types.

At the oak/birch plots (J), a tall-shrub layer of rhododendron (*Rhododendron ponticum*), covering about one-third of the total area, was removed between 1980 and 1982. At 2 of the mixed woods (N and O), selective felling, mainly of pine (*Pinus* spp.) at N and of birch at O, removed much or all of one tree type from part of the site, leaving the rest unaltered. At these 3 'experimental' sites, we examined the changes resulting from the manipulations in more detail than in the general comparative analysis of whole census plots. Similarly, we examined within-site variation in those sites which had both a tall-shrub layer and an upper canopy.

2.2 Bird counts

Most census plots were rectangular, with the ratio of long and short sides never more than 2.5 : 1. Each was marked out in a regular grid of 40 m x 40 m squares to aid mapping of bird sightings.

For mapping bird territories, we used the standard Common Bird Census methods of the British Trust for Ornithology (Marchant 1983), plotting the positions of all birds heard or seen on each of several visits between March–April and June, then deriving territory boundaries for each song bird species from the resulting maps. If a territory overlapped the plot boundary, it was scored as a half, unless there was good evidence that more than three-quarters of it was outside (score 0) or inside (score 1). Where territory boundaries were doubtful, we used the arrangement which gave the minimum score. Crossbills (*Loxia curvirostra*) were not counted, as they were not normally territorial during the period of the counts (their young were already hatched), neither were game birds, corvids, nor birds of prey. Differences between observers were assessed by duplicate counts at a number of sites, and found to be negligible.

For subsequent analyses, the counts were first corrected to territories 10 ha^{-1}. (Throughout the paper, number of 'birds' means number of territories mapped). Bird species were classified in the following ecological groups according to their use of habitat, after Thomson (1910), Komdeur and Vestjens (1982), Haapanen (1965), and our own field observations.

 i. *Open ground* Birds of large open areas with little or no tree or shrub cover only occurred in

Table 1. List of sites, with median altitudes (to nearest 10 m), brief descriptions, top heights and sampling dates (for locations see Figure 1)

A Strone.   220 m asl. Young (<40 yrs) pine plantation, plus some later natural regeneration, top height *c*9 m, sampled 1980–83.

B Gairney.   260 m asl. Uniform stand of tall pine, possibly regenerated after fire, *c*140 yrs old, top height *c*20 m, sampled 1980–83.

C Allachy.   260 m asl. 'Caledonian' pine forest, >150 yrs old, rather open, a little juniper near one end, top height *c*20 m, sampled 1980–83.

D Drum.   320 m asl. 'Caledonian' pine, >150 yrs old, very open, many spreading trees, some juniper, but mostly short, top height *c*18 m, sampled 1980–83.

E Glassel Road.   120 m asl. Mature pine plantation, with some broadleaf understorey and shrub layer, relatively dense upper canopy, top height *c*21 m, sampled 1985.

F Glen Dye.   100 m asl. Mature pine plantation, *c*80–90 yrs old, rather open, very tall trees, with gaps, including a large area of natural regeneration acting as a tall-shrub layer, top height *c*25 m, sampled 1984–85.

G Dinnet Roadside.   160 m asl. Young birch (<40 yrs) colonizing heather moor, very open, and grazed by cattle, includes areas of bog/marsh, top height 8 m, sampled 1980–83 and 1985.

H Huntly Road.   170 m asl. Birch colonizing moor, similar to G but more older trees and generally denser, includes a little bog and a small pond, top height *c*10 m, sampled 1985.

I Ord Hill.   170 m asl. Birch/aspen, mixed age but few really old trees, *c*½ in small clumps, of all ages and spp., the rest nearly all young birch, top height *c*15 m, sampled 1980–83.

J 1. Dinnet Oakwood.   170 m asl. Old oak plantation *c*⅓ with mixed-age birch/aspen/cherry, and another ⅓ with dense rhododendron shrub layer, sampled 1980–81.
2. as above, after removal of rhododendron, top height *c*19 m, sampled 1982–85.

K Potarch.   160 m asl. Mixed wood, mainly mixed-age/spp. conifer, plus some birch and cherry, height very variable, top height *c*14 m, sampled 1984–85.

L Braeroddach.   210 m asl. Mixed wood, mainly birch + some pine, both medium-age, grazed by cattle, some bog areas, top height *c*14 m, sampled 1983–85.

M Craigendarroch.   180 m asl. Mixed wood, mainly oak, plus birch/pine, on steep slope with many boulders, generally fairly uniform except in mixed areas, top height *c*20 m, sampled 1982–85.

N 1. Cambus o' May.   210 m asl. Mature-old birch + many large old pines + small areas of oak and (?) coppice birch + edge of mixed-conifer plantation, grazed by cattle, rather open, top height *c*18 m, sampled 1983–84.
2. As above, after felling/removal of some pine and birch during winter 1984–85, more even distribution of pine/birch, sampled 1985.

O 1. Corsedardar.   210 m asl. Half very young conifer, half an intimate mixture of Douglas fir with medium-age/semi-mature birch and rowan + a few scattered large pine and beech, top height 5–8 m in young part, sampled 1984. *c*14 m in mixed part, sampled 1984.
2. as above, after removal of nearly all birch/rowan from half the mixed area, sampled 1985.

P. Crathie.   280 m asl. Very mixed wood. Several ages of birch + some other broadleaf trees + a wide range of mature-old conifers, juniper abundant both under birch and in gaps, as well as several other shrub-types. A long-established, well-developed wood, top height *c*20 m, sampled 1981–84.

appreciable numbers at one site, so were ignored in all analyses of habitat groups: skylark (*Alauda arvensis*), sedge warbler (*Acrocephalus schoenobaenus*) (might also be put in group (ii) or (iia)), meadow pipit (*Anthus pratensis*).

ii. *Shrub + open* Birds using shrubs or similar cover, usually plus some small open gaps: song thrush (*Turdus philomelos*), ring ouzel (*T. torquatus*) (a single territory, on a craggy area at the top of a hill, but also using shrubby areas in the site), blackbird (*T. merula*), dunnock (*Prunella modularis*), greenfinch (*Chloris chloris*), bullfinch (*Pyrrhula pyrrhula*), yellowhammer (*Emberiza citrinella*).

iia. *Ground cover* Wren (*Troglodytes troglodytes*) (needing tall ground vegetation or similar low cover, or shrubs. Similar to group (ii), and incorporated for some analyses).

iii. *Stem and air* Birds mainly of more open, mature woodland, stem/hole nesters, or stem feeders, or air feeders, or requiring high, open song stations, or canopy nesters but ground foragers: woodpeckers (*Picus viridus* and *Dendrocopus major*), tree creeper (*Certhia familiaris*), mistle thrush (*Turdus viscivorus*), redstart (*Phoenicurus phoenicurus*), wood warbler (*Phylloscopus sibilatrix*), spotted flycatcher (*Muscicapa striata*), tree pipit (*Anthus trivialis*).

iv. *Tall shrub (+ canopy)* Birds preferring a fairly dense tall-shrub layer (or, in some cases, cover at equivalent height), usually also a canopy of some

kind in addition: wood pigeon (*Columba palumbus*), long-tailed tit (*Aegithalos caudatus*), blackcap (*Sylvia atricapilla*), redpoll (*Acanthis flammula*).

iva. *Tall shrub* Canopy more or less irrelevant, but otherwise similar to group (iv) and combined for some analyses: robin (*Erithacus rubecula*), willow warbler (*Phylloscopus trochilus*).

v. *Canopy* Birds either of actual canopy or of 'tops' of trees or shrubs: blue tit (*Parus caeruleus*), coal tit, (*P. ater*), goldcrest (*Regulus regulus*), siskin (*Carduelis spinus*).

vi. *Whole profile* Birds either requiring cover at all levels or able to use almost any level: great tit (*Parus major*), chaffinch (*Fringilla coelebs*).

These ecological groups are essentially related to forest structure. They do not take into account preferences of some bird species for particular tree species or types; for example, great tit is usually only found where broadleaf trees are present, and goldcrest only with conifers. The effect of tree type is, however, examined in the consideration of mixtures.

Another common distinction which we have not made is between 'seed eaters' and 'insect eaters', as this distinction does not normally apply during the nesting period when the counts were done.

The diversity indices 'bird species diversity' (BSD), using numbers of each species, and 'habitat group

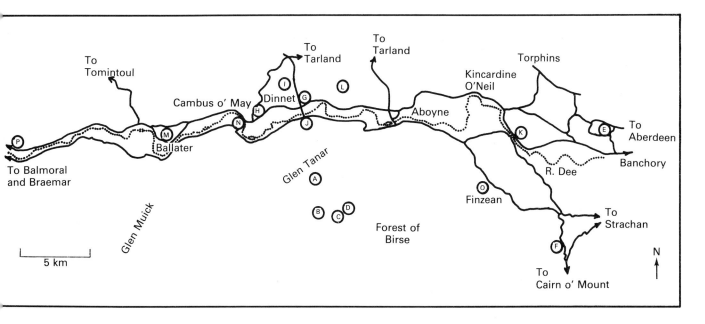

Figure 1. Approximate site locations. Site codes as in Table 1

diversity' (HGD), using numbers in each ecological group, were both calculated using the Shannon Index:

$$-\Sigma[p_i \times \ln(p_i)]$$

where p_i is the proportion of the ith species or group in the population or sample (Shannon & Weaver 1949).

2.3 Habitat survey
This survey was done mainly to obtain measures of forest structure parameters (cover of different layers, and general structural diversity), especially vegetation profiles (cf Moss 1978). Initially, all distinct 'habitat types' (ie areas with distinctive structure, species composition, height, density, etc) found in the census plot were mapped. Within each habitat type, we recorded the cover of vegetation at heights of 0–0.25 m, 0.25–0.5, 0.5–1, 1–2 and thereafter at intervals according to presence of cover, to the nearest metre. Plots of 10 m x 10 m were placed in randomly selected grid squares within each habitat type, near a corner of the square chosen (i) to avoid boundaries of habitat types, and (ii) to be a 'representative' sample of the type, and were moved within the square or to an adjacent square if necessary to satisfy these conditions. Three further constraints were that (i) as far as possible all separate areas of any type should be sampled at least once, (ii) sampling intensity in any habitat type should be approximately proportional to its area, and (iii) the total number of plots in any site should be not more than about 35, but always at least 20.

At each height, cover was estimated to the nearest 10%, with under 5% scored as 'present'. The resulting cover profiles were then examined graphically. Habitat types which did not have distinct profiles were combined, and an average profile was calculated for each profile/habitat type. The overall profile for the census plot was calculated as the weighted mean (proportionally, by relative area) of the average profiles of the recognized habitat types. From the vegetation profiles, we extracted 'total cover' (sum of all layers), cover at 0–1 m (ground layers and low shrub), 2–6 m (tall shrub), 7–12 m (low canopy), 13–18 m (mid-canopy), 19–25 m (high canopy), and 13–25 m ('upper' canopy = average of mid and high). From these data, we calculated foliage height diversity (FHD) using ground, shrub, lower and upper canopy as the constituent groups expressed as the Shannon Index, and the number of distinct profile types (NPT).

FHD measures only the vertical heterogeneity of the vegetation. We also used a reduced version of the transect method of van Berkel (1979) to estimate horizontal heterogeneity (Opdam & van Bladeren 1981). This measure is defined (per transect of 50 points) as $\log_{10}[1 + $ (no. of groups with +ive score) x (no. of different-sized groups +ive) x (no. of different-sized gaps)] for each layer (herb, shrub, lower canopy, upper canopy) separately. These values were then averaged over 6–8 transects, and the resulting mean values for each layer were summed to give an index of total horizontal heterogeneity (HET) over all layers for each site. From the transect data, we also estimated the relative cover of different tree types in the canopy, and the average size of gaps.

2.4 Analyses
Our analyses were in 2 parts. First, from the general survey, we assessed the effects of the following 'vegetation parameters':

— structural composition (cover of different layers) and diversity (FHD, NPT and HET) profile and heterogeneity parameters

— age or stage of development of the stand
— canopy tree type (ie broadleaf, conifer, mixed)
— a tall-shrub layer

on these 'bird parameters':

— number of birds using different parts of the profile (the 'ecological groups' defined above)
— number of birds ⎫
— number of species ⎬ bird summary parameters
— the 2 diversity indices ⎭

Second, using especially our later selective samples and 'experimental' sites, we attempted to define an 'optimal' size for gaps, to derive a minimal 'useful' proportion of secondary types in mixtures, and to suggest the best distribution of tree types within a mixture. We also assessed in greater detail the effects of different combinations of tall-shrub layer and canopy types.

3 Results

3.1 Basic data and general description of bird populations

Table 2 lists the numbers of territories 10 ha^{-1} of species in the 8 ecological groups, plus bird summary parameters for each study area. All song bird species from Newton's (1986) list were present, except for redwing (*Turdus iliacus*) and chiffchaff (*Phylloscopus collybita*) (both seen but never shown to hold territory), whitethroat (*Sylvia communis*) and pied flycatcher (*Ficedula hypoleuca*), which are all uncommon in north-east Scotland. The variety of bird species was therefore much as expected for the area generally.

Numbers in our plots were within Newton's (1986) range of numbers of (territorial) birds, ie 15–150 10 ha^{-1}, varying from 22 at Dinnet Roadside (site G) to 118 at Crathie (site P). Numbers in our conifer woods were generally similar to or higher than those of Moss (1978) and Moss *et al.* (1979) for plantations in southern Scotland.

Data in Table 2 are mean counts over all available years at each site. Variation between years was moderately high, eg total number typically ranged ± 10% of the mean count over 3–5 years. In a few sites the range was wider (>20%).

There was a general trend of increasing number of species with number of birds. However, there were several sites with many birds but few species, eg Strone, site A, or *vice versa*, eg Allachy, C, or Braeroddach, L (Table 2).

Usually, there were fewer bird species in birch and conifer woods than in oak or mixed woods. Some species also were either restricted to, or more numerous in, particular tree types. With the exception of siskins, which were found with all tree types, and reached their highest density (in 1981) in the oakwood (site J), our data were not inconsistent with Newton's (1986) general observations on individual species or groups.

3.2 Whole-wood (general survey) analyses

Correlations and regressions with profile and heterogeneity parameters were calculated using the mean

Table 2. Numbers of birds (territories) 10 ha^{-1} in 8 ecological groups, and bird summary parameters, in 16 Deeside woods (source: original unpublished data

Site	(i)	(ii)	(iia)	(iii)	(iv)	(iva)	(v)	(vi)	Number of Birds	Number of Species	Bird species diversity	Habitat group diversity
A	0	0	1.9	0	0	22.1	8.9	8.3	41.6	6.2	1.66	2.73
B	0	0	6.9	6.1	0	1.4	8.7	14.0	37.1	8.0	1.73	2.71
C	0	0	3.9	6.1	0	3.2	6.1	9.7	29.0	11.3	2.07	4.88
D	0	0	5.2	3.9	0	6.9	7.6	13.4	37.2	8.3	1.83	4.64
E	0	0.6	1.2	13.2	3.0	3.6	10.2	10.8	42.6	11.0	2.13	6.26
F	0	1.5	4.5	18.5	3.7	7.6	11.7	15.6	62.9	15.0	2.39	7.53
G	7.5	0.5	0	0	0	9.6	2.0	2.3	22.1	8.2	1.62	2.04
H	0	2.2	3.0	5.9	1.5	21.6	5.2	11.9	51.3	11.0	2.01	5.90
I	0	2.1	4.0	3.1	2.3	17.0	3.7	13.3	45.6	13.0	2.11	5.97
J1	0	4.9	4.2	12.2	1.1	13.6	10.5	18.5	64.9	16.0	2.43	7.48
J2	0	2.7	0.3	15.5	0.3	9.6	9.0	14.6	52.0	14.3	2.35	4.83
K	0	7.6	1.6	10.9	3.9	12.7	7.5	18.0	62.0	17.5	2.54	8.09
L	0	1.1	0.5	3.1	1.5	7.0	5.8	11.9	30.9	12.0	2.09	4.75
M	0	4.4	0.6	9.4	3.0	9.3	11.1	20.6	58.4	16.5	2.36	6.40
N1	0	4.4	0	13.2	0.8	6.5	12.2	19.6	56.9	16.0	2.43	5.20
N2	0	3.1	0.5	9.3	0	3.6	15.1	14.6	46.2	16.0	2.42	3.54
O1	1.1	5.1	0	2.2	0	32.7	5.0	10.0	56.1	13.0	1.91	3.30
O2	0.6	3.4	1.1	0.6	1.1	33.8	12.1	13.3	66.0	14.0	2.01	3.82
P	0	10.6	4.4	16.0	11.9	33.3	16.0	26.4	118.6	19.0	2.53	7.99

All figures are mean scores for the site over all available years. Site codes as in Table 1
Ecological groups – birds of: (i) open ground, (ii) shrub + open, (iia) ground cover (wren), (iii) stem and air, (iv) tall shrub (+ canopy), (iva) tall shrub, (v) canopy, (vi) whole profile

Table 3. Vegetation profile and heterogeneity parameters for 16 Deeside woods (source: original unpublished data)

Total % cover (summed over 1 m intervals) of:

Site	Ground cover (0–1 m)	Tall shrub (2–6 m)	Lower (7–12 m)	Mid (13–18 m)	High (19–25 m)	Upper (mean of mid and high)	Foliage height diversity	Number of distinct profile types	Horizontal heterogeneity
					Canopy				
A	248	140	13	0	0	0	0.77	3	6.14
B	126	23	90	38	2	20	1.23	1	3.82
C	129	17	53	16	1	8	1.07	4	6.53
D	139	21	48	9	0	4	0.98	3	5.85
E	119	36	97	150	8	79	1.36	4	6.57
F	117	22	14	36	27	31	1.29	5	7.53
G	86	21	2	0	0	0	0.59	3	5.02
H	136	90	11	0	0	0	0.82	2	5.23
I	110	86	86	10	0	5	1.20	4	7.85
J1	159	139	149	68	0	34	1.34	5	7.97
J2	107	118	172	58	0	29	1.32	4	7.64
K	140	103	51	1	0	1	1.05	7	6.99
L	109	73	139	2	0	1	1.10	4	7.11
M	52	56	189	69	2	36	1.25	4	6.37
N1	96	77	149	29	0.5	14	1.26	7	6.80
N2	93	69	129	19	0.5	10	1.24	6	6.75
O1	156	99	27	1	0	1	0.94	4	7.22
O2	163	72	21	1	0	1	0.88	4	6.99
P	139	102	97	31	1	16	1.29	7	8.26

Site codes as in Table 1

data in Table 2. Effects of age, tree type and shrub/canopy combinations were calculated using data from individual years.

3.2.1 Vegetation profiles and horizontal heterogeneity
Correlations of bird parameters (Table 2) with profile and heterogeneity parameters (Table 3) indicated strong relationships between number of birds, number of species and diversity indices, and several vegetation parameters, especially FHD, NPT and HET (Table 4). Ecological groups (iii) and (vi) were also well correlated with many vegetation parameters, but otherwise correlations between individual ecological groups and site characteristics were generally low. Even those that were high (eg group (ii), ground + shrub birds,

with NPT) were all of the group with some general expression of habitat diversity, rather than with anything more specific.

In an attempt to convert these correlations to predictive equations, and to obtain more immediately measurable predictive parameters, we computed a series of multiple regressions, using a step-up procedure, and avoiding FHD, NPT and HET unless they were necessary to produce any significant regression. The predictive values of the best regression equations for each bird parameter were tested by comparing observed and expected values at the 2 sites omitted from the analyses (Table 5). About two-thirds of the predicted values are reasonable for both woods, but

Table 4. Correlation matrix of bird parameters *vs* profile and heterogeneity parameters in Deeside woods (source: original unpublished data)

(i)	(ii)	(iia)	(iii)	(iv)	(iva)	(v)	(vi)	Birds	Species	Bird species diversity	Habitat group diversity	
			Ecological groups					Number of				
−0.55	0.39	−0.07	0.40	0.15	0.15	0.42	0.54	0.41	0.39	0.47	0.35	Total cover
−0.21	−0.05	0.21	−0.31	−0.06	0.51	0	−0.19	0.11	0.36	−0.35	−0.15	Ground cover
−0.30	0.50	−0.29	0.12	0.17	0.51	0.19	0.28	0.42	0.32	0.31	0.23	Tall shrub
−0.40	0.26	−0.16	0.46	0.09	−0.34	0.35	0.57	0.16	0.48	0.57	0.30	Lower canopy
−0.30	0.20	0.19	0.67	0.16	−0.28	0.43	0.57	0.31	0.41	0.50	0.42	Mid-canopy
−0.09	−0.12	0.27	0.48	0.19	−0.17	0.21	0.10	0.14	0.14	0.21	0.34	High canopy
−0.30	0.16	0.24	0.74	0.19	−0.30	0.45	0.55	0.32	0.42	0.51	0.47	Upper canopy
−0.67	0.36	0.30	0.80	0.35	−0.26	0.55	0.77	0.45	0.64	0.76	0.62	FHD
−0.24	0.76	−0.28	0.61	0.55	0.17	0.52	0.63	0.63	0.84	0.84	0.66	NPT
−0.38	0.58	−0.16	0.46	0.49	0.44	0.30	0.48	0.61	0.71	0.70	0.67	HET
−0.39	0.74	−0.13	0.77	0.58	0.06	0.63	0.77	0.67	0.89	0.93	0.73	FHD × NPT
−0.56	0.55	0.08	0.77	0.51	0.08	0.49	0.73	0.62	0.79	0.86	0.77	FHD × HET

For definition of ecological groups, see Table 2. Cover categories as in Table 3
FHD = foliage height diversity, NPT = number of profile types, HET = horizontal heterogeneity
r=± 0.47, P<0.05; r=± 0.59, P<0.01

Table 5. 'Best' regression equations of bird parameters on vegetation parameters, and tests of their predictive ability (source: original unpublished data)

Bird parameter	Regression	R^2	Site E Observed	Site E Expected	Site H Observed	Site H Expected
Ecological group* (ii)	$1.39 \times$ NPT $- 3.12$	.58	1.0	2.5	1.5	0
Ecological group* (iia)	$0.04 \times$ (tall shrub) $- 0.04 \times$ (lower canopy) $+ 0.09 \times$ (upper canopy) $- 1.06$	.47	1.5	3.5	3.0	2.0
Ecological group* (iii)	$20.2 \times$ FHD $+ 0.29 \times$ (high canopy) $- 15.2$	.72	13.0	15.0	4.0	2.0
Ecological group* (iv)	NPT $- 2.668$	.31	3.0	1.5	1.5	0
Ecological group* (iva)	$0.17 \times$ (tall shrub) $- 0.09 \times$ (lower canopy) $+ 8.88$	.50	4.0	6.0	21.0	23.0
Ecological group* (v)	$7.3 \times$ FHD $+ 0.85 \times$ NPT $- 2.9$	.41	10.5	10.5	5.0	5.0
Ecological group* (vi)	$1.29 \times$ NPT $+ 15.82 \times$ FHD $- 8.85$	.72	11.0	18.0	12.0	7.0
Number of birds	$6.25 \times$ FHD $\times$ NPT $+ 20.9$	.45	43	55	51	31
Number of species	$1.93 \times$ NPT $+ 4.65$	.71	11	12	11	9
BSD	$0.12 \times$ FHD $\times$ NPT $+ 1.53$	.87	2.13	2.18	2.01	1.73
HGD	$0.66 \times$ FHD $\times$ HET $+ 0.02$	.59	6.26	5.92	5.90	2.85

Regressions were calculated omitting sites E and H, then the expected bird parameters for each site were calculated from the regressions
All regressions are significant at $P<0.05$
BSD = bird species diversity, HGD = habitat group diversity (Shannon Index)
Shrub and canopy variables are total cover (summed at 1 m intervals) over the range 2–6 m (tall shrub), 7–12 m (lower canopy) and 19–25 m (high canopy), and the mean of 13–18 m and 19–25 m (upper canopy)
FHD = foliage height diversity (Shannon Index), NPT = number of profile types, HET = horizontal heterogeneity (Opdam & van Bladeren 1981)
*See Table 2

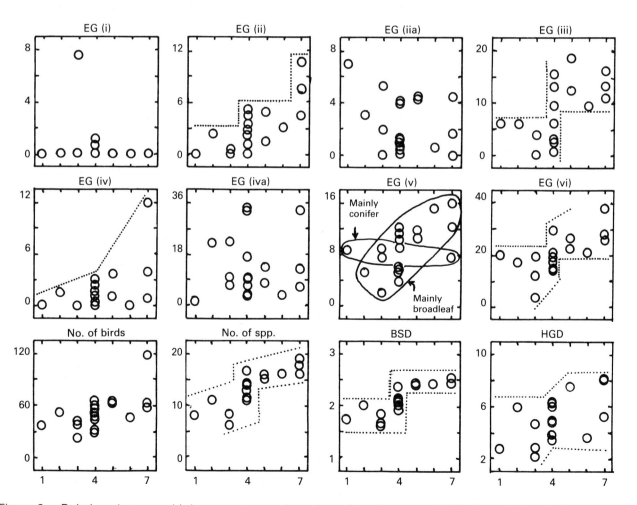

Figure 2. Relations between bird parameters and number of profile types (NPT). Dotted lines indicate step or threshold at NPT=4. EG = ecological group (see text and Table 2) (source: original unpublished data)

the prediction of habitat groups cannot generally be called 'good', neither can the prediction of number of birds. Number of species and BSD, however, were both well estimated and, together with prediction of habitat groups taken as a whole, the regressions provide a fairly good measure of the overall value of a wood for song birds.

We also found that, if plotted against bird parameters, the number of distinct profile types (NPT) frequently showed a step or threshold relationship, in which 4 profile types was the threshold above or below which a wood could be classed as 'good' or 'bad'. This threshold held true for number of birds, number of species, BSD, and ecological groups (ii), (iii) and (vi). Group (v) was related to NPT in broadleaved and mixed woods, but not in coniferous woods (Figure 2). Groups (i), (iia) and (iva), on the other hand, seem to depend more on the actual amounts of particular layers than on any kind of structural heterogeneity.

3.2.2 Age/development of wood

Four classes were defined: young (before canopy closure), medium age (with at least lower canopy), old (with full canopy, <100 years old or, if older, then first generation), and very old (>100 years old, or a multiple-age wood established for several generations). Preliminary analyses of variance suggested that the only major division was between young woods and all others. For tall-shrub birds (group (iv) + (iva)), medium-age woods appeared to be best, and old woods, with little understorey, worst, while canopy birds (group (v)) divided between old and very old woods (best) and the rest. Jonckheere's S-test (Jonckheere 1954) confirmed these orderings of bird parameters between age classes (Table 6i). The ranking of age classes was very similar over all bird parameters. A Kendall coefficient of concordance (see, eg, Siegel 1956) confirms this similarity (W=0.62, P<0.001), indicating that, after canopy closure, the actual age of a wood is relatively unimportant in determining its

Table 6. Tests of ranking of wood types for birds (Jonckheere's S-test) (source: original data)

i. Age/development

	Young	Medium	Old	Very old			S	z
Number of birds	1	3	3	3			260	3.20***
Number of species	1	3	3	3			310	3.82***
Ecological group (cf Table 2)								
(ii) + (iia)	1	3	3	3			308	3.79***
(iii)	1	3	3	3			376	4.63***
(iv) + (iva)	2.5	4	1	2.5			372	3.31***
(v)	1.5	1.5	2.5	2.5			350	3.49***
(vi)	1	3	3	3			368	4.53***
BSD	1	3	3	3			342	4.21***
HGD	1	3	3	3			368	4.53***

ii. Tree type

	(a)	(b)	(c)	(d)	(e)	(f)	S	z
Number of birds	2.5	1	4.5	4.5	2.5	6	594	5.23***
Number of species	1.5	1.5	3.5	5.5	3.5	5.5	602	5.40***
Ecological group								
(ii) + (iia)	3.5	1.5	3.5	5.5	1.5	5.5	376	3.31***
(iii)	2.5	1	5	5	2.5	5	526	4.69***
(iv) + (iva)	3	3	3	3	3	6	228	2.94**
(v)	3.5	1	3.5	3.5	3.5	6	536	5.23***
(vi)	2	1	4	4	4	6	578	4.91***
BSD (1)	1.5	1.5	4.5	4.5	4.5	4.5	544	5.12***
BSD (2)	1.5	1.5	4.5	6	3	4.5	614	5.49***
HGD	4	1	4	4	4	4	280	3.45**

iii. Tall shrub/canopy combinations

	(a)	(b)	(c + d)				S	z
Number of birds	3	2	1				622	5.69***
Number of species	3	2	1				554	5.07***
Ecological group								
(ii) + (iia)	3	2	1				446	4.08***
(iii)	3	2	1				524	4.79***
(iv) + (iva)	3	2	1				418	3.82***
(v)	3	2	1				284	2.59**
(vi)	3	2	1				546	4.99***
BSD	3	2	1				574	5.25***
HGD	3	2	1				404	3.69***

**P<0.01, ***P<0.001
Ranks in each row give the group orders tested against the data for each bird parameter. A high rank indicates a high value of the corresponding bird parameter. z is the normal approximation
BSD (1) and (2) in (ii) are alternative orders tested against the same data
For definitions of age classes and of groups, (a)–(f) in (ii) and (a)–(d) in (iii), see text

overall song bird populations. Data for sites E and H all fell within the range expected for their groups.

3.2.3 Tree type

Bird parameters were compared between different tree types, by analyses of variance and Jonckheere's S, in the same way as for age. Six classes of tree types were defined, according to canopy composition, ie ignoring understorey/shrub layer: (a) conifer, (b) birch/aspen, (c) oak (± other broadleaves), (d) mixed (mainly conifer), (e) mixed (mainly broadleaves) and (f) mixed (equal). Woods were assigned to mixture classes (d, e, f) according to whether there was more or less than 25% of the secondary tree type. The rankings (Table 6ii) appear slightly more variable than for age classes, but the coefficient of concordance is still high (W= 0.72, P<0.001), indicating a significant agreement in overall ranking, in the order: birch<conifer≤mixed (mainly broadleaves)<oak<mixed (mainly conifer) <mixed (equal). Particularly consistent are the ranking of birch/aspen woods (always worst) and mixed (equal) woods (always best). The generally low ranking of broadleaved types other than oak is also notable. Again, data for sites E and H are as expected.

These rankings partly contradict the generally held view that broadleaved trees always support more birds and species than conifers. For example, Newton (1986) states that 'with similar soil and field layer, breeding birds are more abundant in birch/oak than in spruce, and more abundant in spruce than pine', while from our data the order is oak> conifers>birch. This result may be because of uncritical comparison between tree species which confounds tree species with structural characteristics, or because of the tendency to combine all broadleaved species, or not to distinguish between single-species stands and mixtures of species of the same tree type (broadleaf/conifer). While insufficient for a detailed comparison, our data also suggest that pine is not necessarily the worst tree species for song birds. Indeed, one of our richest sites (Glen Dye, site F) was pure pine.

3.2.4 Tall-shrub layer in relation to canopy

We expected woods with both mature canopy and a tall-shrub layer to have richer song bird populations than woods with only one of these layers. We also expected that, where both canopy and tall-shrub layer were present, their spatial distribution would affect the composition of the bird population. We tested these 2 ideas by Jonckheere's S-test, dividing the woods into 4 groups:

a. woods with at least one-third of the census plot containing a tall-shrub component, and at least one-third of the area with upper canopy, especially high canopy, and with canopy and tall-shrub both together and separately (F, J1, P);

b. woods with both upper canopy and tall-shrub layers, shrub over less than one-third of the area but still more than 15%, and/or with less than all

3 possible combinations of tall shrub and/or canopy (I, J2, K, M);

c. woods with no significant upper canopy (A, G, O);

d. woods effectively without a tall-shrub component (B, C, D, L, N).

Even though we thought that the tall-shrub + canopy combination would be important, the results of the tests surpassed all our expectations. Every bird parameter tested gave the ordering (c, d)<(b)<(a) (Table 6iii: W=1, P=0).

3.2.5 Altitude and fertility

Altitude seemed to be relatively unimportant to woodland song birds on Deeside in spring. Both the best and worst of our woods were found at or near both altitudinal extremes. Only at one site (D) might a combination of altitude and exposure be extreme enough to depress the bird populations. Better soils supported more birds, but fertility had little or no effect on numbers of species, confirming Newton's (1986) conclusion.

3.3 Detailed analyses of specific patterns or relationships

3.3.1 Horizontal heterogeneity; is there an 'optimal' gap size?

Woods with a uniform closed canopy did not support a rich song bird population (ie high numbers and many species), while large open areas did not normally contain many woodland birds (cf Tables 2–3). Somewhere between these extremes there must be an optimal range of gap sizes (a 'gap' being any space between tree crowns that is at least the size of a single crown). How wide or narrow is this range? What proportion of the total area should be gaps? To answer these questions, we examined the relation between BSD, percentage of total area covered by gaps >15 m wide, and mean size of gaps >15 m. We chose 15 m as the minimum size because gaps smaller than this will be present in almost any canopy where there has been even a small amount of thinning, removal of dead trees, or simply lack of establishment of a tree in a particular position. Fifteen metres is about the smallest gap likely to be created by removal of a group of trees from the canopy, and is therefore the minimum size to be considered in manipulating forest structure.

If we take a BSD of 2 or less as indicating a poor wood for song birds, 2–2.3 as moderate and >2.3 as good, and plot the range of these bands against percentage cover of gaps >15 m and mean size of gaps >15 m, a clear pattern emerges (Figure 3). The best woods all lie within a quite narrow range, both of percentage cover of gaps and size of gaps, ie 10–35% cover, and mean width 20–35 m. The only 'bad' woods to lie within this range are Strone and Gairney, which both had exceptionally simple profiles. Also, within both the moderate and good groups, the highest BSDs all clustered about 20% cover of gaps, irrespective of gap size, decreasing both above and below this line.

All distributions of gap sizes within woods were highly

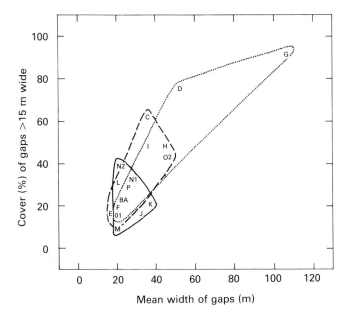

Figure 3. *BSD in relation to percentage cover of gaps ≥15 m (in canopy) and mean width of gaps. Data plotted are the range of cover and gap size for 3 groups of woods:* ——— *BSD>2.3,* – – – *2.0 ≤BSD ≤2.3,* - - - - *BSD <2.0. A–P are site codes (see Table 1)*

skewed, so a mean gap size of 20–35 m implies a maximum gap of perhaps 150 m x 100 m once in 10 ha, or, say, 50 m x 100 m or equivalent 2 or 3 times 10 ha^{-1}.

3.3.2 Optimal composition of mixed woods

What is the minimum proportion of the secondary tree type in broadleaf/conifer mixtures that will markedly improve the value of the wood for song birds? Is there an optimal spatial distribution of tree types in mixtures, eg are clumps better than an even scatter of individual trees?

In 2 sites, selective felling of one component of a mixed canopy, within a single coherent area, had changed the composition of the mixture over part of the site, in both cases with a comparable, coherent area left unchanged. At Cambus o' May (site N), many old pines and some birch were felled in winter 1984–85, changing an area originally containing similar amounts of pine and birch to predominantly birch (+ a few pine), while another part of the site, originally also birch (+ a few pine), remained unaltered. At Corsedardar (site O), also in 1984–85, nearly all birch and rowan (*Sorbus aucuparia*) were removed from about half of the mixed area, where they had previously accounted for 30–50% of the total canopy cover (cf Table 1).

If these changes in proportion of the tree types had affected the bird populations, we would expect, in both sites, a general decline in both numbers and species richness in the felled areas, relative to the corresponding unfelled areas. After correcting all counts to a constant area within each site, we compared overall changes in numbers of each bird species, between years, in felled and unfelled areas (Wilcoxon signed-ranks test), and also noted presence or absence of marked changes in some bird summary parameters (Table 7).

At Cambus o' May, there was no evidence for any effect of removing the old pines, as there was a highly significant decline in numbers of most species in both felled and unfelled areas, both in 1983–84 and 1984–85 (Wilcoxon test). The aggregate parameters 'number of birds' and BSD also declined in the felled area both before and after felling. The 2 areas (felled and unfelled) appeared to be changing differently, but the differences cannot, so far, be attributed to changes in tree type composition.

Table 7. Comparison of bird summary parameters, and overall changes in numbers of individual species, between felled and unfelled areas at 'experimental' sites. Felling was between 1984 and 1985 (source: original unpublished data)

i. Cambus o' May (site N)

		Unfelled			Felled		
Year		1983	1984	1985	1983	1984	1985
Number of birds		17.5	17.5	15	29	16.5	11.5
Number of species		11	12	10	12	12	10
BSD		2.00	2.14	2.09	2.14	2.09	2.01
Wilcoxon test of overall	T		5.5	3.5		2.5	2.0
changes in individual species							
between years	N		12	11		13	10
	P		<0.01	<0.01		<0.01	<0.01

ii. Corsedardar (site O)

		Unfelled		Felled	
Year		1984	1985	1984	1985
Number of birds		21	31	20	22
Number of species		8	11	10	9
BSD		1.52	1.88	1.66	1.74
Wilcoxon test of overall	T		10		24
changes in individual species					
between years	N		12		11
	P		<0.01		NS

Table 8. Bird summary parameters compared with canopy composition of mixed woods (source: original unpublished data)

Mixture type	Site	Proportion of secondary tree type (%, to nearest 5%)	Distribution of secondary type	Number of birds	Number of species	Bird species diversity
Mainly broadleaves	(L)	15	clump	31	12	2.09
	(N2)	20	clump	46	16	2.42
	(M)	10	clump	58	16	2.36
Mainly conifers	(K)	23	clump	62	17	2.54
	(E)	15	even	43	11	2.13
Approx 'equal'	(N1)	30	clump	57	16	2.43
(primary : secondary ratio	(P)	25	clump	119	19	2.53
3 : 1)	(O1)	30	even	56	13	1.91
	(O2)	20–25	even	66	14	2.01

'Even' in 4th column indicates a more-or-less even scatter of single trees or very small clumps (2 or 3 trees at most)
'Clump' indicates that the secondary tree type has an appreciably clumped distribution, ie a larger scale of pattern

At Corsedardar, there was no obvious change between years in anything except BSD in the felled area, but all bird parameters tested improved markedly in the unfelled area, suggesting that in this case there was some detrimental effect of removing part of the mixture. The remaining birch in the mixed area is due to be felled before 1986, which should provide a further test of the effect of removing a tree type from the mixture.

If, however, we compare whole mixed woods, rather than sub-plots, for differences in song bird populations related to canopy composition and clumping of tree types (Table 8), 2 trends can be seen. First, with the possible exception of the mixed oak/pine/birch plot at Craigendarroch (site M), woods with less than about 20% of the secondary tree type had fewest birds and bird species, and lower BSD. Second, a clumped distribution of the secondary tree type was better than an even scatter of individual trees. We did not sample any woods with very large (2 ha or more) clumps so cannot say whether these would be better or worse than smaller clumps.

3.3.3 Combinations of tree and shrub types
We have data from 4 sites where there were distinct areas with and without a tall-shrub layer. At 3 (Glassel

Road, Glen Dye and Potarch), we can simply compare the summary bird parameters over the 2 areas (Table 9). In nearly all cases (the only exception was number of birds, not the most important parameter, at Potarch), areas with a tall-shrub layer, as expected, consistently contained more birds of more species, with higher BSD, than areas without one.

At the fourth site, Dinnet Oakwood, we monitored the consequences of removal, in 1980 and 1981, of a shrub layer of rhododendron, which formerly covered about one-third of the area. The census plot consisted of 3 blocks of almost equal areas. These were: oak with rhododendron in 1980–81 (but not thereafter); oak always without rhododendron; and oak (also without rhododendron) mixed with birch, aspen and bird cherry (*Prunus padus*). Comparing successive pairs of years (one pair before/during treatment and 2 after) within each of these areas, there was a drastic decrease in the richness of the bird population in the former rhododendron area after its removal (Table 10). The apparent partial recovery (indicated by number of species and BSD in 1984–85) was entirely due to a small influx of stem and air (group iii) and canopy (group v) birds, all in low numbers and, from examination of the territory maps, usually only holding parts of their territories in the area from which rhododendron

Table 9. Bird summary parameters in areas with and without a tall-shrub layer within 3 woods, showing the general increase in the richness of the song bird population with the presence of a tall-shrub layer (source: original unpublished data)

Site	Bird parameter	With tall shrub 1984	With tall shrub 1985	Without tall shrub 1984	Without tall shrub 1985
Glassel Road (E)	Number of birds		20		16
	Number of species		11		7
	BSD		2.17		1.74
Glen Dye (F)	Number of birds	41	40	33	38
	Number of species	13	13	11	10
	BSD	2.37	2.37	2.18	2.05
Potarch (K)	Number of birds	38	45	43	34
	Number of species	16	17	12	12
	BSD	2.56	2.62	2.07	1.86

Table 10. Bird summary parameters, and overall changes in numbers of individual species between successive pairs of years in 3 sub-plots in Dinnet Oakwood (site J) (source: original unpublished data)

2-year period	Oak originally with rhododendron[1]			Oak always without rhododendron[2]			Oak with other broadleaf spp. and without rhododendron[3]		
	1980–81	1982–83	1984–85	1980–81	1982–83	1984–85	1980–81	1982–83	1984–85
Number of birds	20.5	5	8	12	16	17	20.5	23	20
Number of species	12	6	11	15	13	13	11	12	15
BSD	2.43	1.71	2.18	2.34	2.36	2.32	2.54	2.23	2.39
Wilcoxon tests of overall T		4	9.5		23	42		46	40
changes in individual									
species (between years) N		13	9		13	14		14	14
P		<0.01	NS		NS	NS		NS	NS

[1]Area with rhododendron present in 1980–81, removed thereafter

[2]Area of oak with rhododendron never present ⎫ These 2 areas provide partial controls for comparison with the rhododendron area, to assess the effects on the bird population of removing the shrub layer between 1980 and 1982

[3]Area with much birch/aspen/bird cherry mixed with the oak ⎭

had been removed, the territories being centred on adjacent areas. In the other 2 areas, there was no significant change between periods. Further monitoring will show whether the loss of the original (largely shrub-related) species will eventually be offset by an increase in species using the more open air space in the cleared area.

The within-wood analyses, therefore, confirm the original survey conclusion of the great importance of a tall shrub + canopy combination. Can we also say whether any particular type of shrub or canopy, or combination, is better for song birds than another? We have data for several woods, all with approximately equivalent amounts of tall shrub, in all combinations of conifer and broadleaf (deciduous), plus one wood with a broadleaved (evergreen) shrub layer (Dinnet Oakwood before rhododendron removed), and one (Crathie) with a mixture of broadleaved and conifer types in both shrub layer and canopy. In the results below: (a) = conifer under conifer (Glen Dye), (b) = conifer under broadleaves (Potarch), (c) = broadleaved deciduous under conifer (Glassel Road), (d) = broadleaved deciduous under broadleaf (Dinnet Oakwood 1982–85), (e) = broadleaved evergreen under broadleaf (Dinnet Oakwood 1980–81), and (f) = mixed under mixed (Crathie). Jonckheere tests on number of birds, number of species, and BSD indicate the following rankings:

Number of birds
(c)<(d)<(a,e,b)<(f) S=76, z=3.94   P<0.001

Number of species
(c)<(d,a,e)<(b,f) S=52, z=2.88   P<0.002

BSD
(c)<(d,a,e)<(b,f) S=42, z=2.31   P<0.01

Combining these groups gives an overall ranking of (c)<(d)≤(a,e)≤(b)≤(f); ie an evergreen shrub layer (whether conifer or broadleaf) was consistently better (for song birds) than a deciduous shrub layer, and a mixed shrub layer, at least in combination with a mixed canopy, better than either. The relatively high ranking of Glen Dye, in which both canopy and shrub layers were entirely pine, indicates that the structural characteristics of the shrub/canopy combination were probably more important than their species composition.

4 Discussion
The generally low ranking of birch/aspen woods and of mixtures where the main component was broadleaved species, indicating that they were relatively poor habitat for song birds, is perhaps surprising. However, because both birch and aspen tend to colonize in fairly homogeneous even-aged blocks, structural diversity is likely to be low in these woods. Also, they rarely develop a distinct tall-shrub layer of sufficient extent and density to support many shrub-living birds (ecological groups (ii), (iv) and (iva)). Similarly, in mixtures, a small proportion of broadleaved species, if suitably clumped, may contribute a greater number of additional species to those of pure conifer stands than vice versa.

The importance of structural diversity has been emphasized in our results, supporting the suggestions of MacArthur and MacArthur (1961), with the major proviso that, as well as FHD, it is also necessary to take into account some measure of horizontal heterogeneity (eg NPT or HET). Our observed variation among tree types does not indicate tree species effects, but rather effects of differences in the cover profiles characteristic of those types.

Mixtures (of tree types) increase species richness (of bird populations), not only by increasing structural diversity but also by providing habitat for birds specific to, or most common in, each individual tree type (eg goldcrest in conifers, blue tit in broadleaves). At least some aggregations of the secondary tree type should be large enough to support complete territories of the type-specific birds. From observed territory sizes, we can suggest that, for most bird species 'preferring' a particular tree type, a single clump of 50–100 m diameter, or a cluster of smaller clumps of equivalent total area, will provide sufficient of the correct tree type to enable establishment of at least one territory. This will not be sufficient markedly to improve overall species richness in a 10 ha total area, as many of the 'type' species will be competing for the suitable habitat and only one or a few birds will successfully hold territory. Nevertheless, it does give some indication of a possibly optimal clump size in mixtures .

Indicators of a wood with a structure attractive to many song bird species include the number of distinct profile types. While this number appears to be a good general guide, it is an index that is not always easy to define precisely. Especially, differences in canopy height, if mainly within the same canopy class (low, mid, high), are not likely to matter to most song birds. (Crossbills, however, seemed to require high canopy.) Also, differences in actual amounts of cover in the tall-shrub range were generally more important than the same differences in canopy layers, and may be further confused by the intermingling of low canopy with the tops of tall shrubs. However, in practice, most profile types seem to be distinguishable from each other on the ground, and we had little or no difficulty in assessing this parameter in our woods. One point to note is that profile types covering only very small areas (<40 m x 40 m) should usually be ignored or, alternatively, combined with whichever other type they most resemble.

5 Conclusions

From our data and analyses, we can state a series of 'desiderata' for a rich song bird population, as a guide to the sort of woodland structure for which a forester should aim in order to encourage a wide variety of song birds. These 'desiderata' are not all entirely compatible with maximizing an economic crop, but most can be achieved at little cost. Given that many foresters are willing to 'give up' about 10% of the total area of a forest to 'conservation purposes', it would, for example, be possible to establish a near-optimal structure over 10 ha in a forest one km^2, leaving the rest entirely for intensive timber growing. A potentially more fruitful approach, however, would be to spread the '10%' more widely and attempt to integrate it into the more general management of the forest. The first method might provide an extremely rich wood in a small area, but would have little or no effect on the rest of the forest. The second, while almost certainly never attaining the same maximum richness anywhere, might still make the whole forest significantly richer in birds, and the total effect could be much greater. What combination of these methods is best for any particular forest must be decided by the forester, taking into account any existing features of the area, such as topography, water bodies, open areas, as well as his own management requirements.

The 'desiderata' (all apply primarily to a 10 ha area) are as follows.

1. The wood must be already established, with at least one-third mature or old trees. There is little a forester can do with a very young wood to encourage woodland song birds, because the necessary habitats simply are not there. Three options for improving the structure of the ensuing mature wood, however, are (i) to stagger plantings, in order to generate as wide a variety of ages as possible and provide some degree of 'edge' habitat, (ii) to use existing older trees as a 'nurse crop' for under-planting, and (iii) to plant mixtures of tree types, in suitable-sized blocks. Much of the possible management for song birds, though, starts with first thinnings and fellings, and with the second and subsequent rotations.

2. The wood must contain at least 4 distinct profile types. This is another essential feature, and may at first seem a difficult one to attain. However, a single tree species, at 2 ages more than 15 years apart, and with and without a shrub layer, or at different spacings, or thinned and unthinned, immediately provides at least 4 distinct profiles, possibly more. Clearings immediately add 1 to the number of profile types.

3. It should have a tall-shrub layer (not necessarily a dense one) over about one-quarter to one-third of its area. This layer can be of genuine shrubs (eg juniper (*Juniperus communis*), rose (*Rosa* spp.), elder (*Sambucus nigra*), hazel (*Corylus avellana*), rhododendron, and perhaps bramble (*Rubus* spp.)) or small trees (preferably evergreen of some sort, including young conifers), and may be achieved by planting, by coppicing (where appropriate), or simply by not removing regeneration.

4. It should have an 'upper canopy' (>12 m), preferably including some 'high canopy' (>20 m), over at least one-third of its area. This simply means that there should be about one-third or more 'pole' and 'high forest'. Ideally, pine in some areas should be left to grow beyond about 80 years old, spruces 60 years, birch 60–90 years, and other trees to equivalent ages, albeit in a well-thinned stand, possibly acting as a 'nurse' for under-plantings or natural regeneration (see also 5).

5. Shrub layer and canopy should overlap over about one-third of their respective areas. Maximum bird richness requires canopy and shrub, both separately and together. The combination is, however, easily achieved by (i) planting or restocking next to pole or mature forest, (ii) not removing regeneration, especially at the edges of mature thinned stands (the understorey will always extend a little way in), and (iii) under-planting.

6. There should be gaps >15 m wide in the canopy, covering about 20% of the total area, mostly ≤50 m wide, but with one or a few (10 ha^{-1}) up to 100 m wide. Gaps larger than 100 m should

preferably include some 'shrubs'. The extent to which this layout is attainable will depend very much on the practicability of appropriate thinning and felling regimes. Basically, it implies a small-scale thinning/extraction programme, analogous to efficient muirburn. Long corridors, eg rides, are not an adequate substitute for genuine gaps, but a length : breadth ratio of up to about 5 : 1 is probably acceptable for widths of up to 40 m, especially if there is some shrub or understorey in the gap. Generally, the proportion of gap is more critical than the size of gaps, especially in relatively dense stands. In mature stands, already well thinned, a few larger gaps would probably be sufficient, especially if there was also some regeneration or under-planting (see 3–5 above).

7. The canopy should be a mixture of tree types (broadleaf/conifer) in a ratio between about 3 : 1 and 5 : 1 (in either direction), the secondary type mostly arranged in clumps or blocks not less than 25 m wide, and with some clumps or aggregates of clumps totalling ≥c1 ha. Like number of profile types, this requirement may appear at first almost impossible. However, remembering the 2 methods of 'giving 10% to conservation' noted above, a forester wanting to cut broadleaved planting to the absolute minimum could, if he chose the first method, limit broadleaved species to as little as 2% of the total plantings in one km^2, though ornithologists would probably consider that to be a distinctly 'suboptimal' strategy. Additionally, readily colonizing broadleaved species such as birch and rowan could be encouraged, or at least not immediately removed, especially in cleared areas (before subsequent replanting), and even used as a nurse for young conifers, probably after some initial thinning.

8. Large-scale even-age planting, and clearfelling in large blocks (≫c5 ha) should be avoided.

9. Some dead wood (not too small, ie large branches, stumps and stems) is useful to encourage woodpeckers, tits and other hole-breeders (lack of nest holes is often a limiting factor to some bird species). Often less than 0.5% (ground cover), or just 2 or 3 dead trees and a few stumps or fallen branches, is sufficient. Total removal of all dead wood may even be counter-productive, as many hole-breeding species, particularly great spotted woodpecker, will make their holes in dead or rotten wood by preference but, if that is denied them, may then start to attack live wood. Against this factor, however, must be set the (small) risk of potential pathogens, if too much dead wood is left in a stand.

The end result of forest management according to the above *desiderata* should be a wood something like that shown in Figure 4, and the 3 most important general strategies for achieving it are as follows.

1. Planting, thinning, extraction and restocking in small blocks or strips, generally not more than c200–250 m wide, but with a length : breath ratio that can be up to 5 : 1. Initial plantings can be on a much larger scale, provided subsequent thinning, etc, reduces the final scale of pattern to the above ratio or less.

2. Encouragement (or non-removal) of natural re-generation of all kinds, together with some under-planting, to provide a tall-shrub layer and, in conjuction with strategy 1 and with a variety of planted age classes, to multiply the variability produced by 1.

3. Planting (including under-planting and replanting), or encouraging regeneration, in mixtures (conifer + broadleaf), with the secondary tree type suitably clumped.

Finally, comparison of the pine plantation at Glen Dye, and the mixed conifers at Potarch, with the 'Caledonian' pinewoods at Glen Tanar shows clearly that plantations need not be poorer than 'natural' woods in song birds and can, indeed, be considerably richer, if the above guidelines are followed.

6 Summary
In 16 woods in Deeside, we analysed the relationships between song bird populations and structural characteristics of the woods, with the aim of deriving recommendations for woodland management to enhance song bird populations.

Bird populations were assessed by a mapping method (British Trust for Ornithology Common Bird Census), and bird species were assigned to one of 8 'ecological groups', according to their nesting and foraging habits. These groups, and the summary parameters, 'number of birds', 'number of species' and 'bird species diversity' (BSD), were compared with vegetation profiles and diversity/heterogeneity parameters, derived from detailed surveys of the census plots.

The main conclusions, from regressions of bird parameters on vegetation parameters, and statistical comparisons among different ages of woods, tree types, and amounts and distributions of tall shrubs, were as follows.

1. The quality of habitat for woodland song birds generally improved with age of wood.

2. Birch was the 'worst' single type for song birds and oak the 'best', with conifers intermediate. Mixtures of conifers and broadleaved species were usually 'better' than pure stands of a single tree type, and mixtures with the main component conifer were 'better' than those that were mostly broadleaved trees. The secondary tree type in mixtures needed to be at least 20% of total canopy to be effective. It also should be concentrated in clumps or similar aggregations, rather than evenly spread or in thin lines.

142

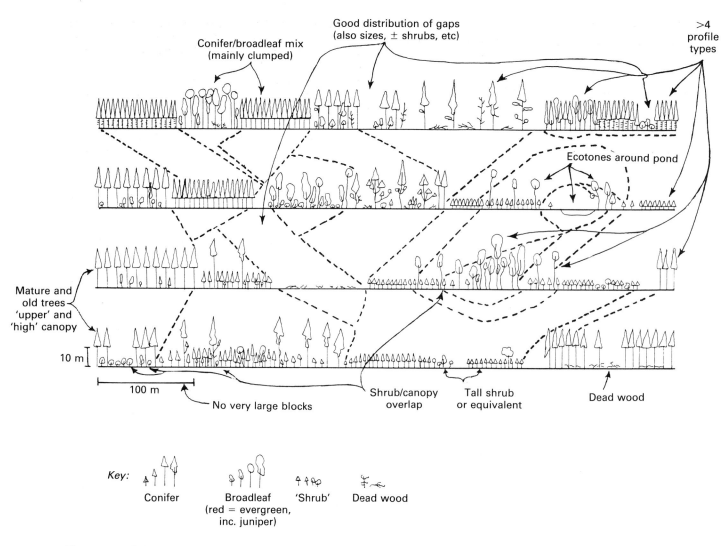

Figure 4. Schematic representation of a desirable forest structure. The Figure represents 4 parallel transects over a total area of c15 ha, and stand densities are all drawn half-size, in relation to broadleaves and 'shrub', for greater clarity

3. The combination of canopy >12 m high, especially where some trees were >20 m, with a tall-shrub layer or equivalent, was especially conducive to a rich song bird population. The structural aspect was much more important than the tree/shrub species involved, though evergreen 'shrubs' (including young conifers) appeared to be 'better' than deciduous broad-leaved types.

4. The number of distinct vegetation/cover profiles in a wood was a fairly good general guide to its attractiveness to many song bird species. More than 4 distinct profiles 10 ha^{-1} usually indicated a 'good' structure, favouring a rich, diverse, song bird population, and less than 4 a 'poor' structure, supporting few species.

5. Small gaps (15 m ≤ gap size ≤ 50 m) in the canopy were important.

From our analyses, we derived the following 'desiderata', which are further discussed in terms of their practicability (often they are far more practicable than appears at first sight).

— The wood must contain at least one-third mature or old trees, and a variety of other age classes.

— It must contain at least 4 distinct profile types in 10 ha.

— It should have canopy over about one-third of its area, with a tall-shrub layer over a similar proportion, and these should overlap over about half their range.

— There should be gaps ≥15 m wide in the canopy, over about 20% of the total area, mostly small (≤c50 m wide) or, if larger than 100 m, including shrubs or young trees.

— There should be a mixture of tree types, suitably clumped. Uniform, large-scale, even-age blocks (≫c5 ha) should be avoided.

— A small amount of dead wood should be allowed to remain in the stand.

An example of a 'desirable' woodland structure is given, and strategies are suggested for achieving the above 'desiderata'.

7. Acknowledgements

We thank all the landowners who gave permission to work in their woods, and the foresters, keepers, wardens and other estate staff for their co-operation and, in many cases, active assistance. Many colleagues in and out of the Institute helped with fieldwork, and discussion of ideas, especially Lynda Hepburn and Jos Vestjens.

8 References

Haapanen, A. 1965. Bird fauna of the Finnish forests in relation to forest succession. I. *Ann. zool. fenn.,* **2,** 153–196.

Jonckheere, A.R. 1954. A distribution-free k-sample test against ordered alternatives. *Biometrika,* **41,** 133–145.

Komdeur, J. & Vestjens, J.P.M. 1982. *De relatie tussen bosstructuur en broedvogelbevolking in Nederlandse naaldbossen.* Doktoraalverslag, LH Natuurbeheer/Boosteelt, Wageningen.

MacArthur, R. & MacArthur, J. 1961. On bird species diversity. *Ecology,* **42,** 594–598.

Marchant, J. 1983. *BTO common bird census instructions.* Tring: British Trust for Ornithology.

Moss, D. 1978. Diversity of woodland songbird populations. *J. Anim. Ecol.,* **47,** 521–527.

Moss, D. 1979. Even-aged plantations as a habitat for birds. In: *The ecology of even-aged forest plantations,* edited by E.D. Ford, D.C. Malcolm & J. Atterson, 413–427. Cambridge: Institute of Terrestrial Ecology.

Moss, D., Taylor, P.N. & Easterbee, N. 1979. The effects on song-bird populations of upland afforestation with spruce. *Forestry,* **52,** 129–147.

Newton, I. 1986. Principles underlying bird numbers in Scottish woodlands. In: *Trees and wildlife in the Scottish uplands,* edited by D. Jenkins, 121–128. (ITE symposium no. 17.) Abbots Ripton: Institute of Terrestrial Ecology.

Opdam, P. & van Bladeren, G.J. 1981. *De vogelbevolking van beheerde en onbeheerde delen van het Forstamt hasbruch en relatie tot de bosstructuur.* (RIN-rapport 81/21.) Leersum: Research Institute for Nature Management.

Shannon, C.E. & Weaver, W. 1949. *The mathematical theory of communication.* Urbana, IL: University of Illinois Press.

Siegel, S. 1956. *Nonparametric statistics for the behavioral sciences.* New York: McGraw-Hill.

Thomson, A.L. 1910. *British birds and their nests.* Edinburgh: Chambers.

Van Berkel, C.J.M. 1979. *Onderzoek naar kwantitatieve methoden voor het beschrijven van vegetatiestructuren.* Leersum: Stageverslag LH Wageningen, Plantenoecologie, Research Institute for Nature Management.

ERRATUM

TREES AND WILDLIFE IN THE SCOTTISH UPLANDS

The caption to Figure 4 on page 142 should read:

Schematic representation of a desirable forest structure. The Figure represents 4 parallel transects over a total area of c 15 ha, and stand densities are all drawn at half actual density for great clarity. Disregard the reference to red in the figure.

The forest's potential for recreation and landscape

DAME SYLVIA CROWE
B/59 Ladbroke Grove, London

1 Introduction

Forests can provide unique opportunities for public enjoyment and participation, and are also capable of contributing to the beauty and fertility of the country-side. These benefits can only be realized if forestry planning and practice take account of all the possible side benefits, in addition to their prime objective of timber production. Few extensive land uses offer so many opportunities for recreation and amenity as do the forests. Once they are established and the trees have passed the thicket stage, it is possible to allow public access, even into working and commercial forests, on a scale only rivalled by that available on areas of hill grazing and far in excess of anything which is practicable in most agricultural areas.

The attractions which visitors find in forests are many and varied, and can be greatly increased by sympathetic forest management. The attractions of forests include the opportunity to take long walks in beautiful surroundings, free from roads and traffic, now becoming a rare experience elsewhere.

There is also the feeling of remoteness and mystery engendered by the enclosing trees, and the opportunity to see and study wildlife and woodland flowers, and, in deciduous forests, the ever-changing pageant of the seasons.

Enjoyment can be found in any forest. Trees themselves, of any species, are things of beauty, but the attraction can be immeasurably increased by sympathetic forest management. In almost every case, measures to increase the ecological richness and diversity of the forests will also result in visual enhancement, and attraction to the public.

Some of the least attractive forests are those consisting of large areas of single-age monoculture. This statement is particularly true of unbroken conifer plantations, because these discourage undergrowth, resulting in a diminution of wildlife. Such plantations are also visually monotonous. Nevertheless, limited areas of pure conifers can be magnificent in maturity, as can be seen to perfection within the stands of giant redwood (*Sequoia sempervirens*) in California. Even in Britain, there are examples of the grand cathedral effect of mature stands of Scots pine (*Pinus sylvestris*) or Douglas fir (*Pseudotsuga menziesii*).

2 The forest's potential for recreation and landscape

In general, variety in age and species produces the forest type most popular with human visitors, as well as with other species of life. Deciduous trees, more-over, not only provide variety in themselves but also encourage the growth of shrubs and ground flora, which, in addition to their inherent beauty and interest, provide food and habitats for a wide range of life. Anyone who has seen the carpet of primroses (*Primula vulgaris*), followed by wood anemones (*Anemone nemorosa*) and bluebells (*Endymion non-scriptus*) in woods worked on the old coppice and standard system will rejoice to learn that the type of timber produced by this method is now finding a profitable outlet for fuel and joinery. This forest practice is one of many which can increase the attraction of forests for visitors.

3 Site planning

The careful adjustment of planting patterns and species to physical features of the site produces a landscape of interest and variety, far removed from that produced by a solid blanket of monoculture. Not only will careful regard to the site produce at least some variety in crop species, but some areas will be revealed, such as rocky outcrops and scree, where planting is uneconomic and which can best be left to colonization by such native tree species as rowan (*Sorbus aucuparia*) and the local plant associations.

A wide outlook on maximum benefits of land use will also recognize the value of other landscape features. Mountain streams are not only vital to the welfare of the river systems, by replenishing water and providing for the spawning of fish, they are also a magnet of attraction for visitors. Keeping the forest back from the stream edge, to give space, air and light to the waterways, loses little in the way of timber, and adds much to the pleasures and fertility of the countryside.

3.1 Scale

Large areas of newly planted forests are relatively unattractive, and a far more acceptable landscape results from smaller areas of felling and replanting, planned to enhance and accentuate the natural lie of the land. In our forests today, there are many examples of felling which, far from appearing as gashes on the landscape, add interest by their shape and the retention of outstanding groups of trees. Some years ago, a head forester in Devon showed me, with justifiable pride, how he had felled to open up a view down a valley, shaping the boundaries of the coup to frame and accentuate the view. Repton could not have done better.

3.2 Climatic factors

On our often windswept forestry sites, felling large areas at a time can open the way to serious windblow;

and there can, as so often, be practical as well as aesthetic reasons for limiting the extent of felling coups and shaping them to the lie of the land. In Britain's windy climate, shelterbelts can play a vital role and their use could be extended with advantage. While straight strips of woodland are acceptable as shelterbelts within the rectangular field pattern of the lowlands, there is an added beauty in the sweeping shape of shelterbelts on the northern hills. Belts of woodland often occur at the line where hillsides merge into the plain, and give a satisfying definition to the land form, as well as serving to check runoff and erosion.

3.3 Design within the forest

The traditional forest ride is long and straight, but is now sometimes being replaced by rides inflecting to the contours of the land. These rides provide far more attractive walks, and, by avoiding the wind tunnel effect, they are more conducive to bird life. There are examples in the forests today (even along the straight 'wind tunnels') where verges are allowed to develop their natural flora. There are some particularly attractive examples in Friston Forest, in Sussex, where a host of wild flowers and their attendant bees and butterflies make the forest rides a favourite haunt for naturalists and walkers.

A management regime which delays cutting the verges till late summer, and cuts each side in alternate years, encourages the floral display. These rides provide a refuge for many of the downland flowers eliminated from the open downs by changes in farming practices, notably the replacement of sheep grazing by that of cattle, resulting in a coarser sward, inimical to many of the downland flowers. In historic terms, Friston Forest is comparatively recent and its attraction for the public will increase as it matures and the beech (*Fagus sylvatica*) is released from the nurse crop of conifers.

4 Public reaction to forests

Fortunately, the old practice of planting rectangular blocks of forestry irrespective of land formation and the pattern of the landscape has given way to a more sympathetic and enlightened approach. Due regard is now paid to the character and contours of the land. When the results of this policy become evident, there is likely to be a far more sympathetic attitude to forestry by the public. There are many reasons for the public's lack of enthusiasm for forestry in the past. Although the Highlands in ancient times had been under forest, recent generations, since the clearances for sheep grazing and timber, had known and loved the open, treeless hills. The hills of Britain, owing to an ancient and varied geological history, are exceptionally varied and subtly modelled, and their whole character can be effaced by unsympathetic planting. Yet the character of these hills can even be accentuated when plantations complement the land form, running up the sheltered valleys and down from the exposed hill

breasts, and incorporating sufficient variety in species and spacing to allow the forest to inflect to the character and contours of the land.

Hill lands require a very different approach from flat lands. On the great plain of northern Brazil, the solid square blocks of woodland appear appropriate, as do the rectangular woods of the Dutch polders. Even within the patchwork of fields in the English lowlands, solid blocks of woodland add emphasis to the pattern, giving punctuation to the lines of hedges. On hills, by contrast, not only does the vertical elevation expose the whole plantation to a map-like view, but the contoured landscape cannot accept the rectangular shapes which are quite acceptable in a flat land.

5 Recreation in the forests

The development in forests of planned visitor attraction is comparatively recent and has achieved great success. One of the earliest forest visitor centres was established at Grizedale in the Lake District, and proved to be a pioneer in providing the type of visitor attraction now found in many forests. These attractions provide signposted walks, hides for bird-watching, and information centres, the latter ranging from the small and simple to quite elaborate buildings with literature and slide displays. There are also many camp-sites, one of the earliest having been established in the Forest of Dean. These sites have been augmented by cabin and even chalet development in more remote areas. Other forms of recreation include orienteering and, as in the Forest of Dean, canoeing.

A perpetual watch is necessary on the extent and impact of recreational activities to guard against the very real danger that over-use may damage the environment, to the detriment both of the forest's main purpose and of its quality as a recreational resource. Careful planning can ensure that short, easy walks and look-out points are provided for the casual visitor, while ensuring that other parts of the forests remain remote and only visited by those prepared for effort and long walks in their desire to experience the true spirit of the forest. One means of ensuring that some areas remain quiet and remote is by limiting car access and parking to areas designed to take such pressure. Considerable care and planning skill are required to ensure that car-parking, even in the most popular areas, does not infringe on the spirit of the forest or disrupt the views with a litter of cars. This objective can be achieved by careful siting and by screening car-parks with land form and/or planting.

The United States Forest Service was a pioneer in catering for the public enjoyment of its forests, and foresters in the UK have been able to learn many useful lessons from its experiences. It must, however, be appreciated that problems in the 2 countries are very different. The scale of the USA is such that a far greater visitor pressure can be accommodated than could be tolerated in the limited area of the UK forests.

An important aspect of planning in all forests frequented by the public is the design of forest furniture, ranging from noticeboards to forest cabins. The Forestry Commission now sets a high standard of design, relying on straightforward simplicity and the use of sturdy timber structures.

6 Town forests

There are many examples in the UK of forests and woodlands close to conurbations which serve as recreational areas for the townspeople, and more are being established by the new towns. On the whole, however, we have lagged behind many other European countries in this provision, and do not have the equivalent of the Bois de Boulogne or the Amsterdam Bos. This omission is one we should rectify. For example, a journey from Heathrow airport to London reveals a welter of eye-sores amid a network of worked-out gravel pits. This area would appear to offer an opportunity to plant a matrix of forestry to absorb all the discordant elements. Our country abounds in unrealized opportunities to effect a transformation which would immeasurably improve the suburban landscape, provide opportunities for recreation, and augment our timber supplies.

7 Summary

Forestry is one of the land uses offering most opportunities for public enjoyment and participation. The basic visual attraction of forests is the beauty of the trees themselves. They also provide for the outdoor enjoyments of walking, camping and studying nature. Diversity in forests of age, species and management regimes increases their interest and attraction.

There is beauty to be found in stands of tall conifers, in deciduous woodlands, and in the patterns of old coppice and standard. The visual advantage of comparatively small coupes, shaped to the lie of the land, coincides with climatic advantages in Britain's windy climate.

The old practice of planting square blocks on hillsides has been superseded by planting in sympathy with the lie of the land, which allows forestry to contribute to the beauty of the landscape. Enlightened management is making the interior of forests attractive to visitors both visually and by providing recreational facilities. Care is necessary to ensure that over-use and sophistication do not impinge on the spirit of the forest.

The USA has pioneered forest recreation. In learning from its experience, we must remember that our areas are very small by comparison and may need different treatment.

Britain has lagged behind in the provision of town forests and an extended field of enterprise waits to be implemented here.

Managing forests for wildlife in Sweden

V MARCSTRÖM

Department of Zoophysiology, University of Uppsala, Sweden

1 Introduction

Modern wildlife resources are a product not only of present land use but very much also of past events, especially in the long rotation of northern forests. This paper gives some information about the development and current use of Fennoscandian and particularly Swedish forests. My main theme is the relationship between forest management and wildlife, focusing on game animals and related species. I will also discuss some ecological problems relevant to future forest policy.

2 The development and extent of forest ecosystems

At the end of the last Ice Age, 9000–10 000 years ago, Scandinavia was colonized by forest ecosystems and by man (Tenow 1974). The first agriculture began 5000 years later, but was a step-wise development punctuated by long periods of stagnation. The rapidly increasing human population of the 17th and 18th centuries progressively opened up the landscape, with a culmination in the 19th century. Browsing by cattle formed rather extensive heathland in southern Sweden and Norway and in Denmark. Much woodland was also converted into pastures and arable land. Continuous forest was reduced by heavy cutting in many regions, generally into a mosaic, part-open, landscape.

As forest products found new and wider uses, necessitating a change from exploitative to sustained-yield forestry, a reforestation law was introduced early in the present century. Two decades later, the felling of young stands was forbidden, although rational thinning was, of course, still permitted. In recent years, the previous mosaic landscape has been split increasingly into 2 contrasting areas: arable land and forests. Farmers have removed hedges, scrub and copses, while foresters have planted abandoned small fields, meadows and pastures with spruce (*Picea* spp.) or pine (*Pinus* spp.). As a result of these and other changes in land management, the stock of trees has increased throughout the 20th century, and Sweden probably has more forest today than in any other period since the last Ice Age.

In Sweden, woodland now accounts for 23.5 Mha, 57% of the land area and just under 1% of the world's dense woodland. The sawmill industry is the largest in Europe, producing about 8% of the world's sawn softwood. Sweden is the world's third largest exporter of paper, paperboard and fibreboard. Wood provides about 19% of all Swedish exports, and forest products play a crucial role in the trade balance. Forestry accounts for over half of Sweden's net export.

Forestry is also very important in Finland, where 76% of the land area is wooded, and in some regions in Norway, where 23% of the total land area is covered by productive forests. Though the area of woodland has tripled in Denmark during the last 100 years, less than 12% of the land is wooded and forestry has less economic importance.

Half the Swedish woodland is owned by private persons, one-quarter by forest companies and one-quarter by public bodies. Most public forests are owned by the state, and are situated mainly in the north. The largest forest company owns 1.7 Mha and the next largest 1.4 Mha. Private ownership is predominant in southern Sweden and is distributed among about 240 000 holdings in the whole country. In Finland and in Norway, 63% and 75% of the forests are private.

About two-thirds of Sweden's forests are within the northern temperate coniferous belt, while the southern part of the country has temperate mixed forests. Our relatively dry climate favours Norway spruce (*Picea abies*) (47% of the conifer forest), Scots pine (*Pinus sylvestris*) (38%) and birch (*Betula pubescens and B. verrucosa*) (10%), with aspen (*Populus tremula*), oak (*Quercus robur and Q. petraea*) and other deciduous species about 5% altogether. Lodgepole pine (*Pinus contorta*) has been introduced on 300 kha, mainly in northern areas, but is restricted to a planting of 30 kha yr^{-1}.

The rotation cycle in Swedish forestry is fairly long, about 70 years in the southernmost parts and about 140 years in the extreme north. Due to a bad reforestation programme in the late 1920s to the 1940s, we have a somewhat uneven age distribution (Table 1). Twenty-three per cent of Swedish woodland is 0–20 years old, only 22% is 21–60 years old, 28% is 61–100 years old, and 27% is more than 100 years of age.

The distribution of age classes does not differ greatly

Table 1. Percentage of woodland area in the different age classes of the stands on forest land in Sweden, Norway and Finland

Country	Age class (years)			
	0–20	21–60	61–100	>100
Sweden	23	22	28	27
Norway	27	19	30	25
Finland	19	29	30	22

between the 3 Nordic countries. However, in Finland, 30% of the stands are 21–60 years old, and only 22% more than 100 years old. In Norway, almost 27% of the woodland is 0–20 years old, and about 25% is more than 100 years old. The area to be planted each year is about 30 kha.

A wide zone along the Scandinavian mountain range in the west of Sweden is of special interest. In this area, there are 3 forest zones. Highest up is the sub-alpine birch forest. Below this zone is a belt of conifers (600 kha) of very low productivity, which is to remain untouched by forestry. Below this zone again is a conifer belt of higher productivity of 1.5 Mha. The use of this land for tree production has been much debated, and forest management is to be severely restricted. About 1 Mha of this lowest forest is older than 100 years, and present plans allow for only 10–15% to be felled or otherwise managed.

Five per cent of the Swedish land area is subject to some form of nature protection. Approximately 575 kha are national parks, destined to remain in their natural state for recreation and research. Nature reserves, with various regulations for land use and other activities, cover 854 kha. Animal protection zones totalling 350 kha have been established, especially for bird protection but a few for seals and beaver (*Castor fiber*).

3 Forestry during the 20th century

3.1 Silvicultural practices

In the past 100 years, Sweden has developed from a purely agrarian society to an industrial nation, and Swedish forestry has developed enormously. Forest management and harvesting techniques have changed in the course of time and have also varied considerably between different parts of the country (Juhlin Dannfelt 1952; Nordström 1959). Clearcutting was common in southern and central Sweden during the later 19th and early 20th centuries, and many plantations were established. However, the 1920s and 1930s saw a return to older forestry methods, including selective cutting (characterized by the removal of single mature trees or small groups) and the 'dimension system' (the felling of all trees over a certain size). It was expected that natural regeneration would cover the felled areas.

From the late 1940s, clearcutting became more usual again, with modern silvicultural methods developing in reaction to the failure of the selective system. There seem to be many reasons why clearcutting is a suitable system of forest management in northerly regions, including cost and efficiency. This modern approach is characterized by large clearcut areas, active generation of stands, removal of deciduous trees from mixed stands, thinning operations, application of fertilizers to well-grown stands, and drainage. Different branches of forest research have developed rapidly and have been very important to the whole forestry sector.

In recent years, about 230 kha have been cut annually. This figure is almost 1% of the woodland. Corresponding figures for Finland are 170 kha (0.9%), and for Norway 40 kha (0.7%). The figure for Norway is relatively low because topography and high altitude make many areas inaccessible or fairly unproductive.

Vigorous regrowth of deciduous trees like birch and aspen may be a serious threat to young conifers on some clearcut areas, and has therefore been restricted by the use of herbicides. About 100 kha of forest land were sprayed each year during the late 1960s. However, aerial application has been forbidden in Sweden since 1980, and from 1984 the use of chemicals in forestry has become a political matter. Local authorities have tended to stop all spraying, so that few areas are now treated. The use of chemicals for silviculture seems to have attracted less controversy in Finland, where a few per cent of clearcut areas are still sprayed to control deciduous species, and in Norway where 30% are similarly treated.

Nitrogen fertilization is used to increase growth rates in suitable stands. Approximately 135 kha each year are treated in Sweden, under regulations which are intended to avoid undesirable environmental effects. In Finland, about 100 kha have been treated yearly, but little fertilizer is used in Norway. Drainage of bogs and swamp forest is another way to increase timber production. In recent years, ditches have been dug to drain 35–45 kha annually in Sweden. Finland has drained 80–90 kha each year, but less will be drained in the future, and Norway drains only limited areas.

In Sweden, there are 1–4 thinning operations in each rotation. The first cleaning or unmerchantable thinning is usually when the stands are 2–3 m high. Up to 25% of the timber is removed in thinning operations. Tending and harvesting systems have become mechanized and more efficient since the Second World War. Farm tractors began to replace horses for haulage during the 1940s, and the chainsaw was used more and more during the 1950s. A breakthrough for mechanization in Swedish silviculture came with the use of cross-country forestry tractors in the 1960s, followed by the introduction of processing machines and harvesters. In recent years, mechanization has also affected thinning and planting preparations such as scarification.

3.2 Changes in forest habitat

The large changes in woodland management during the 20th century are reflected in the character of the forests. Dimension cutting of the early decades sometimes produced rather large clearings, and gave rise to promising young stands. In other situations, however, the dimension method and the selective system resulted in uneven-aged and poorly stocked stands with many openings. Berried shrubs flourished in the senescent forest communities, especially bilberry (*Vaccinium myrtillus*), and the turnover of nutrients was slow. With local intrusion of deciduous species, especially birch, productivity was very variable and usually comparatively low. In recent decades, many of these low-yielding forests have been felled and subsequently replanted, often with government subsidies.

Perhaps surprisingly, forest fires were common as recently as the beginning of the present century, and often resulted in extensive open areas. However, they seldom led to monocultures because of variations in landscape, site quality and natural regeneration. Remnants of virgin forest were present here and there, and some sites contained many dead trees, waterlogged areas and other wetlands. On the whole, there was an appreciable diversity within rather restricted forest areas.

The clearcutting method, on the other hand, produces large areas with less diversity. In the 1950s and 1960s, there were some unnecessarily large clearcuttings, but these are less common now. The new vegetation on clearcut areas is dominated by light-demanding species, typified by a short-lived growth of rosebay willowherb (*Chamaenerion angustifolium*), raspberry (*Rubus idaeus*) and cowberry (*Vaccinium vitis-idaea*). In mesotrophic dwarf-shrub areas, there is usually a transition from bilberry to the wavy hair-grass (*Deschampsia flexuosa*) after clearcutting, although bilberry can stand increased light exposure rather well at high altitudes.

The somewhat excessive herbicide spraying of the 1960s helped to produce conifer monocultures. Because the use of chemicals is now restricted in Swedish forestry, and it is comparatively expensive to remove deciduous species in other ways, the proportion of deciduous trees will increase in the forests. The clearing of thicket stages and the thinning of somewhat older stands have also decreased because of the cost and the low value of small trees. On large clearcut areas, managed according to modern methods, abundant grass and herbaceous vegetation remains as long as the ground is exposed to light, but it decreases as the canopy begins to close. Raspberry and willowherb, too, give way to bilberry once again, although the area covered by bilberry has decreased in some modern woods (Huse 1965).

4 The Forestry Act
In 1979, the Swedish parliament established guidelines for forest policies in a new Forestry Act. This Act provides a framework of regulations for felling, planting and other forest management. Its 21st paragraph deals with forestry's responsibility for fauna and flora, water resources, local climate and recreation. The leading principle is that the value of the forest as an environment for man and other forms of life must be maintained, with special consideration near settlements and in areas of scientific or social importance. Areas of clearcutting should be as small as possible,

and final felling should be avoided on waste land or non-productive land. Nest trees of threatened or rare animals must be spared, including some birds of prey, and the stands surrounding some nests of raptors and owls must also be left uncut. Various fruit-bearing trees should remain, and it is recommended that old deciduous trees, whether living or dead and preferably in groups, should be left, as well as single dead conifers and some windthrows. Production of extensive monocultures is to be avoided, and restrictions are placed on the use of foreign tree species. Capercaillie (*Tetrao urogallus*) leks must be left uncut if possible, and areas with extensive black grouse (*Tetrao tetrix*) displaying grounds should not be drained or otherwise disturbed. Further recommendations are given by Ahlén *et al.* (1979) and by Bleckert *et al.* (1984).

Norway and Finland have similar guidelines for forest policy, in which nature conservation and other public interests are stressed.

5 Status of the most important game species
Wildlife populations may be affected by many environmental factors, habitat being one of the most important. Silviculture may thus affect the population density of many forest animals. This is certainly true for game species, whose cover, food quantity and quality may vary very much from time to time because of silvicultural practices, successional stage, and so on. Although our knowledge of relationships between forest management and fauna is incomplete, it seems that the impact of modern forestry is mainly negative for some species, but generally positive for others.

5.1 Ungulates
The Swedish big game fauna contains 4 cervids, elk (*Alces alces*), red deer (*Cervus elaphus*), fallow deer (*Dama dama*), roe deer (*Capreolus capreolus*), and wild boar (*Sus scrofa*). Norway lacks wild boar and fallow deer, but has considerable numbers of red deer and wild reindeer (*Rangifer tarandus*). The populations of red deer, fallow deer, roe deer and wild boar are currently small in Finland, but the North American white-tailed deer (*Odocoileus virginianus*) is present in a large continuous area in the south-west, and wild reindeer are found in some eastern areas.

5.1.1 Elk and roe deer
These 2 species are the most important ungulates in Sweden. They have increased greatly during the present century, with parallel if less marked increases in Norway and Finland. In the early 1900s, fewer than 2000 elk were killed in Sweden each year (Figure 1), and there were no large changes until the end of the 1930s. There was then a more obvious increase, and the population 'exploded' in the 1970s, reaching an all-time peak of approximately 400 000 individuals early in the 1980s. Because of increasing browsing in young pine stands, damage to cultivated fields, and numerous car and train accidents, the elk stock had to be

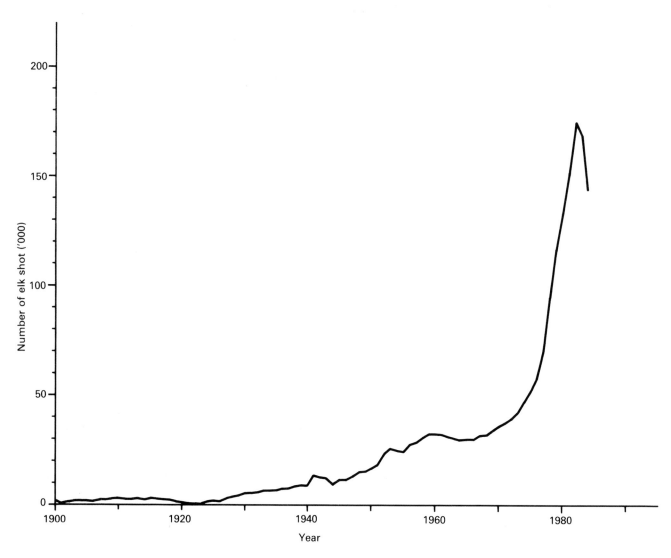

Figure 1.   Number of elk killed legally in Sweden 1900–84

reduced. More than 175 000 were harvested in 1982. Although the population was further reduced in the following years, large areas of Sweden still have denser elk populations than anywhere else in the world. The roe deer population has also increased considerably, with 100 000 now being harvested annually.

The small roe deer and elk populations of the 19th century were mainly the result of uncontrolled hunting and of predation by large predators. A few landowners in Scania saved roe deer from extinction through hunting. Formerly, large predators were numerous in Sweden; for instance, more than 5000 wolves (*Canis lupus*) were killed in Sweden in the 1830s (Hemberg 1914). Land use was very probably a further important factor. Extensive pasturing and haymaking reduced

the nutrient supply for wild herbivores over large areas (Ahlén 1966, 1975).

The increase of roe and elk populations during the last 50 years has been favoured in many ways, including the introduction of modern hunting regulations and game conservation, and a reduction in the number of large predators. The total wolf population in Sweden is currently less than 10 individuals. Cattle are now feeding on cultivated fields and not competing for food with wild browsers. Moreover, there have been very important changes in the forest habitat.

The maturing forests of the selective system adopted in 1920–45 produced a lot of berried shrubs, especially bilberry, which is a highly preferred food for most browsing game species in the woods. This factor was of less importance for elk, however, which in winter feed mainly on twigs and shoots from deciduous and coniferous trees (Westman 1958; Markgren 1969). Browse of this kind was rather limited at that time, a crucial factor in areas with long snow cover, and thus little access to the field layer. Modern forestry has radically increased the amounts of grass, herbs and young trees on the clearcuttings, and has been an essential factor in the increase of the elk population in the past 15 years. The fact that chemicals cannot be widely used to restrict competing deciduous vegetation on clearcuttings may be a problem for forestry, but it is without doubt beneficial for the twig-eating elk. In compensation, a moderate elk population may be useful for forestry by keeping down the deciduous species in coniferous plantations. As the canopy begins to close, the dwarf shrubs reappear, but there is an overall decrease in the amount of winter food above the snow surface, and very little ground vegetation is present in dense spruce plantations.

The problem of elk damage to pine is further complicated in some northern regions, where part of the elk population is very mobile. The elk feed mainly on grass, herbs and dwarf shrubs while there is no snow, and are then dispersed over the whole landscape. In winter, however, they tend to congregate in restricted areas for nutritional, climatological and topographical reasons (Sandegren et al. 1982, 1986; and others), where they can seriously damage the pine plantations. These seasonal migrations vary in length between areas but often average some tens of kilometres, and population densities in these winter quarters may reach 8–10 km^{-2}. As there is little damage in some breeding areas and browsing may even be beneficial on clearcuttings, there is an intricate management problem in reducing forest damage by shooting in winter areas without also reducing the elk population too much in the breeding areas.

The Scandinavian roe deer occupies a rather different feeding niche from the elk. Roe are selective feeders, preferring herbs during summer. They select evergreen parts of dwarf shrubs (mainly heather, bilberry, and cowberry), as well as field crops in winter (Hagen 1958; Strandgaard 1972; Huseby 1976; Cederlund et al. 1980). The roe deer apparently lacks physiological adaptations for subsisting on a purely woody diet over long periods (Brüggemann et al. 1963; Drozdz et al. 1975; Cederlund & Nyström 1981). Nevertheless, buds, shoots and twigs of trees and different shrubs are very important as emergency food during severe snow. The roe deer is able to paw for the field layer vegetation up to a maximal snow depth of c50 cm (Raiby 1970; Cederlund et al. 1980). In north Sweden, where snow is deep in winter and where there is limited cultivated land, roe deer densities are lower.

Roe deer are attracted to young conifer plantations, especially those with a diverse field layer. Middle-aged monocultures are little used, but in deep snow roe are often found in mature stands of conifers with plenty of dwarf shrubs within which the deer can reach the field layer. In the northernmost regions with very deep snow, roe deer also eat tree lichens (Formozov 1946; Markgren 1966), and they often overwinter in old conifer stands where these are abundant. The occurrence of old lichen-rich forests may have been an important factor in the extension of the roe deer's range so far to the north (Marcström 1978).

Supplementary feeding is used to help roe deer over the hardest part of the winter in many parts of Sweden. Though mortality because of malnutrition and dehydration cannot be eliminated entirely (Borg 1970), many animals are saved in some years. Nevertheless, the value of different artificial foods is not well known, and social factors may also influence survival near feeding stations. There is scope for more research on this subject.

5.1.2 Fallow and red deer
Scattered populations of fallow deer are found in southern and central Sweden. Their numbers and harvest by man have both increased considerably during the last 50 years. Two hundred and seventy were shot in 1940 and 2980 in 1984. The fallow deer feeds to a large extent in cultivated areas but also in woodland. It causes some damage on farms, as well as in the woods. Modern forestry seems not to have had any big impact on the population development of this species.

The red deer is rare in Sweden, although its numbers have increased in southern and central parts of the country. The bag has grown from 30 to 531 in the last 45 years. The red deer is a mixed feeder (Ahlén 1965a, 1975; Lavsund 1975), with food habits somewhat between elk and roe deer. It feeds on field crops, herbs, dwarf shrubs and grass but can subsist on a twig and bark diet in winters with deep snow. The red deer can adapt to a variety of forest types. In spruce monocultures, it is sometimes responsible for severe bark-stripping, leading to fears that dense populations could cause expensive damage (Ahlén 1965b).

5.2 Wild boar
After early extinction in Scandinavia, free-living wild boar herds, which originally escaped from game parks, have been reported in the 1970s in parts of central and southern Sweden. The current population estimate is under 500 individuals, but it is likely to increase quickly. There is some debate about whether free-living wild boar should be permitted in Sweden, because there is a risk of severe damage to agriculture. However, as an investigation (Kristiansson 1985) has shown that crop damage is not widespread, it is likely that the wild boar has come to stay. Because wild boar spend much of their life in the forest, they may well be affected by changes in woodland management. However, modern forestry will probably not have any major impact on

their population density, except perhaps where dense stands make them difficult to shoot.

5.3 Mountain hare (*Lepus timidus*)

The mountain hare is a very popular game animal in Scandinavia. It is a typical browser, feeding on twigs when the field layer is covered with snow. It prefers and perhaps needs a variety of food species (Sperber 1974; Lindlöf *et al.* 1974; Pehrsson 1980; Bryant *et al.* 1983; Jokinen 1983). Its living conditions are affected by silvicultural measures in much the same way as many of the cervids. The earliest successional stages in modern forestry are very favourable, producing excellent grazing for the hare in summer, and sprouting shoots of deciduous species are valuable during winter (Marcström 1978; Angelstam *et al.* 1982). As the young conifers grow and suppress the deciduous bushes and shrub layer, there is less food for hares which, unlike elk, do not feed on conifers in winter. Data on mountain hares are rather sparse for the selective period of Swedish forestry, but the animals may have been numerous at this time. A big increase in hare numbers recently may be associated with a reduction in numbers of foxes (*Vulpes vulpes*) due to sarcoptic mange (Lindström & Mörner 1984).

Aspen and other deciduous trees have often been felled to help hares in winter. The value of this management has not been studied scientifically, but, as hares in some areas can bark the whole aspen and consume all the thinner twigs, there is probably no winter 'food surplus' for these animals.

5.4 Small mammals

Small rodents, particularly species of the vole genera (*Microtus* and *Clethrionomys*), are a very important part of the forest ecosystem. They have a characteristic 3–4 year population cycle in central and northern Fennoscandia (Siivonen 1948; Hagen 1952; Lack 1954; Angelstam 1983), and can be a major problem, especially in peak years, by gnawing the bark from seedlings and young trees (see Larsson 1973). Vole damage, in particular, has increased in recent decades. Grass-rich clearcut glades and, above all, abandoned agricultural land are extremely favourable habitats for these small marauders, which can increase in numbers very rapidly. The problem is most marked on good soil, where seedlings risk being smothered by grass in summer and being consumed by innumerable small rodents in winter. It is likely that vole numbers have increased because of modern forestry practices.

The balance within modern forests is further tipped in favour of the voles because there is less opportunity for owls to breed as old trees with nest holes are gradually eliminated in many areas. Legal protection has not affected owl numbers to any extent. The situation is reminiscent of the protection afforded to some insects of the virgin forest, whereby the individual is protected but its habitat may be converted without opposition to a few cubic metres of firewood.

However, predators probably cannot prevent small mammal populations increasing or cause rapid population declines in central and northern Scandinavia (Lack 1954; Chitty 1960; Myllymäki 1970; and others), although predation may be a primary cause of non-cyclicity of small rodents in other regions (Pearson 1966; Pitelka 1973; Erlinge *et al.* 1983).

5.5 Tetraonids

Capercaillie, black grouse and hazel grouse (*Tetrastes bonasia*) are present in most of our coniferous forests. Willow grouse (*Lagopus lagopus*) are normally restricted to the uplands and some other areas, as well as a few northerly islands. They all tend to fluctuate in numbers between years. In parts of Norway and Sweden, a 3–4 year cycle has been shown to synchronize with the small mammal cycle (see Hagen 1952; Lack 1954; Myrberget 1974; Angelstam 1983). In Finland, on the other hand, there have been 6–7 years between the 3 latest population peaks (Rajala 1978; Lindén & Rajala 1981), and in northernmost Sweden the changes in tetraonid numbers have been rather irregular.

Besides these more or less regular short-term fluctuations, more prolonged population changes have been recorded at least for capercaillie, black grouse and hazel grouse. For example, the generally dense Swedish populations of the 1920s, early 1930s and mid-1940s tended to decline through the 1950s and parts of the 1960s, when the populations of these species reached their minima for this century. More recently, there has been a considerable recovery in tetraonid populations in central and northern Sweden, but numbers are still remarkably low further south. Long-term population trends among tetraonids have been more or less similar throughout Fennoscandia, although the Finnish tetraonid population is at present extremely sparse in large parts of the country.

There is a lot of information on Fennoscandian tetraonid habitats (see Seiskari 1962; Marcström 1978; Hjort 1982; Angelstam 1983; Wegge 1986), with many references on habitat use by capercaillie and black grouse in a report from a comprehensive study in Norway edited by Myrberget (1984). Much evidence indicates that capercaillie have suffered from forest exploitation, at least in some regions. In Fennoscandia, this species is to a large extent restricted to mature forests, and its habitat has been greatly reduced by the extensive felling of older forest. Capercaillie usually avoid cleared areas and young stands, but are found in somewhat older plantations, as well as in middle-aged forests, especially where there is reasonable plant species diversity.

The best capercaillie areas in Sweden nowadays are senescent and variable-aged coniferous forests, which may often contain some deciduous trees, preferably aspen. In such habitats, there are still many bogs and other wet areas, and dwarf shrubs (especially bilberry) are abundant. These areas tend to be residual forest from the selective system, with low tree density and volume, and are now rather rare. Mature, dwarf shrub or herb-rich spruce forest with a certain complexity also makes good capercaillie habitat. All such areas have little in common with uniform, dense and well-tended plantations.

In contrast to capercaillie, black grouse in Scandinavia prefer more open terrain and earlier successional stages. They therefore have a more advantageous relationship with modern forestry, at least in Sweden. In times gone by, it was often the forest edges which produced black grouse. The more open landscape developed by smallholdings, forest fires and grazing was beneficial. These areas have now mostly become dense scrub or plantations, and many heaths have been afforested in south Sweden. On the other hand, modern forestry has provided clearcut areas which suit black grouse. Clearings with a developing herb-rich vegetation, some berries and deciduous plants are a real benefit to them.

The considerable population fluctuations in tetraonid numbers are most likely to be caused by a number of factors. The trend for black grouse bags to increase more than those of capercaillie (Angelstam 1983; Figure 2) probably reflects the impact of modern forestry, whereas the comparatively large bag of both species after 1980 is at least to some extent an effect of the low fox numbers in large parts of central and northern Sweden.

Hazel grouse need considerably less extensive habitat than capercaillie. Selective cutting created excellent hazel grouse habitat, in old and uneven-aged conifer stands with spruce thickets and groves of aspen, willow or other deciduous trees, and the younger or middle-aged pine or mixed forests can also be favourable habitats if they are dense and untended. Hazel grouse seem to avoid clearcuttings as well as young stands of the type preferred by black grouse, and seldom use thinned stands and older monocultures.

Willow grouse, which occur mainly in the high moun-

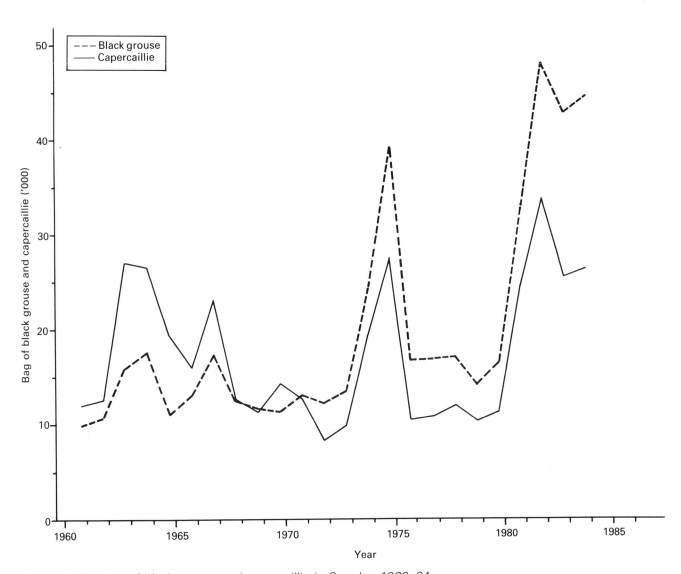

Figure 2. The bag of black grouse and capercaillie in Sweden 1960–84

154

tains, have increased their range in some upland regions. They have moved into the large clearcuttings, and are now shot in areas where they were not present earlier.

5.6 The 4 large carnivores

The brown bear (*Ursus arctos*), the wolf, the lynx (*Felis lynx*) and the wolverine (*Gulo gulo*) are the 4 large carnivores in Sweden. They decreased very much in numbers during the 19th century, except for the wolverine which has increased during the present century. Hunting, rather than land use, is the main factor determining the present population density of these carnivores.

5.7 The red fox

The red fox is the most important predator on small game in Fennoscandia, and seems to have a significant effect on hare and grouse numbers in some regions (Jenson 1970; Lindlöf 1978; Marcström 1986).

The population density of the red fox is generally considered to have increased after the 1920s and 1930s, though no accurate figures are available. Heavy hunting pressure in some areas probably produced fairly sparse fox populations in earlier days. With high prices for furs, foxes were taken with all possible methods, including poison. They have been hunted less intensively in recent decades. As fox density has been found to be limited by food supply in the north of Scandinavia (Englund 1965, 1970; Lindström 1982), the increasing volume of garbage and mortality of prey animals due to road traffic have probably benefited fox populations, as may the dense small mammal populations on abandoned farmland and grass-covered clearcuttings.

5.8 Pine marten (*Martes martes*)

There have been some studies on home range and activity of the pine marten in Fennoscandia (Pulliainen & Heikkinen 1980; Pulliainen 1981), but the breeding behaviour and population ecology of this species are relatively unknown. Martens were hunted intensively in the past, and there were fears that the species would not adapt well to modern forestry. However, their numbers have increased in many parts of Sweden since the 1930s and 1940s. Perhaps the factors causing the fox population to increase are also important for the marten.

6 The future

Because forestry is such an important sector of the Swedish economy, the woodlands will most likely be used to their capacity for future long-term timber production. Continued research and technical development will lead to even more efficiency and to increased rationalization. It has been said that Swedish large-scale forestry, step-by-step, will approach a level of mechanization that could be characterized by 'no foot on the ground, no hand on the tree'. It is to be hoped that the future increases in demand and competition for timber will not result in extensive use of marginal areas for timber production. Many of these habitats are better suited to produce wildlife and recreation.

While some browsing game animals have been favoured by modern forestry and have consequently increased in number, animals which are adapted to virgin forest or mixed stands with considerable diversity have suffered. Because the foresters have desired to obtain a high degree of uniformity, they have sometimes applied the same treatment to unplantable areas as to areas to be replanted.

The increased value of hunting should make production of wildlife more profitable. By restricting the size of clearcuttings, and mixing forest blocks producing food for game with stands providing cover, it is possible to increase wildlife production considerably within the scope of economically sound forestry. Improved management of rocky and scrub-covered areas, marshes, lake shores, springs, streambanks, powerline clearings, public refuges, and other marginal regions could further maximize the carrying capacity for wildlife. However, better understanding of the habitat requirements of tetraonids and of some other game species is necessary for management recommendations. In order to standardize description of these habitats, we have developed a special field form (Figure 3) for describing the woodland environment (Marcström *et al.* 1983), and we have started investigations in different parts of the country.

How to utilize abandoned fields, meadows and pastures has been a question of considerable importance in forestry and agriculture during the past 2 decades. These areas are often well suited to produce game, but, instead, they have been planted with trees on a large scale, and monocultures of spruce have taken over. Further development in this direction will result in unfavourable conditions for most game species. In recent years, environmental conservation and preservation of the rural landscape have received increasing attention. A careful assessment of the potential of various areas and the establishment of treatment priorities are necessary. As modern technology makes it possible to control the forest environment, it is hoped that future silviculture and other forms of land use will produce a complex ecosystem where timber, wildlife and recreation are effectively produced side by side.

7 Summary

Methods of managing and harvesting forests in Sweden have changed with time. Clearcuttings were common during the latter 19th and early 20th centuries. In the following period (1920–45), selective cutting was dominant. The failure of this system resulted in the large-scale forestry which has been predominant during the last decades.

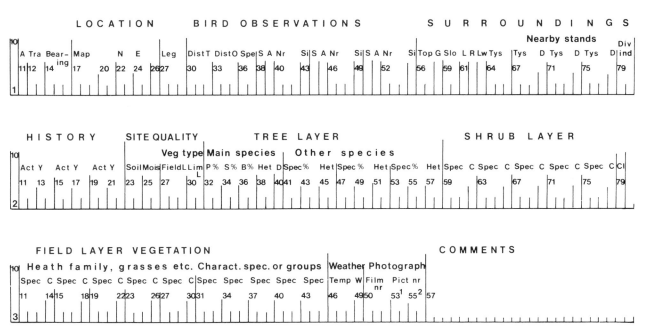

Figure 3. Field form for description of woodland grouse habitat (source: Marcström et al. 1983)

The changes in forest habitat have affected wildlife populations. Some species have been favoured and others prejudiced in a complex pattern of relationships. Capercaillie and, to some extent, hazel grouse managed well during the selective period, but they have suffered considerably where modern forestry has been practised most intensively. On the other hand, the number of black grouse has increased in regions with extensive areas of clearcuttings and young stands. The moose, primarily a browser and twig consumer, has also gained from the large amount of excellent food produced after clearcutting. For other wildlife species, the effects have been both positive and negative. The future carrying capacity for most forest-living animals will be greatly affected by the way in which various silvicultural measures are applied. Middle-aged and mature conifer monocultures cannot support much game, especially not in northern regions with long periods of snow. As forest and wildlife are among the few renewable natural resources, their management should be planned with a long-term ecological perspective. Instead of pure monocultures, a diverse forest ecosystem is necessary for the sustained production of valuabie timber, wildlife and recreation.

8 Acknowledgements

I am grateful to Matti Helminen and Timo Tanninen, Office for National Parks, National Board of Forestry, Helsinki, Finland, and to Olav Hjeljord, Institute of Nature Conservation, Agricultural University of Norway, Oslo, for information about forestry in Finland and Norway, and to Gunnar Olofsson, National Board of Forestry, Östersund, Hans Liedholm and Anders Håkansson, National Board of Forestry, Jönköping, and Olle Zachrisson, Department of Forest Site Research, Swedish University of Agricultural Sciences, Umeå, for valuable information about forestry in sub-alpine woodland. Robert Kenward, ITE, Furzebrook, helped with the English, and Ingrid Lukell, Department of Zoophysiology, Uppsala University, drew the figures.

Information on forest statistics was obtained from the following sources.

Kalhyggen. Stockholm: Jordbruksdepartementet Ds Jo 1974:2. 1974. 250 pp.

Naturmiljön i siffror. Miljöstatistisk årsbok 1983–84. Stockholm: Sveriges officiella statistik. Statistiska centralbyrån. 1984. 199 pp.

Statistical yearbook of forestry 1985. (Official statistics of Sweden.) Jönköping: National Board of Forestry. 1985. 248 pp.

Swedish forest – facts about Swedish forestry and wood industries. Jönköping: National Board of Forestry. 1985. 109 pp.

Swedish trade policy. (Fact sheets on Sweden.) Stockholm: The Swedish Institute. 1983. 2 pp.

Urskogar – Inventering av urskogsartade områden i Sverige: 5. Fjällregionen. (SNV PM 1511.) Jönköping: Skogsstyrelsen. 1984. 209 pp.

Yearbook of forest statistics 1984. (Official statistics of Finland.) Helsinki: The Finnish Forest Research Institute. 1985. 232 pp.

9 References

Ahlén, I. 1965a. Studies on the red deer, *Cervus elaphus* L., in Scandinavia. I. History of distribution. *Viltrevy*, **3**, 1–88.

Ahlén, I. 1965b. Studies on the red deer, *Cervus elaphus* L., in Scandinavia. III. Ecological investigations. *Viltrevy*, **3**, 177–376.

Ahlén, I. 1966. Landskapets utnyttjande och faunan. *Sver. Nat. Årsb.*, **57**, 73–99.

Ahlén, I. 1975. Winter habitats of moose and deer in relation to land use in Scandinavia. *Viltrevy*, **9**, 45–192.

Ahlén, I., Boström, U., Ehnström, B. & Pettersson, B. 1979. *Faunavård i skogsbruket.* Jönköping: Skogsstyrelsen.

Angelstam, P. 1983. *Population dynamics of tetraonids, especially the black grouse* (Tetrao tetrix L.) *in boreal forests.* PhD thesis, University of Uppsala.

Angelstam, P., Lindström, E. & Widén, P. 1982. Cyclic shifting of predation and other inter-relationships in a south taiga small game community. *Proc. int. Congr. game Biol., 14th,* 53–60.

Bleckert, S., Carlsson, K., Carlsson, L., Haglund, T., Norén, M. & Pettersson, R. 1984. *Skyddsvärda fågelbiotoper i södra Sveriges skogar.* Jönköping: Skogsstyrelsen.

Borg, K. 1970. On mortality and reproduction of roe deer in Sweden during the period 1948–1969. *Viltrevy*, **7**, 121–149.

Brüggemann, J., Giesek, D. & Karst, K. 1963. Untersuchungen am Panseninhalt von Reh- und Rotwild. *Proc. int. Congr. Game Biol., 6th,* 139–144.

Bryant, J.P., Chapin, F.S. & Klein, D.R. 1983. Carbon/nutrient balance of boreal plants in relation to herbivory. *Oikos*, **40**, 357–368.

Cederlund, G. & Nyström, A. 1981. Seasonal differences between moose and roe deer in ability to digest browse. *Holarct. Ecol.*, **4**, 59–65.

Cederlund, G., Ljungkvist, H., Markgren, G. & Stålfelt, F. 1980. Foods of moose and roe deer at Grimsö in central Sweden. *Viltrevy*, **11**, 169–247.

Chitty, D. 1960. Population processes in the vole and their relevance to the general theory. *Can. J. Zool.*, **38**, 99–113.

Drozdz, A., Weiner, J., Gebczynska, Z. & Krasinska, M. 1975. Some bioenergetic parameters of wild ruminants. *Pol. ecol. Stud.*, **1**, 85–101.

Englund, J. 1965. Studies of food ecology of the red fox (*Vulpes vulpes*) in Sweden. *Viltrevy*, **3**, 377–485.

Englund, J. 1970. Some aspects of reproduction and mortality rate in Swedish foxes (*Vulpes vulpes*) 1961–1963 and 1966–1969. *Viltrevy*, **8**, 1–82.

Erlinge, S. et al. 1983. Predation as a regulating factor on small rodent populations in southern Sweden. *Oikos*, **40**, 36–52.

Formozov, A.N. 1946. Snow cover as an integral factor of the environment and its importance in the ecology of mammals and birds. Transl. from: *Material for fauna and flora of the USSR. New series: Zoology,* **5**, 1–152. (Occasional paper no. 1.) Edmonton: Boreal Institute, University of Alberta.

Hagen, Y. 1952. *Rovfuglene og viltpleien.* Oslo: Gyldendal Norsk Forlag.

Hagen, Y. 1958. Litt om undersøkelser over vinternaering hos rådyr og elg. *Jeger Fisker*, **10**, 1–12.

Hemberg, 1914. Vargen. In: *Vårt villebråd 1,* edited by G. Kolthoff. Stockholm: Centraltryckeriet.

Hjort, I. 1982. Attributes of capercaillie display grounds and the influence of forestry – a progress report. In: *Proc. Woodland Grouse Symp., 1981,* edited by T.W.I. Lovel, 26–35. Lower Basildon: World Pheasant Association.

Huse, S. 1965. Skogskjøtselens betydning for viltets livsvilkår. *Norsk Skogbr.*, **11**, 197–199.

Huseby, K. 1976. *Rådyrets ernaering. Hovedoppgave ved Norges Landbrukshøgskole.* (Unpublished.)

Jensen, B. 1970. Effect of a fox control programme on the bag of some other game species. *Proc. int. Congr. Game Biol., 9th,* 480.

Jokinen, M. 1983. The role of plant chemistry in the food choice of hares – a review. *Suom. Riista*, **30**, 51–59.

Juhlin Dannfelt, M. 1952. Svensk skogsvård under ett halvsekel. *Svenska Skogsv. För. Tidskr.*, **50**, 118–136.

Kristiansson, H. 1985. *Vildsvinets biologi och skadegörelse.* (Institute of Zoology report.) University of Lund.

Lack, D. 1954. *The natural regulation of animal numbers.* Oxford: Clarendon.

Larsson, T-B. 1973. *Smågnagarskador på skogskulturer i Sverige 1900–1970.* (Abstract in English: *Small rodent damage in Swedish forestry during the period 1900–1970.*) (Research notes no. 18.) Institute of Forest Zoology, Royal College of Forestry.

Lavsund, S. 1975. *Kronhjortens* Cervus elaphus *utbredning i Sverige 1900–1973.* (Abstract in English: *The distribution of red deer,* Cervus elaphus *L., in Sweden 1900–1973.*) (Research notes no. 18.) Institute of Forest Zoology, Royal College of Forestry.

Lindén, H. & Rajala, P. 1981. Fluctuations and long-term trends in the relative densities of tetraonid populations in Finland, 1964–1977. *Finn. Game Res.*, **39**, 13–34.

Lindlöf, B. 1978. Det är räven som tar de flesta vuxna skogshararna. *Jaktmarker Fiskevatten*, **65**, 274–276.

Lindlöf, B., Lindström, E. & Pehrson, A. 1974. On activity, habitat selection and diet of the mountain hare (*Lepus timidus* L.) in winter. *Viltrevy*, **9**, 27–43.

Lindström, E. 1982. *Population ecology of the red fox* (Vulpes vulpes) *in relation to food supply.* PhD thesis, University of Stockholm.

Lindström, E. & Mörner, T. 1984. The spreading of sarcoptic mange among Swedish red foxes (*Vulpes vulpes* L.) in relation to fox population dynamics. *Proc. Symp. Ecopathology of Wild Canids, Nancy, France.* In press.

Marcström, V. 1978. Silviculture and higher fauna in Sweden. *Proc. int. Congr. Game Biol., 13th,* 401–413.

Marcström, V. 1986. Predation on two islands in Sweden. In: *Proc. Woodland Grouse Symp., 1984.* Lower Basildon: World Pheasant Association. In press.

Marcström, V., Brittas, R., Engren, E. & Winqvist, T. 1983. *Field form for description of woodland grouse habitat.* Uppsala: Swedish University of Agricultural Sciences.

Markgren, G. 1966. Om rådjuren i Nordsverige och deras vinterekologi. *Zool. Revy*, **28**, 97–107.

Markgren, G. 1969. Reproduction of moose in Sweden. *Viltrevy*, **6**, 127–299.

Myllymäki, A. 1970. Population ecology and its application to the control of the field vole, *Microtus agrestis* L. *Eppo Publ. Ser. A,* **58**, 27–48.

Myrberget, S. 1974. Variations in the production of willow grouse (*Lagopus lagopus*) in Norway 1963–1972. *Ornis Scand.*, **5**, 163–172.

Myrberget, S. 1984. Hvorfor varierer norske rype-bestander noenlunde regelmessig? In: *Rypeforskning. Statusrapport 1983,* edited by J.B. Steen, 143–149.

Nordström, L. 1959. Skogsskötselteorier och skogslagstiftning. In: *Sveriges skogar under 100 år,* 241–262. Stockholm: Kungl. Domänstyrelsen.

Pearson, O.P. 1966. The prey of carnivores during one cycle of mouse abundance. *J. Anim. Ecol.*, **35**, 217–233.

Pehrsson, Å. 1980. *Intake and utilization of winter food in the mountain hare* (Lepus timidus) *– a laboratory investigation.* PhD thesis, University of Stockholm.

Pitelka, F.A. 1973. Cyclic pattern in lemming populations near Barrow, Alaska. In: *Alaskan arctic tundra,* edited by M.E. Britton. (Paper no. 25.) Calgary: Arctic Institute of North America.

Pulliainen, E. 1981. Winter habitat selection, home range, and movements of the pine marten (*Martes martes*) in a Finnish Lapland forest. In: *Proc. Conf. Worldwide Furbearers,* edited by J.A. Chapman & D. Pursley, 1068–1087. Falls Chard: R.R. Donelly & Sons Co.

Pulliainen, E. & Heikkinen, H. 1980. Näädän talvisesta käyttäyty-misestä Metsä-Lapin itäosassa. (Summary in English: Behaviour of the pine marten (*Martes martes*) in E. Finnish Forest Lapland in winter. *Suom. Riista*, **28,** 30–36.

Raiby, M. 1970. Vinterdøslighet hos rådyr i forhold till klima. *Fauna*, **23,** 284–290.

Rajala, P. 1978. Status of tetraonid populations in Finland. In: *Proc. Woodland Grouse Symp., 1978*, edited by T.W.I. Lovel, 32–34. Lower Basildon: World Pheasant Association.

Sandegren, F., Bergström, R., Cederlund, G. & Dansie, E. 1982. Spring migration of female moose in central Sweden. *Alces*, **18,** 210–234.

Sandegren, F., Bergström, R. & Sweanor, P.Y. 1986. Seasonal moose migration related to snow in Sweden. *Alces*, **21.** In press.

Seiskari, P. 1962. *On the winter ecology of the capercaillie,* Tetrao urogallus, *and black grouse,* Lyrurus tetrix, *in Finland.* (Papers on game research no. 22.) Helsinki: Finnish Game Foundation.

Siivonen, L. 1948. *Structure of short-cyclic fluctuations in numbers of mammals and birds in the northern hemisphere.* (Papers on game research no. 1.) Helsinki: Finnish Game Foundation.

Sperber, I. 1974. Food utilization of *Lepus timidus* in the winter. *Proc. int. Congr. Game Biol., 11th,* 175–177.

Strandgaard, H. 1972. The roe deer (*Capreolus capreolus*) popu-lation at Kalø and the factors regulating its size. *Dan. Rev. Game Biol.,* **7,** (1).

Tenow, O. 1974. *Det nordiska skogslandskapets och skogsbrukets utveckling fram till 1900-talet – en kort översikt.* (Internal report no. 2.) Barrskogslandskapets ekologi.

Wegge, P. 1986. Spacing pattern and habitat use of capercaillie hens in spring. In: *Proc. Woodland Grouse Symp., 1984.* Lower Basildon: World Pheasant Association. In press.

Westman, H. 1958. Älgens skadegörelse på ungskogen. *K. Skogs-högsk. Skr.,* **28**.

Managing forests for wildlife in Germany

H NIEMEYER

Niedersächsische Forstliche Versuchsanstalt, 34 Göttingen, Federal Republic of West Germany

1 Introduction

This paper considers the conservation of a wide range of wildlife living in German forests, and also the management of those species harmful to forestry. The need to manage the total range of wildlife as part of modern forest protection plans is widely accepted by German foresters, especially in the state forests, and many ideas are encapsulated in a practical guide entitled *Biotop-Pflege im Walde* (Arbeitskreis Forstliche Landespflege 1984).

2 Historical development of woodlands, forestry and wildlife

A long period of deforestation in natural woodlands in Germany started about 1000 years ago in order to make agriculture possible. Before this time, three-quarters of Germany was covered with woods consisting of about 90% broadleaved trees, especially oak (*Quercus* spp.), beech (*Fagus sylvatica*) and wild fruit trees which provided fodder for pigs and browse for cattle. Clearing for agriculture mostly ended, but the devastation of the remaining woods continued, and the woodland area was reduced to about 30% of the country (nearly the same as today) at the close of the 13th century. Forest pasturage and a coppicing for fuelwood prevented natural regeneration and the natural spread of conifers. The devastation of the natural forests accelerated in the 18th century through industrialization and the increase of human population density. As a result, especially in the northern part of Germany, no fully stocked forest stand could be found in the second half of the 18th century.

In northern Germany, heather (*Calluna vulgaris*) covered most of the land surface, and for centuries the farmers used the underlying peat for bedding for their cattle. This practice led to denuded soils which were degraded to podzols. In addition, the prevailing wind from the North Sea caused the sand to drift and form dunes. Early in the 19th century, when the destruction of forests and soils was at its height, a forester visiting some plantations reported that for several days he travelled through sand storms, passed abandoned farms, and the only creature he met was a dead fox which 'probably died of total resignation'.

Afforestation by both planting and sowing started on a large scale in some areas in the middle of the 18th century. The trees used were mostly conifers, primarily Norway spruce (*Picea abies*). A century later, Scots pine (*Pinus sylvestris*) was used as a vigorous pioneer species in the dry and sandy northern plains. The first Chair for forest science was established in 1787 in Freiburg, and methods of forest inventory, regulation and valuation were developed during the 18th and 19th centuries in many German countries. Unfortunately, knowledge of the biological and ecological implications of forestry and trees did not evolve simultaneously; the necessity to reforest large areas within the shortest possible time led to the planting of forests which very often were not in accordance with our recent knowledge of the site requirements of species and provenances. Serious problems with several biotic and abiotic factors have resulted, causing severe damage.

In the case of wildlife, the consequences of the revolution in 1848 were at least as fatal for all game species as for some social classes of people. When the totalitarian government of the numerous sovereigns in German countries ended, everybody was allowed to hunt. Within a few years, roe (*Capreolus capreolus*) and, especially, red deer (*Cervus elaphus*) became nearly extinct. As a result, new hunting regulations became obligatory.

The main regulations were that hunting was permitted only in hunting grounds of sufficient size. Such a district or chase could be owned or leased. Nonetheless, it was not until 1935 that hunters were forced by law to manage the population density of their deer in accordance with an annual licence issued by the local hunting authority. Both this law and the Federal Law for Hunting, enacted first in 1952, obliged the hunters to keep the population density of all game species in accordance with the requirements of landscape, agriculture, forestry and nature protection; even the conservation of wildlife habitat in relation to the diversity of fauna and to the biological balance was demanded by law. As a result of these regulations, the game stocks recovered, for example in the Prussian state forests (and in the Federal Republic (Figure 1)).

The Hunting Law interacts with other laws, namely the Federal Forest Law (from 1975), the Federal Law on Nature Protection (from 1976), and the forest protection regulations of the Federal states which are also obligatory (eg the Forest Protection Regulations of Lower Saxony (Table 1)). Maintaining species diversity, as well as economic and ecological objectives, is an important element in these laws (Table 1). Forest Law particularly emphasizes economy, the Nature Protection Law emphasizes ecology, and the Hunting Law hunting; these different emphases give rise to political tension and interaction between different interests in the rural community, and engender a great deal of public discussion.

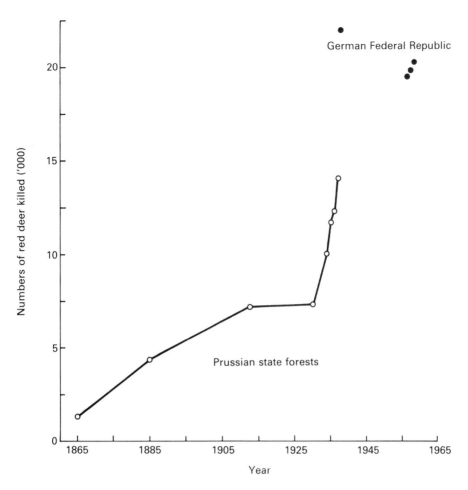

Figure 1. Numbers of red deer killed in Germany 1865–1955 (source: Müller-Using 1960)

Table 1. Objects of environmental laws regarding forestry and wildlife in West Germany

Bundeswaldgesetz (Federal Forest Law) 1975	Bundesnaturschutzgesetz (Federal Law of Nature Protection) 1976	Bundesjagdgesetz (Federal Law of Hunting) 1976	Nds Forstschutzvorschrift (Forest Protection Regulations of Lower Saxony) 1960
1. Conserve or augment forest, secure its regular management for the following reasons: – economical use – ecological meaning – capacity of ecosystem – climate – water economy – prevention of air pollution – soil fertility – landscape amenity – agricultural infrastructure – recreation of people 2. Promote forestry 3. Balance the interests of public good and forest owners	1. Protect, care for and develop nature and landscape so that: – capacity of ecosystem – capacity of natural resources – flora and fauna – diversity, peculiarity and amenity of nature and landscape (as the basis of human life and recreation) will be secured and sustained 2. These requirements are to be weighed against each other and against other needs of the public 3. Regular agriculture and forestry are highly important for the protection of landscape, and normally serve the aims of this law	1. 'Hunting right' is the right to hunt and to appropriate certain species of mammals and birds (game) 2. Hunting right includes the obligation to 'keep the game' 3. 'Game keeping' aims at the conservation of a diverse and healthy game stock and at the tending of its habitat 4. 'Game keeping' has to avoid injuries to agriculture, forestry and fishery	1. Prognoses of population dynamics of important pests are prescribed and are prerequisite for control actions 2. Pesticides for control of forest pests, including herbicides, will be used only to avoid really important economic or silvicultural injuries when these are strongly predicted 3. The pesticides used should have the lowest possible side-effects on the environment 4. Biological, physical or silvicultural control methods should be preferred to chemical ones

The lengthy gestation of the legislation may give a wrong impression of the development and realization of the basic ecological principles, but these principles have been discussed in theory and put into practice for more than 50 years (eg Schwerdtfeger 1942). Diversifying silviculture in relation to site requirements was recommended in the 18th century (Kremser & Otto 1973), but was not widely applied in Germany before the end of the Second World War.

3 Silviculture in relation to site conditions (The most important pre-condition for managing forest for wildlife)

Silviculture based on site conditions is believed to take into account all the objectives of the different laws shown in Table 1. Silviculture, in this context, provides the best synthesis of ecological and economic demands in sustaining the long-term stability and diversity of the woodland ecosystem. It aims to favour also wildlife, especially its diversity, and to minimize the risk of biotic diseases in the forest (Otto 1972, 1985; Kremser & Otto 1973).

documented experiences of many foresters over the past 200 years contribute much to our current knowledge. In Lower Saxony, a plan for silviculture covering all state forests has been devised on this basis (Kremser & Otto 1973). This plan is used consistently, and its adoption accelerated the reconstruction or conversion of forests destroyed by windthrow in 1972. This disaster destroyed about 100 000 ha of woodland and forced forest owners to reforest very rapidly. One of the most remarkable results was a major decline in the extent of Scots pine from 72 000 ha to 36 000 ha, and of spruce from 113 000 ha to 92 000 ha.

In the case of Scots pine, about 50% of its former area will remain stocked with this species, but 24% will change to Douglas fir (*Pseudotsuga menziesii*) and 19% to oak (Table 2).

4 Managing forests for wildlife

Silviculture in relation to site conditions also favours wildlife. In general, the greater the diversity of forest, the better the conditions for diverse animal commun-

Table 2.   Amounts (ha) of clearfelling and reafforestation between 1975 and 1995 in Lower Saxonian state forests (source: Otto 1985)

	Felled	Replanted							
		Oak	Beech	Other hardwoods	Spruce	Douglas	Pine	Larch	Other softwoods
Oak	1400	1400	•	•	•	•	•	•	•
Beech	1300	300	800	•	100	100	•	•	•
Other hardwoods	50	•	•	50	•	•	•	•	•
Spruce	6500	2600	200	•	1700	1000	1000	•	•
Douglas fir	850	150	•	•	100	600	•	•	•
Pine	29500	5600	400	•	1200	7100	14500	500	200
Larch	300	100	•	•	•	100	•	100	•
Other softwoods	1100	300	•	100	•	•	400	•	300
TOTALS	41000	10450	1400	150	3100	8900	15900	600	500

Ecological mapping of forest sites has been the practice in most Federal states since 1945. In Lower Saxony, for example, this mapping now covers the total area of state forests and started in private forests some years ago. The basis is a grid of soil pits 100–400 m apart. The properties of soil, topography, and vegetation result in an 'ecological key-number' consisting of 4 figures. The first figure represents the index for soil humidity and topography (both factors with more than 40 combinations); the second figure represents the key for the nutrient potential of the soil; and the third and fourth figures represent the indices for the geological substratum and for soil class and structure, with 77 combinations. In addition, the influence of climate is expressed in terms of meteorologically and geographically defined 'growth areas', to which the 'ecological key-numbers' are assigned.

Given knowledge of all ecological parameters for a given site, it is no longer a problem to find correlations between site conditions and growth of tree species or provenances by experiment or survey. In addition, the

ities. But what is being done or should be done in practical forest management?

4.1 Size of stand

Stand units should be as small as possible in relation to the results of the mapping and diversity of sites. The aim should be to increase the diversity of tree species and ages in each area.

4.2 Age and space structure of stands

In pure stands of Scots pine, Dierschke (1973) found that the number of breeding bird species was a function of the space structure provided by the trees. In Scots pine forests 1–3 years old, 5 bird species were found to be breeding; in stands 3–35 years old, 6–8 species; in stands 25–45 years old, only 4; while there were 8–9 bird species in pine stands 40–100 years old. All bird species showed specific preferences for particular age classes.

From this evidence it can be seen that the higher the range of tree ages in a given area, the higher the number of bird species. This statement is true also for invertebrates; in a 60-year-old pine stand, Engel (1941) found 247 species of arthropods in the tree crowns, but 281 species in a comparable stand 112 years old. Similarly, Roth *et al.* (1983) recorded 64 species (17 families) of beetles in a 39-year-old stand of spruce and 86 beetle species (23 families) in an 85-year-old stand.

4.3 Number of tree species

Creating mixed stands of more than one tree species is a highly effective method of increasing the diversity of the entire forest ecosystem, especially if the mixed tree species are of several ages. Of course, the species used for reafforestation must suit the local conditions shown by the site mapping. In most sites, several tree species will show sufficient growth to be economic. Very important, however, are the growth relations of the species to be combined and their light requirements, including their tolerance of shade. The number of animal species is increased by mixing broadleaved species with conifers. For example, in stands of Scots pine alone, 7 bird species were recorded in 60–100% of sample sites, compared with 14 bird species in mixed stands of Scots pine and broadleaves (Dierschke 1973). Table 3 shows higher

biotope suits them better than dense stands or even a self-sown forest without clearings. These climatic conditions favour rapid mobilization of the nitrogen reserve of the soil for plants and a rich growth of various species of flowering herbs, as an essential basis for a high diversity of invertebrates (especially Hymenoptera), and for mammals and birds (especially where older stands are adjacent). The high importance of flowering plants for parasitic Hymenoptera (Chalcididae, Proctotrupidae, Ichneumonidae, etc) and for parasitic Diptera (Tachinidae) is discussed below.

An important pre-condition for a high diversity of flowering plants is the prohibition of weeding by mowing or by using herbicides which kill herbs or prevent their flowering. Often the control of weeds such as raspberries (*Rubus idaeus*) or grasses, except some species of small-reed (*Calamagrostis*), is unnecessary. Their competitive power is mostly overestimated, and their value for wildlife, including invertebrates, and for nutrient circulation is often underestimated (Huss 1982). If the anticipated competition from weeds in a plantation is too high, it is usually possible to reduce competition by applying low dosages of selective herbicides. Low doses do not usually

Table 3. Fauna recorded in the crowns of trees in different stands of Scots pine (source: Altenkirch 1982; after Engel 1941, 1942)

| | | Numbers of pine looper moth (*Bupalus piniarius*) | | | |
| | Number of arthropod species | Young larvae per crown 1936 | Imagines m^{-2} 1937 | Old larvae per crown 1937 | Pupae m^{-2} 1938 |
Stand					
Pine, 60 years old	247	577.0	23	106.5	2.1
Pine, 112 years old + pine (self-sown) 20–40 years old	281	212.0	2.6	104.5	0.7
Pine, 112 years old + oak 45 years old	309	161.5	0.8	49.0	0.3

total numbers of arthropods in both a mixed stand of pine and oak and in a well-structured pine stand than in a pure, even-aged Scots pine stand.

4.4 Method of regeneration

The way in which regeneration following clearfelling is carried out, whether by planting on small or on large areas or by natural seeding, with or without clearings, probably has the greatest influence on the total number of animal species. In Schleswig-Holstein, the northernmost state of the Federal Republic, Heydemann and Müller-Karch (1980) found that small open glades of at most a few hectares had by far the greatest number of animal species of all terrestrial ecosystems. The abundance was due to the shelter provided, which induced relatively high temperatures and humidity. Protection from wind ensured a low risk of small flying arthropods being blown away and of flowers being destroyed. Clearings were particularly important for the Aculeata, represented in Schleswig-Holstein by about 500 of species, of which 40% are found in glades or clearings. Most species of Aculeata need high temperatures (above 14°C), so that this

prevent herbs from flowering but can nevertheless prevent the risk of an economically meaningful reduction in the growth or quality of the forest trees (Reinecke 1985). Plates 1, 2 and 3 show examples of the conversion of a monotonous cover of grasses or of cleavers (*Galium aparine*) into vegetation of much higher diversity by the correct use of herbicides.

Where clearings in naturally regenerating woodlands are small, ie less than about 200 m^2, artificial replanting seems to be unnecessary. Where larger gaps are replanted, if possible with another species, they may be cared for as outlined above. Choice of planting space should also take ecological implications into account. For both economic and ecological reasons, German forestry has for some years been tending towards wider spacing, epecially the planting distance between rows. This has been increased from 1 m or 1.5 m to 2.5 m, 3 m or even 4 m, according to the demands of different tree species. However, minimum densities are necessary for good-quality timber and to reduce risks from air pollution. Minimum densities ha^{-1} include the following.

Scots pine	8000–10000
Norway spruce and Douglas fir	2500– 3000
European larch (*L. decidua*)	2000– 3000
Japanese larch (*L. kaempferi*)	3000– 4000
Beech (mixed with spruce or European larch)	7000–10000
Pedunculate oak (*Quercus robur*), mixed with beech or small-leaved lime (*Tilia cordata*)	8000–11000
European oak (*Q. petraea*) including mixed beech	8000– 9000

4.5 Preparation of the ground before planting

Ground vegetation not only absorbs ions released by mineralization but also prevents losses of nutrients which may, without ground vegetation, amount to 500 kg nitrogen ha^{-1}. (The nutrients would later circulate through the trees (Ulrich 1981).) Organic matter, in the form of tree stumps or brash, has an important function as the breeding place of some arthropods. Heydemann and Müller-Karch (1980) found that 72% of the local surface-living species of Hymenoptera bred in old tree stumps.Therefore the removal of stumps to permit deep ploughing, eg for planting pines and oaks by machine in sandy soils or in podzols with hardpan, has some ecological disadvantages, although cost-effective. With deep ploughing, the growth of pine or oak plants is good, provided that the humus layer and the upper layers of soil retained on the stumps are not removed by stump pulling. If much of the upper soil humus is removed, large losses of young plants are to be expected as a result of drying; loss of humus also encourages an increase of the weevil *Brachyderes incanus,* which can destroy large parts of a plantation if not controlled by insecticide.

4.6 Cleaning and thinning

These 2 operations provide opportunities to increase the diversity of wildlife species. Secondary (ie naturally regenerating in this case) tree species and shrubs should be preserved, eg willows (*Salix* spp.), rowan (*Sorbus aucuparia*) and other *Sorbus* species, aspen (*Populus tremula*), hazel (*Corylus avellana*) and others which are important for insects and game. Unless these species become dominant in the stand, there should be no significant loss in economic productivity of the primary tree crop. For example, Erler (1983) found in a plantation of 6-year-old Douglas fir that naturally growing silver birch (*Betula pendula*), rowan, American black cherry (*Prunus serotina*), bird cherry (*Prunus padus*) and alder buckthorn (*Rhamnus frangula*) inhibited the growth of Douglas fir when the fir and one of these hardwoods were less than 1 m apart. However, when such trees were 1–2 m apart, survival and growth of the Douglas fir were favoured, no matter what height the hardwoods had reached. This interaction depends on the shade tolerance of the forest trees. Thinning within the economic (primary) tree species of a stand should be done early in the cycle. Sufficient trees should be removed to allow the remaining stand of mature trees to develop full crowns

and strong stems, so that they can withstand storms and heavy snowfalls. Early thinning of plantations is also best for vertebrate and invertebrate wildlife because it allows maximum light penetration into the stands during their darkest phases. To protect rare vertebrates which are sensitive to disturbance (eg wild cat (*Felis silvestris*), sparrowhawk (*Accipiter nisus*), stock dove (*Columba oenas*) or capercaillie (*Tetrao urogallus*)), all thinning and harvesting must be done in autumn or winter.

4.7 Particular habitats

Woods may include particular habitats such as extremely old or dead trees, forest edges, wetlands and open waters within the forests, ecosystems on limestone, and dunes and other dry sites within the forest area. Forest administrations in Germany are responsible for protecting or even augmenting all these special habitats. Leaflets on some of these subjects have been prepared to advise practical foresters.

4.7.1 Forest edges, if well structured, are important not only for protection against wind, sun and fire and for amenity, but also for wildlife and habitat conservation. The 'edge effect' is well known, especially the high diversity of forest edges compared to adjacent open areas or dense stands (Figure 2).

Forest edge of a stand consisting of shade-tolerant trees:

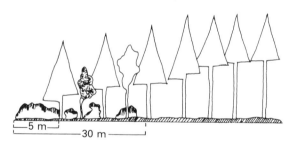

Forest edge of a stand consisting of light-demanding trees:

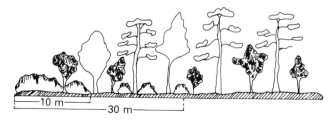

Figure 2. Basic structure of the outer edges of forests (source: Arbeitskreis Forstliche Landespflege 1984)

In principle, forest edges should be managed separately from the rest of the forest; they should, as far as possible, be stocked *permanently* with shrubs or trees which should regenerate naturally, independently of the felling cycle of the stand itself. The appropriate depth of the 'edge' is about 30 m on forest boundaries exposed to wind or sun, but on leeward or shady sides a depth of 15–20 m should be sufficient. All outside edges should contain 3 irregularly overlapping zones of (i) brush, (ii) secondary trees or shrubs which grow to a lower height than the third zone and which regenerate naturally, and (iii) primary trees (comprising the stand itself).

In planning the structure of the forest edge, it is important to distinguish whether the stand contains light-demanding or shade-tolerant tree species. When the stand is composed of light-demanding trees, the outer edge should consist of brush and (secondary) broadleaved trees to a depth of about 10 m. Behind that, there should be a sparse stocking of primary light-demanding trees, eg oak or Scots pine, which can overlap into the outer zone. When the stand is composed of shade-tolerant trees, the structure of the edge can be more simple. The outer edge should be a narrow zone of brush bounding a broader zone thinly stocked with mature, single broad-crowned primary trees, such as Norway spruce, silver fir (*Abies alba*) or Douglas fir, with some shade-tolerant broadleaved trees planted under them.

Inside the forest, a strip 5 m wide on both sides of paths should be kept free of trees. Along streams and in boggy places, a broad margin at least 10 m wide on both sides should be left for the natural development of vegetation. All these recommendations represent aims, more or less accepted in practical forestry, but realized in few areas so far.

4.7.2 Keeping old and dead trees is an effective and cheap way in which forestry management can increase the diversity of animals and plant species which depend on these micro-habitats. The animals include rare species such as stag-beetle (*Lucanus cervus*), oak cerambycid (*Cerambyx cerdo*), hornet (*Vespa crabro*), several woodpeckers including some which do not occur in Scotland (*Dendrocopos minor, D. medius, D. leucotos, Picoides tridactylus*), stock dove, Natterer's bat (*Myotis nattereri*), noctule (*Nyctalus noctula*), forest dormouse (*Dryomys nitedula*) and pine marten (*Martes martes*).

Foresters should check whether the following specific points are practical:

— allow a long rotation period between consecutive harvests;
— select some individual trees so that they can be retained in the next rotation;
— with some tree species, such as fir, beech, Scots

pine (perhaps Norway spruce), extend the felling period with a selective harvesting of the thickest stems;
— retain a few trees 100 ha^{-1} until they die and are destroyed by nature (in these trees, the black woodpecker (*Dryocopus martius*), for example, will peck out nest holes which will be used later by several other species of birds, as well as by mammals and insects);
— keep the root plates of windblown trees standing upright to provide breeding places for sand wasps (Sphecidae), some bird species such as wren (*Troglodytes troglodytes*), robin (*Erythacus rubecula*) and, near brooks, grey wagtail (*Motacilla cinerea*), and even kingfisher (*Alcedo atthis*);
— if thinning is done near open waters, cut the willow, birch, alder or poplar at a height of about 1 m from the ground to allow the willow tit (*Parus montanus*) to excavate nesting holes;
— do not remove brash and pulled stumps totally but heap them together to provide shelter and breeding or feeding places for some mammals, birds and invertebrates.

4.8 Managing forests in favour of particular species
There is one rare species, the capercaillie, for which specialized management (ie retention and wide spacing of old trees, with an undergrowth of bilberry (*Vaccinium myrtillus*) is necessary in refuges or places where this bird is to be reintroduced. These areas should be at least some hundred hectares in extent (Müller 1978, 1980; Aschenbrenner 1985).

4.9 Natural forest reserves ('Naturwaldreservate')
Until 1980 in the FRG, there were 326 semi-natural forest reserves, with a total area of 8318 ha (Krause & Wolf 1981). Most woodland plant associations recorded in Germany are represented in these reserves (Jahn 1982). The reserves are mostly small, with about 90% being less than 50 ha in extent. Lower Saxony is now planning to increase both the number and size of its reserves to some 3000 ha in total. The status of a 'natural forest reserve' given by the forest administration is by far the strongest means of protection. All forestry practices, including protection against pests and diseases, are strictly prohibited, and, in addition, potential influences of forestry in neighbouring areas are to be avoided where practicable.

The main aim in these reserves is the study of the dynamics of the semi-natural woodlands and their fauna and flora under a minimum of human influence. Though not really forest management, it can nevertheless be highly effective in protecting wildlife, especially when the number and area of the reserves can be significantly increased.

5 Managing forests for protection from wildlife
5.1 Insects
Large-scale and widespread deaths of trees from attacks by insects, rodents or fungi may be an

important part of the dynamics of natural forest ecosystems in the northern hemisphere, in addition to the effects of windblows or wild fires. All these events prevent the forests from remaining too long in the climax stage. They induce new cycles of succession in plant and animal life, keep the diversity high, and maintain evolution. This pattern is what we try to achieve by our silviculture, according to site conditions, and by all the other measures mentioned above. The aim is to keep diversity high, not only on a large timescale and in the big areas of natural forests, but, wherever possible, also within the limited scales of our European economic forests.

There are hints that the higher the diversity of the ecosystem, the lower the frequency and the rate of spread of insect infestations causing severe damage. For example, in the case of the fauna of the tree crowns of the different pine stands shown in Table 3, the number of arthropod species in the old stand mixed with oak was higher than in the younger, even-aged, pure pine stand (Altenkirch 1982; after Engel 1941, 1942). The reverse was the case with the population density of the pine looper moth (*Bupalus piniarius*). The cause is difficult to identify, but an important parasite of the pine looper moth, the wasp *Ichneumon nigritarius*, has 13 species of butterflies as secondary hosts. Seven species of these butterflies live on broadleaved trees, another 3 species on herbs, and 3 other species on pine or spruce (Thalenhorst 1939). The inference is that the moth is less likely to reach pest status in forests where it has many parasites than in places where its parasites are scarce. Another well-known example is the case of the pine shoot moth (*Rhyacionia buoliana*) and its hymenopterous parasite *Orgilus obscurator* (Braconidae) (Bogenschütz 1974; Altenkirch 1982). The female of this parasite can live for about 20 days when feeding on flowers (especially on wild carrot (*Daucus carota*)) but without flowers it can live only 4 days. Yet 4 days is too short a time to allow all a female's eggs to be oviposited, as confirmed in laboratory experiments and field investigations by Syme (1966) and Leius (1967) in Canada, and by Györfi (1951, 1962) and Hassan (1967) in Europe.

With regard to the pine beauty moth (*Panolis flammea*), striking observations suggest that heterogeneous pine forests, consisting of many small stands of different ages, were much less damaged than adjacent dense and even-aged forests (Escherich 1942), perhaps because the more homogeneous forests had fewer secondary hosts, fewer parasites, and fewer natural checks on the moth. However, under certain conditions, the opposite can also be true; in Lower Saxony, the last 2 outbreaks of the nun moth (*Lymantria monacha*) have had their centres in mixed stands of Scots pine, Norway spruce, larch and birch, and not in the pure pine stands. Obviously, the reason is the very specific ecological demands and behaviour of this particular species.

5.2 Game animals

Despite their potential harmfulness, these insect species and also some harmful game species are considered to be indispensable parts of the natural ecosystem. Even if we could exterminate them, we would not do so. However, for some years, great efforts have been made by specialized forest scientists and game biologists to advise practical foresters on habitat management for game, especially deer. The following 2 types of measures are proposed.

i. Lay out cultivated deer pastures with grasses, herbs and coppice providing long-term browsing facilities inside quiet and sheltered areas where the deer can feed according to their natural diurnal activity rhythm.
ii. Improve the conditions of life for ungulates in the forests by silviculture and forest management in order to achieve wildlife habitats in which game populations of low density can live in balance with each other and their habitat.

These measures need to be supported by successful regulation of the density and structure of the game populations through hunting. The basis of an improvement in the life conditions for game is the same as described above for the management of forests for all kinds of wildlife.

6 Summary

Due to agriculture and excessive exploitation, there have been no natural forests in Germany for more than 1000 years. Large-scale reafforestation with Scots pine, Norway spruce and some other species started in the 18th century. In these early stages of forestry, the site requirements of the different species and provenances were not known as well as they are now. However, silviculture practices in accordance with site conditions became common after the end of the Second World War. This is now the most important pre-condition both for managing forests to conserve wildlife and for protecting the forests against wildlife pests. Country-wide site mapping within forests has led to official guidelines for an ecologically based silviculture obligatory for all state forests.

Concrete suggestions are given which are substantiated by the results of investigations into the diversity of animal communities in forests managed for wildlife. The basic idea is to take advantage of site variation as a means of increasing the diversity of forest ecosystems. For example, the following practices are now encouraged: small stand units; mixed ages to provide a higher degree of space structure within a given area; mixed stands (eg conifers mixed with broadleaved trees); clearfelling on as small areas as possible to take advantage of the high diversity of ecosystems in small openings; wide spaces between planting rows; saving the vegetation cover and organic material when preparing the ground; weeding only if really necessary by using selective herbicides to reduce the growth of competing plants instead of killing them; preserving secondary trees and shrubs when cleaning or thinning. The overall aim is to provide a rich flowering vegetation with a rich fauna of dependent invertebrate and vertebrate species.

The management of particular habitats, such as forest edges or old and dead trees, is described briefly, as is the development of German 'natural forest reserves' to preserve and study the dynamics of undisturbed semi-natural forest plant associations and wildlife. Managing forests for protection from wildlife pests is based on the same site-dependent type of silviculture and on all the measures recommended to encourage the development of forest ecosystems of high diversity. It is believed that the higher the diversity, the lower the frequency and rate of spread of insect infestations which can cause severe damage. Recommendations concerning game species aim to improve conditions which create a balance between the animals and their habitat, and which allow the game to develop natural diurnal activity rhythms. It is essential that the density and the structure of game populations are controlled in relation to the requirements of nature protection, forestry and agriculture.

7 References

Altenkirch, W. 1982. Ökologische Vielfalt – ein Mittel natürlichen Waldschutzes? *Forst- u. Holzwirt,* **37,** 211–217.

Arbeitskreis Forstliche Landespflege. 1984. *Biotop-Pflege im Walde, ein Leitfaden für die forstliche Praxis.* Greven: Kilda.

Aschenbrenner, H. 1985. *Rauhfusshühner, Lebensweise, Zucht, Krankheiten, Ausbürgerung.* Hannover: M. & H. Schaper.

Bogenschütz, H. 1974. Fehlanzeige in Sachen biologischer Schädlingsbekämpfung? *Allg. Forstz.,* **29,** 1040.

Dierschke, F. 1973. Die Sommervogelbestände nordwestdeutscher Kiefernforsten. *Vogelwelt,* **94,** 201–225.

Engel, H. 1941. Beiträge zur Faunistik der Kiefernkronen in verschiedenen Bestandestypen. *Mitt. Forstw. Forstwiss.,* **12,** 334–361.

Engel, H. 1942. Über die Populationsbewegung des Kiefernspanners (*Bupalus piniarius*) in verschiedenen Bestandestypen. *Z. angew. Entomol.,* **29,** 116–163.

Erler, J. 1983. Einfluss von Weichhölzern in einem Douglasienjungwuchs. *Forst- u. Holzwirt,* **38,** 87–91.

Escherich, K. 1942. *Die Forstinsekten Mitteleuropas.* Band 5. Berlin.

Györfi, J. 1951. Die Schlupfwespen und der Unterwuchs des Waldes. *Z. angew. Entomol.,* **33,** 32–47.

Györfi, J. 1962. Der Einfluss der Waldpflanzen auf die Vermehrung der Schlupfwespen. *Anz. Schädlingsk.,* **35,** 20–22.

Hassan, E. 1967. Untersuchungen über die Bedeutung der Kraut- und Strauchschicht als Nahrungsquelle für Imagines entomophager Hymenopteren. *Z. angew. Entomol.,* **60,** 238–265.

Heydemann, B. & Müller-Karch, J. 1980. *Biologischer Atlas Schleswig-Holstein.* Neumünster: Karl Wachholtz.

Höregott, H. 1960. Untersuchungen über die qualitative und quantitative Zusammensetzung der Arthropodenfauna in den Kiefernkronen. *Beitr. Ent.,* **10,** 891–915.

Huss, J. 1982. Die Bekämpfung der Konkurrenzvegetation von Waldverjüngungen in der forstlichen Praxis. *Allg. Forstz.,* **37,** 398–400.

Jahn, G. 1982. Wald- und Gebüschgesellschaften in Norddeutschland, ihre Gefährdung sowie Möglichkeiten ihrer Förderung durch Waldbau. *Forst- u. Holzwirt,* **37,** 150–156.

Krause, A. & Wolf, G. 1981. Naturwaldreservate in der Bundesrepublik Deutschland, eine Zwischenbilanz. *Forst- u. Holzwirt,* **36,** 20–21.

Kremser, W. & Otto, H.-J. 1973. Grundlagen für die langfristige, regionale waldbauliche Planung in den niedersächsischen Landesforsten. *Aus dem Walde,* no. 20.

Leius, K. 1967. Influence of wild flowers on parasitism of tent caterpillar and codling moth. *Can. Ent.,* **99,** 444–446.

Müller, F. 1978. Rauhfusshühner als Biotop-Indikatoren. (Jagd + Hege 6.) St Gallen: Jagd+Hege-Verlags AG.

Müller, F. 1980. *Wildbiologische Informationen für den Jäger.* Band 3. Stuttgart: Jagd+Hege-Verlag F. Enke.

Müller-Using, D. 1960. *Grosstier und Kulturlandschaft.* Göttingen: Musterschmidt-Verlag.

Otto, H.-J. 1972. Die Ergebnisse der Standortkartierung im pleistozänen Flachland Niedersachsens, Grundlage waldbaulicher Leitvorstellungen. *Aus dem Walde,* no. 19.

Otto, H.-J. 1985. Sylviculture according to site conditions as a method of forest protection. *Z. angew. Entomol.,* **99,** 190–199.

Reinecke, H. 1985. *Begleitwuchsregulierung.* Privately published. (Plesseweg 12, D-3400 Göttingen.)

Roth, M., Funke, W., Günl, W. & Straub, S. 1983. Die Käfergesellschaften mitteleuropäischer Wälder. *Verh. Ges. Ökol.,* **10,** 35–50.

Schwerdtfeger, F. 1942, 1981. *Waldkrankheiten.* Hamburg: Paul Parey.

Syme, P. D. 1966. The effect of wild carrot on a common parasite of the European pine shoot moth. *Bi-mon. Res. Notes, Dept For. Can.,* **22,** 3–4.

Thalenhorst, W. 1939. Über das Auftreten von *Ichneumon nigritarius* als Parasit des Kiefernspanners und anderer Lepidopteren. *Mitt. Forstw. Forstwiss.,* **10,** 65–74.

Ulrich, B. 1981. Destabilisierung von Waldökosystemen durch Biomassenutzung. *Forstarchiv,* **52,** 199.

The management of native woods for wildlife

K J KIRBY

Nature Conservancy Council, Peterborough

1 Introduction

Most broadleaved, semi-natural or native woodland is in southern Britain (Evans 1984), and the recommendations for management to meet nature conservation objectives tend to be biased towards lowland conditions and situations. The aim of this paper is to draw together those elements which are most relevant to upland woods, excluding the large, commercial plantations of conifers which were mainly established in this century. In the first part of the paper, the philosophy and practice of woodland management are examined in general terms and in relation to issues which have arisen in particular woods. The second part deals with the way that nature conservation management objectives for woodland might be integrated with other forms of land use.

2 Objectives of management for nature conservation in woodland

All woods contain wildlife; so what are the objectives of management for wildlife in native woods? The following are suggested.

    i. To manage woods to maintain rare species or communities.
    ii. To manage areas so as to increase the number of woodland species or the populations of those species.
    iii. To manage the woodland to favour natural and semi-natural communities of plants and animals on the site.

The first objective emphasizes the criterion of rarity, the second diversity, the third naturalness (Ratcliffe 1977). These objectives are not mutually exclusive, but may lead to different approaches to management. Usually, the Nature Conservancy Council (NCC) is most concerned with the maintenance or development of natural (semi-natural) communities as the general objective, with the others becoming important only in specific sites or circumstances.

3 Why manage at all?

If natural communities are to be favoured, why should we manage for wildlife at all? Should we not leave 'nature' to itself? In Britain, the natural forest cover has all but disappeared. Less than 3% of the land area has remained as woodland throughout the whole of the past 1000 years, and even this remnant has been modified by grazing, burning, felling or replanting. The larger forest mammals such as wild boar (*Sus scrofa*) and beaver (*Castor fiber*), which must have influenced the structure and composition of the woods, have gone. Despite this long history of management, many

of the variations in the structure and composition of the surviving semi-natural woodland can be related to soil and climatic factors and to the probable composition of the former natural forest cover. Such past-natural features (Peterken 1977) have survived only in situations where man's influence is part of the ecosystem. They may not now survive removal of management; for example, without direct intervention by man the ground flora is unlikely to survive in a wood where rhododendron (*Rhododendron ponticum*) is spreading.

4 Levels of intervention

The structure and composition of a wood may be controlled directly or indirectly by man, but with different levels of intervention. For example, in the Morrone Birkwoods near Braemar, Deeside, and in other Highland woods, regeneration is limited by red deer (*Cervus elaphus*) browsing; in many Welsh woods, sheep grazing is the critical factor; in an East Anglian coppice wood it could be the demand for rake handles or firewood which determines how and when a stand is cut and regenerated. Thus, there are situations (i) where there is no on-site active management (although changes in the management of surrounding areas could have effects within the wood); (ii) where there is limited control of key elements that would otherwise lead to deleterious changes, eg control of stock or deer numbers, removal of invasive rhododendron; and (iii) where there is direct management of the tree and shrub layer, either with or without associated work on other parts of the wood, eg rides, bogs, and water bodies.

If the primary concern on a site is maintenance of as near natural woodland as possible, then there should be a presumption in favour of low intensity and indirect intervention. Some nature reserves, or parts of them, are treated in this way deliberately. Many other sites at present are also effectively treated thus by neglect. Higher levels of intervention may be required to meet other objectives, for example to combine wood production with nature conservation. Intervention may also be justified purely on nature conservation grounds, where the aim is to increase (maintain) a diversity of conditions within a wood or to enhance the population of a particular rare species. For example, glades might be created to provide suitable areas for the chequered skipper butterfly (*Carterocephalus palaemon*).

The degree of intervention which is necessary or desirable varies according to the size and nature of the site. If there is a large enough block of woodland, it should contain patches of all age classes including saplings and over-mature trees (Pickett & Thompson 1978). Plants and animals which require open glades or scrubby conditions can then maintain their populations through naturally created gaps in the woodland. However, many woods in lowland Britain are now too small to contain such a continuity of open conditions. In some woods which were not managed intensively enough for glade maintenance in the 1950s and 1960s, butterfly populations have declined (Collier 1978). In parklands, continued pollarding and the planting of replacement trees may be the only effective way to ensure the survival of the dead-wood fauna in the old pollard trees.

Traditional forms of woodland management, such as coppicing, ceased in Scotland earlier than in England and Wales (Peterken 1981). On the predominantly acid soils of much of the uplands, it is less likely that coppicing or the restoration of coppicing in oak (*Quercus* spp.) woodland will produce the same benefits in wildlife terms as in the neglected mixed coppices in southern Britain. Minimum intervention is thus more likely to be an appropriate treatment for Scottish semi-natural woods than in England and Wales.

The next sections take a series of issues which are raised frequently in discussions about the management of woods.

5 Grazing and natural regeneration

Peterken (1986) outlines the way in which the structure and composition of woods in Scotland have been influenced by grazing. Miles and Kinnaird (1979) review the relation between grazing and regeneration, and illustrate how animals may both create the conditions necessary for regeneration and hamper subsequent growth of seedlings. Often regeneration appears to be lacking because too many animals (deer, sheep or cattle), which spend much of their time on the open hill, are concentrated in small areas of woodland at particular times of the year. If the overall numbers of deer on the surrounding hills were reduced, the area of woodland could expand and a better balance between deer and wood might be achieved. To be effective, deer numbers would often need to be reduced over very large areas, so such a solution is usually impracticable. The common alternative, whereby sections of the wood are fenced off, is generally successful in terms of increasing regeneration, although not always of the trees currently dominant. There is, however, scope for examining systems where stock are not totally excluded from a wood, or not excluded for the whole of the year, which might, for example, make it easier to retain rich bryophyte communities and diverse field and shrub layers, as well as placing less restriction on agriculture. The practicality of this form of management is the subject of joint research between the Nature Conservancy Council and the Hill Farming Research Organisation. Tree shelters (Tuley 1982) placed on seedlings which occur naturally may also provide an alternative to large-scale fencing, although only with respect to tree regeneration.

Peterken (1986) has also explored the question of whether, even where grazing levels are reduced, regeneration would occur inside the existing woodland boundary. There is a tendency for birch (*Betula* spp.) and pine (*Pinus* spp.) particularly to invade open ground (Miles 1978), and for the boundaries of woods to shift in consequence. Most woods contain gaps which are large enough to support seedling or sapling growth, however, and there is no shortage of 'seedlings' (though these may actually be saplings several years old, the growth of which has been suppressed) of the main native species in most woods (Table 1). If

Table 1. Frequency of 'seedling'[1] occurrence by species in 200 m² quadrats in different woodland types in Scotland (source: original data)

Woodland type	Ash, ash/elm	Alder	Oak	Birch
Stand type group (Peterken 1981)	3,1	7	6	12
Number of quadrats examined	18	39	40	55
Number containing no seedlings of any species	1	7	4	6
Number containing seedlings of the following species:				
Ash (*Fraxinus excelsior*)	14	17	6	1
Oak (*Quercus robur, Q. petraea*)	2	3	18	1
Rowan (*Sorbus aucuparia*)	8	19	31	39
Birch (*Betula pendula, B. pubescens*)	3	7	14	29
Other native trees and shrubs[2]	14	20	12	16
Non-native trees and shrubs[3]	1	2	5	1

The records are biased towards western Scotland, but are all from 'unenclosed' woodland, although grazing levels varied and there was no selection for areas where seedlings were particularly abundant. Plots with a combined tree and shrub layer of less than 5% were excluded

[1]'Seedling' is used here to mean any small stem (other than obvious coppice regrowth) less than 1 m high, regardless of its age

[2]Hazel (*Corylus avellana*), willows (*Salix* spp.), elm (*Ulmus glabra*), alder (*Alnus glutinosa*), aspen (*Populus tremula*), hawthorn (*Crataegus monogyna*)

[3]Sycamore (*Acer pseudoplatanus*), spruce (*Picea* spp.), beech (*Fagus sylvatica*), rhododendron (*Rhododendron ponticum*)

left to themselves, and where grazing pressures were low, most woods could maintain themselves more-or-less on their existing sites. In some cases, regeneration may depend on bare soil or peat being exposed as trees are blown over (in the absence of rooting wild boars) or on rotting logs to provide favourable sites for seedling growth. Gaps created by felling may thus be less favourable to regeneration than naturally created ones. The degree of bare soil exposed may affect the species balance in the regeneration. In a fenced enclosure in Cawdor Wood (Nairn), with a dense ground cover of great wood-rush (*Luzula sylvatica*), birch and raspberry (*Rubus idaeus*) are springing up along single-spaced furrows ploughed through part of the plot, but in the unploughed half the main regeneration is oak at densities of 2–10 10 m^{-2}.

General recommendations for management on heavily grazed sites are to (i) reduce grazing levels around native woods, (ii) reduce grazing levels within woods by fencing all or part of the area, (iii) protect individual seedlings by using tree shelters.

6 Non-native trees and shrubs

As a rule, the more of a site which is occupied by species not native to the site, the less valuable it is for nature conservation. Non-native species in this context means species introduced to Britain, such as rhododendron, sycamore (*Acer pseudoplatanus*), spruce (*Picea* spp.), larch (*Larix* spp.), lodgepole pine (*Pinus contorta*). It also includes beech (*Fagus sylvatica*) whose native range in Britain does not include Scotland, and it includes Scots pine (*Pinus sylvestris*) if it is used in woods where there is no evidence that it had been present within historical times. (The argument can even be extended to include non-native provenances or non-native genetic stock of species native to the site.) Adopting this general principle, it is possible to develop a range of conservation management responses to particular situations.

Rhododendron might be placed at one extreme of the spectrum of response. Although it can provide valuable cover for small birds and mammals in woods where shrub growth is otherwise lacking (French *et al.* 1986), its disadvantages outweigh this benefit. These include the way in which it spreads, the suppression of the ground flora, the poor associated insect fauna, and the way it hampers other activities within the wood, including forestry. Unfortunately, it is also one of the more difficult species to control (Shaw 1984; Tabbush & Sale 1984). In sites where it is already well established, the priority should be to control spread and establish 'rhododendron-free' zones, and only then to seek to eradicate the main colonies.

The establishment of large stands of conifers in broadleaved woods, or introduced conifers in native Scots pine stands, is undesirable from a conservation point of view. Young under-planted (or naturally regenerating) introduced conifers should be removed

as soon as possible, before they have a significant effect on the ground flora. Where thicket or older stands exist with no surviving broadleaves (or native pine) within them, the ideal is to remove them immediately. In practice, often it may make little long-term difference to the site if they are grown on, preferably with heavy thinning, until they can be removed commercially. Higher priority should be given to removing under-planted conifers than to removing pure stands where no remnants of the former tree cover survive. Scattered individual 'specimen' trees, often of considerable size, in woods which are otherwise of native species, seldom detract significantly from the nature conservation value of the site and may provide nesting platforms for large raptors. While regeneration from such trees should be controlled, the trees themselves could be left until they die naturally or until there are commercial reasons to remove them.

The non-native broadleaves which create most problems for nature conservation in Scotland are beech and sycamore. As with other non-native species, it is desirable that these be removed, but both species regenerate well on many sites, and in woods allowed to develop to a future-natural state beech would often replace oak, and sycamore would replace ash or elm. As big or over-mature trees, they may be of interest for their lichens. There may also be circumstances where it is preferable to accept the more (future-)natural structure provided by natural regeneration of beech and sycamore than to create disturbance by felling them and replanting with native species.

7 Planting of native species within existing woods

Past management (particularly oak coppice management) selected against some species which were formerly a natural component of the woods (Tittensor 1970). Such species may reinvade under the less intensive management now prevailing, so that pure oakwoods become mixtures of oak, birch, hazel (*Corylus avellana*), holly (*Ilex aquifolium*) and rowan (*Sorbus aucuparia*). There is a general presumption against reintroducing such species by planting, because this would not be retaining an existing past-natural feature and would be interfering with future-natural development. Exceptions may be made where the evidence for a species actually having been present is very strong, and where the past location of the species is clear. Enrichment planting experiments have been carried out on sites such as Arriundle National Nature Reserve (Lochaber), where, because of its isolation, natural recolonization of the site would be very slow. The case for reintroduction of appropriate species is also stronger where the management system is a compromise between timber production and conservation such that the principle of planting has already been agreed; the site may already be partly plantation. If a completely new area of woodland is being created, it is usually desirable to plant a variety of native species, according to the site conditions, to increase the range of associated plants and animals that may be able to colonize the new wood.

Where planting takes place, a wide spacing between the planted trees will allow more opportunity for natural regeneration to fill any gaps. The overall woodland pattern should then be more natural than where close spacing is used. The use of tree shelters, by increasing tree survival and growth, can reduce the need for close spacings of 3.5 m or less (which are current forestry practice). Planted trees should preferably be of local stock to maintain the genetic diversity between and within native woodlands. Gordon (1985) points out that possible gains from the use of seed from selected stands are insignificant compared to the effects of management on the crop, so that one objection to the use of local seed may be eliminated.

8 Silvicultural systems and modifications to the tree and shrub layers

Many native woods in Scotland were formerly managed as coppice. In southern Britain, restoration of coppicing is often recommended because of the diversity of conditions that it creates, the historical/cultural value of working coppices, and because it can produce a saleable crop. On some base-rich soils, mainly in the lowlands of Scotland, these same conditions may apply. They are, however, less appropriate to the many former oak coppices on acid soils in western Scotland, most of which should be allowed to develop into high forest by singling and thinning of the oak.

Many native woods are more-or-less even-aged, although differences in age of 20–30 years between different blocks may not always be apparent. It is often suggested that group felling and regeneration of such stands should be encouraged to increase the structural diversity of the wood. The argument is that, if this management is not done, the whole wood will die or blow over at some future date. This may be the case, but it could also be the way that these woods would behave under natural conditions. It is more likely that windblow or death by other causes will be patchy and will be spread over a period of perhaps 50–100 years. A felling and regeneration programme spread over 45 years could actually produce a more uniform wood in the long term than a policy of minimum intervention. Large over-mature trees tend to be rare in Scottish woods, so that it is generally more valuable to maintain a mature stand, even if it is even-aged, than to create a diversity of age classes at the expense of losing maturity.

Heavy thinning or small group felling (up to 0.5 ha) as an alternative to large-scale clearfelling is desirable in even-aged stands where it is necessary to combine timber production with nature conservation. Singling and thinning of former oak coppices may be justified in large, relatively uniform, young stands, but it is seldom necessary or desirable to fell mature stands purely on nature conservation grounds.

9 Development of new woods

The more dynamic nature of Scottish woodland means that there is greater opportunity for developing new woods of high conservation value than in England and Wales, either by imaginative planting as on Rhum (Wormell 1968) or through natural regeneration such as occurs within new plantation fences. Planting should be of native species chosen to match the ground conditions, and should leave open areas amongst the more densely planted stands. Where possible, new planting should be linked to existing woodland or other features such as streams or rock outcrops. Once a new woodland has been established, most of the points made above will apply.

10 Treatment of streams, rides, bogs, and other open areas

The treatment of these features is covered in books on conservation management (Brooks 1980; Peterken 1981; Kirby 1984a; Smart & Andrews 1985). In Scotland, because of the predominance of acid rocks and soils, particular attention should be paid to any base-rich areas which are likely to contain species absent from much of the site; drainage of bogs and ditching of streams should be avoided; and, as in commercial conifer stands, any new planting should be kept well back from water bodies, to avoid direct runoff and erosion into streams.

The application of these ideas to a particular site is illustrated by Figure 1.

11 Management of woods for wildlife at the landscape scale

The foregoing represent nature conservation recommendations expressed largely without reference to other land uses. On a small proportion of nature reserves and Sites of Special Scientific Interest (SSSIs), nature conservation is either the sole object of management, or there is scope through compensation arrangements under the Wildlife and Countryside Act 1981 to ensure that nature conservation requirements can predominate should there be a conflict with other land uses. SSSIs include only the minority of native woodland areas in Scotland, although locally where such woodland is scarce they may cover the majority of sites. For example, while 90% of semi-natural woods in Caithness and over 80% of the native pinewoods are scheduled as SSSIs, only some 25% of semi-natural woodland in Sutherland is covered; expressed as a percentage of all woodland in Sutherland, the figure is about 4%. Another way to look at this pattern is to compare the distribution of any one type of woodland on a 10 km square basis with the distribution of SSSIs for this type (Figure 2). The distribution of scheduled sites broadly mirrors that of the resource as a whole, but many large woodland areas and parts of the Districts are omitted. A similar pattern for birch woodland throughout Scotland is shown in Kirby (1984b).

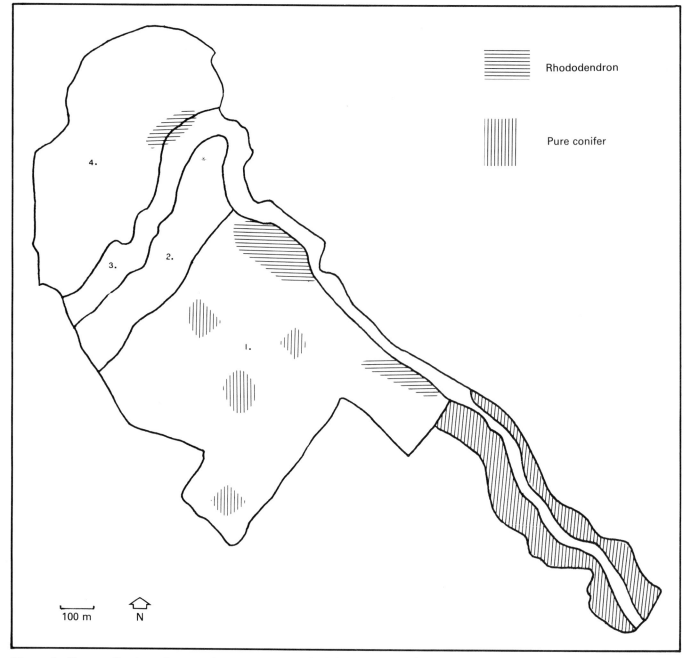

Rhododendron

Pure conifer

100 m

N

Figure 1. The application of general management principles to a particular site

The following example is based on an actual site, but is simplified so that it may be used as a guide to, rather than as a definitive statement of, NCC's views on how this site might be managed, from *the nature conservation point of view*. The aim is to maintain and, if possible, increase the areas of semi-natural woodland, in most of which oak is likely to remain the major native tree component, although increases in, for example, birch, holly or other native species would not be considered undesirable. The lichen communities contain some rare species which it is desirable to protect.

Management suggestions

Area

1. Oak woodland with trees 200–300 years old particularly important for lichens. Regeneration of native species apparently limited by deer browsing.
   a. Control rhododendron spread and eventually aim to eliminate it from the site.
   b. Remove any regeneration of conifers. Look to the long-term removal of the small blocks within the oak stand.
   c. Any felling of old oak is undesirable.
   d. Oak seedlings are frequent; some gaps already occur in the canopy and more will be created by conifer removal. In the long term, deer fencing of all or part of the block may be necessary. In the short term, tree shelters might be placed over existing seedlings to protect them.

2. A block of mature beech, including some old pollards, which like the oak have a rich lichen flora.
   a. Retain existing mature beech for their lichens.
   b. Control spread of beech into the oak stand.
   c. Favour any oak regeneration amongst the beech.

3.   Gorge with a rich flora, but with some invasion by beech, sycamore and rhododendron.
     a.   Remove sycamore, beech and rhododendron regeneration where possible, but in the gorge itself this may create too much disturbance to the soil and flora.
     b.   Aim to thin heavily, and eventually remove, the conifers nearest to the gorge in the south-east corner of the site to reduce shading of the gorge.
4.   Formerly oak woodland as 1, partially replanted with larch about 70 years ago, much of which has recently been felled; the felled areas have been replanted with oak, beech and larch.
     a.   Retain the remaining mature oak.
     b.   Fell any remaining old larch as it becomes economic to do so.
     c.   Encourage natural regeneration of oak and favour oak in any thinning of the newly planted trees to restore the area to oak high forest.
     d.   Control natural regeneration of rhododendron and non-native trees.

Work such as fencing the main oak block (1) and control of rhododendron would involve high costs to the owner, although there could be some forestry benefits; restrictions on felling of oak and beech and the removal of conifers reduce the income from the site. Any management plan would need to balance these aspects against the gains in nature conservation terms.

Nature conservation is a proper constraint on the productive use of land, and not an 'optional extra'. If other land uses (forestry, urbanization, agriculture, mineral extraction) were given free rein, there would be continued decline in the area and nature conservation value of semi-natural woodland, as occurred over the last 40 years (Parr 1981). The present (and currently proposed) SSSIs would probably be insufficient to maintain the full range of woodland species and communities, and it would be necessary, as has happened in Caithness, to schedule a much higher proportion of the total resource to ensure its survival. How, and how far, is it possible to influence the management of woods outside the statutorily designated sites to take nature conservation into account, while keeping constraints on production to the minimum?

12 Defining the resource and priorities
The first step is to catalogue the native woodland resource. The total figures for broadleaved woodland broken down by species or age class provided by the Forestry Commission censuses (Forestry Commission 1983) are useful, but the categories used (scrub, coppice, broadleaved high forest) are too broad for most nature conservation purposes and do not give information about particular sites. Hence, NCC has organized its own surveys which concentrate on the categories of woodland most likely to be of nature conservation value and which provide site-specific information. These surveys include detailed field descriptions of individual sites, as well as more general surveys such as that carried out by ITE on the deciduous woodland cover of Scotland (Bunce *et al.* 1979; Parr 1981), and work currently in progress to identify ancient and semi-natural woodland.

Even without detailed site information, it is possible to predict which sites are most likely to be of nature conservation value.

  i.   The longer a wood has been present on a site, the more likely it is to be of nature conservation value. Three categories may be distinguished: those thought to be 'ancient' (continuous wood-

land cover back to 1600 at least); those classed as long established which are at least 100 years old, but may be much older; and 'recent' woods, less than 100 years old.
 ii.   Semi-natural woods or old (more than 100 years) plantations of native species are generally more valuable than young plantations or plantations of non-native species.
iii.   Regardless of their origin, woods composed of native species are valuable in a country where native woodland of any sort is sparse. They provide reservoirs of populations of common woodland species, even if those sites of recent origin lack the more specialized species. In Sutherland, 60% of the semi-natural woodland area identified by NCC was in blocks more than 10 ha in extent, but these comprised only 22% of the number of sites (Walker 1985).

The results of the general surveys noted earlier may then be used in a general woodland conservation strategy based on the following series of priorities.

  i.   Maintain the areas of semi-natural woodland scheduled as SSSIs.
 ii.   Maintain areas of semi-natural woodland (and mature plantations of native trees) on ancient or long-established sites.
iii.   Maintain other large areas of semi-natural woodland, those greater than 10 ha for example, as a reservoir of the more common species.
 iv.   Encourage the natural spread of native woodland around existing native woodland sites, especially when linking together other small fragments.
  v.   Plant new woods of native trees.

Figure 3 illustrates some of the different categories and priorities for conservation in a particular block of land in west Argyll.

13 Conservation through management
Most native woods were used in the past (Anderson 1967; Callander 1986). Often that is the reason why they survived, but they are now considered to have little or no economic value. Outside the areas where

Map A

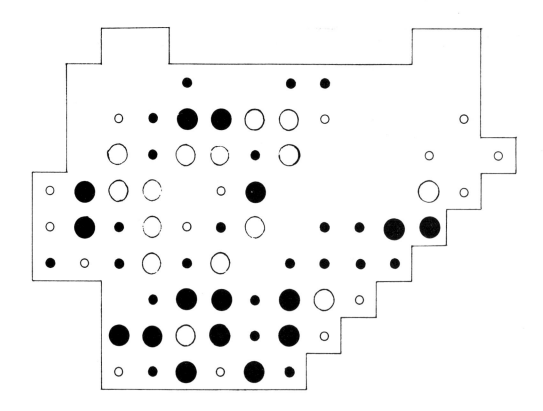

Map B

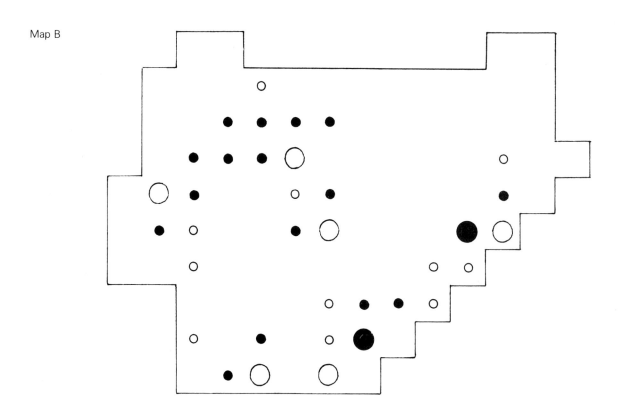

Figure 2. Distribution of semi-natural areas on the Nature Conservancy Council woodland inventory by 10 km² in Caithness and Sutherland (source: Walker 1985; unpublished data)

The inventory lists ancient and long-established woodland sites plus selected recent woodland sites of known or likely conservation value. All semi-natural stands on the inventory contribute to Map A, while Map B includes only those within SSSIs or NNRs.

- ○   1– 10 ha of woodland 10 km⁻²
- ● 11– 50 ha of woodland 10 km⁻²
- ◯ 51–100 ha of woodland 10 km⁻²
- ● > 101 ha of woodland 10 km⁻²

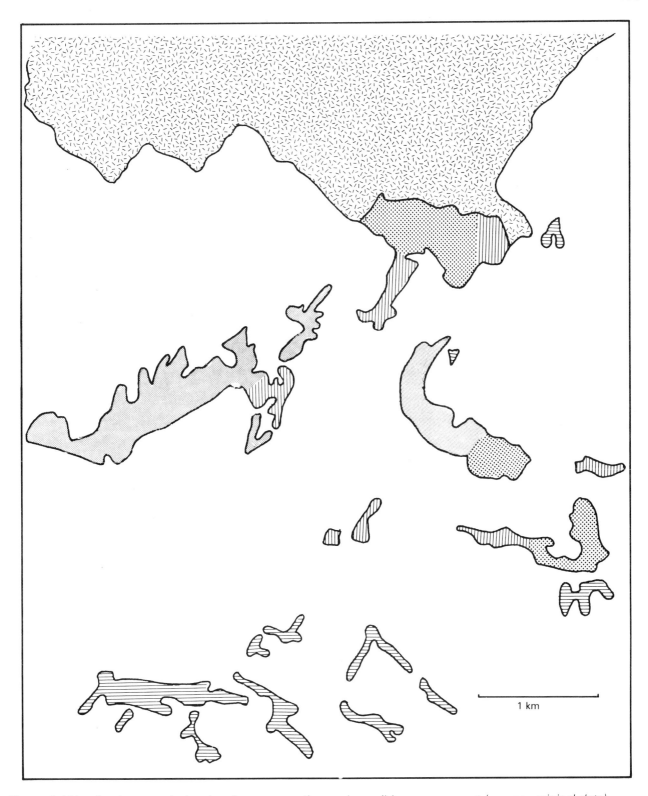

Figure 3. Woodland types, their value for conservation and possible management (source: original data)

The woodland in this area in west Argyll has been classified according to its likely history and current composition, based on a variety of map and survey sources. Priorities for conservation are determined and suggestions for management made, taking account of other land uses in the area.

ANCIENT SEMI-NATURAL WOODLAND

1. The 2 large blocks plus small outliers of semi-natural woodland are shown as woodland on the maps of General Roy (1750), and are rich in lichens and vascular plants. They are possible Sites of Special Scientific Interest and are also prominent in the landscape. Management should take account of their conservation importance, but some production of oak and ash for timber (both widespread components in these woods) and alder coppice for firewood is possible without detracting from their wildlife value.

continued overleaf

174

LONG-ESTABLISHED SEMI-NATURAL WOODLAND

2.　Numerous small fragments of semi-natural woodland, mainly birch, at least 100 years old (shown on the OS 6″ first edition maps) often occur along streams. They are generally of little productive value, and their future survival is largely a matter of chance and variations in the grazing pressure of surrounding land. In places, it might be possible to fence some sections so that stock is excluded. The more substantial blocks of birch woodland could perhaps be enriched with oak to increase their timber potential or managed on a rotational exclosure basis so that there are always areas available for stock shelter, while providing the opportunity for woodland regeneration. Although of high nature conservation value, they are unlikely to be designated as SSSIs.

LONG-ESTABLISHED PLANTATIONS BROADLEAF CONIFER

3.　Various mixed plantations were established in the 19th century. Some are now pure conifers, others are broadleaves. The broadleaved areas should remain so, being managed to produce hardwoods as economically as possible, and perhaps some of the conifers might be returned to mixed plantations in the next rotation. Their conservation value is likely to be low compared to the previous 2 categories, but higher than the following area.

RECENT PLANTATIONS

4.　The largest block of woodland in the sample area is that of least inherent conservation interest. It is a block of new conifer plantations established this century. While its main function is to supply softwood timber and pulp, the open areas or small patches of birch within it have some potential for wildlife which could be developed with relatively little loss of production (Ratcliffe & Petty 1986).

nature conservation is the main objective (SSSIs, NNRs), the future survival of native woodland may be enhanced if new uses can be found for it.

In some cases, this exploitation could be through inclusion within forestry schemes. There is scope for producing wood (firewood or better) from many sites, using the methods outlined earlier, without spoiling their conservation value. The new forestry grants and management guidelines (Forestry Commission 1985) should help to reduce total conversion to conifers, but timber production is likely to be worthwhile only on the better soils, in the more accessible sites, and where the main species are oak and ash. If the birch improvement programme is successful (Kennedy & Brown 1980), the scope could be widened (Ogilvy 1986). Similarly, the potential for sustained firewood production from native woods on farms particularly should be further explored.

Semi-natural woods may also be included within productive forest (most significantly within the forest fence), without being directly included in production plans. Their contribution in terms of landscape, recreation and the reduction in the acidity of streams may help to make large conifer planting schemes in the uplands more acceptable. The suggestion that 5% of the woodland area in upland plantations could be allocated to broadleaves with minimal loss of timber production (Forestry Commission 1985) is to be welcomed.

Woods open to hill grazing may not have much

potential for timber production at present, and are a largely unquantified element in the hill farming pattern. Some farmers believe that their woods are important areas for grazing and shelter, but others regard them as a nuisance, either because they could be cleared to provide better grazing or because stock become lost within them. The new felling licence procedures may help to maintain the total area under native woodland on the hills by reducing deliberate clearance. However, gradual attrition of woodland may continue through over-grazing, leading to a lack of regeneration, and death or felling of individual trees. What is not clear is whether the new broadleaf grant scheme will encourage more positive management, such as the fencing off of parts of woods, at least for a period, to allow a burst of regeneration.

Integration of different land uses has been happening in many upland woods for the last 60–80 years. The woods provide grazing and shelter, landscape and wildlife conservation, as well as small amounts of timber. Recommendations for the management of upland woods for wildlife in combination with other objectives have been made before, eg Goodier and Ball (1974), Goodier et al. (1983) and Brown (1983).

Unfortunately, most grants and advice have presumed a single main use for each site (agriculture, forestry or nature conservation) and the incentives have been insufficient to prevent broadleaved woods declining in area or changing to conifers. The new broadleaf grant recognizes that there may be a variety of objectives in any particular site and that timber production need not be the most important. Can we now solve the practical problems of implementing the recommendations for multiple-use forestry?

14 Summary

Management for wildlife in the native woods of Scotland must take account of the different character of many of the woods compared to those in the rest of Britain. The main nature conservation aim should be to encourage the development of natural and semi-natural plant and animal communities. Maintenance of past-natural features which are difficult (impossible) to re-create should generally take precedence over the development of future-natural ones. Lower levels of intervention are often more appropriate than in the woods of southern Britain because, in Scotland, the recent management has generally been less intense.

A reduction in the level of grazing in and around woods, not necessarily complete exclusion of grazing, would frequently benefit wildlife. If the concern is only with regeneration, tree shelters placed over naturally occurring seedlings may be a partial alternative to fencing.

Non-native species should be removed, except where excessive disturbance to the soil or other parts of the site would result. Planting even of native species should be limited within existing woods, but, if it is unavoidable, it should be at wide spacing, with trees of local provenance. High forest management is more appropriate for many Scottish woods, even former oak coppices, than trying to restore the coppice cycle. Felling of mature timber, even if the stand is even-aged, is seldom desirable from a conservation point of view.

Nature conservation must not be confined to the minority of woods which are designated as Sites of Special Scientific Interest. Surveys which allow the broad categorization of woodland according to its history, current composition and size can be used to indicate the likely conservation value of other sites.

Outside designated conservation areas, recognition of the present and potential uses of native woodland may reduce the risk that a site will be cleared or replanted with introduced species.

The new broadleaved woodland policy may provide the necessary stimulus to develop the new forms of management that will maintain the nature conservation value of upland woods, as well as allowing some agricultural or forestry production.

15 References

Anderson, M.L. 1967. *A history of Scottish forestry.* London: Nelson.

Brooks, A. 1980. *Woodlands.* Wallingford: British Trust for Conservation Volunteers.

Brown, I.R. 1983. *Management of birch woodland in Scotland.* Perth: Countryside Commission for Scotland.

Bunce, R.G.H., Munro, R.C. & Parr, T.W. 1979. *Deciduous woodland survey of Scotland.* (CST report no. 250.) Banbury: Nature Conservancy Council.

Callander, R. 1986. The history of native woodlands in the Scottish Highlands. In: *Trees and wildlife in the Scottish uplands,* edited by D. Jenkins, 40–45. (ITE symposium no. 17.) Abbots Ripton: Institute of Terrestrial Ecology.

Collier, R.V. 1978. *The status and decline of butterflies on Castor Hanglands NNR.* (CST note no. 8.) Peterborough: Nature Conservancy Council. (Unpublished.)

Evans, J. 1984. *Silviculture of broadleaved woodland.* (Forestry Commission bulletin no. 62.) London: HMSO.

Forestry Commission. 1983. *Census of woodlands and trees, Scotland.* Edinburgh: FC.

Forestry Commission. 1985. *Guidelines for the management of broadleaved woodland.* Edinburgh: FC.

French, D.D., Jenkins, D. & Conroy, J.W.H. 1986. Guidelines for managing woods in Aberdeenshire for song birds. In: *Trees and wildlife in the Scottish uplands,* edited by D. Jenkins, 129–143. (ITE symposium no. 17.) Abbots Ripton: Institute of Terrestrial Ecology.

Goodier, R. & Ball, M.E. 1974. The management of upland broadleaved woodlands for nature and landscape conservation. *Forestry,* **47** (Supplement), 59–71.

Goodier, R., Kirby, K.J. & Wormell, P. 1983. *The establishment, management and conservation of upland native woodlands.* Paper presented to British Ecological Society meeting on Ecology and Upland Land Use, York. (Unpublished.)

Gordon, A.G. 1985. Are EEC seed regulations really in Britain's interest? *For. & Br. Timber,* **14,** (11), 22–25.

Kennedy, D. & Brown, I.R. 1980. Breeding better birch. *For. & Br. Timber,* **9,** 44–45.

Kirby, K.J. 1984a. *Forestry operations and broadleaf woodland conservation.* (Focus on nature conservation no. 8.) Peterborough: Nature Conservancy Council.

Kirby, K.J. 1984b. Scottish birchwoods and their conservation – a review. *Trans. bot. Soc. Edinb.,* **44,** 205–218.

Miles, J. 1978. The influence of trees on soil properties. *Annu. Rep. Inst. terr. Ecol. 1977,* 7–11.

Miles, J. & Kinnaird, J.W. 1979. Grazing with particular reference to birch, juniper and Scots pine in the Scottish Highlands. *Scott. For.,* **33,** 280–289.

Ogilvy, R.S.D. 1986. Whither forestry? The scene in AD 2025. In: *Trees and wildlife in the Scottish uplands,* edited by D. Jenkins, 33–39. (ITE symposium no. 17.) Abbots Ripton: Institute of Terrestrial Ecology.

Parr, T.W. 1981. Scottish deciduous woodland; a cause for concern. In: *Forest and woodland ecology,* edited by F.T. Last & A.S. Gardiner, 12–15. (ITE symposium no. 8.) Cambridge: Institute of Terrestrial Ecology.

Peterken, G.F. 1977. Habitat conservation priorities in British and European woodlands. *Biol. Conserv.,* **11,** 223–236.

Peterken, G.F. 1981. *Woodland conservation and management.* London: Chapman & Hall.

Peterken, G.F. 1986. The status of native woods in the Scottish uplands. In: *Trees and wildlife in the Scottish uplands,* edited by D. Jenkins, 14–19. (ITE symposium no. 27.) Abbots Ripton: Institute of Terrestrial Ecology.

Pickett, S.T.A. & Thompson, J.N. 1978. Patch dynamics and the design of nature reserves. *Biol. Conserv.,* **13,** 27–38.

Ratcliffe, D.A. 1977. *A nature conservation review.* Cambridge: Cambridge University Press.

Ratcliffe, P.R. & Petty, S.J. 1986. The management of commercial forestry for wildlife. In: *Trees and wildlife in the Scottish uplands,* edited by D. Jenkins, 177–187. (ITE symposium no. 17.) Abbots Ripton: Institute of Terrestrial Ecology.

Roy, General. 1750. *The military survey of Scotland 1747–1755.* Edinburgh: National Library of Scotland. (Unpublished.)

Shaw, M.W. 1984. *Rhododendron ponticum* – ecological reasons for the success of an alien species in Britain and features that may assist in its control. In: *Weed control and vegetation management in forests and amenity areas. Asp. appl. Biol.*, **5**, 231–242.

Smart, N. & Andrews, J. 1985. *Birds and broadleaves handbook.* Sandy: Royal Society for the Protection of Birds.

Tabbush, P.M. & Sale, J.S.P. 1984. Experiments on the chemical control of *Rhododendron ponticum* L. In: *Weed control and vegetation management in forests and amenity areas. Asp. appl. Biol.*, **5**, 243–253.

Tittensor, R. 1970. History of Loch Lomond oakwoods. *Scott. For.*, **24**, 100–118.

Tuley, G. 1982. Tree shelters increase the early growth of broadleaved trees. In: *Broadleaves in Britain, future management and research*, edited by D.C. Malcolm, J. Evans & P.N. Edwards, 176–182. Edinburgh: Institute of Chartered Foresters.

Walker, G.J. 1985. *Sutherland: Inventories of ancient, long-established and semi-natural woodlands.* Peterborough: Nature Conservancy Council. (Unpublished.)

Wormell, P. 1968. Establishing woodland on the Isle of Rhum. *Scott. For.*, **22**, 207–220.

The management of commercial forests for wildlife

P R RATCLIFFE and S J PETTY
Forestry Commission, Wildlife & Conservation Research Branch, Glenbranter

1 Introduction

This paper describes the wildlife associated with the sequential growth stages of conifer forests in upland Scotland, and discusses management practices and options which might maximize this wildlife while maintaining the profitability of the timber crop. Our use of the term 'wildlife' refers entirely to birds and mammals.

Commercial forests in the British uplands are mainly concerned with the production of fast-growing, small-diameter spruce (*Picea* spp.) and pine (*Pinus* spp.). The age at which crops are felled is governed primarily by the increasing risk of windthrow with increased height (Busby 1974) and by economic constraints (Busby & Grayson 1981). Forests are zoned according to their susceptibility to windthrow, the sites most at risk being managed under a 'no-thinning' regime (Grayson 1981). A major consequence of short rotation forestry is that very large areas of forest are always in the early growth stages (Ratcliffe 1985a) (Figure 1).

2 Sequential growth stages of conifer forests

Foresters have loosely defined different growth stages in commercial forests. Moss *et al.* (1979) used these stages to catalogue the successive changes in song bird populations, and Ratcliffe *et al.* (1986) redefined them to aid the management of red deer (*Cervus elaphus*).

The changing area occupied by each growth stage through time affects most wildlife species in some way, and provides valuable data on which to base the predictive management of commercial forest eco-systems. The interface between each stage can easily be redefined to suit studies of particular wildlife species or communities, and the application of computer models (Ratcliffe *et al.* 1986) can provide rapid tabulated and graphical output describing future changes in forest structure (Figure 2) and associated wildlife numbers. To examine the effects of sequential changes in the growth of forests on groups of species having widely differing requirements, we can define

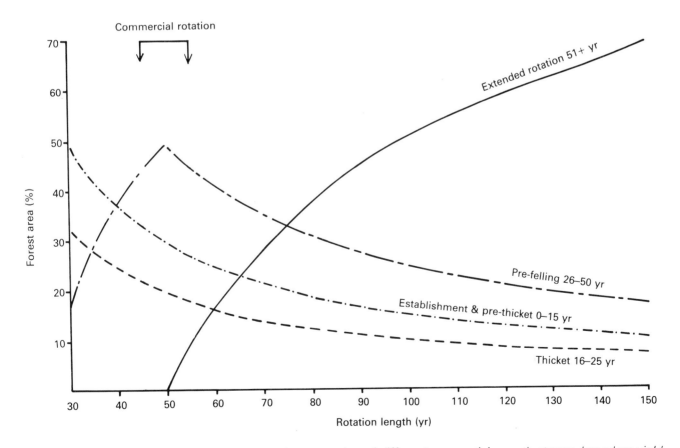

Figure 1. *The influence of rotation length on the proportion of different sequential growth stages, based on yield class 12 Sitka spruce*

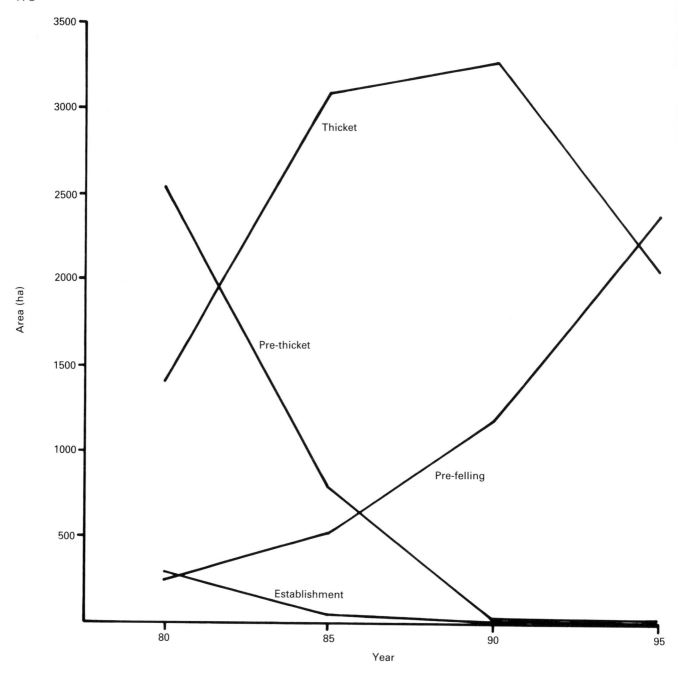

Figure 2. Predicted changes in sequential growth stages at Glenorchy Forest, Argyll (source: Ratcliffe et al. 1986)

these stages (Figure 3) as a means of estimating changing levels in resources (Figure 4).

2.1 Establishment

Moorland is usually ploughed to achieve cultivation, drainage and weed suppression (Thompson 1984) and phosphate fertilizer is normally applied (Busby 1974). Trees are planted at a density of about 2000 ha^{-1}, regularly spaced at approximately 2 m × 2 m. Domestic grazing stock are usually excluded and in about 55% of afforested areas, mainly in north and central Scotland, red deer are also excluded by fencing (Ratcliffe 1984). These establishment techniques inevitably result in an increase in vegetation which in turn leads to an increase in the numbers of small rodents (Charles 1981), and their mammalian and avian predators, such as the fox (*Vulpes vulpes*), wild cat (*Felis silvestris*), weasel (*Mustela nivalis*), short-eared owl (*Asio flammeus*) and kestrel (*Falco tinnunculus*) (Newton 1983; Staines 1983).

Temporal cycles in the abundance of short-tailed field voles (*Microtus agrestis*) which are unrelated to forest succession also modify predator/prey interactions during the establishment phase. The abundance of prey attracts less widely distributed species such as the long-eared owl (*Asio otus*) and barn owl (*Tyto alba*), if suitable nest sites are available (Newton 1983), and has led to increases in some rare species such as the red kite (*Milvus milvus*) in central Wales (Newton *et al.* 1981), and the hen harrier (*Circus cyaneus*) throughout the uplands (Watson 1977). Following afforestation,

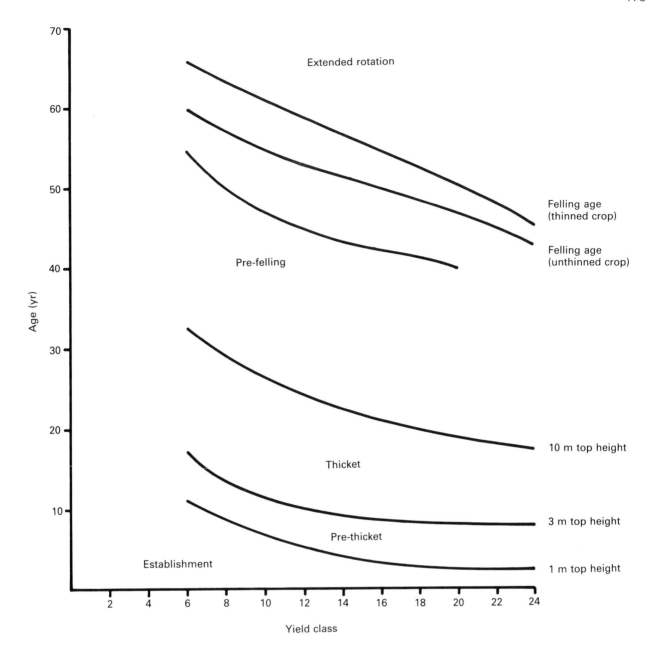

Figure 3. Model of sequential growth changes in Sitka spruce forests (source: Ratcliffe et al. 1986)

some moorland song bird populations increase in density while others are lost (Moss *et al.* 1979). Species favouring scrub habitats, such as whinchat (*Saxicola rubetra*), redpoll (*Carduelis flammea*), and willow warbler (*Phylloscopus trochilus*), also increase in numbers, though these species are absent prior to afforestation and in the older growth stages (Figure 5).

A wide variety of forbs appears during the early years (Hill 1979) and roe bucks (*Capreolus capreolus*) colonize and establish territories at this stage, followed later by does. When red and roe deer have not been excluded, they will make substantial use of these areas for feeding, and it is likely that there will be a marked loss in botanical diversity at densities as low as 3 red deer km^{-2} (Kraus 1985) compared to densities of

5–40 km^{-2} in Scottish forests (Ratcliffe 1984, 1985a). The presence of domestic ungulates, particularly sheep, adds to this problem.

2.2 Pre-thicket

In the pre-thicket stage, trees reach a height of about 1–3 m. Browsing by deer on the commercial tree crop diminishes, and a degree of cover is provided for roe deer (Staines & Welch 1984). Red deer will use these areas, but as cover is below optimum, and their increase in numbers is slower, they seldom achieve the densities of roe deer (Ratcliffe & Rowe 1985). Mammal and bird predators continue to feed on field voles, and many of the moorland birds will have been replaced by an increasing number of species associated with young conifers. True woodland birds such as

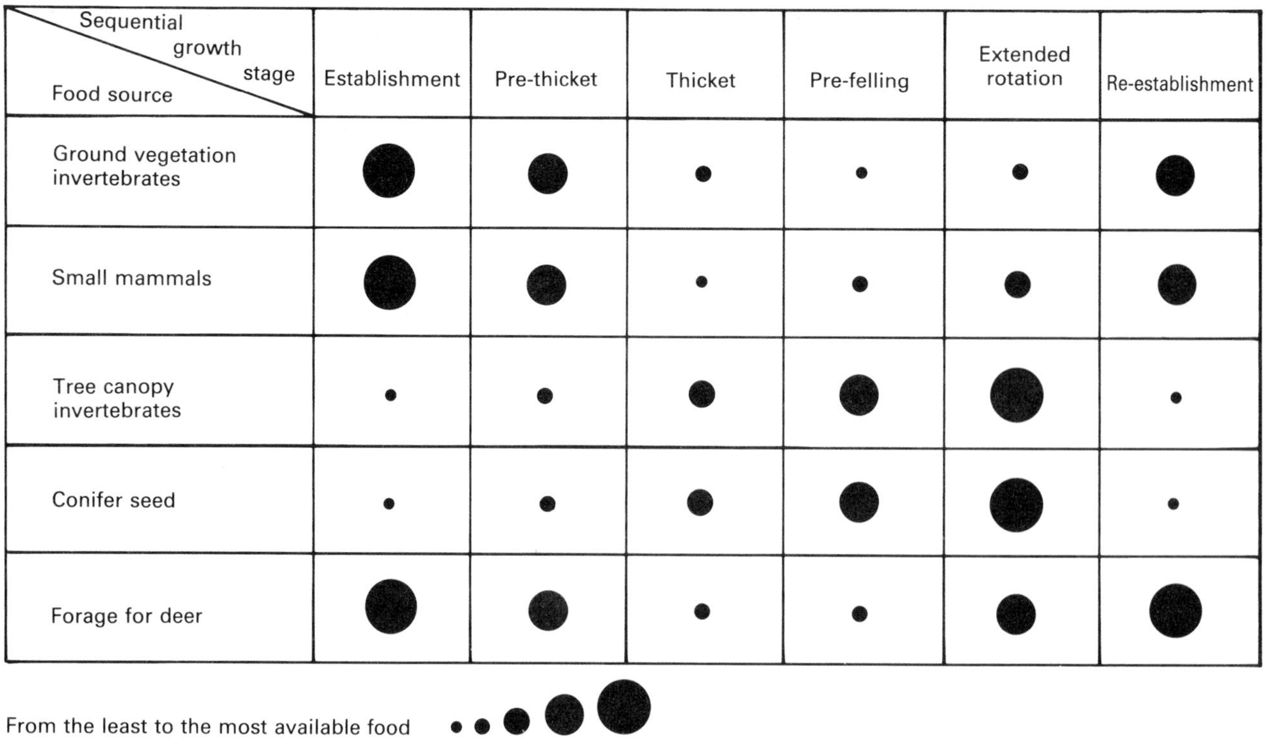

Food source \ Sequential growth stage	Establishment	Pre-thicket	Thicket	Pre-felling	Extended rotation	Re-establishment
Ground vegetation invertebrates	⬤	⬤	•	•	•	⬤
Small mammals	⬤	⬤	•	•	●	⬤
Tree canopy invertebrates	•	•	●	⬤	⬤	•
Conifer seed	•	•	●	⬤	⬤	•
Forage for deer	⬤	⬤	•	•	●	⬤

From the least to the most available food • • ● ⬤ ⬤

Figure 4. The availability of major food resources in relation to sequential growth stage

goldcrest (*Regulus regulus*), coal tit (*Parus ater*), and chaffinch (*Fringilla coelebs*) also become established (Figure 5).

2.3 Thicket

At this stage, tree height is between 3 m and 10 m and canopy closure occurs. When light intensity begins to fall, a decline in the abundance of vascular plants commences (Hill 1979), and, ultimately, under dense, vigorously growing conifers, ground vegetation is completely eliminated, except along road-, ride- and streamsides. These habitats may together account for about 15% of the forest area. However, very large areas of uniform growth are uncommon, and, by the thicket stage, many forests have developed an uneven height and density (structural diversity) due to local variations in site quality. This development results in small vegetated glades within thickets, which, due to the close proximity of food and shelter, support the highest densities of red deer found in Great Britain (Ratcliffe 1984). Subsequently, in the later thicket stage, roe deer appear to decline (Staines & Welch 1984).

Woodland song birds will have completely replaced their moorland counterparts (Figure 5), but a few scrub species persist in glades, together with forest edge species such as the tree pipit (*Anthus trivialis*) (Moss *et al.* 1979).

All the raptors associated with the previous stages, which depend on open conditions for hunting, will now have disappeared, and trees in the thicket stage are too small or too dense to allow access for breeding by woodland birds of prey, such as the sparrowhawk (*Accipiter nisus*) (Newton *et al.* 1977) and tawny owl (*Strix aluco*) (Petty unpubl.).

2.4 Pre-felling

Tree height is from 10 m up to that predicted at the age of felling (Figure 3). Crops gradually become more open as suppressed trees die and thinning and windthrow occur. A limited ground vegetation usually returns, but it is of low quality for herbivores. Deer use this stage less than any other, though roe deer can maintain low densities as the vegetation starts to recolonize (Staines & Welch 1984). Passerine populations are dominated by species which feed on invertebrates in the canopy, with goldcrest and coal tit reaching their greatest densities, while the lightly vegetated forest floor provides both foraging and breeding sites for woodcock (*Scolopax rusticola*), robin (*Erithacus rubecula*) and song thrush (*Turdus philomelos*) (Moss *et al.* 1979). Coniferous trees may produce heavy cone crops and, as trees mature and crown volume increases, the potential for higher cone production also increases. Conifer seeds provide a rich food source for common crossbill (*Loxia curvirostra*) and siskin (*Carduelis spinus*), 2 species which are specially adapted to utilize this bonanza (Newton 1972), and which have greatly expanded their range in Britain as a result of the expansion of commercial forestry (Sharrock 1976). High densities of crossbills and siskins provide abundant prey for sparrowhawks in

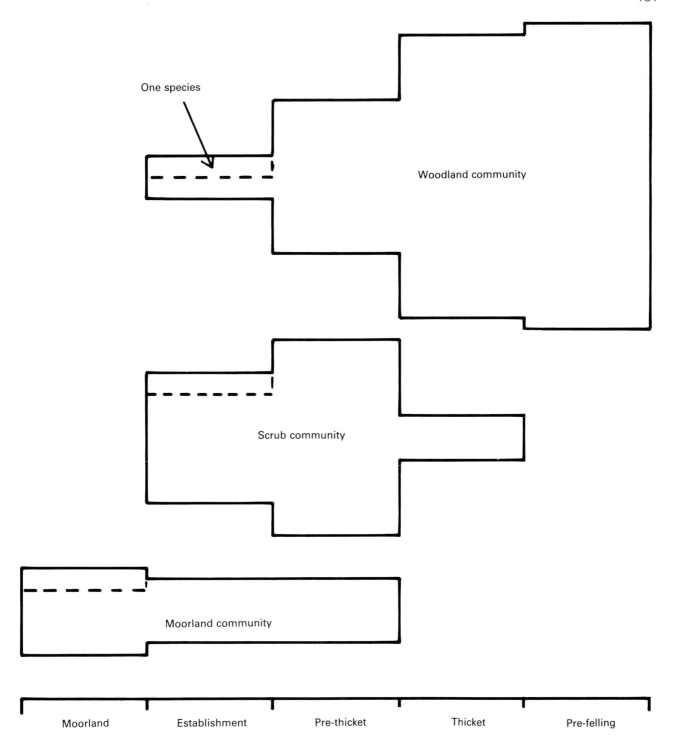

One species

Woodland community

Scrub community

Moorland community

| Moorland | Establishment | Pre-thicket | Thicket | Pre-felling |

Figure 5. Changes in song bird community structure resulting from afforestation of open moorland (source: Moss et al. 1979)

early spring when other forest passerines are scarce and when sparrowhawk productivity attains high levels (Petty 1979, unpubl.). The increasingly open structure of the forest enables sparrowhawks to hunt and allows access for breeding. Red squirrels (*Sciurus vulgaris*) are also largely dependent on conifer seed for food and may colonize commercial forests at this stage (Tittensor 1975).

2.5 Extended rotation
This stage continues beyond the usual age of felling

based upon economic constraints and windthrow risk (Figure 3), and seldom occurs in British commercial forests. However, it is a stage which has important benefits for the conservation and management of wildlife (and presumably for other vertebrate groups and invertebrates). The management option of maintaining extended rotations is discussed later.

2.6 Re-establishment
Re-establishment or restocking of trees usually follows clearfelling, but can occur prematurely following

the clearance of windblown areas. It involves the planting of trees amongst the stumps and branches left from the previous crop.

The size of felled areas depends upon economic and environmental considerations (Low 1985), but they are usually much smaller than areas being planted for the first time. Deer utilize these areas similarly to the establishment phase, but in small areas, where cover and food are close at hand, red and roe deer usage can be very high. On larger sites, red deer use the central areas, far from cover, less heavily than the edges (Thirgood 1984). The developing plant communities are unlike those prior to afforestation, and the variety of species present depends on soil type, seed sources and grazing pressure.

In north Wales, in the absence of deer, rich soils were colonized by broadleaved tree seedlings and forbs. This colonization resulted in a diverse scrub layer which supported a diverse bird community, including willow warbler and wren (*Troglodytes troglodytes*) and the less common blackcap (*Silvia atricapilla*), whitethroat (*S. communis*), and garden warbler (*S. borin*) (Currie & Bamford 1981; Bibby *et al.* 1986a). In Northumberland, where selective feeding by roe deer eliminated broadleaved plants and a grassy vegetation resulted, the bird community was similar to that present on newly afforested sites, with meadow pipit (*Anthus pratensis*) the most abundant species (Leslie 1981).

Site quality may affect the response of particular plants to browsing (Burdekin & Ratcliffe 1985), and hence may modify vegetation composition. Vole populations fluctuate on grassy sites (Petty unpubl.), and short-eared owls may be attracted to the largest of these (Leslie 1981). Tawny owls become established in the surrounding forest, increasing their productivity in response to the periodic abundance of vole prey (Petty 1983).

3 Spatial diversity

In addition to the temporal changes described, the spatial aspects of commercial forests are also important. Afforested areas usually succeed each other annually in a step-wise fashion across land acquisitions, resulting in a fairly uniform monoculture of conifers. Large areas of uniform spruce crops with low diversity can support only the restricted wildlife associated with that particular growth stage.

However, with the recent attainment of completed commercial rotations in many areas, crops have been felled and new areas have been re-established. This has resulted in an increased spatial diversity which may be further increased by windthrow, creating an intimate mosaic of stands of different ages. This is an important characteristic of second rotation forests and

has innumerable benefits to wildlife, but it can also increase the carrying capacity for deer still further.

4 Habitat improvements

Benefits to wildlife following afforestation have usually occurred fortuitously and many more improvements are possible by careful, planned management. Prescriptions should include the management of important sites, the requirements of particular species, and the diversification of the remaining forest (Smart & Andrews 1985). Specialist organizations, such as the Forestry Commission (FC), Institute of Terrestrial Ecology, Nature Conservancy Council, Royal Society for the Protection of Birds, and local naturalist organizations, may be able to provide information on the presence of important species or habitats and on their subsequent management.

4.1 Tree species

Commercial forestry aims to plant the most profitable species on a particular site type (Busby 1974). In the uplands, this often leads to Sitka spruce (*Picea sitchensis*) being the most widely used species. The tree species used is of less importance, for example to bird communities, than is the ensuing structure of the forest (Moss 1978), though spruce is usually richer for birds than pine or larch (*Larix* spp.) (Newton 1983). Some structural diversity will develop in extensive, relatively even-aged, plantations due to variation in aspect, drainage and nutrient status, but this diversity can be increased considerably by the use of other species in groups or in mixtures.

The recent introduction of a new broadleaved woodland policy by the FC has provided a much needed stimulus to secure a place for broadleaves within all commercial forests (Forestry Commission 1984). Although this policy is not confined to native species, many upland sites will not profitably grow broadleaved crops. Indigenous species have greater conservation benefits and we suggest therefore that these should be the only broadleaves planted on such sites, ie sessile oak (*Quercus petraea*), alder (*Alnus glutinosa*), birch (*Betula pubescens*), rowan (*Sorbus aucuparia*), holly (*Ilex aquifolium*), aspen (*Populus tremula*), bird cherry (*Prunus padus*), and goat willow (*Salix caprea*). Additionally, ash (*Fraxinus excelsior*), wych elm (*Ulmus glabra*), and hazel (*Corylus avellana*) could be encouraged or planted on well-drained base-rich soils. Native conifers are equally important and should also be encouraged or planted on suitable sites. An extension of the use of Scots pine (*Pinus sylvestris*), rather than lodgepole pine (*P. contorta*) or Sitka spruce, will assist the spread of species associated with native pinewoods (Bunce & Jeffers 1977). The crested tit (*Parus cristatus*), for example, has extended its range, albeit at lower densities, into the pine plantations on the north-east coast of Scotland, and the capercaillie (*Tetrao urogallus*) has extended its range still further into areas of mixed woodland (Sharrock 1976). Bark-stripping damage by red deer is much less severe on

Scots pine than on the faster-growing lodgepole pine. This factor, in addition to other wildlife benefits, seems a justifiable reason for planting it in preference to lodgepole pine in some areas.

All areas of ancient or semi-natural woodland should be retained and, if possible, expanded. These areas, if large enough, will support their own distinctive wildlife (Lowe 1977; Newton & Moss 1977; Fuller 1982). Additionally, many areas of the uplands support broadleaved trees, particularly birch, which have established themselves naturally, either on moorland or within conifer plantations. The planting and/or retention of native trees both in pure crops along road- or streamsides or interspersed throughout plantations provide immense benefits to wildlife. Bibby et al. (1986b) have shown that single broadleaved trees and small groups scattered through conifer crops will encourage some rarer song birds not normally found in conifer plantations, while Newton and Moss (1981) demonstrated that pine/birch mixtures supported higher densities of song birds than pure pine crops. In non-commercial broadleaved areas, there is no reason to create densely stocked plantations, the aim being to re-create native woodland conditions with glades and irregular spacing.

The presence of broadleaves will provide seed sources and the potential for natural regeneration at the re-establishment phase. Many upland sites will readily grow birch and a limited range of other native species. Birch can be difficult to transplant and direct sowing of seed on to previously cultivated sites lacking adjacent seed sources may be a useful alternative (Brown 1983). Birch reverses podzolization and acidification accentuated by conifers, and there may be important silvicultural benefits to be gained from birch/conifer mixtures (Miles 1981).

Among the broadleaves, the relatively low palatability of birch to herbivores (Bobek et al. 1972; Mitchell et al. 1982) is an advantage, though it may require protection in some areas when deer densities are high (Lowe 1977; Miles & Kinnaird 1979).

4.2 Extended rotations
The absence of this mature stage in British commercial forests reduces the carrying capacity of the habitat for birds and mammals characteristic of climax forest ecosystems. A provision allowing at least a small proportion of commercial crops to continue beyond normal rotation age, with some being left to reach biological maturity, would greatly enhance conditions for wildlife (Bunce & Jeffers 1977; Currie & Bamford 1982a).

The natural thinning or removal of tree stems allows more light to penetrate the canopy, with a consequent increase in vegetation. Indeed, it is the presence and development of glades and both a field and shrub layer which benefits a large variety of birds, including wood

warbler (Phylloscopus sibilatrix), spotted flycatcher (Muscicapa striata) and redstart (Phoenicurus phoenicurus) (Currie & Bamford 1982a). These species are more frequently found in mature broadleaved woodlands in Britain (Fuller 1982), but they also occur in mature conifer forests in northern Europe (Haapanen 1965, 1966). The open nature of this habitat provides suitable flying conditions for bats and some raptors.

Older trees produce more cones, and therefore will support more red squirrels, crossbills, and siskins. Pines produce cones regularly, providing a steady, dependable food supply, while cone crops from spruces are irregular and unpredictable. Rajala and Lampio (1963) showed that heavy spruce and pine cone crops alternated, perhaps as a consequence of the dependence of flowering of both species on similar weather conditions, but with spruce cones maturing in the same year and pine a year later (Moller 1983).

Squirrels feed much more efficiently on spruce than on pine, due to the higher calorific value of spruce seeds and to the relative ease of stripping the spruce cones (Danilov 1938), and there is abundant evidence that red squirrels prefer spruce cones over pines (see Moller (1983) for a review). However, most of this work was done in mixed Norway spruce and Scots pine forests in continental Europe, where it is relatively easy for a sedentary animal to switch from the dependable but less nutritious food supply of pine seed to the sporadic but more nutritious supply of spruce seeds in years of abundance. In Scotland, where spruce and pine tend to be more segregated, red squirrels in pine forests cannot always take advantage of the irregular bumper crops of spruce seeds, neither can the low-density populations in spruce forests make use of the dependable crop of pine seed. In contrast, birds like common crossbills and siskins are highly mobile and can move long distances to exploit the irregular spruce cone crops. The conservation of red squirrels may be dependent upon increasing rotation length to provide larger biomasses of conifer seed, but it seems likely that mixtures of pine and spruces would also provide considerable benefits.

Only 4 species of bat are recorded in any numbers in Scotland; these are the Natterer's bat (Myotis nattereri), Daubenton's bat (M. daubentoni), pipistrelle bat (Pipistrellus pipistrellus) and brown long-eared bat (Plecotus auritus), all of which depend, to some extent, on trees for roosting and feed in open woodland. Extended rotation forests with large dead trees, woodpecker holes or the provision of bat boxes to simulate natural roosts will almost certainly lead to an increase in these species (Stebbings & Walsh 1985).

With extended rotations, a smaller proportion of the forest will be occupied by the younger sequential growth stages (Figure 1), which will result in a reduction in the overall carrying capacity for deer (Ratcliffe 1985a), an important benefit considering the great difficulties currently experienced in controlling deer populations (Ratcliffe 1984, 1985b; Ratcliffe & Rowe 1985).

4.3 Felling coupe size

Decisions on the size of areas to be felled provide an opportunity to modify the spatial diversity of forests. It is often unwise to perpetuate the large even-aged blocks created in the first rotation, and the opportunity should be taken to increase spatial diversity by the creation of a mosaic of blocks of different ages (Hibberd 1985). The use of natural features and roads for the boundaries of felling coupes will avoid conflicts with landscaping objectives and reduce the risk of windthrow at the edges of standing crops. The retention of even small groups of trees on felled areas will improve the site for birds (Currie & Bamford 1981; Bibby et al. 1986a).

Bibby et al. (1986a) showed that the composition of song bird communities on re-establishment sites in Wales was unrelated to area. They also found that song bird density decreased adjacent to thicket stage conifers but not when adjacent to broadleaves, open or pre-felling stage conifers. Small felling coupes provide a high edge to area ratio, and may sustain higher numbers of some song birds. In Sweden, forest bird density increased near the edge of felled areas (Hansson 1983). Large felling coupes may be more attractive to some larger and scarcer species, such as curlews (Numenius arquata) and short-eared owls (Leslie 1981), while kestrels may breed in old crow nests near the edge of felled areas and exploit the increased abundance of voles (Petty 1985). Hen harriers have bred recently on re-establishment sites (Petty unpubl.). A range of felling coupe sizes will provide and perpetuate a dynamic spatial diversity which will support a wide range of wildlife species.

The less intensive use of large re-establishment areas by red deer (Section 2.6) suggests opportunities to restrict browsing damage by felling and replanting large areas only. Unfortunately, this suggestion conflicts with the requirement for at least some smaller coupes to enhance bird diversity.

4.4 Deer control

Selective grazing by high densities of deer causes damage to commercial tree crops and drastically reduces botanical diversity (Kraus 1985). Native red deer are hybridizing with Japanese sika deer (Cervus nippon) in some areas, creating a threat to the genetic purity of red deer (Lowe & Gardiner 1975; Harrington 1982; Ratcliffe 1987). The spread of sika deer is related to the expansion of commercial forestry, and this fact raises the question of creating unafforested sanctuaries for native red deer. High densities of deer in upland forests are undesirable and pose difficult

problems which should be anticipated at the afforestation and re-establishment stages. Sites for high seats (Rowe 1979) and deer control clearings or glades should be selected before planting. These clearings should usually be 0.2–1.0 ha in extent, and well distributed throughout the forest, selecting if possible areas naturally favoured by deer (Ratcliffe 1985b). Glades should be sited so as not to conflict with landscape design. Indeed, they may be beneficial both to landscaping and to wildlife conservation.

4.5 Streams, lochans and bogs

In order to reduce acidity and generally improve water quality, conifers should not be planted close to streamsides (at least 5 times the stream width on either bank) (Mills 1980). Groups of broadleaves, such as alder, bird cherry, ash and willow, will further enhance these areas for wildlife. Lochans and bogs provide attractive areas for a number of birds, including divers and waders. Dense plantations closely surrounding these areas may result in the loss of fly-ways for divers and provide cover for nest predators, such as crows (Corvus corone) and foxes. Otters (Lutra lutra) will benefit from riverside trees, particularly ash and alder, and from dense vegetation along riversides. King and Potter (1980) provide recommendations for otter conservation, and it may be possible to encourage them further by providing artificial holts (Vincent Wildlife Trust unpubl.). Virtually all species of bats have recently been shown to be dependent upon water, and small permanent pools may provide flight areas and an abundance of flying insects for them (Neville unpubl.).

4.6 Steep banks and crags

These features provide important nesting areas for many raptors, including merlins (Falco columbarius), kestrels, peregrine falcons (F. peregrinus) and golden eagles (Aquila chrysaetos). Many such features occur close to watercourses and can be effectively incorporated by extending these unplanted places. Crags which are isolated by plantations should remain unplanted on the downhill side for a distance of at least twice the height of the crag, including any steep ground at the base. This distance will depend on the adjacent land form and should be large enough to provide unrestricted access by birds on to the crag when the trees have reached their full height.

4.7 Other topographic features

These features include old buildings which provide nest and roost sites for swallows (Hirundo rustica), barn owls, kestrels and bats, small open areas such as those used traditionally for display by black grouse (Tetrao tetrix), and badger setts (Meles meles). Unplanted areas around these sites may encourage their continued use and badger gates in fences will allow badgers to move freely without causing damage (Rowe 1976).

4.8 Artificial nest sites for birds

When an absence of natural nest sites is thought to

limit the presence or to control the density of birds, artificial nest sites may improve the situation.

Nest boxes suit a wide range of cavity-nesting song birds (Du Feu 1985), and the density of pied fly-catchers (*Ficedula hypoleuca*) and tits can be dramat-ically increased by their use in broadleaved and mixed woodland, and in conifers adjacent to these areas (Currie & Bamford 1982b). However, nest boxes for song birds in spruce plantations appear to be little used, perhaps because the coal tit is the only cavity-nesting species present and appears to be dependent on ground holes (Currie & Bamford 1982b). Large boxes will provide barn owls with suitable nest sites in derelict buildings which lack suitable nesting ledges (Du Feu 1985), while tawny owls in coniferous forest will almost completely abandon natural sites in preference for nest boxes (Petty 1983), though this may not be desirable. Although kestrels readily used nest boxes in Holland (Cavé 1968), they did not do so in newly afforested and re-established sites in Wales and north-east England (Petty 1985). Kestrels and long-eared owls bred in artificial crow nests sited in old shelterbelts scattered throughout a newly afforested area in south Scotland (Village 1981, 1983). Large boxes sited along the forest edge adjacent to lochs and rivers have been used successfully by goldeneyes (*Bucephala clangula*) (Dennis & Dow 1984) and goosanders (*Mergus merganser*) (Petty unpubl.). Large trees supporting the nests of buzzards (*Buteo buteo*) and goshawks (*Accipiter gentilis*), and some trees with large supportive whorls of branches should be re-tained, as nest sites are often scarce in conifer plantations. Saurola (1978) constructed artificial plat-forms which were used by goshawks, and larger platforms can provide nest sites for golden eagles and ospreys (*Pandion haliaetus*).

Rafts providing undisturbed nest sites can be floated in lochs when disturbance and/or changing water levels are affecting the breeding of waterfowl. They have been successfully used for divers (*Gavia* spp.) (Merrie 1979), and may be used by other waterfowl.

4.9 Dead wood
Dead trees, particularly large ones, provide some birds with nest sites and an important supply of invertebrate food, and should only be removed if it is necessary to control the spread of fungal or insect pathogens. Conifers do not develop natural holes as readily as broadleaves. Holes excavated by woodpeckers are important and their absence may limit the presence of other hole-nesting birds. Pines and broadleaved trees support more of the larger wood-boring beetles favoured by great spotted woodpeckers (*Dendrocopus major*), and consequently their density is often low in spruce forests. Many wind-snapped and windthrown trees in upland forests are particularly valuable in providing nest sites for redstart and spotted flycatcher, while both these species and song thrush, blackbird (*Turdus merula*) and wren nest in the root plates of windthrown trees.

5 Additions to the fauna
Many forests in the uplands are experiencing coloniz-ation by indigenous (eg pine martens (*Martes martes*)), non-indigenous (eg mink (*Mustela vison*)), desirable (eg wild cat and goshawk) and non-desirable (eg sika deer) wildlife species. Most of these events are unmanaged, though a notable exception is the active management by the Forestry Commission aimed at increasing the range and density of the goshawk in upland spruce forest (Petty unpubl.) and the red squirrel in east England (Rowe 1983).

The destruction of native woodlands resulted in many woodland species being reduced to low numbers or becoming extinct (Ritchie 1920). Some, like the pine marten and wild cat, have recently shown a remark-able increase in their range with the increase in commercial afforestation (Staines 1983). This passive spread of indigenous species is generally considered to be desirable, and is logically only a short step away from the reintroduction of formerly native species. The programme to reintroduce the white-tailed eagle (*Haliaeetus albicilla*) in Scotland (Love 1983) gained almost unanimous approval and few would question the introduction of capercaillie and goshawk. An equally sound case exists for reintroducing the red kite into Scotland, from where it disappeared during the last century (Baxter & Rintoul 1953). At present, it is restricted to a small area in central Wales from where it seems unable to expand, probably because of the illegal use of poisons in the surrounding areas (Davis & Newton 1981).

The reintroduction of large carnivores is a highly controversial subject. The lynx (*Felis lynx*) has apparently been absent from Britain since the early post-glacial period, but would probably thrive in upland commercial forests where it might be expected to have a controlling influence on woodland deer pop-ulations, especially roe deer (Pulliainen 1981). How-ever, its impact on hill sheep would require careful study. Land use changes, which have occurred since the extinction of the wolf (*Canis lupis*) in Scotland, appear to exclude any case for the reintroduction of this species, except perhaps on an island.

Norway spruce (*Picea abies*), though an important component of Scandinavian forests, has been absent from Great Britain as a native tree throughout the post-glacial period (Godwin 1975). It follows that the characteristic sedentary animals of European spruce forests are largely absent from Great Britain. The similarities between Scandinavian forests of Norway spruce and Scottish exotic Sitka spruce forests raise the logical, but perhaps controversial, consideration of the introduction of some non-indigenous animals. Such species include the ural owl (*Strix uralensis*), hazel hen (*Tetrastes bonasia*) and the three-toed and black woodpeckers (*Picoides tridactylus* and *Dryocopus martius*), none of which can be expected to colonize British spruce forests naturally. The possible consequences of introductions should be carefully considered beforehand and monitored afterwards, preferably under controlled circumstances (Anon 1979; De Bont 1985).

The conclusions of the World Wildlife Fund Manifesto on Animal Re-Introductions in 1976 seem to apply equally to introductions and provide succinct advice: 'we believe that conservation of existing populations and ecosystems should always take priority and only where this has been achieved should releases be undertaken, with the aim of maintaining ecosystems that are as natural as possible and as functional as necessary' (Anon 1979).

6 Research
Our current research is aimed at understanding the ecology of certain species of wildlife in commercial forests. For the future, we identify an urgent need to determine the effects of specific management practices and options (ie thinning and felling coupe size) on a wider range of species, progressing ultimately to studies of whole communities. Multidisciplinary teams will be necessary to achieve results which are cost-effective.

7 Summary
This paper describes the wildlife of different growth stages of newly planted forests, showing how moorland species are gradually replaced, through the pre-thicket and thicket stages, by a predominantly woodland community. The younger and older growth stages hold the most diverse wildlife communities, in contrast to the thicket stage. The effects of second generation forests on wildlife are discussed, and it is suggested that they may be similar in subsequent rotations. Modifications to current forest management practices are proposed which will greatly enhance upland forests for birds and mammals, our aim being to increase both the spatial and structural diversity of even-aged forests. These proposals involve not planting conifers close to important habitats, such as watercourses and ancient woodlands, the planting and maintenance of native tree species, the careful design of felling coupes, and the extension of conifer rotations. The benefits gained from providing artificial nest sites for birds, and the consequences of introducing additional species of birds and mammals are discussed. The beginning or end of the rotation is the most opportune time to exercise modifications. New directions for future research are suggested which concentrate on a multidisciplinary approach to a wider range of species. Active management is necessary to ensure that upland forests become diverse ecosystems which complement the magnificent scenery among which we choose to plant trees for commercial gain.

8 Acknowledgements
We thank Ian Newton and Roderick Leslie for their constructive comments on an earlier draft of this paper, John Williams who drew the figures, and Lena Birchall for typing successive drafts.

9 References
Anon. 1979. *Wildlife introductions to Great Britain.* London: Nature Conservancy Council

Baxter, E.V. & Rintoul, L.J. 1953. *The birds of Scotland.* Edinburgh: Oliver & Boyd.

Bibby, C.J., Phillips, B.N. & Seddon, A.J.E. 1986a. Birds of restocked conifer plantations in Wales. *J. appl. Ecol.* In press.

Bibby, C.J., Aston, N. & Bellamy, P.E. 1986b. Effects of broadleaf trees on birds of upland conifer plantations. *Proc. int. Conf. Bird Census and Atlas Work, 9th, Dijon, 1985.* In press.

Bobek, B., Weiner, J. & Ziellinski, J. 1972. Food supply and its consumption by deer in a deciduous forest in southern Poland. *Acta theriol.,* **17,** 187–202.

Brown, I.R. 1983. *Management of birch woodland in Scotland.* Perth: Countryside Commission for Scotland.

Bunce, R.G.H. & Jeffers, J.N.R., eds. 1977. *Native pinewoods of Scotland.* Cambridge: Institute of Terrestrial Ecology.

Burdekin, D.A. & Ratcliffe, P. 1985. Deer damage to Sitka – what does it really cost? *For. & Br. Timber,* **14,** (8), 26–27.

Busby, R.J.N. 1974. *Forest site yield guide to upland Britain.* (Forestry Commission forest record no. 97.) London: HMSO.

Busby, R.J.N. & Grayson, A.J. 1981. *Investment appraisal in forestry.* London: HMSO.

Cavé, A.J. 1968. The breeding of the kestrel, *Falco tinnunculus* L., in the reclaimed area Oostelyk flevoland. *Neth. J. Zool.,* **18,** 313–407.

Charles, W.J. 1981. Abundance of the field vole *Microtus agrestis* in conifer plantations. In: *Forest and woodland ecology,* edited by F.T. Last & A.S. Gardiner, 135–137. Cambridge: Institute of Terrestrial Ecology.

Currie F.A. & Bamford, R. 1981. Bird populations of sample pre-thicket forest plantation. *Q. Jl For.,* **75,** 75–82.

Currie, F.A. & Bamford, R. 1982a. The value to birdlife of retaining small conifer stands beyond normal felling age within forests. *Q. Jl For.,* **76,** 153–160.

Currie, F.A. & Bamford, R. 1982b. Songbird nestbox studies in forests in north Wales. *Q. Jl For.,* **76,** 250–255.

Danilov, D.N. 1938. The calorific value of main food-stuffs of the squirrel. *Zool. Zh.,* **17,** 734–738.

Davis, P.E. & Newton, I. 1981. Population and breeding of red kites in Wales over a 30-year period. *J. Anim. Ecol.,* **50,** 759–772.

De Bont, A.F. 1985. Effects on the ecosystem of release of animals with a proposal to minimize some of the hazards. *Trans. int. Union Game Biol.,* 17th, 117–123.

Dennis, R.H. & Dow, H. 1984. The establishment of a population of goldeneyes *Bucephala clangula* breeding in Scotland. *Bird Study,* **31,** 217–227.

Du Feu, C. 1985. *Nestboxes.* (BTO field guide no. 20.) Tring: British Trust for Ornithology.

Forestry Commission. 1984. *Broadleaves in Britain. A consultative paper.* Edinburgh: FC.

Fuller, R.J. 1982. *Bird habitats in Britain.* Calton: Poyser.

Godwin, H. 1975. *The history of the British flora.* Cambridge: Cambridge University Press.

Grayson, A. J. 1981. Current Forestry Commission thinking on thinning. *For. & Br. Timber,* **10,** (8), 46–49.

Haapanen, A. 1965. Bird fauna of Finnish forests in relation to forest succession. *Ann. Zool. Fenn.,* **2,** 153–196.

Haapanen, A. 1966. Bird fauna of Finnish forests in relation to forest succession. *Ann. Zool. Fenn.,* **3,** 176–200.

Hansson, L. 1983. Bird numbers across edges between mature conifer forest and clearcuts in central Sweden. *Ornis Scand.,* **14,** 97–103.

Harrington, R. 1982. The hybridisation of red deer (*Cervus elaphus* L. 1758) and Japanese sika deer (*C. nippon* Temminck 1838). *Trans. int. Union Game Biol.,* 14th, 559–671.

Hibberd, B.G. 1985. Restructuring of plantations in Kielder Forest District. *Forestry,* **58,** 119–129.

Hill, M.O. 1979. The development of a flora in even-aged plantations. In: *The ecology of even-aged plantations*, edited by E.D. Ford, D.C. Malcolm & J. Atterson, 175–192. Cambridge: Institute of Terrestrial Ecology.

King, A. & Potter, A. 1980. *A guide to otter conservation for water authorities.* London: Vincent Wildlife Trust.

Kraus, P. 1985. Vegetationsbeeinflussung, Schälschadensintensität und Wildbretgewichte als Indikatoren der relativen Ratwilddichte. *Trans. int. Union Game Biol., 17th,* 969–978.

Leslie, R. 1981. Birds of north-east England forests. *Q. Jl For.,* **75,** 153–158.

Love, J. 1983. *The return of the sea eagle.* Cambridge: Cambridge University Press.

Low, A.J. 1985. *Guide to upland restocking practice.* (Forestry Commission leaflet no. 84.) London: HMSO.

Lowe, V.P.W. 1977. Pinewoods as habitats for mammals. In: *Native pinewoods of Scotland*, edited by R.G.H. Bunce & J.N.R. Jeffers, 103–108. Cambridge: Institute of Terrestrial Ecology.

Lowe, V.P.W. & Gardiner, A.S. 1975. Hybridization between red deer (*Cervus elaphus*) and sika deer (*Cervus nippon*) with particular reference to stocks in N.W. England. *J. Zool.,* **177,** 553–566.

Merrie, T.D.H. 1979. Success of artificial island nest sites for divers. *Br. Birds,* **72,** 32–33.

Miles, J. 1981. Effects of trees on soil. In: *Forest and woodland ecology*, edited by F.T. Last & A.S. Gardiner, 85–88. Cambridge: Institute of Terrestrial Ecology.

Miles, J. & Kinnaird, J.W. 1979. Grazing: with particular reference to birch, juniper and Scots pine in the Scottish Highlands. *Scott. For.,* **34,** 280–289.

Mills, D.H. 1980. *The management of forest streams.* (Forestry Commission leaflet no. 78.) London: HMSO.

Mitchell, B., McCowan, D. & Wilcox, N.A. 1982. Effects of deer in a woodland restoration enclosure. *Scott. For.,* **36,** 102–112.

Moller, H. 1983. Foods and foraging behaviour of red (*Sciurus vulgaris*) and grey (*Sciurus carolinensis*) squirrels. *Mammal Rev.,* **13,** 81–98.

Moss, D. 1978. Diversity of woodland song-bird populations. *J. Anim. Ecol.,* **47,** 521–527.

Moss, D., Taylor, P.N. & Easterbee, N. 1979. The effects on song-bird populations of upland afforestation with spruce. *Forestry,* **52,** 129–147.

Newton, I. 1972. *Finches.* (New naturalist no. 55.) London: Collins.

Newton, I. 1983. Birds and forestry. In: *Forestry and conservation*, edited by E.H.M. Harris, 21–30. Tring: Royal Forestry Society.

Newton, I. & Moss, D. 1977. Breeding birds of Scottish pinewoods. In: *Native pinewoods of Scotland*, edited by R.G.H. Bunce & J.N.R. Jeffers, 26–34. Cambridge: Institute of Terrestrial Ecology.

Newton, I. & Moss, D. 1981. Factors affecting the breeding of sparrowhawks and the occurrence of their song-bird prey in woodlands. In: *Forest and woodland ecology*, edited by F.T. Last & A.S. Gardiner, 125–131. Cambridge: Institute of Terrestrial Ecology.

Newton, I., Davies, P.E. & Moss, D. 1981. Distribution and breeding of red kites in relation to land use in Wales. *J. appl. Ecol.,* **18,** 173–186.

Newton I., Marquiss, M., Weir, D.N. & Moss, D. 1977. Spacing of sparrowhawk nesting territories. *J. Anim. Ecol.,* **46,** 425–441.

Petty, S.J. 1979. Breeding biology of the sparrowhawk in Kielder Forest, 1975–78. *Tyneside Bird Club occas. Rep. no. 2, 1–18.*

Petty, S.J. 1983. A study of tawny owls *Strix aluco* in an upland spruce forest. *Ibis,* **125,** 592.

Petty, S.J. 1985. A negative response of kestrels *Falco tinnunculus* to nestboxes in upland forests. *Bird Study,* **32,** 194–195.

Pulliainen, E. 1981. Winter diet of *Felis lynx* L. in SE Finland as compared with the nutrition of other northern lynxes. *Z. Säugetierk.,* **46,** 249–259.

Rajala, P. & Lampio, T. 1963. The food of the squirrel (*Sciurus vulgaris*) in Finland in 1945–1961. *Suom. Riista,* **16,** 155–185.

Ratcliffe, P.R. 1984. Population dynamics of red deer (*Cervus elaphus* L.) in Scottish commercial forests. *Proc. R. Soc. Edinb.,* **82B,** 291–302.

Ratcliffe, P.R. 1985a. Population density and reproduction of red deer in Scottish commercial forests. *Acta zool. fenn.,* **172,** 191–193.

Ratcliffe, P.R. 1985b. *Glades for deer control in upland forests.* (Forestry Commission leaflet no. 86.) London: HMSO.

Ratcliffe, P.R. 1987. The distribution and current status of sika deer, *Cervus nippon*, in Great Britain. *Mammal Rev.* In press.

Ratcliffe, P.R. & Rowe, J.J. 1985. A biological basis for managing red and roe deer in British commercial forests. *Trans. int. Union Game Biol., 17th,* 917–925.

Ratcliffe, P.R., Hall, J. & Allen, J. 1986. Computer predictions of sequential growth changes in commercial forests as an aid to wildlife management, with reference to red deer. *Scott. For.* In press.

Ritchie, J. 1920. *The influence of man on animal life in Scotland.* Cambridge: Cambridge University Press.

Rowe, J.J. 1976. *Badger gates.* (Forestry Commission leaflet no. 68.) London: HMSO.

Rowe, J.J. 1979. *High seats for deer management.* (Forestry Commission leaflet no. 74.) London: HMSO.

Rowe, J.J. 1983. Squirrel management. *Mammal Rev.,* **13,** 173–181.

Saurola, P. 1978. Artificial nest construction in Europe. In: *Birds of prey management techniques*, edited by T.A. Geer, 72–81. British Falconers Club.

Sharrock, J.T.R., ed. 1976. *The atlas of breeding birds in Britain and Ireland.* Berkhamsted: Poyser.

Smart, N. & Andrews, J. 1985. *Birds and broadleaves handbook: a guide to further the conservation of birds in broadleaved woodland.* Sandy: Royal Society for the Protection of Birds.

Staines, B.W. 1983. The conservation and management of mammals in commercial plantations with special reference to the uplands. In: *Forestry and conservation*, edited by E.H.M. Harris, 38–51. Tring: Royal Forestry Society.

Staines, B.W. & Welch, D. 1984. Habitat selection and impact of red (*Cervus elaphus* L.) and roe (*Capreolus capreolus* L.) deer in a Sitka spruce plantation. *Proc. R. Soc. Edinb.,* **82B,** 303–319.

Stebbings, B. & Walsh, S. 1985. *Bat boxes: a guide to their history, function and construction and use in the conservation of bats.* London: Fauna & Flora Preservation Society.

Thirgood, S.J. 1984. *The effects of distance from cover upon the utilization of re-stocked Sitka spruce* (Picea sitchensis L.) *plantations by red deer* (Cervus elaphus L.) *and roe deer* (Capreolus capreolus L.). Hons thesis, University of Aberdeen.

Thompson, D.A. 1984. *Ploughing of forest soils.* (Forestry Commission leaflet no. 71.) London: HMSO.

Tittensor, A.M. 1975. *Red squirrel.* (Forestry Commission forest record no. 101.) London: HMSO.

Village, A. 1981. The diet and breeding of long-eared owls in relation to vole numbers. *Bird Study,* **28,** 215–224.

Village, A. 1983. The role of nest-site availability and territorial behaviour in limiting the breeding density of kestrel. *J. Anim. Ecol.,* **52,** 635–645.

Watson, D. 1977. *The hen harrier.* Berkhamsted: Poyser.

The economics of wildlife in private forestry

ELIZABETH H W JEFFERY, M A ASHMOLE and F M MACRAE
Fountain Forestry Limited, Perth

1 Introduction

All forests are wildlife habitats and can be altered as such to give a greater diversity of species or changed in one direction or another to encourage one particular species. Each individual land use exists within economic constraints and any one use (wildlife conservation or commercial forestry) must be valued more than another to be continued in isolation. These values may be quantifiable or based on personal preferences. However, while the value of a diversity of wildlife is not quantifiable, any change in productivity of a forest can be calculated. Both sets of values change through time, and recent attitudes on the value of these uses are dependent on a finite resource. Some types of land of interest both to conservation and forestry have become more scarce.

If wildlife conservation and forestry are to be amalgamated, it is important to integrate any wildlife conservation prescriptions into woodland management plans. In the case of afforestation, this integration is best carried out at the planning stage, before establishment begins. It is therefore essential that costings are prepared on the change in production incurred by the adjustments to the management plan so that either an individual owner can make a choice between the uses of his land or the manager can justify his actions.

2 The case for forestry

2.1 The need for timber

Britain uses almost 40 Mm^3 of raw timber each year, but produces less than 4 Mm^3. It is the economic and logistical problems involved that have led successive governments to support expansion within the industry with a positive overall forest policy. In recent years, the onus has been placed on the private sector to carry out the bulk of new planting and the major expansion of our forest resource lies here. Spurred on by grants for planting and by tax incentives, private owners have invested in the industry, the majority using professional forest managers to oversee their investments.

The forest industry has reacted to the call, and modern forest management has been transformed by new techniques in afforestation and harvesting methods. This increase in activity from the forest industry, particularly that directed towards afforestation, has meant changes in characteristics of the environment.

This process of increased specialization presents anxieties and has not been welcomed by all. Even when foresters themselves were anxious to avoid the conflict of interest which the economic pressures unleashed, they were forced to adopt practices which radically altered the nature of the countryside. Calls are now being made for planning constraints on forestry and a halt on certain operations altogether, totally against the present policy.

It is clear that a shift is taking place in the relative values of alternative uses of land, and management should be channelled accordingly. The growing need for a home timber resource will not go away, and further developments and refinements within the industry are to be encouraged. It is essential therefore that a policy for land use, backed up by sound economic facts, should be reached, if we are to avoid black or white decisions and conflict of one use *versus* another.

2.2 The alternatives

Within the forest, wildlife may be considered in 3 different contexts.

  i. The forest is the natural habitat for wildlife.
  ii. The forest can cater for wildlife, if the forest is suitably modified.
  iii. Forestry management cannot be modified to take account of wildlife, and the wildlife must be conserved in other habitats.

Point (iii) is a black and white case of afforestation *versus* nature conservation, ie commercial forestry is acknowledged to be the primary land use.

In the past, the existence of more attractive investment opportunities elsewhere has kept most hill land under-developed. Now, when investment in forestry is more profitable, problems occur in areas owned by people who hold a resource enjoyed by society at large. The area may contain a rare species of wildlife, or a scarce specialized habitat, or the land may be of value as an interesting habitat which, though not scarce nationally, happens to be close to a population centre. In such cases, the decision to plant trees or to preserve the original habitat must surely be political. If the economic benefit of timber production is deemed to be more than offset by non-market benefits which accrue to someone other than the owner of the land, then someone must sustain the revenue loss. In the past, this loss has generally fallen on the proprietor, but by methods such as compensation the loss may be shared by society. We would suggest that, because of over-riding economic factors, we can no longer afford the luxury of vast tracts of the uplands being left barren for specialist interests which do not take into account a valuation of the assets.

Point (i) can be seen in terms of casual multiple land use, ie no deliberate decision is taken to produce more than one product from an area, but this situation happens inadvertently. The wildlife may consist of species which in no way affect the profitability of the forest or, alternatively, of other species which have a bearing on the return and type of management, but the vast majority of wildlife within the woodland area does not affect its profitability. In some cases, however, such species as deer can be an asset in terms of sporting revenue or a liability in terms of the damage they cause within the plantation. Financial calculations can easily be undertaken to discover how different courses of action affect management and profitability. As the intensity of management and capital commitment increases, so casual multiple use declines because, in order to safeguard the timber which is the primary product, management will not tolerate subsidiary products, such as deer, which represent the multiple land use.

Point (ii) is of most significance to the forest manager and can have the greatest impact on the management of a forest unit, producing deliberate multiple land use. It is this aspect on which we wish to concentrate.

3 Altering the forest

The aim of wildlife conservation is to preserve biological diversity under free-living conditions. The preservation or creation of suitable habitats is the means of achieving this diversity. In forests, prescriptions to increase the number of habitats have concentrated on the following 4 main aspects of the system (Steele 1972):

    i. plant diversity
    ii. structural diversity
    iii. shelter
    iv. other features

3.1 Plant diversity

The tree species influences the presence of other plants, and the species composition of the vegetation is important in determining the variety of insects present. These insects are the start of the food chains which are the basis of wildlife conservation. In general, a far greater number of insect species depend on native trees and shrubs than on non-natives.

Diversity of plant species can be affected by either altering the tree species itself or by encouraging shrub growth in areas which have not been planted. In some areas, afforestation will reintroduce native species which have been absent for many years. By leaving areas clear of trees, 'ecological freeways' are created, whereby the existing wildlife communities are represented throughout the life of the crop. An environmental link is forged to maintain these communities, which may then be further developed, should the opportunities arise at a later date.

3.2 Structural diversity

Although the variety of insects depends to a large extent on the plant species present, their presence has less influence on vertebrate animals such as birds and mammals. These animals are much less affected by the species of tree in a forest than by the structure of woodland. As the canopy closes, pressures are exerted on wildlife communities generally. The communities consequently change as the forest alters throughout its life-time. This effect is often seen in birds which can show well-marked succession through different stages of a woodland.

Like birds, mammals are also affected by the structure of the forests. Being less mobile, they tend to live in one layer of woodland, usually the field layer. A well-developed field layer is of major importance to wildlife conservation.

In even-aged plantations, structural diversity can be altered by increasing rotation lengths and by reducing the size of felling coups to leave some forest cover throughout clearfelling regimes. The concept of the 'normal forest' is one to be aimed at, not only in terms of production but also for conservation.

Restocking techniques can be altered to include systems such as natural regeneration which will give a multistoried canopy. The development of the field layer is encouraged by thinning as heavily as practicable.

3.3 Shelter

Woodlands modify local climate by maintaining higher humidity, reducing windspeeds, lessening temperature fluctuations and providing shade. Sheltered situations in woodlands favour many plants and animals which cannot survive the more extreme conditions outside the forest. The systems mentioned above to increase structural diversity will also maintain a level of shelter in the forest throughout its life.

3.4 Other features

Features which can readily be created or maintained in the forest area are ponds, which will produce habitats for aquatic flora and fauna, and the preservation of old over-mature and dying trees, which may provide very specialized niches for lichens, insects and nesting birds. Paths, rides and glades normally present within the plantation provide open, light but sheltered conditions, and have a very long edge in relation to the area occupied. A glade or ride is of most value to wildlife if the central grassy area merges gradually through taller herbaceous vegetation and shrubs into the trees. An abrupt transition provides less variety of habitat and shelter.

Taking these 4 main aspects into consideration, the methods which can be used to change the habitat within the forest can be summarized as follows.

i. Leave land bare to encourage species which are not permanent forest dwellers by increasing edges.
ii. Plant a variety of tree species, particularly adding native hardwoods.
iii. Alter silvicultural techniques such as ploughing and thinning to encourage natural regeneration.
iv. Increase rotation lengths and reduce the size of felling coupes to leave some forest cover throughout clearfelling regimes.
v. Create or maintain features such as ponds, over-mature and large individual trees to provide specialized alternative habitats.

All these options can be costed by the forest manager to find the reduction in productivity by carrying out one or a combination of them. Carrying out these options does not always incur a straightforward loss of production. In some cases, there are benefits to the forest. Open spaces can be at a premium during harvesting; they can be used effectively for vermin control, and the increase in game numbers can produce a sporting income. Water is always an advantage in the forest, and lochs can double as fire ponds.

By calculating the net discounted revenue for the highly productive option and for the less commercially valuable but environmentally desirable option, the cost of conservation or 'opportunity cost' can be found by subtraction. What is not calculated is whether the benefits outweigh the losses or *vice versa*. Until a method is available to put a value on the conservation benefits, no comparison can be made.

4 Illustration
An example of these ideas put into practice is a plantation of some 250 ha in the Ochil Hills in Perthshire, where the owner made a conscious decision to allow for wildlife conservation in his management plan. The area lies on fertile, well-drained soils, derived from andesite and basalt lavas between 200 m and 400 m above sea level. Aspect is south-easterly and rainfall averages 1200 mm yr^{-1}.

The entire site was considered to be plantable with Sitka spruce (*Picea sitchensis*), giving an anticipated yield class of 14–16. Planting began in 1969 and continued over a period of 7 years, but only on 81% of the land. The species were mixed, although Sitka spruce was planted over 84% of the area. Old steadings and paddocks were left bare, and planting was kept back from the main stream. Wide rides and roadlines were retained (to the extent that Forestry Commission grants were reduced). Mixed hardwoods were also planted, particularly in groups by the streamside, and old mature trees were retained.

Eight ponds were constructed, and the larger ones were stocked with brown trout (*Salmo trutta*) from the nearby stream. The ponds have been naturally colonized over the years by a range of aquatic vegetation.

An area of Norway spruce (*Picea abies*) was respaced at 11 years from planting, and the produce sold for Christmas trees. Regrowth of vegetation under the remaining crop is much enhanced.

The actual cost of these operations was calculated at the planning stage:

Estimated cost of conservation

Total area	247.1 ha
Plantable areas left unplanted	47.7 ha = 19%
Normal roads and rides unplanted	= 10%
Therefore, additional unplantable area due to conservation considerations	= 9%

9% lost to timber production:

	Value
Area lost to thinnings only 1%	4,810
Area lost for whole rotation 8%	132,090
Cost of conservation	£136,900

Estimated value of conservation

Potential enhanced game rent over rotation	149,500
Potential game rent if fully planted	35,000
Potential hay rent from paddocks	3,000
Net potential income	£118,500

Therefore, net loss of income over rotation = £18,400

Additional unquantifiable values
i. Decreased protection costs due to time-saving layout.
ii. More effective control of pests leading to decreased crop damage.
iii. Amenity and conservation value.

5 Conclusion
Land use is dynamic, always under the influence of changes in demand. More pressure is being brought to bear on our finite land resource by different groups. Forests are ideal habitats for much of our native wildlife, and the preservation or creation of suitable habitats is the means of achieving wildlife conservation. Subsequently, the need consciously to amalgamate the main role of forestry, timber production, with conservation is increasing.

In private forestry, it is essential that each option can be costed so that the course of action taken can be justified. This is one of the basic principles of management. Private forest management companies, which have carried out so much of the new planting in this country in recent years, often have overall control of large areas, and are in an ideal and unique position to produce overall management policies for these areas. All the forestry options can be costed by the manager, who then has the resources to hand to carry out the plan. However, there is currently little information on the conservation of wildlife. Research is urgently required as major policy decisions are currently being made with few hard facts from this side of the case. If these facts were available, then a model of the options could be produced to enable individual owners to choose between various courses of action. The same information could then be used by government to produce a positive policy for these areas, backed up by sound economic facts.

6 Summary
As a result of government policy, the private forest industry is in an expansionary stage. The subsequent changes in our landscape brought about by new planting have not always been welcomed by conservationists. It is clear that a shift is taking place in the value of alternative uses of our uplands.

Forestry and wildlife conservation are compatible, with a little compromise from both sides. Forests can, with a little alteration at initial planning stages, contain a greater variety of habitat.

There must be a basis of comparison between options. Foresters can already cost each situation, but we need to be able to value the non-market benefits of the options of wildlife conservation.

The private forest companies are already in a position to provide the best overall management. If the information on wildlife is made available to them, they will then be able to cost all the options and, having decided on which course to embark, they have the resources required to carry through the plans.

7 Reference
Steele, R.C. 1972. *Wildlife conservation in woodlands.* (Forestry Commission booklet no. 29.) London: HMSO.

Summary of discussion

H G MILLER
Department of Forestry, University of Aberdeen, Aberdeen

The present expansion of Britain's forest estate is arguably the most radical change imposed on the uplands of Britain since the destruction of the natural forest cover. Inevitably, this change provokes concern, the more so because the new forests are seldom composed of indigenous species. Under these circumstances, meetings between foresters and conservationists can degenerate into ritualized displays of mutual antagonism. Fortunately, such did not occur in this meeting, reflecting in part the proper restraint of the contributors, and in part the growing awareness that there are great areas of common interest.

Foresters become foresters because they value the countryside and they like to regard themselves as natural conservers. Their business life, however, like that of other business managers, is spent resolving conflicting interests, usually through assigning monetary costs or values. It inevitably seems to the forest manager that wildlife conservationists have appropriated an excessive and unrealistic luxury when they make their interests, no matter how *outré*, primary and apparently seldom open to assessment or compromise. By contrast, the conservationist points out that in Britain all forestry is stimulated by public money, either directly or through grants and fiscal measures, and queries whether the solution offered by the forester is in the best public interest. What must be clear is that Britain's forests will be increasingly managed to achieve multiple objectives. In part, this begs the questions of what these objectives should be and what are the criteria for success. Government policy, however, is that there should be further expansion of commercial forests and that the management of these forests should pay proper regard to conservation interests. There is then a great need for further discussion and research in order to define the different conservation needs and to devise and cost the means of achieving them.

It was suggested early in the meeting that there are 2 distinct strands. These were concerned with (i) long-existing forests and their wildlife, where conservation may be properly the sole or major object of management, even if it has to be costed against a different enterprise, and (ii) maximizing the conservation values of our new forests (created since the Napoleonic wars) without so impairing their financial viability that they are not managed at all.

Despite the amount of research that the ancient and semi-natural forests have attracted, it seems that there is still much that needs to be known. Generally, these ancient forests have to be subjected to some form of management if their conservation interest is to be retained. Indeed, as in the case of coppice woodlands, much of the interest may stem from previous forms of management. The difficulties entailed in such management should not be underestimated. Trees are long-lived organisms and, when it is time to regenerate them, the climate, soil and pathological factors may be very different from those that were operative when the parent trees first took root. There is both the continual change resulting from altering physical conditions with time and the often observed tendency for trees to belong to more or less cyclical successions involving generations of 2 or 3 species. In these circumstances, it becomes hard to define aims and requirements which are frequently expressed as loose *desiderata* rather than as objectives sufficiently closely defined to guide management operations.

In his paper, Dr Staines offered 2 wide objectives that might apply to managing ancient forests. These aims were (i) maintenance of diversity, and (ii) preservation of rarities and unique populations of scientific or historical interest. These seem useful guidelines, although they beg the questions of what is rare, how unique is unique (for any community becomes unique if sufficiently closely defined) and, in particular, what is meant by the label 'of scientific interest'. There must be some fear that one man's scientific interest is a commonplace for his neighbour.

Research can be directed to further honing of definitions, but this would probably serve little purpose. Instead, attention should be given to the precise requirements of a range of different, and even mutually exclusive, objectives so that the best compromise management can be devised. It is striking how often this boils down to the 2 questions: (i) what is the minimum space definitely needed to achieve a particular objective, and (ii) what is the minimum interference with other land uses that is consistent with that objective? Until these 2 problems can be more objectively defined, the wildlife conservationist will continue to regard the forester as unsympathetic, and the forester will regard the conservationist as unduly demanding.

There is the danger that conservationists may lose public sympathy by making demands that seem, perhaps wrongly, to be elitist and obstructionist. The public are aware that there is a high degree of subjectivity in stating conservation requirements, and are quickly exasperated by unduly dogmatic demands.

It is in the interest of all that the necessary information be obtained to ensure that those decisions regarding conservation that have impact on other land users (as they almost invariably do) are objective and defensible. This point is particularly important as conservationists now argue a right to influence land use decisions in areas outside Sites of Special Scientific Interest.

The idea of increased use of conservation criteria in non-designated areas was raised in various forms, some speakers from the floor suggesting that conditions should be attached to all forms of government subsidy, whether forestry, agricultural or otherwise. Perhaps this is the way forward, but it can only be viable in the long term if landowners and users are convinced of the validity of the decisions being made. Again, the need for research to establish clear, objective and supportable criteria for conservation requirements seems to be clear.

Much the same series of points can be made when discussing conservation in relation to Britain's new forests. There is an undercurrent of a suggestion that Britain has no need to expand its forest estate because other countries will provide the timber needed, so that the land (and perhaps other resources) can be left to the conservationist. This view may be valid but, as Mr Jeffers pointed out, it makes the somewhat questionable assumption that continued timber importation will remain both financially feasible and morally justifiable.

In 1980, the world consumed 3340 Mm^3 equivalent of timber, with half used as fuel. The *per capita* consumption was 1.24 m^3 in the developed world (0.14 m^3 as fuel) against 0.53 m^3 (0.45 m^3 as fuel) in the developing world. Between 1970 and 1980, consumption increased by 22% in the developed world and by 33% in the developing world. Both the population and the consumption *per capita* are increasing rapidly in the developing world, concomitant with a fast-shrinking forest resource. For example, in Ethiopia it is estimated that forests covered 40–60% of the land area at the start of this century, but today they cover less than 4%. The morality, not to mention financial advisability, for any European country to assume that it has no productive role to play in ensuring the world's supply of timber must be questioned.

If, as the government clearly believes, Britain is to expand its forest estate, the question then is how to harmonize this development with legitimate conservation requirements. The new forests have very limited diversity, both in structure and species. The latter derives not from the perversity of foresters but because, in silvicultural terms, Sitka spruce (*Picea sitchensis*) is the most suitable species for most sites. This fact, however, does not preclude the introduction of limited species diversity and the gradual development of structural diversity with time. The large variations in soil fertility, drainage and exposure in our uplands will impose increasing structural diversity on

our forests. Changes in patterns of finance for forestry (and perhaps of perception by foresters) are allowing an increasing, albeit limited, variety in species.

The forest manager needs guidance as how best to use the limited flexibility he is being offered for the good of conservation. Our new forests offer new opportunities for conservation. The need for precise guidance, rather than ill-formed pious hopes, calls for an accelerated research effort. To pay dividends, however, the research should be planned and conducted by multidisciplinary teams involving both foresters and conservationists. The joint ITE/FC work on the interactions between deer and forestry is a classic example of what can be achieved.

In many respects, the main requirements are already known. The list of woodland practices and features suggested by Dr Young as favourable for Lepidoptera is probably as good a summary as any, and is equally applicable to most other fauna and flora. Yet these *desiderata* are far from well defined. Questions remain, such as how diverse a structure is needed? What size of open space or broadleaved island should be the target (to achieve the objectives, not simply to please the objector)? What is the influence of the shape of such islands? What should be aimed for when discussing 'corridors'? Accepting the conservation benefits of retaining some trees beyond financial maturity, what are the requirements in terms of numbers and for how long (the ideal of a treatment/response curve should not be totally unattainable)? What are the considerations when planning size of felling coupes, for clearly it is not the simplistic notion of aiming for the smallest possible? These, and related, questions can be answered, but demand research.

To close with the above list, however, would be vastly to over-simplify the problem. It is unfortunately true that every action has a cost (or there can be no management, for the manager is a cost to somebody), and frequently has an undesirable or unforeseen consequence. Mr Ogilvy rightly pointed out that foresters in the future will tolerate red deer (*Cervus elaphus*) throughout much of their forest. Mr Nicol pointed out that both the rabbit (*Orictolagus cuniculus*) and the grey squirrel (*Sciurus carolinensis*) are on the increase. Establishing broadleaved species then becomes difficult and expensive, but not impossible. However, more research is desperately needed to help in managing our forests so that browsing animals do not become uncontrollable pests. The interaction with hunting may offer one solution, but this solution is unlikely to be universally applicable (nobody in Britain hunts grey squirrels and, for good reason, it would not be permissible for capercaillie (*Tetrao urogallus*) and black grouse (*Tetrao tetrix*).

Integration, with an improved matrix of forest and farmland, is often regarded as an important goal.

Circumstances alter cases and, in areas of large-scale topography and vistas, intricate patterns of varying land use would be inappropriate. Nevertheless, as Mr Nicholson pointed out, increased management of forest areas to accommodate domestic animals would inevitably lead to diversity and, probably, improved conservation value. Further discussion of such ideas, however, is hampered by a lack of valid research data. Until suitable mangement scenarios can be devised, tried and properly costed, there is unlikely to be much advance. Conservation decisions must be seen to be based on scientific criteria, rather than on dimly perceived and exclusive metaphysics.

Perhaps one of the most useful ways forward would be to ensure the promotion and continuation of sympathetic and constructive dialogue between forest manager and conservationist. In organizing this meeting, Professor Jenkins has done much to forward such a dialogue. Forest managers must come to appreciate what they can do to help and must respond constructively. Conservationists must show more willingness to understand that management operations, whether in a national park or a commercial forest, cost money that has first to be raised. They cannot, by remaining on the side-lines, opt out of this problem. There is a crying need for these 2 groups of land managers to be educated in each other's problems. At the same time, it must be appreciated that management decisions must be taken on fairly hard and fast information (a definitive statement, even if it subsequently proves to be slightly wrong, is better than no statement, particularly when this absence is hedged around by criticism). Research should be aimed at establishing precisely the conservation requirements of different species and the benefits to be gained by realistic changes in forest practice.

In advocating this approach, it should finally be emphasized that the greatest good will come from understanding the ecological requirements of the species to be conserved or of the hydrology of the bogs to be preserved (conservation of amenity must always remain subjective). Site-specific research is of limited value for it is only through understanding the processes involved that we can intelligently deduce the responses that the forest manager and conservationist should make on other sites. That they should both respond is essential, because advance can only come through the partnership that results from an awareness of each other's requirements.

Appendix

LIST OF PARTICIPANTS

Mr J Atterson, Forestry Commission, North Scotland Conservancy, 21 Church Street, Inverness, IV1 1EL.

Mr M A Ashmole, Fountain Forestry Limited, Isla Road, Perth, PH2 7HF.

Dr I P Bainbridge, The Royal Society for the Protection of Birds, 17 Regent Terrace, Edinburgh, EH7 5BN.

Dr Jean Balfour, CBE, Kirkforthar House, Markinch, Glenrothes, Fife, KY7 6LS.

Mr N Black, Highland Regional Council, Glenurquhart Road, Inverness, IV3 5NX.

Mr J W Blackwood, Nature Conservancy Council, Northminster House, Peterborough, PE1 1UA.

Dr J M Boyd, 57 Hailes Gardens, Colinton, Edinburgh, EH13 0JH.

Dr I R Brown, University of Aberdeen, Department of Forestry, St Machar Drive, Aberdeen, AB9 2UU.

Mr D A Burdekin, Forestry Commission, Alice Holt Lodge, Wrecclesham, Farnham, Surrey, GU10 4LG.

Mr R F Callander, Haughend, Finzean, Aberdeenshire AB3 3PP.

Mr C Claridge, Highland Regional Council, Glenurquhart Road, Inverness, IV3 5NX.

Dr H Q P Crick, University of Aberdeen, Department of Zoology, Culterty Field Station, Newburgh, Ellon, Aberdeenshire, AB4 0AA.

Mr R H Dennis, The Royal Society for the Protection of Birds, RSPB Highland Office, Munlochy, Ross & Cromarty, IV8 8ND.

Mr J W Dodds, Fountain Forestry Limited, Isla Road, Perth, PH2 7HF.

Dr R Fairley, Countryside Commission for Scotland, Battleby, Redgorton, Perth, PH1 3EW.

Mr J A Forster, Careers Advisory Officer, University of Aberdeen, Regent Walk, Aberdeen, AB9 1FX.

Professor C H Gimingham, University of Aberdeen, Department of Plant Science, St Machar Drive, Aberdeen, AB9 2UD

Mr R Goodier, Nature Conservancy Council, 12 Hope Terrace, Edinburgh, EH9 2AS.

Mr D Hammerton, Clyde River Purification Board, Rivers House, Murray Road, East Kilbride, Glasgow, G75 0LA.

Dr G Howells, Nature Conservancy Council, Plas Penrhos, Ffordd Penrhos, Bangor, Gwynedd, LL57 2LQ.

Mr F A Hunter, Ministry of Agriculture, Fisheries and Food, Slough Laboratory, London Road, Slough, Bucks, SL3 7HR.

Mr T Huxley, Countryside Commission for Scotland, Battleby, Redgorton, Perth, PH1 3EW.

Dr H A P Ingram, The University of Dundee, Department of Biological Sciences, The University, Dundee, DD1 4HN.

Mr A A Johnston, North East River Purification Board, Woodside House, Persley, Aberdeen, AB2 2UQ.

Dr K J Kirby, Nature Conservancy Council, Great Britain Headquarters, Northminster House, Peterborough, PE1 1UA.

Mr R Leslie, Forestry Commission, 231 Corstorphine Road, Edinburgh, EH12 7AT.

Mr A J Lilburn, Mains of Coull, Aboyne, Aberdeenshire, AB3 4TS.

Professor G A Lodge, University of Aberdeen, Department of Agriculture, School of Agriculture Building, Aberdeen, AB9 1UD.

Dr R Lorrain-Smith, 9 Fyfe Grove, Baildon, Shipley, West Yorkshire, BD17 6DN.

Mr J McCarthy, Nature Conservancy Council, 12 Hope Terrace, Edinburgh, EH9 2AS.

Miss Jane MacKintosh, Nature Conservancy Council, 12 Hope Terrace, Edinburgh, EH9 2AS.

Mr A F MacPherson, Tilhill Forestry Limited, Old Sauchie, Sauchieburn, Stirling, FK7 9QG.

Mr D McPhillimy, Friends of the Earth, 53 George IV Bridge, Edinburgh, EH1 1EJ.

Mr F MacRae, Aros, Knockbain Road, Dingwall, Ross-shire, IV15 9NR.

Professor V Marcström, Institute of Zoophysiology, University of Uppsala, N. Parkvagen 21 A, 75245 Uppsala, Sweden.

Mr E M Matthew, Nature Conservancy Council, Wynne-Edwards House, 17 Rubislaw Terrace, Aberdeen, AB1 1XE.

Mr P K Matthews, Economic Forestry Limited, 27 Rutland Square, Edinburgh, EH1 2BW.

Professor H G Miller, University of Aberdeen, Department of Forestry, St Machar Drive, Aberdeen, AB9 2UU.

Mr P Neville, University of Aberdeen, Department of Zoology, Tillydrone Avenue, Aberdeen, AB9 2TN.

Mr S A Neustein, Forestry Commission, Northern Research Station, Roslin, Midlothian, EH25 9RE.

Mr A H Nicol, Timber Growers United Kingdom, Estates Office, Ballogie, Aboyne, Aberdeenshire, AB3 5DT.

Dr H Niemeyer, Forest Director, Niedersächsische Forstliche Versuchsanstalt, 34 Göttingen, Federal Republic of West Germany.

Mr J Y Ogilvie, Forestry Commission, South Scotland Conservancy, 55–57 Moffat Road, Dumfries, DG1 1NP.

Mr R S D Ogilvy, Fountain Forestry Limited, Bogallan Nursery, North Kessock, Inverness, IV1 1XE.

Mr J Oswald, Glen Tanar Estate, Glen Tanar, Aboyne, Aberdeenshire, AB3 5EU.

Dr W H Parry, University of Aberdeen, Department of Forestry, St Machar Drive, Aberdeen, AB9 2UU.

Dr I D Pennie, 5 Badcall, Scourie, Sutherland, IV27 4TH.

Dr G F Peterken, Nature Conservancy Council, Great Britain Headquarters, Northminster House, Peterborough, PE1 1UA.

Mr S Petty, Wildlife Research Branch, Forestry Commission, Invernoaden Gate, Glenbranter, Strachur, Argyll, PA27 8DL.

Dr P H Pitkin, Nature Conservancy Council, 12 Hope Terrace, Edinburgh, EH9 2AS.

Professor P A Racey, University of Aberdeen, Department of Zoology, Tillydrone Avenue, Aberdeen, AB9 2TN.

Dr D A Ratcliffe, Nature Conservancy Council, Great Britain Headquarters, Northminster House, Peterborough, PE1 1UA.

Mr P R Ratcliffe, Wildlife Research Branch, Forestry Commission, Invernoaden Gate, Glenbranter, Strachur, Argyll, PA27 8DL.

Mr I H Robinson, University of Aberdeen, Department of Zoology, Tillydrone Avenue, Aberdeen, AB9 2TN.

Mr I Ross, Belrorie, Dinnet, Aboyne, Aberdeenshire, AB3 5PH.

Mr A A Rowan, Private Forestry and Services, Forestry Commission, 231 Corstorphine Road, Edinburgh, EH12 7AT.

Mr R F Sheridan, Glendye Estate, Banchory, Kincardineshire, AB3 1DJ.

Mr R C Steele, Director General, Nature Conservancy Council, Northminster House, Peterborough, PE1 1UA.

Mr J T Stoakley, Forestry Commission, Northern Research Station, Roslin, Midlothian, EH25 9RE.

Mr G Tuley, Forestry Commission, Kincardine Forest District, Kirkton of Durris, Banchory, Kincardineshire, AB3 3BP.

Mr C Watt, Department of Agriculture and Fisheries for Scotland, Atholl House, Guild Street, Aberdeen, AB9 2ZL.

Dr W Williams, Nature Conservancy Council, Wynne-Edwards House, 17 Rubislaw Terrace, Aberdeen, AB1 1XE.

Miss Esther Woodward, Grampian Regional Council, Department of Physical Planning, Woodhill House, Ashgrove Road West, Aberdeen, AB9 2LU.

Dr M R Young, University of Aberdeen, Department of Zoology, Tillydrone Avenue, Aberdeen, AB9 2TN.

Mr R W Youngson, Red Deer Commission, 82 Fairfield Road, Inverness, IV3 5LH.

The following staff from the Institute were also present:

Mr J W H Conroy, Mr R P Cummins, Mr D D French, Miss Alison Hester, Professor D Jenkins, Dr J Miles, Dr G R Miller, Mr I A Nicholson, Mr R A Parr and Dr B W Staines, Institute of Terrestrial Ecology, Hill of Brathens, Banchory, Kincardineshire, AB3 4BY.

Dr J E G Good and Dr M O Hill, Institute of Terrestrial Ecology, Bangor Research Station, Penrhos Road, Bangor, LL57 2LQ.

Dr Ann Booth, Professor F T Last, Dr P A Mason and Dr A D Watt, Institute of Terrestrial Ecology, Bush Estate, Penicuik, Midlothian, EH26 0QB.

Dr R E Kenward and Dr M G Morris, Institute of Terrestrial Ecology, Furzebrook Research Station, Wareham, Dorset, BH20 5AS.

Mr A H F Brown, Dr R G H Bunce, and Professor J N R Jeffers, Institute of Terrestrial Ecology, Merlewood Research Station, Grange-over-Sands, Cumbria, LA11 6JU.

Dr I Newton and Dr R C Welch, Institute of Terrestrial Ecology, Monks Wood Experimental Station, Abbots Ripton, Huntingdon, PE17 2LS.